CRAIG BROWN

One on One

FOURTH ESTATE · *London*

Fourth Estate
An imprint of HarperCollins*Publishers*
77–85 Fulham Palace Road
Hammersmith, London W6 8JB

This Fourth Estate paperback edition published 2012

First published in Great Britain by Fourth Estate in 2011

Copyright © Craig Brown 2011

Craig Brown asserts the moral right to
be identified as the author of this work

A catalogue record for this book is
available from the British Library

ISBN 978-0-00-736064-2

Excerpt from 'Chelsea Hotel' from *Stranger Music: Selected Poems and Songs*
by Leonard Cohen © 1993. Reprinted with permission. All rights reserved.
Excerpt from T.S. Eliot, *The Waste Land*,
reprinted by permission of Faber and Faber Ltd.

Set in Minion by G&M Designs Limited,
Raunds, Northamptonshire
Printed and bound in Great Britain by
Clays Ltd, St Ives plc

MIX
Paper from
responsible sources
FSC™ C007454

FSC is a non-profit international organisation established to promote
the responsible management of the world's forests. Products carrying the
FSC label are independently certified to assure consumers that they come
from forests that are managed to meet the social, economic and
ecological needs of present or future generations,
and other controlled sources.

Find out more about HarperCollins and the environment at
www.harpercollins.co.uk/green

tions *This is Craig Brown*, ... *...ost Diaries*. Among his creations are Wallace Arnold, t... ...n social commentator, and Bel Littlejohn, the *Guardian* columni... ...nd installation artist, whose exhibition 'I Wish I Could Disappear Now and Forever Into th... Ground, Buried and Forgotten' was shortlisted for the Turner P... His radio series include *1966 and All That* and *As Told to Craig Brown*. Since 1986, he has written the parodic diary in *Private Eye*.

From the reviews of *One on One*:

'For anyone who likes to be provoked to both laughter and thought'

ANDREW RAWNSLEY, *Observer*

'Who but Brown could think up such an elegant device? Brown's glorious book is an original, and a complete delight'

MIRANDA SEYMOUR, *Sunday Times*, Books of the Year

'Laugh-out-loud on every page, humane and absurd at once'

NICOLA SHULMAN, *Daily Telegraph*, Books of the Year

'A brilliant reinvention of biography as the interesting bits'

PHILIP HENSHER, *Daily Telegraph*, Books of the Year

'*One on One* is entirely a work of non-fiction, and a very thoroughly researched one, too, while still as funny and perceptive as anything else Brown has given us … relish *One on One* from first chapter to 101st'

CHRISTOPHER HART, *Sunday Times*

'A rich and hugely enjoyable book that looks with affection and melancholy on the whirling roundabouts of history and celebrity, and reminds us that the paths of glory lead, handshake by handshake, pratfall by pratfall, to the grave'

SAM LEITH, *Guardian*

'Delightfully eccentric'

ANTHONY HOROWITZ, *Sunday Telegraph*, Books of the Year

'Rich with bite-size wonders'

POLLY SAMSON, *Daily Telegraph*, Books of the Year

'Out of truth comes absurdity; out of levity comes profundity, and out of chaos comes order, as Craig Brown's mighty wheel revolves' *Scotsman*

'For pure entertainment, it's hard to beat' *Spectator*, Books of the Year

'An original conceit flawlessly executed'

PEREGRINE WORSTHORNE, *New Statesman*, Books of the Year

'The book that made me laugh most'

JULIAN BARNES, *TLS*, Books of the Year

'This book is a treat. If history is gossip well told, then Brown's book is a triumph of the genre. By Jove! It's a clinker'

SEBASTIAN SHAKESPEARE, *Literary Review*

Other books by Craig Brown

The Lost Diaries
The Agreeable World of Wallace Arnold
Rear Columns
A Year Inside: Parliamentary Sketches
The *Private Eye* Book of Craig Brown Parodies
Hug Me While I Weep for I Weep for the World: The Lonely Struggles of Bel Littlejohn
The Craig Brown Omnibus
1966 and All That
Fame, Sex, Money, Power: A Beginner's Guide
This is Craig Brown
The Little Book of Chaos
The Marsh Marlowe Letters
Imaginary Friends: Collected Parodies 2000–2004
The Hounding of John Thomas
Craig Brown's Greatest Hits
Welcome to My Worlds!: The Dread Decades of Wallace Arnold
The Tony Years

For Frances

CONTENTS

Tossed upon ocean waters,
Two wooden logs meet;
Soon a wave will part them,
And never again will they touch.
Just so are we; our meetings
Are momentary, my child.
Another force directs us,
So blame no fault of man.
Ga Di Madgulkar

We have as many personalities
as there are people who know us.
William James

The earth keeps turning round and gets nowhere.
The moment is the only thing that counts.
Jean Cocteau

When Arthur Miller shook my hand I could only think
that this was the hand that had once cupped
the breasts of Marilyn Monroe.
Barry Humphries

ADOLF HITLER

IS KNOCKED DOWN BY

JOHN SCOTT-ELLIS

Briennerstrasse, Munich
August 22nd 1931

Earlier this year, the Nationalsozialistische Deutsche Arbeiterpartei – the second largest political party in Germany – moved into new offices at Briennerstrasse 45, near Königsplatz. As he approaches his forty-third birthday, its leader, Adolf Hitler, is enjoying success as a best-selling author: *Mein Kampf* has already sold 50,000 copies. He now has all the trappings of wealth and power: chauffeur, aides, bodyguards, a nine-room apartment at no. 16 Prinzregentenplatz.* His stature grows with each passing day. When strangers spot him in the street or in a café, they often accost him for an autograph.

His new-found sense of self-confidence has made him less sheepish around women. A pretty nineteen-year-old shop assistant named Eva Braun has caught his eye; she works in the shop owned by his personal photographer, Heinrich Hoffmann. He has even begun dating her. Walking along Ludwigstrasse on this bright, sunny day in Munich, what can possibly go wrong?

A few hundred yards away, young John Scott-Ellis is taking his new car for a spin. He failed to distinguish himself as a pupil at Eton College. 'I had advantages in that I wasn't stupid and was quite good at most games,' he remembers, 'yet I squandered all this because of an ingrained laziness or lack of will … I was a mess … I cheated and felt no remorse and when threatened with the sack – "You have come to the end of your tether," is what Dr Alington once greeted me with – I always managed to put on a tearful act and wriggle out.'

---

* 'The flat was all in brown and white, really rather ugly and quite plain,' wrote Deborah Mitford in her diary on June 7th 1937, after going with her sister Unity and their mother for tea with Herr Hitler.

He has emerged with few achievements to his name. A letter from his father to his mother, written in John's second year at Eton, reads:

Dear Margot,

I enclose John's reports. As you will see they are uniformly deplorable from beginning to end ... I'm afraid he seems to have all his father's failings and none of his very few virtues.

Of course we may have overrated him and he is really only a rather stupid and untidy boy but it may be he is upset by the beginning of the age of puberty. But I must say the lack of ambition and general wooliness of character is profoundly disappointing.

Try and shake the little brute up.

Yours

T.

After leaving Eton last year, John went to stay on one of his family's farms in Kenya (they own many farms there, as well as a hundred acres of central London between Oxford Street and the Marylebone Road, 8,000-odd acres in Ayrshire, the island of Shona and a fair bit of North America too).

It was then decided that he should spend some time in Germany in order to learn a language. In 1931, aged eighteen, he has come to Munich to stay with a family called Pappenheim. He has been in the city for barely a week before he decides to buy himself a small car. He plumps for a red Fiat, which his friends ('very rudely') refer to as 'the Commercial Traveller'. On his first day behind the wheel, he invites Haupt. Pappenheim, a genial sixty-year-old, to join him. Thus, he hopes to find his way around Munich, and to avoid any traffic misdemeanours.

They set off. John drives safely up the Luitpoldstrasse, past the Siegestor. The Fiat is handling well. The test run is a breeze. On this bright, sunny day in Munich, what can possibly go wrong?

While Adolf Hitler is striding along the pavement, John is driving his Fiat up Ludwigstrasse. He takes a right turn into Briennerstrasse. Crossing the road, Hitler fails to look left. There is a sudden crunch.

'Although I was going very slowly, a man walked off the pavement, more or less straight into my car,' recalls John. Many drivers, before and since, have used those very same words, often to magistrates.

The pedestrian – in his early forties, with a small square moustache – is down on one knee. John is alarmed, but the man heaves himself to his feet. 'He was soon up and I knew that he wasn't hurt. I opened the window and naturally, as I hadn't a word of German, let Haupt Pappenheim do the talking. I was more anxious about whether a policeman, who was directing the traffic, had seen the incident.'

All is well. The policeman has not noticed, or if he has, he is unconcerned. The man with the little moustache brushes himself down, and shakes hands with John and Haupt. Pappenheim, who both wish him well.

'I don't suppose you know who that was?' says Haupt. Pappenheim as they drive away.

'Of course I don't, who is he?'

'Well, he is a politician with a party and he talks a lot. His name is Adolf Hitler.'

Three years later, in 1934, Adolf Hitler is sitting in a box at the small rococo Residenztheater* waiting for the opera to begin. By now he is the German Chancellor, the talk of the world. In the adjoining box is the twenty-one-year-old John Scott-Ellis, celebrating the first night of his honeymoon by taking his young German bride to the opera. John looks to his left. Isn't that the very same fellow he knocked down three years ago?

The young man leans over. He seems to want to say something. Hitler's bodyguards are taken aback. Who is he, and what the hell does he want?

John Scott-Ellis introduces himself. He seizes the moment and asks the Führer if he remembers being knocked over in the street three years ago. To his surprise, Hitler remembers it well. 'He was quite charming to me for a few moments.' Then the orchestra strikes up, and the overture begins. The two men never meet again.

Over the years,[†] John often tells this tale of his unexpected brush with Adolf Hitler. 'For a few seconds, perhaps, I held the history of Europe in my rather clumsy hands. He was only shaken up, but had I killed him, it would have changed the history of the world,' he concludes of his own peculiar one on one.

---

* Now the Cuvilliés-Theater.

[†] In 1946 he inherits the title Baron Howard de Walden. He dies in 1999, aged eighty-six. Hitler dies in 1945, aged fifty-six.

JOHN SCOTT-ELLIS
TALKS OF THE BOCHE WITH
RUDYARD KIPLING

Chirk Castle, Wrexham, North Wales
Summer 1923

In the summer of 1923, John Scott-Ellis is still only ten years old, yet he has already lunched with G.K. Chesterton and George Bernard Shaw.

John lives in a vast thirteenth-century castle. His father, the eighth Baron Howard de Walden, dabbles in the arts, writing operas, poetry and plays. At one time he owned the Haymarket Theatre, putting on a good many highbrow productions, including works by Henrik Ibsen. When these failed to make money, he was persuaded to stage a comedy called *Bunty Pulls the Strings*; it ran for three years.

The eighth Baron's castle acts as a tremendous draw to artists and writers. Young John is now used to passing the time of day with Hilaire Belloc, Augustus John, George Moore or Max Beerbohm. Some of these grandees are more friendly than others. Belloc teaches him all sorts of tricks with paper, such as how to make a bird which flaps its wings when you pull its tail. By cutting out two triangles and placing them on a sheet of paper in a particular way, he also shows him an easy way to prove Pythagoras' Theorem. 'While I remember how to do this, I am sad to have forgotten his absolute proof of the Trinity, which he demonstrated in a somewhat similar fashion,' John recalls in old age. He remembers, too, the Irish novelist George Moore ('always rather preoccupied') tackling his father with a problem he was finding impossible to solve.

'I keep on writing down "she was in the habit of wearing a habit", and it isn't right and I can't think how to alter it.'

'What about, "she was used to wearing a habit"?' suggested Lord Howard de Walden. Moore went away happy.

In the summer of 1923, Rudyard Kipling comes to stay at Chirk. The great author and the young boy go for a walk around the garden together. It was in such a setting that Hugh Walpole observed of the five-foot-three-inch Kipling, 'When he walks about the garden, his eyebrows are all that are really visible of him.'

At the age of fifty-seven, Kipling encourages children to call him Uncle Ruddy. He finds it hard to make friends with adults, but speaks to children as equals, which is how he writes for them too. 'I would sooner make a fair book of stories for children than a new religion or a completely revised framework for our social and political life,' he explains.

Among children, he becomes a child. On a trip to South Africa, he lay himself flat on the deck to teach a little boy how to play with soldiers. But he can be short-tempered with those who lack his sense of adventure. He once handed his revolver to a youngster and urged him to fire it. Seeing him hesitate, Kipling snapped, 'At your age I would have given *anything* to shoot a revolver!'

But Kipling and John operate on the same wavelength. Kipling has long been fascinated by the paranormal, so he is perhaps attracted by the boy's unusual powers: John is able to throw a pack of cards face down on the floor and then pick out the four aces. 'I claim absolutely no strange powers but probably I had, or even have, this ESP slightly higher than others,' he recollects. One afternoon, a visiting Admiral with an interest in psychic matters asks him to throw two dice, and wish for high. 'For about twenty throws or more I never threw less than four and frequently double sixes.' The Admiral then tells him to wish for low. 'I started with double ones and continued in much the same vein.'

On their walk around the garden, John chats with Rudyard Kipling about Germans. Kipling says he hates them. Their talk turns to aeroplanes. Kipling says they are always trying to knock down his chimneys.

John asks him if he would ever travel in an airship.

'What!' exclaims Kipling. 'Locked in a silver coffin with lots of Boche?!'

Such a quote may seem almost too good to be true, but Kipling has a curious capacity to become his own caricature. Dining with Somerset Maugham at the Villa Mauresque, the conversation turned to a mutual friend. When Kipling declared, 'He's a white man,' Maugham thought to himself, 'This is characteristic. How I wish, in order to fulfil my preconceptions of him, he would say he was a pukka sahib.'

'He's a pukka sahib all right,' continued Kipling.

After their walk, Kipling accepts John's invitation to take a look at John's collection of his complete works in their smart red-leather pocket edition. Kipling offers to sign them for him, but as if by magic, Kipling's formidable wife Carrie suddenly swoops into the room and tells him not to. This, too, is characteristic. Carrie spends her time protecting her husband from his readers, and is often derided for it. To Lady Colefax she is 'a super-bossy second-rate American woman, the sort of woman you could only speak to about servants'. A young boy called Henry Fielden was in the habit of dropping in at Kipling's house, Bateman's, to borrow books. Once when he arrived he saw Kipling standing at the window, so he waved, and Kipling waved back. But when Henry knocked on the front door, a maid told him that Mr Kipling was not at home. Henry insisted that they had just waved to each other, and the maid rushed away in confusion. A short while later, a furious Mrs Kipling appeared, saying through tight lips that her husband would be down in a minute.

The day after their interrupted book-signing, Kipling takes John to the sheepdog trials in Llangollen. John notes how comfortable Kipling is in the company of the shepherds, 'getting them to talk and explain all about the trials and their lives'. On their way home, Kipling promises to write a story about these very shepherds. 'But sadly,' observes John, by now an old man, 'he never got round to it.'

RUDYARD KIPLING

HERO-WORSHIPS

MARK TWAIN

Elmira, New York State
June 1889

In 1889, Rudyard Kipling is twenty-three years old, though he looks closer to forty. He arrives in San Francisco on May 28th, after a twenty-day voyage from Japan.

He is greedy for life. He witnesses a gunfight in Chinatown, lands a twelve-pound salmon in Oregon, meets cowboys in Montana, is appalled by Chicago, and falls in love with his future wife in Beaver, north Pennsylvania.

Before he leaves the United States, he is determined to meet his hero, Mark Twain. He goes on a wild-goose chase – to Buffalo, then Toronto, then Boston – before tracking him down to Elmira, where a policeman tells him he spotted Twain 'or someone very like him' driving a buggy through town the day before. 'He lives out yonder at East Hill, three miles from here.'

At East Hill, he is informed that Twain is at his brother-in-law's house downtown. He finds the house and rings the doorbell, but then has second thoughts. 'It occurred to me for the first time Mark Twain might possibly have other engagements than the entertainment of escaped lunatics from India.'

He is led into a big, dark drawing room. There, in a huge chair, he finds the fifty-three-year-old author of *Tom Sawyer* with 'a mane of grizzled hair, a brown mustache covering a mouth as delicate as a woman's, a strong, square hand shaking mine and the slowest, calmest, levellest voice in all the world ... I was shaking his hand. I was smoking his cigar, and I was hearing him talk – this man I had learned to love and admire 14,000 miles away.'

Kipling is transfixed. 'That was a moment to be remembered; the landing of a twelve-pound salmon was nothing to it. I had hooked Mark

Twain, and he was treating me as though under certain circumstances I might be an equal.'

The two men discuss the difficulties of copyright before moving on to Twain's work. 'Growing bold, and feeling that I had a few hundred thousand folk at my back, I demanded whether Tom Sawyer married Judge Thatcher's daughter and whether we were ever going to hear of Tom Sawyer as a man.'

Twain gets up, fills his pipe, and paces the room in his bedroom slippers. 'I haven't decided. I have a notion of writing the sequel to *Tom Sawyer* in two ways. In one I would make him rise to great honor and go to Congress, and in the other I should hang him. Then the friends and enemies of the book could take their choice.'

Kipling raises a voice of protest: to him, Tom Sawyer is real.

'Oh, he *is* real. He's all the boys that I have known or recollect; but that would be a good way of ending the book, because, when you come to think of it, neither religion, training, nor education avails anything against the force of circumstances that drive a man. Suppose we took the next four and twenty years of Tom Sawyer's life, and gave a little joggle to the circumstances that controlled him. He would, logically and according to the joggle, turn out a rip or an angel.'

'Do you believe that, then?'

'I think so; isn't it what you call kismet?'

'Yes; but don't give him two joggles and show the result, because he isn't your property any more. He belongs to us.'

Twain laughs. They move on to autobiography. 'I believe it is impossible for a man to tell the truth about himself or to avoid impressing the reader with the truth about himself,' Twain says. 'I made an experiment once. I got a friend of mine – a man painfully given to speak the truth on all occasions – a man who wouldn't dream of telling a lie – and I made him write his autobiography for his own amusement and mine ... good, honest man that he was, in every single detail of his life that I knew about he turned out, on paper, a formidable liar. He could not help himself.'*

---

* Twain is equally flexible with the truth of stories about other people's lives. As a young journalist, he regularly makes up stories and puts them in the local newspaper. When someone falls out with his older brother, he gets his own back by writing a story headlined 'Local Man Resolves to Commit Suicide'.

As Twain walks up and down talking and puffing away, Kipling finds himself coveting his cob pipe. 'I understood why certain savage tribes ardently desire the liver of brave men slain in combat. That pipe would have given me, perhaps, a hint of his keen insight into the souls of men. But he never laid it aside within stealing reach.'

Twain talks of the books he likes to read. 'I never cared for fiction or story-books. What I like to read about are facts and statistics of any kind. If they are only facts about the raising of radishes, they interest me. Just now for instance, before you came in, I was reading an article about mathematics. Perfectly pure mathematics. My own knowledge of mathematics stops at "twelve times twelve" but I enjoyed that article immensely. I didn't understand a word of it; but facts, or what a man believes to be facts, are always delightful.'

After two hours, the interview comes to an end. The great man, who never minds talking, assures his disciple that he has not interrupted him in the least.*

Seventeen years on, Rudyard Kipling is world famous. Twain grows nostalgic for the time he spent in his company. 'I believe that he knew more than any person I had met before, and he knew I knew less than any person he had met before … When he was gone, Mr Langdon wanted to know about my visitor. I said, "He is a stranger to me but is a most

---

* Kipling himself proves less gracious with journalists. Just three years later, in 1892, during his ill-fated time living outside Brattleboro in Vermont, a journalist from the Boston *Sunday Herald* drops by. The two men have an altercation outside the house. 'I refuse to be interviewed,' says Kipling. 'It is a crime. I never was. I never will be. You have no more right to stop me for this than to hold me up like a highwayman. It is an outrage to assault a man on the public way. In fact this is worse.'

The journalist won't take no for an answer, and tries every ploy. 'Mr Kipling, you are a citizen of the world, and you owe it something and it owes you.'

'Yes, and that little debt has got to be paid me first, and I shall never pay mine.'

'You were a member of the press, and the profession wants to know what you have to say. You owe it something.'

'Damn little.'

'… Why, Mr Kipling, I wouldn't have missed this interview, to use your favourite word, for anything.'

'You haven't got anything anyway.'

'Oh yes I have. I've got enough to tell people to keep away from you.'

'That's what I want … Say I am a boor, for I am, and I want people to learn it and let me alone.'

With that, Rudyard Kipling slams the door.

remarkable man – and I am the other one. Between us, we cover all knowledge; he knows all that can be known, and I know the rest."'

Twain, now aged seventy, is addicted to Kipling's works. He rereads *Kim* every year, 'and in this way I go back to India without fatigue … I am not acquainted with my own books but I know Kipling's books. They never grow pale to me; they keep their colour; they are always fresh.'

The worshipped has become the worshipper.

MARK TWAIN

BIDS FAREWELL TO

HELEN KELLER

Stormfield, Connecticut
February 1909

As Helen Keller's carriage draws up between the huge granite pillars of Mark Twain's house, the most venerable author in America is there to greet her, though she can neither see him nor hear him. Her companion Annie Sullivan – her eyes and ears – tells Helen that he is all in white, his beautiful white hair glistening in the afternoon sunshine 'like the snow spray on gray stones'.

Twain and Keller first met fifteen years ago, when he was fifty-eight and she was just fourteen. Struck deaf and blind by meningitis at the age of eighteen months, Helen had, through sheer force of will, discovered a way to communicate: she finds out what people are saying by placing her fingers on their lips, throat and nose, or by having Annie transpose it onto the palm of her hand in letters of the alphabet.

Taken up as a prodigy by the great and the good,* she formed a special friendship with Twain. 'The instant I clasped his hand in mine, I knew that he was my friend. He made me laugh and feel thoroughly happy by telling some good stories, which I read from his lips … He knew with keen and sure intuition many things about me and how it felt to be blind and not to keep up with the swift ones – things that others learned slowly or not at all. He never embarrassed me by saying how terrible it is not to see, or how dull life must be, lived always in the dark.'

Unlike other people, Twain has never patronised her. 'He never made me feel that my opinions were worthless, as so many people do. He knew

---

* She is, in a way, the Nelson Mandela of her age: however great you are, you can't feel really good about yourself until you have shaken hands with Helen Keller. Albert Einstein declares himself 'a great admirer'; Alexander Graham Bell feels that 'in this child I have seen more of the Divine than has been manifest in anyone I ever met before'; Winston Churchill calls her 'the greatest woman of our age'; and to H.G. Wells she is 'the most wonderful being in America'.

that we do not think with eyes and ears, and that our capacity for thought is not measured by five senses. He kept me always in mind while he talked, and he treated me like a competent human being. That is why I loved him …'

For his part, Twain is in awe. 'She is fellow to Caesar, Alexander, Napoleon, Homer, Shakespeare and the rest of the immortals. She will be as famous a thousand years from now as she is today.' Shortly after their first meeting, Twain formed a circle to fund her education at Radcliffe College, which led to her publishing an autobiography at the age of twenty-two, which in turn led her to become almost as celebrated as Twain himself.

But the intervening years have struck Twain some heavy blows. One of his daughters has died of meningitis,* another of an epileptic fit in a bath-tub, and his wife Livy has died of heart disease. Throughout Helen's stay he acts his familiar bluff, entertaining old self, but she senses the deep sadness within.

'There was about him the air of one who had suffered greatly. Whenever I touched his face, his expression was sad, even when he was telling a funny story. He smiled, not with the mouth but with his mind – a gesture of the soul rather than of the face.'

But for the moment, he welcomes them into the house for tea and buttered toast by the fire. Then he shows them around. He takes Helen into his beloved billiard room. He will, he says, teach her how to play just like his friends Paine, Dunne and Rogers.

'Oh, Mr Clemens, it takes sight to play billiards.'

'Yes, but not the variety of billiards that Paine and Dunne and Rogers play. The blind couldn't play worse,' he jokes.

They go upstairs to see his bedroom. 'Try to picture, Helen, what we are seeing out of these windows. We are high up on a snow-covered hill. Beyond, are dense spruce and firwoods, other snow-clad hills and stone walls intersecting the landscape everywhere, and, over all, the white wizardry of winter. It is a delight, this wild, free, fir-scented place.'

---

* 'It is one of the mysteries of our nature that a man, all unprepared, can receive a thunder-stroke like that and live,' he writes after receiving a telegram saying, 'Susy was peacefully released today.'

He shows the two women to their suite. On the mantelpiece there is a card telling burglars where to find everything of value. There has recently been a burglary, Twain explains, and this notice will ensure that any future intruders do not bother to disturb him.

Over dinner, Twain holds forth, 'his talk fragrant with tobacco and flamboyant with profanity'. He explains that in his experience guests do not enjoy dinner if they are always worrying about what to say next: it is up to the host to take on that burden. 'He talked delightfully, audaciously, brilliantly,' says Helen. Dinner comes to an end, but his talk continues around the fire. 'He seemed to have absorbed all America into himself. The great Mississippi River seemed forever flowing, flowing through his speech, through the shadowless white sands of thought. His voice seemed to say like the river, "Why hurry? Eternity is long; the ocean can wait."'

Before Helen leaves Smithfield, Twain is more solemn. 'I am very lonely, sometimes, when I sit by the fire after my friends have departed. My thoughts trail away into the past. I think of Livy and Susy and I seem to be fumbling in the dark folds of confused dreams …'

As she says goodbye, Helen wonders if they will ever meet again. Once more, her intuition proves right. Twain dies the following year. Some time later, Helen returns to where the old house once stood; it has burnt down, with only a charred chimney still standing. She turns her unseeing eyes to the view he once described to her, and at that moment feels someone coming towards her. 'I reached out, and a red geranium blossom met my touch. The leaves of the plant were covered with ashes, and even the sturdy stalk had been partly broken off by a chip of falling plaster. But there was the bright flower smiling at me out of the ashes. I thought it said to me, "Please don't grieve."'

She plants the geranium in a sunny corner of her garden. 'It always seems to say the same thing to me, "Please don't grieve." But I grieve, nevertheless.'

HELEN KELLER

AND ...

MARTHA GRAHAM

66 Fifth Avenue, New York
December 1952

Before she taught Helen Keller each new word and phrase, Annie Sullivan used to say, 'And ...'

'AND open the window!'

'AND close the door!'

Everything life had to offer began with this little word.

The first word Helen ever learned was w-a-t-e-r. In Helen Keller's dark, silent childhood, her teacher placed her hand beneath the spout of a well.

'As the cool stream gushed over one hand she spelled into the other the word *water*, first slowly, then rapidly. I stood still, my whole attention fixed upon the motions of her fingers. Suddenly I felt a misty consciousness as of something forgotten – a thrill of returning thought; and somehow the mystery of language was revealed to me. I knew then that "w-a-t-e-r" meant the wonderful cool something that was flowing over my hand. That living word awakened my soul, gave it light, hope, joy, set it free! ... I left the well-house eager to learn. Everything had a name, and each name gave birth to a new thought. As we returned to the house every object which I touched seemed to quiver with life. That was because I saw everything with the strange, new sight that had come to me.'

Now aged seventy-two, Helen Keller still dreams of being like other women: what must it be like, she wonders, to see and hear? However much she gains the upper hand over her disabilities, there are still many perfectly simple and basic things within easy reach of everybody else that she can never hope to master, or perhaps even to comprehend: dance, for instance.

She has gained the respect of some of the most distinguished people in the world, but sometimes she thinks she would swap it all for the chance to dance. 'How quickly I should lock up all those mighty warriors, and hoary sages, and impossible heroes, who are now almost my only

14

companions; and dance and sing and frolic like other girls!' she confesses to a friend.

But she abhors self-pity; when she feels it looming, she forces herself to count her blessings. '... I must not waste my time wishing idle wishes; and, after all, my ancient friends are very wise and interesting, and I usually enjoy their society very much indeed. It is only once in a great while that I feel discontented, and allow myself to wish for things I cannot hope for in this life.'

Dance comes to symbolise the carefree land from which she is for ever exiled. 'There are days when the close attention I must give to detail chafes my spirit, and the thought that I must spend hours reading a few chapters, while in the world without other girls are laughing and singing and dancing, makes me rebellious; but I soon recover my buoyancy and laugh the discontent out of my heart. For, after all, every one who wishes to gain true knowledge must climb the Hill Difficulty alone, and since there is no royal road to the summit, I must zigzag it in my own way ... Every struggle is victory.'

Still fêted wherever she goes, Helen Keller is taken by a friend to meet the electrifying Grande Dame of modern dance, Martha Graham. Graham is immediately taken by what she calls Helen's 'gracious embrace of life', and is impressed by what appears to be her photographic memory. They become friends. Before long, Helen starts paying regular visits to the dance studio. She seems to focus on the dancers' feet, and can somehow tell the direction in which they are moving. Martha Graham is intrigued. 'She could not see the dance but was able to allow its vibrations to leave the floor and enter her body.'

At first, Graham finds it hard to understand exactly what Helen is saying, but she soon grows accustomed to what she calls 'that funny voice of hers'. On one of her visits, Helen says, 'Martha, what is jumping? I don't understand.'

Graham is touched by this simple question. She asks a member of her company, Merce Cunningham, to stand at the barre. She approaches him from behind, says, 'Merce, be very careful, I'm putting Helen's hands on your body,' and places Helen Keller's hands on his waist.

Cunningham cannot see Keller, but feels her two hands around his waist, 'like bird wings, so soft'. Everyone in the studio stands quite still, focusing on what is happening. Cunningham jumps in the air while Keller's hands rise up with his body.

'Her hands rose and fell as Merce did,' recalls Martha Graham, in extreme old age. 'Her expression changed from curiosity to one of joy. You could see the enthusiasm rise in her face as she threw her arms in the air.'

Cunningham continues to perform small leaps, with very straight legs. He suddenly feels Keller's fingers, still touching his waist, begin to move slightly, 'as though fluttering'. For the first time in her life, she is experiencing dance. 'Oh, how wonderful! How like thought! How like the mind it is!' she exclaims when he stops.

Helen Keller and Martha Graham appear together in a documentary film, *The Unconquered*, in 1953. Still wearing her hat, Keller stands in the middle of a group of dancers 'feeling' the dance, while Graham and her dancers circle around her. She has a look of ecstasy upon her face.

Almost half a century later, Martha Graham, now aged ninety-six, is busy dictating her autobiography. Her hands are crippled with arthritis. She looks back on Helen Keller, who died over twenty years ago, as 'the most gallant woman I have ever known'. And then it suddenly strikes her why, way back in the 1950s, Helen had been quite so excited by her visits to the studio.

'The word "and" is inseparable from the dance, and leads us into most of the exercises and movements. It led her into the life of vibration. And her life enriched our studio. And to close the circle, all of our dance classes begin with the teacher saying, "AND ... one!"'

MARTHA GRAHAM

SILENCES

MADONNA

316 East 63rd Street, New York
Autumn 1978

By 1978, Martha Graham has a formidable reputation. Over the course of her career, she has danced at the White House for eight US presidents, and baffled almost as many.*

Her work is adored and reviled in roughly equal measure. The Graham technique, taught at the school she founded half a century ago, is tense, percussive, sexually explicit. It is her belief that female dancers should 'dance from the vagina'. One of her acolytes explains that 'Martha's premise was that an act of lovemaking was an act of murder.'

Aged eighty-four, she maintains a ferocious temper, storming in or out at the drop of a hat. She has been known to pull the cloth from a restaurant table, scattering everything to the floor before making her exit. Nowadays, she is spotted only rarely in her school, though rumour has it that she is always there, like a demanding ghost.

The nineteen-year-old Madonna Ciccone has just taken her first trip in an aeroplane. She arrives in New York City from Michigan, with $35 and a bag of dance tights, determined to make her name as a dancer. After she tells the cab driver to take her to the centre of everything, he drops her off in Times Square.

She auditions for a dance company, but fails. They tell her she has drive but no technique, and advise her to enrol in the Martha Graham Dance School. Within twenty-four hours she has signed up for beginners' classes, paying her way by working in a fast-food restaurant.

'I dug this place. The studios were Spartan, minimalist. Everyone whispered, so the only sounds you heard were the music and the instructors,

---

* She unites both sides in the Cold War: after a sexually explicit production of *Phaedra*, her work is condemned as 'pornographic' in the House of Representatives, and in the Soviet Union she is attacked as a disturbing influence on the young.

and they spoke to you only when you were fucking up – which was pretty easy to do around there. It's a difficult technique to learn. It's physically brutal and there is no room for slouches … At one time in my life, I had fantasized about being a nun, and this was the closest I was ever going to get to convent life.'

The topic of Martha Graham provides the backdrop to every conversation. 'I wanted to meet the mother superior, the woman responsible for all this.' She hears that Graham visits the building often, and she even sits in on classes from time to time, either to check up on the teaching staff or to scout for talent. Madonna grows obsessed with meeting her, much as a visitor to Loch Ness might long to meet the monster. 'She stayed pretty hidden. I had heard she was vain about growing old. Maybe she was really busy, or really shy, or both. But her presence was always felt, which only added to her mystique and to my longing to meet her … She had a serious Garbo vibe about her and seemed like she really wanted to be left alone.'

Madonna begins to daydream about running into her. 'I was gonna be fearless and nonchalant. I would befriend her and get her to confess all the secrets of her soul.'

With this aim in mind, she signs on for extra classes, and lingers in the hallways in the hope of catching a glimpse. Sometimes, she invents excuses to enter the offices. And then, one day, quite by chance, it happens.

Madonna is in the middle of her 11 a.m. class. She has drunk too much coffee. Against the rules, she nips out 'with my bladder at bursting point'. She heaves open the heavy door to the hallway and steps outside the classroom, only to find herself face to face with Martha Graham. 'There she was, right in front of me, staring into my face. OK, not exactly in front of me, but my appearance must have taken her by surprise: no one ever left the tomb-like classrooms until classes were over.'

Graham stops dead in her tracks. Madonna is paralysed and, for the first time in her life, and possibly the last, struck dumb. 'She was part Norma Desmond in *Sunset Boulevard*. The rest of her was a cross between a Kabuki dancer and the nun I was obsessed with in the fifth grade, Sister Kathleen Thomas. In any case, I was overwhelmed, and all my plans to disarm her and win her over were swallowed up by my fear of a presence I'd never encountered before.'

Graham doesn't say a word. 'She just looked at me with what I thought was interest but was probably only disapproval. Her hair was pulled back severely, displaying a pale face made up like a porcelain doll. Her chin jutted out with arrogance and her eyes were like shiny brown immovable marbles. She was small and big at the same time.'

Madonna waits for words to spring from Martha Graham's mouth, and daggers to fly out of her eyes. 'I ignored the aching in my lower abdomen. I forgot that I had a big mouth and that I wasn't afraid of anyone. This was my first true encounter with a goddess. A warrior. A survivor. Someone not to be fucked with.'

Martha Graham says nothing, but flicks her long skirts and disappears into a room, closing the door behind her. 'Before I could clear my throat, she was gone. I was left shaking in my leotard, partly because I still had to go to the bathroom but most because I had encountered such an exquisite creature. I was truly dumbfounded … Much has happened in my life since then but nothing will diminish the memory of my first encounter with this woman – this life force.'*

Ten years later, Madonna is by far the most famous female pop star in the world. Her performances incorporate elaborate dance routines: tense, percussive, sexually explicit. One day, someone from the Martha Graham Dance School contacts her office, saying that the school is facing bankruptcy. 'Give it one day,' comes the reply. The very next day, Madonna's office rings back, offering $150,000. When Martha Graham, now aged ninety-four, is presented with the cheque, she bursts into tears.

---

* Their respect was, eventually, mutual. Before she died, Martha Graham expressed her approval of Madonna's performances: 'She is naughty and dares you to react. But she only puts onstage what most women hide, and yes, it may not be respectable … Respectable! Show me any artist who wants to be respectable.'

MADONNA

INDUCES QUEASINESS IN

MICHAEL JACKSON

The Ivy restaurant, Beverly Hills, Los Angeles
March 15th 1991

Wondering who might be sufficiently glamorous to accompany her to the Academy Awards, where she is due to perform, Madonna has a brainwave. 'How about Michael Jackson? Oh my God, what a great idea! Don't you love it?' she exclaims to her manager, Freddy DeMann, who used to manage him.

DeMann negotiates with Jackson, and reports back: he has managed to arrange a preliminary dinner. The two biggest-selling stars in the world are booked to meet at the Ivy in Beverly Hills, ten days before the ceremony.

In the past, Jackson has been puzzled by Madonna. Though he is an astute businessman, he can't fathom her appeal. 'She's always in your face, isn't she?' he once complained to a friend. 'I don't get it. What is it about her? She's not a great dancer or singer. But she does know how to market herself. That must be it.'

Two years ago, he was somewhat put out to discover that she was being advertised by Warner Brothers as the 'Artist of the Decade'. It was only in a trade publication, but even so. 'It makes me look bad,' he explained. 'I'm the artist of the decade, aren't I? Did she outsell *Thriller*? No, she did not.'

At their table at the Ivy, Madonna wears a black jacket and hot-pants with lacy stockings. Around her neck hangs a crucifix. Jackson is wearing black jeans, a red shirt and matching jacket, topped off with a fedora. He keeps his dark glasses on.

'I had my sunglasses on, and I'm sitting there, you know, trying to be nice. And the next thing I know, she reaches over and takes my glasses off. Nobody has ever taken my glasses off ... And then she throws them across the room and breaks them. I was shocked. "I'm your date now," she told me, "and I hate it when I can't see a man's eyes." I didn't much like that.'

As the dinner progresses, Madonna thinks she has spotted Michael Jackson taking a crafty peek at her breasts. Grinning, she snatches his hand and places it upon them. Jackson recoils. When all is said and done, this is not his style. But Madonna is not the kind of person to take no for an answer; later during their dinner, she saucily drops a piece of bread down her cleavage, then fishes it out and pops it into her mouth. The effect on Jackson is one of instant queasiness.

'Oh my God, you should see the muscles on that woman! I mean, she's got muscles in her arms way bigger than mine. They're, like, rippling, you know? I wanted to know how she got muscles that big, but didn't want to ask because I was afraid she'd make me show her *my* muscles.'

Their exploratory dinner at the Ivy cannot, therefore, be judged a great success, but at least it is not so disastrous as to derail their joint entrance at the Academy Awards ceremony at the Shrine Auditorium in Los Angeles.

Both of them have made an effort. They cut a dash together, Jackson in a white-sequinned suit with a large diamond brooch, plus gloves and gold-tipped cowboy boots, Madonna preferring a Marilyn Monroe look, with a skin-tight low-cut gown, also white-sequinned, and $20 million-worth of jewels, on overnight loan from Harry Winston.

Afterwards, they go to Swifty Lazar's annual Oscar night party at Spago. As she is making her entrance, Madonna is asked by a Hollywood reporter how she managed to convince the normally reclusive Michael Jackson to accompany her. 'Oh, Michael's coming out more,' she replies. Cynics detect a sneaky joke.

Once inside Spago and away from the cameras, it is not long before Madonna drifts towards her former lover Warren Beatty, leaving Jackson all alone. He is rescued by his old friend Diana Ross. 'Well, I just don't understand it, Michael,' Ross says loudly, so that everyone can hear. 'I mean, she's supposed to be with you, isn't she? So, what is she doing with him?'

'I don't know,' whispers Michael Jackson. 'I guess she likes him better.'

'Well, I think she's an awful woman,' says Diana Ross, reassuringly. 'Tacky dress, too.'

It is the very last time that Michael Jackson and Madonna will go out on a date together. However, a month or two later, Jackson asks Madonna to appear in his new video. Madonna, very excited, thinks they should do something 'utterly outrageous'. As the title of the song is 'In the Closet', she thinks it would be a good idea if she were to appear as a man, and Jackson as a woman. Jackson is not so sure; might it not just confuse everyone? After all, the song is intended to be solidly heterosexual: the title, 'In the Closet' refers only to the singer's desire to keep a relationship between himself and his girlfriend under wraps. Jackson's sister Janet has always been sceptical about Madonna ('If I took off my clothes in the middle of a highway, people would look at me, too. But does that make me an artist?'), but she expresses enthusiasm for the project. 'What a statement!' she says.

In the end, Jackson decides against, and the model Naomi Campbell appears in the video instead. The very first lines of the song are spoken in a breathy whisper by, of all people, Princess Stephanie of Monaco. 'There's something I have to say to you, if you promise you'll understand. I cannot contain myself: when in your presence I'm so humble. Touch me. Don't hide our love … woman to man.'

Naomi Campbell writhes around in a desert, wearing very little. She smooths her breasts with her hands while the gyrating Michael Jackson, in a sleeveless white T-shirt and black jeans, performs energetic thrusts, cupping his hands hither and thither around his pelvis while singing:

> *Because there's something*
> *About you baby*
> *That makes me want*
> *To give it to you!*

The two of them barely look at one another, let alone touch.

MICHAEL JACKSON

INTRIGUES

NANCY REAGAN

The White House, Washington DC
May 14th 1984

A month or so ago, Michael Jackson's lawyer, John Branca, was contacted by the White House to ask whether Jackson might donate his song 'Beat It' for advertisements against drink-driving.

Jackson was reluctant: 'That's tacky. I can't do that,' he told Branca. But he then had second thoughts. 'You know what? If I can get some kind of an award from the White House, then I can give them the song. How about that?' He wants to be on a stage at the White House with President Reagan. 'And I sure want to meet Nancy.'

Within days, they have a deal. The President has agreed to present Michael Jackson with a special humanitarian award, and the First Lady will be there too.

Fans gather at dawn to peer through the fence of the White House. At 11 a.m. the South Lawn is thronging with media, along with hundreds of White House staff, most of them clutching cameras.

The President arrives in a navy-blue suit. The First Lady wears a white Adolfo suit with gold buttons, trimmed with gold braid. Jackson wears an oversize military jacket with sequins, plus floppy gold epaulettes and a gold sash, a single white glove, checkered with rhinestones, and droopy dark glasses.

'Well, isn't this a thriller?' chuckles the President, behind his dais. 'I'm delighted to see you all here. Just think: you all came to see me. No, I know why you're here, and with good reason – to see one of the most talented, most popular and one of the most exciting superstars in the world today – Michael Jackson. Michael – welcome to the White House.'

After dutifully peppering his speech with the titles of some of Jackson's hits – 'Off the Wall', 'I Want You Back' – the jovial President gets down to business. 'At this stage of his career, when it would seem he has achieved everything a musical performer can hope for, Michael Jackson is taking time to lead the fight against alcohol and drug abuse ... Michael Jackson is proof of what a young person can accomplish free of drink or drug abuse.* People young and old respect that, and if Americans follow his example then we can face up to the problems of drinking and driving. And we can, in Michael's words, Beat It.

'Nancy spends a great deal of her time with young people talking about the problems of drink and drug abuse, so I speak for both of us when I say thank you, Michael, for the example that you're giving to millions of young Americans ... Your success is an American dream come true.'

Amidst applause, Jackson comes to the podium to receive his award. 'I'm very, very honoured,' he says in his high-pitched voice. 'Thank you very much, Mr President.' He then giggles to himself before adding, 'And Mrs Reagan.'

The President and Mrs Reagan usher Jackson inside, leaving him and his entourage to tour the White House. Jackson shows an interest in a portrait of his namesake, the seventh President of the United States, Andrew Jackson, who is in a similar military uniform, though without the sequins.

Afterwards, Jackson is to have a private meeting with the Reagans, along with one or two children of staff members. But when he is ushered into the Diplomatic Reception Room, he is confronted by seventy-five adults.

He turns on his heels, running down the hall into the rest room off the Presidential Library. He locks the door, and refuses to come out. 'They said there would be kids. But those aren't kids!' he protests to Frank Dileo, his manager.

Dileo has a word with a White House aide, who immediately rounds on an assistant. 'If the First Lady gets a load of this, she's going to be mad as hell. Now you go get some kids in here, damn it.'

---

* 'A Ceremony on the S. Lawn to honor young Michael Jackson who is the sensation of the pop music world – believed to have earned $120 mil. last year,' writes Reagan in his diary that evening. 'He is giving proceeds from one of his biggest selling records to the campaign against drunk driving ... He is totally opposed to Drugs & Alcohol & is using his popularity to influence young people against them. I was surprised at how shy he is.'

Twenty-five years later, when Jackson dies, an autopsy reveals traces of lidocaine, diazepam, nordiazepam, lorazepam, midazolam and ephedrine in his blood. The cause of death is given as 'acute propofol intoxication'. Propofol is an anaesthetic generally employed in major surgery. A total of thirteen puncture wounds are discovered on Jackson's neck, both arms, and both ankles.

Dileo shouts through the rest-room door, 'It's OK, Michael. We're going to get some kids.'

'You'll have to clear all those adults out of there before I come out,' demands Jackson.

An aide runs into the Reception Room. 'OK, out! Everybody out!' A member of Jackson's entourage arrives in the rest room. 'Everything is OK.'

'Are you sure?' asks Michael.

At this point, Frank Dileo grows edgy. 'OK, Mike, outta there. I mean it.'

Michael Jackson returns to the freshly vacated Reception Room. A handful of children are waiting. While he signs a copy of *Thriller* for the Transport Secretary, the Reagans arrive. They usher Jackson into the Roosevelt Room to meet a few more aides and their children.

As Jackson talks to the children, Nancy Reagan whispers to one of his staff, 'I've heard he wants to look like Diana Ross, but looking at him up close, he's so much prettier than she is. Don't you agree? I mean, I just don't think she's that attractive, but *he* certainly is.'

Jackson's employees are forbidden from discussing their employer, so he does not reply.

'I just wish he would take off those sunglasses,' continues Mrs Reagan, adding, 'Tell me, has he had any surgery on his eyes?'

There is still no reply. 'Certainly his nose has been done,' whispers Mrs Reagan, peering hard at Jackson, who is now talking to her husband. 'More than once, I'd say. I wonder about his cheekbones. Is that make-up, or has he had them done too? It's all so peculiar, really. A boy who looks just like a girl, who whispers when he speaks, wears a glove on one hand and sunglasses all the time. I just don't know what to make of it.' She lifts her eyes to the ceiling and shakes her head.

The Jackson aide begins to think it may be rude to say nothing at all to the First Lady. 'Listen, you don't know the half of it,' he says, with a conspiratorial smile. But the First Lady reacts as though she disdains such idle gossip.

'Well, he *is* talented. And I would think that's all that *you* should be concerned about,' she snaps.

NANCY REAGAN

DISAPPOINTS

ANDY WARHOL

The White House, Washington DC
October 15th 1981

'The funny thing about movie people,' says Andy Warhol to the First Lady over tea in the White House, 'is that they talk behind your back before you even leave the room.'

Nancy Reagan's eyes, already preternaturally wide, grow still wider. She looks at Warhol as though he were unbalanced.

'*I* am a movie person, Andy,' she replies.

The interview has been stiff throughout. Mrs Reagan never reacts well to criticism, and can spot it from a great distance. It is written in her stars. 'Cancers tend to be intuitive, vulnerable, sensitive and fearful of ridicule – all of which, like it or not, I am,' she explains in her autobiography. 'The Cancer symbol is the crab shell: Cancers often present a hard exterior to the world, which hides their vulnerability. When they're hurt, Cancers respond by withdrawing into themselves. That's me all right.'

Warhol himself has been notably crab-like in his advance on the Reagans. Two months before the 1980 presidential election, he befriended the Reagans' son Ronald Junior, then their daughter Patti. Both sides are happy: the younger Reagans mix with the most famous artist in America, and in turn Warhol mixes with America's imminent first family. Warhol likes Ronald Junior. 'He turned out to be a really nice kid. God, he was so sweet ... and he's very smart. Lispy and cute.' At their first lunch together, Warhol is tongue-tied. 'I didn't know what to talk to him about. I was too shy and he was too shy.' Warhol finds himself asking an awkward question about whether or not his father dyes his hair. Ronald Junior tries to change the subject. His mother, Nancy, is, he tells Warhol, 'very sweet and very adorable'.

Warhol seizes the moment. 'So then I got sneaky and brought *Ordinary People* up, and I told him how much I hated Mary Tyler Moore, that after

I saw the movie if I saw her on the street I'd just kick her. And at that point he was almost going to say something about Nancy, but then somehow he got the drift of it and changed the subject. Because I think the mother in *Ordinary People* is just like Mrs Reagan. Really cold and shrewd.'

They discuss what to order. Warhol tells Ronald Junior that he has never eaten frogs' legs, 'and he was so sweet he ordered them just so I could try it. He's really sweet, a beautiful body and beautiful eyes. But he just doesn't have a pretty nose. It's too long.'

Two weeks later, Patti Davis, Ronald Junior's older sister, drops by the *Interview* office. 'She looked sort of pretty to me, but then looking at her later on the video, how could these kids have missed their parents' good looks? I mean, Dad was so gorgeous.'

Between Ronald Reagan's election and his inauguration, Andy Warhol goes out with Ronald Reagan Junior and his wife Doria to see the movie *Flash Gordon*. By the end of the evening, he has given Doria a job on *Interview* magazine.

Warhol doesn't encounter Nancy Reagan until March 1981, when, by chance, he spots her eating in the same restaurant. 'We were leaving and didn't want to go by the President's table because it was too groupie-ish – everybody else was stopping at the table – so we went the other way, but then they called us over. Jerry Zipkin was yelling, and I met Mrs Reagan, and she said, "Oh you're so good to my kids."'

The possibility of an interview with Nancy Reagan is mooted in September 1981. By now Nancy has taken to ringing Warhol's sidekick Bob Colacello at the office, fussing about Ron and Doria, 'causing no end of envy to Andy'. Colacello negotiates with the White House for an interview with Mrs Reagan; they give their approval, thinking it might lighten her imperious image. But, perhaps sensing Colacello has overtaken him on this particular social ladder, Warhol affects to pooh-pooh the idea. 'I think she is too old and it's old-fashioned. We should have younger people. What is there to ask her? About her movie career? Oh, it'll never happen anyway.'

But it does. A month later, Warhol and Colacello leave for Washington. Colacello warns Warhol not to ask her any 'sex questions'. This upsets Warhol. 'I just couldn't believe him. I mean, I just couldn't believe him. Did he think I was going to sit there and ask her how often do they do it?'

The two of them, plus Doria, arrive early at the White House and are placed in a reception room. There they remain; when the First Lady arrives, she fails to lead them to somewhere more grand or more intimate. Warhol, ever-alert to matters of status, is affronted; a waiter brings them each a glass of water, and Warhol is further affronted.

The interview never really gets going. 'We talked about drug rehabilitation, and it was boring. I made a couple of mistakes but I didn't care because I was still so mad at being told by Bob not to ask sex questions.'

Soon, it is all over. Before ushering them out, Nancy Reagan gives Doria a piece of Tupperware ('not wrapped up or anything') and socks for Ron Junior. Colacello tells Nancy what a good mother she is, and asks what they are doing for Christmas. Nancy says they will stay at the White House, 'because nobody ever stays at the White House'.

Warhol leaves feeling he has been snubbed. A glass of water! When he gets home, his phone is ringing. 'It was Brigid asking me what kind of tea Mrs Reagan served us, and then I started thinking and I got madder. I mean, she could have put on the dog – she could have done it in a good room, she could have used the good *china*! I mean, this was for her daughter-in-law, she could have done something really great for this interview but she didn't. I got madder and madder thinking about it.'

ANDY WARHOL

BLANKS

JACKIE KENNEDY

1040 Fifth Avenue, New York
December 20th 1978

Somehow, Andy Warhol has no luck with Presidents or First Ladies. They never seem to hit it off. After a party for *Newsweek* in 1983, he observes, 'It was a boring party. No stars. Just Nancy Reagan and President and Mrs Carter.'

But they have their uses. On November 22nd 1963, he was walking through Grand Central Station when the news came through that President Kennedy had been assassinated. Warhol paused to absorb this and then, in a matter-of-fact manner, said to his assistant, 'Well, let's get to work.'

Within months, he had produced any amount of pictures of Jackie Kennedy, some adapted from a photograph of her smiling just before her husband was shot, some from photographs of her at his funeral, others a combination of the two.

As the years roll by, the paths of America's most famous widow and America's most famous artist cross on a regular basis. He is mesmerised by her fame. Possibly as a result, she is often standoffish towards him.* This makes him touchy. In 1977, Warhol is invited to a fundraising dinner Jackie has organised. 'The dinner was a horror. They put us at such a nothing nobody table,' he records in his diary. 'So here we were in this room where we didn't even *recognise* anybody except each other and this girl comes over to me and says, "I know you have a camera, and you can take pictures of everyone here except Mrs Onassis."' A few minutes later, Warhol enters the main room and finds not only that 'there was *everybody*

---

* The fault is probably mutual. 'She was full of complexities and contradictions,' a longtime friend of Jackie Kennedy tells her biographer. 'There was a great sense of competition and hostility. Taking people up, making much of them, then a drop and no one ever knew why.'

we knew', but 'there were 4,000 photographers taking pictures of Jackie. And that horrible girl had come over to tell me *I* couldn't!'

The following year, Warhol is irritated to be told that Diana Vreeland doesn't think he is avant-garde any more, and Jackie doesn't either. That November, he hears that Jackie has thrown a party without inviting him. 'Robert Kennedy Jr told Fred that they had a big question about whether to invite us and decided not to. Jackie really is awful, I guess.'

A week later, things look up. He receives an invitation to Jackie's Christmas party. Warhol invites his friend Bob Colacello. They arrive late. 'Warren Beatty and Diane Keaton were there and Bob heard – *overheard* – Jackie saying that something Warren did in the hall was "disgusting", but we were never able to find out what it was.'

Over dinner at Mortimer's afterwards, someone says Beatty has had sex with Jackie. Bianca Jagger says Warren has probably just made it up, because he made up that he slept with *her*, and when she saw him in the Beverly Wilshire she embarrassed him by screaming, 'Warren, I hear you say you're fucking me. How can you say that when it's not true?'

Then Bianca says that Warren has a big cock, and Steve Rubell asks how would she know, and she says all her girlfriends have slept with him. Colacello is 'in heaven' because Jackie is so nice to him, even sharing her glass of Perrier with him when the butler forgot to bring his, and saying, 'It's *ours*.'

But the next day, Jackie has turned turtle. She calls Warhol three or four times at his office. 'But I didn't call back, because the messages were complicated – they were like, "Call me at this number after 5.30, or before 4.00 if it's not raining."' Finally, she catches him at home. She is frosty. 'She sounded so tough. She said, "Now Andy, when I invited you, I invited *you* – I didn't invite Bob Colacello."' She complains that Colacello 'writes things'. This leads Warhol to suspect that 'something must have happened there that she doesn't want written about. She was thinking about it all day, I guess.' Could she be referring to the disgusting thing Warren Beatty did in her hall?

She punishes Warhol for his tardiness and his uninvited guest by asking her friends not to invite him to their parties. Warhol gets wind of his exclusion; their relationship deteriorates further. She never invites him to another Christmas party. It rankles. He records each fresh omission in his diary. 'Shook hands with Jackie O.,' he writes after attending a black-tie charity do at the Helmsley Palace. 'She never invited me to her Christmas party again, so she's a creep. And now I wouldn't go if she did. I'd tell her to go mind her own business. I mean, I'm the same age, so I can tell her off. Although I do feel like she's older than me. But then, I feel like everybody's older than me.'

Warhol never quite gets over his exclusion from Jackie's party list. In 1985, he is still fulminating. 'I don't understand why Jackie O. thinks she's so grand that she doesn't owe it to the public to have another great marriage to somebody big. You'd think she'd want to scheme and connive to get into history again.'

On Saturday, April 26th 1986, he attends the Cape Cod wedding of Arnold Schwarzenegger and Maria Shriver,* and notes, 'Jackie never smiled at anyone, she was a sourpuss.' At the reception, he blanks her. 'I didn't look at Jackie, I felt too funny.' The two of them never see each other again. Less than a year later, Andy Warhol dies unexpectedly, following an operation to remove his gall bladder.

Twenty-two years after his death, archivists are sifting through 610 cardboard boxes, filing cabinets and a shipping container full of the belongings of Andy Warhol. They find, among much else, a piece of old wedding cake, various empty tins of chicken soup and $17,000 in cash. They also come across a photograph of Jackie Kennedy swimming naked. It is signed by her, 'For Andy, with enduring affection, Jackie Montauk' – a reference to Warhol's estate on Long Island. No one knows how on earth it came to be there, or the story behind it; but it undoubtedly dates from a time before their falling-out in 1978.

---

* He gives the newlyweds a painting of the bride by himself. Another work of art – a sculpture – is a gift from Kurt Waldheim. 'It was really ugly,' notes Warhol. He also notes that 'Watching this story book wedding, you just wonder about what it'll be like when the divorce comes.'

JACKIE KENNEDY

IS ILL-AT-EASE WITH

HRH QUEEN ELIZABETH II

Buckingham Palace, London
June 5th 1961

It is barely four months since President Kennedy's inauguration. Mrs Kennedy is still finding her feet.

Jackie is unsure of herself. In public, she smiles and waves. In private, she bites her nails and chain smokes. She is prone to self-pity. She is overheard saying, 'Oh, Jack, I'm so sorry for you that I'm such a dud,' to which Kennedy replies, 'I love you as you are.' Is each of them telling only half the truth?

Socially, she is an awkward mix of the gracious and the paranoid. 'At one moment, she was misunderstood, frustrated and helpless. The next moment, without any warning, she was the royal, loyal First Lady to whom it was almost a duty to bow, to pay medieval obeisance,' is the way her English friend Robin Douglas-Home puts it. 'Then again, without any warning, she was deflating someone with devastating barbs for being such a spaniel as to treat her as the First Lady and deriding the pomp of politics, the snobbery of the social chamber.'

But now, on their whistle-stop tour of Europe, Jackie suddenly appears formidable. The French take to her as one of their own: born a Bouvier, she has French ancestry, and spent a year at the Sorbonne. She speaks fluent French and has arrived with a wardrobe of clothes specially designed for her by Givenchy. At a banquet at Versailles, President de Gaulle greets her by saying, 'This evening, Madame, you are looking like a Watteau.'*

The political editor of *Time* reports that, 'Thanks in large part to Jackie Kennedy at her prettiest, Kennedy charmed the old soldier into unprecedented flattering toasts and warm gestures of friendship.' At a press

---

* Jackie is particularly gratified when de Gaulle replies to her thank-you letter to him 'promptly and at length', while her husband's goes unanswered.

conference, President Kennedy says, 'I do not think it altogether inappropriate to introduce myself ... I am the man who accompanied Jacqueline Kennedy to Paris, and I have enjoyed it.'

Over dinner in Vienna, Jackie Kennedy charms Mr Khrushchev. As the evening unwinds, the Soviet Chairman draws his chair closer and closer to her. He compliments her on her white evening gown, and their subsequent conversation encompasses everything from dogs in space to folk dances in Ukraine. At the end of it, Khrushchev promises to send her a puppy as a present.

But the next morning, Khrushchev is back to his grumpy old self. He has no interest in charming the President, still less in being charmed by him. Kennedy emerges from their meeting feeling humiliated. On the flight from Vienna to London, both Kennedys appear downhearted, their gloom increased by the President's perennial back problems. Their doctor administers drugs to buck them both up: amphetamines and vitamins for the First Lady and novocaine for the President, who is also taking the powerful painkiller Demerol.

In London the next day, the President informs the avuncular British Prime Minister, Harold Macmillan, of the battering he has received. 'The President was completely overwhelmed by the ruthlessness and barbarity of the Russian Chairman,' records Macmillan. 'It reminded me in a way of Lord Halifax or Neville Chamberlain trying to hold a conversation with Herr Hitler. For the first time in his life Kennedy met a man who was impervious to his charm.'

In the morning, they attend the christening of Jackie's niece Christina Radziwill. From there, they go to an informal lunch with the Prime Minister and a number of friends and relations, including the Ormsby-Gores and the Duke and Duchess of Devonshire. The Duchess, an old friend of the President,* has mixed feelings about Jackie. 'She is a queer fish. Her face is one of the oddest I ever saw. It is put together in a very wild way,' she observes to her old friend Patrick Leigh Fermor.

That evening, the Kennedys attend a dinner at Buckingham Palace. It proves a minefield. The guest list has been the subject of negotiation:

---

* The Duchess of Devonshire is given pride of place at Kennedy's inauguration. 'Our fast young sister went over that ocean & had loving *tete a tetes* with your ruler,' writes her sister Nancy to another sister, Jessica, adding, 'Andrew says Kennedy is doing for sex what Eisenhower did for golf.'

traditionally, divorcees are not invited, so the Queen has been reluctant to welcome Jackie's sister Princess Lee Radziwill, who is on her second marriage, or her husband Prince Stanislaw Radziwill, who is on his third. Under pressure, she relents, but, by way of retaliation, singularly fails to invite Princess Margaret or Princess Marina, both of whose names Jackie has put forward. Jackie's old paranoia returns: she sees it as a plot to do her down. 'The Queen had her revenge,' she confides to Gore Vidal.* 'No Margaret, no Marina, no one except every Commonwealth minister of agriculture they could find.' Jackie also tells Vidal that she found the Queen 'pretty heavy-going'. (When Vidal repeats this to Princess Margaret some years later, the Princess loyally explains, 'But that's what she's *there for*.')

Over dinner, Jackie continues to feel awkward, even persecuted. 'I think the Queen resented me. Philip was nice, but nervous. One felt absolutely no relationship between them.'

The Queen asks Jackie about her visit to Canada. Jackie tells her how exhausting she found being on public view for hours on end. 'The Queen looked rather conspiratorial and said, "One gets crafty after a while and learns how to save oneself."'† According to Vidal (who is prone to impose his own thoughts on others), Jackie considers this the only time the Queen seems remotely human.

After dinner, the Queen asks if she likes paintings. Yes, says Jackie, she certainly does. The Queen takes her for a stroll down a long gallery in the palace. They stop in front of a Van Dyck. The Queen says, 'That's a good horse.' Yes, agrees Jackie, that is a good horse. From Jackie's account, this is the extent of their contact with one another, but others differ. Dinner at Buckingham Palace, writes Harold Macmillan in his diary that night, is 'very pleasant'.

Nine months later, Jackie pays another visit to the Queen at Buckingham Palace, this time by herself. She is more in the swing of things now. 'I don't think I should say anything about it except how grateful I am and how charming she was,' she tells the television cameras as she makes her escape.

---

* Always an unwise move.

† On French President Nicolas Sarkozy's state visit to Britain in March 2008, he asks the Queen whether she ever gets bored. 'Yes, but I don't say so,' she replies.

HRH QUEEN ELIZABETH II

THE DUKE OF WINDSOR

4, route du Champ d'Entraînement, Bois de Boulogne, Paris
May 18th 1972

The Queen is to pay a state visit to Paris to 'improve the atmosphere' before Britain's entry into the Common Market. But before the visit takes place, word arrives at Buckingham Palace that her uncle David, once King Edward VIII, now the Duke of Windsor, has throat cancer, and is days from death.

The Queen's Private Secretary, Sir Martin Charteris, contacts the British Ambassador in Paris, Sir Christopher Soames, who in turn arranges a meeting with Jean Thin, the Duke of Windsor's doctor. The Ambassador comes straight to the point. Dr Thin recalls: 'He told me bluntly that it was all right for the Duke to die before or after the visit, but that it would be politically disastrous if he were to expire in the course of it. Was there anything I could do to reassure him about the timing of the Duke's end?'

Unversed in royal protocol, Thin is taken aback. He can offer no such reassurance. The Duke may die before, during or after his niece's state visit to France, but he is not in the business of making predictions. The Palace is put out. Will the Duke prove as much of a nuisance in death as in life? As it turns out, the prospect of the Queen's visit gives the Duke a new lease of life; more than ever, he seems determined to cling on.

And so he does. He is still alive when the royal party lands at Orly Airport on May 15th. Each evening, Sir Christopher telephones Dr Thin to see how his patient is coming along. Dr Thin reports that His Royal Highness is unable to swallow and on a glucose drip, but still intent on welcoming his monarch.

At 4.45 p.m. on May 18th, the royal entourage arrives after a day at the Longchamp races. The Duchess of Windsor greets the Queen, the Duke of Edinburgh and the Prince of Wales with a succession of shaky curtseys, ushering them into the orchid-laden drawing room for tea. For the next fifteen minutes, no one mentions the Duke of Windsor's health. 'It was as if they were pretending that David was perfectly well,' the Duchess says later. She complains that the Queen was 'not at all warm', though she may simply be irritated by the Windsors' jumpy pugs.

The only member of the royal visitors to have been here before is the Prince of Wales, who called by last October, hoping to patch things up between his black-sheep uncle and the rest of the family. The very next month, Uncle David was diagnosed with cancer, so the Prince's account in his diary of his visit provides a glimpse, albeit a sniffy glimpse, into the Windsors' life as it was lived, not long ago: 'Upon entering the house I found footmen and pages wearing identical scarlet and black uniforms to the ones ours wear at home. It was rather pathetic seeing that. The eye then wandered to a table in the hall on which lay a red box with "The King" on it ... The whole house reeks of some particularly strong joss sticks and from out of the walls came the muffled sound of scratchy piped music. The Duchess appeared from a host of the most dreadful American guests I have ever seen. The look of incredulity on their faces was a study and most of them were thoroughly tight. One man shook hands with me twice, muttered something incomprehensible in French with a strong American accent and promptly collapsed into the arms of a strategically placed black footman.'

The Duchess (dismissed by Charles after their meeting as 'a hard woman – totally unsympathetic and somewhat superficial') leads the Queen up the stairs, where the Duke is sitting in a wheelchair, crisply dressed for the occasion in a blue poloneck and blazer. These garments conceal a drip tube, which emerges from the back of the collar and then swoops down to flasks concealed behind a curtain. He has shrivelled to ninety pounds. As the Queen enters, he struggles to his feet and, with some effort, manages to lower his neck in a bow. Dr Thin worries that this may cause the drip to pop out, but all is well, and it stays put.

The Queen greets her uncle with a kiss, and asks how he is. 'Not so bad,' he replies. From this moment on, the opinions of two of the witnesses to their meeting divide. The Duchess, who is by nature unforgiving, portrays the Queen as unsympathetic and coldly dutiful. 'The Queen's face showed no compassion, no appreciation for his effort, his respect. Her manner as much as stated that she had not intended to honour him with a visit, but that she was simply covering appearances by coming here because he was dying and it was known that she was in Paris.' However, the Duke's Irish nurse, Oonagh Shanley, remembers the Queen chatting perfectly amiably to her uncle, whose voice, reduced to a whispery rasp, is barely audible.

Some say their meeting comes to an end when the Duke is overcome by a coughing fit, and is wheeled away. It is certainly a very short time before the Queen leaves the room, to rejoin the Duke of Edinburgh and the Prince of Wales downstairs.

Rightly or wrongly, the Duchess of Windsor senses that they wish to be off. She escorts them to the front door of the villa, where the four of them pose together for photographers. Inevitably, the Duke of Edinburgh attempts a few jokes. Equally inevitably, the Duchess considers them inappropriate. The royal party leaves. The entire visit has taken less than half an hour.

Ten days later, the Duke of Windsor dies. Nearly 60,000 people come to Windsor to pay their respects. There is a question as to whether or not Trooping the Colour, scheduled for two days before his funeral, should be cancelled, as a mark of respect. But the Queen insists that it should go ahead, so it does.

THE DUKE OF WINDSOR

LOOKS ON AGHAST WITH

ELIZABETH TAYLOR

4, route du Champ d'Entraînement, Bois de Boulogne, Paris
November 12th 1968

Both now in their seventies, the Duke and Duchess of Windsor potter along as stately relics of their former glamour. They occupy their time either entertaining or being entertained by what has come to be known as the jet set. After jetting into Paris, and before jetting out, their ever-changing friends – foreign aristocrats, shipping millionaires, misplaced royalty, international playboys, amusing bachelors, the higher echelons of show-business – are delighted to receive the call from the Windsors.

Thirty years ago, they were the most glamorous couple in the world; that title, only ever temporary, is now held by Richard Burton and Elizabeth Taylor, who are, by chance, both making movies in Paris. The balance of fame, perhaps also of wealth,* dictates that it is the Windsors who make eyes at the Burtons, though the latter are far from displeased, as the Windsors reinforce their sense of having arrived, their craving for being centre-stage, particularly when off-stage.

The Windsors visit the Burtons on their separate sets, and the two couples dine together regularly. In honour of Burton's Welsh roots, the Duchess makes a point of wearing her Prince of Wales brooch – the fleur de lys in white and yellow diamonds. Elizabeth Taylor looks at it covetously: she is celebrated for her jewellery collection.† Dining with the Windsors and the Rothschilds before the European premiere of *The*

---

* 'I have worked out that with average luck, we should, at the end of 1969, be worth about $12 million between us. About $3 million of that is in diamonds, emeralds, property, paintings, so our annual income will be in the region of ½ million,' Burton writes in his diary.

† After the Duchess's death, Taylor buys it at auction for $449,625, bidding over the telephone while sitting by her swimming pool. 'All along I knew my friend the duchess wanted me to have it,' she tells the press, pointing out that 'It's the first time I've ever had to buy myself a piece of jewellery.'

Taming of the Shrew, she wears roughly $1,500,000-worth – so much that the couple have to be protected by eight bodyguards on their short journey to the Paris Opera House. Earlier the same day, Burton spends $960,000 buying her the jet plane on which they flew into Paris. 'Elizabeth was not displeased,' he confides to his diary.

Elizabeth remains enchanted by the fairy-tale glamour of the Windsors, but Burton, less convinced that the world he has created is the world he wants, his unease fuelled and allayed by three bottles of vodka a day, is beginning to find them a little wearing. Unlike the Duchess, the Duke lacks zip: another of their acquaintances finds himself mesmerised by the way that he 'always had something of … riveting stupidity to say on any subject'.

On November 12th, the Burtons grace a dinner for twenty-two at the Windsors' home. As they enter the room, Burton recognises only two people, the Count and Countess of Bismarck, and then only by name. 'He, the Count, looks as much like one's mental picture of the iron chancellor as spaghetti. Soft and round and irresolute. He couldn't carve modern Germany out of cardboard.'

The Duke and Duchess seem, through his jaded eyes, much diminished. 'It is extraordinary how small the Duke and Duchess are. Two tiny figures like Toto and Nanette that you keep on the mantelpiece. Chipped around the edges. Something you keep in the front room for Sundays only. Marred royalty. The awful majesty that doth hedge around a king is notably lacking in awfulness. Charming and feckless.'

Elizabeth notes that she and Richard are the only two people without titles in the entire room. She is offended that she has not been placed next to the Duke, and Richard is furious that he has not been placed next to the Duchess. Instead, he is between another Duchess and a Countess, both 'hard-faced and youngish'.

One of them tells him that she saw him in *Hamlet*, and asks how he could possibly remember all those lines. Burton says that he doesn't bother, that he improvises, that Shakespeare is lousy, that Hamlet's character is so revolting that one could only say some of his lines when drunk. 'I mean, the frantic self-pity of "How all occasions do inform against me, and spur my dull revenge". You have to be sloshed to get around that. At least *I* have to be.'

He thinks he may have shocked her. Another lady, 'not a day under seventy, whose face had been lifted so often that it was on top of her head', asks him if it is true that all actors are queer. Yes, he replies, and that's why he married Elizabeth, because she was queer too, but they have an arrangement.

'What do you do?'

'Well, she lives in one suite, and I in another, and we make love by telephone.'

After dinner, Taylor looks on in horror as Burton approaches the Duchess of Windsor and says, 'You are without any question, the most vulgar woman I've ever met.' Before long, he has picked up the seventy-two-year-old Duchess and is swinging her around 'like a dancing singing dervish'. The room falls silent. Watching the event with the Duke, Taylor is terrified that Burton will drop her or fall down and kill her. Meanwhile, Burton, who has long suspected that his lifestyle is a betrayal of his origins, is overcome with self-pity and starts pining for the Welsh valleys. 'Christ! I will arise and go now and go home to Welsh miners who understand drink and the idiocies that it arouses ... I shall die of drink and make-up.'

Arriving back at the Plaza Athénée, Taylor is furious, and locks Burton in the spare bedroom. He tries to kick the door down, 'and nearly succeeded which meant that I spent some time on my hands and knees this morning picking up the battered plaster in the hope that the waiters wouldn't notice that the hotel had nearly lost a door in the middle of the night'.

In the morning, Taylor berates him for his misbehaviour, complaining that they'll never be invited again. 'Thank God,' he replies, adding, 'Rarely have I been so stupendously bored.'

That weekend, he reluctantly agrees to accompany Taylor to a grand fancy-dress party at the Rothschilds' château in the country. Also at the party is Cecil Beaton, who spots them across the room. 'I have always loathed the Burtons for their vulgarity, commonness and crass bad taste,' he writes in his diary the next day. 'She combining the worst of US and English taste, he as butch and coarse as only a Welshman can be.'

ELIZABETH TAYLOR

UNNERVES

JAMES DEAN

Marfa, Texas
June 6th 1955

She is the former child star, now Queen of Hollywood. He is the up-and-coming method actor, surly and unpredictable. Though Elizabeth Taylor is a year younger than James Dean, she belongs to an earlier generation of old-fashioned, glamorous, self-confident, untouchable stars, whereas he heralds a new generation: scruffy, grunting, brooding, callow. They are to act together in *Giant*, Elizabeth Taylor as the wife of a Texas cattle baron, James Dean as the troublesome ranch-hand who strikes oil.

They are introduced a few days before filming begins. To everyone's surprise, he charms her, and takes her for a ride in his brand-new Porsche. Taylor ends the day convinced that he is a perfect gentleman, and that others have tarred him with the wrong brush.

The following day, Taylor, expecting a warm welcome after their pleasant introduction, goes up to Dean and says hello. He glares at her over the rims of his glasses, mutters something incomprehensible to himself and strides off as though he hasn't seen her. It dawns on her that, after all, his reputation for moodiness may be justified.

Their first four weeks are to be spent on location in the small, sleepy town of Marfa, Texas, where the temperatures frequently rise to 120 degrees in the shade. On their first day of filming, his friend Dennis Hopper has never seen James Dean so nervous on a set.

Their first scene involves Dean firing a shot at a water tower, Taylor stopping her car, and Dean asking her in for tea. But Dean is so nervous that he can barely get the words out. 'At that time there wasn't anybody who didn't think she was queen of the movies, and Jimmy was really fuckin' nervous. They did take after take, and it just wasn't going right. He was really getting fucked up. Really nervous,' recalls Hopper. 'Well, there were around four thousand people watching the scene from a hundred yards away, local people and visitors. And all of a sudden Jimmy turned and walked off towards them. He wasn't relating to them or anything. He got half-way, unzipped his pants, took out his cock, and took a piss. Then he dripped off, put his cock back, zipped up his pants, and walked back to the set and said, "OK, shoot.'"

This is not the sort of behaviour to which Elizabeth Taylor is accustomed. On the way back from the location, Hopper says to Dean, 'Jimmy, I've seen you do some way-out things before, but what was *that*?'

'I was nervous,' explains Dean. 'I'm a method actor. I work through my senses. If you're nervous, your senses can't reach your subconscious and that's that – you just can't work. So I figured if I could piss in front of these two thousand people, man, and I could be cool, I figured if I could do that, I could get in front of that camera and do just anything, anything at all.'

As the filming continues, Dean irritates the cast and crew with his habit of coming to a halt in the middle of a take and shouting, 'Cut – I fucked up!' He attributes it to the perfectionism required of a method actor. His co-star Rock Hudson, one of the old school, is less forgiving of the solipsistic neurosis that powers Dean's acting. The director, George Stevens, also grows irritated by Dean's random behaviour, regarding it as unprofessional. 'I'd get so mad at him, and he'd stand there, blinking behind his glasses after having been guilty of some bit of preposterous behaviour, and revealing by his very cast of defiance that he felt some sense of unworthiness.' Stevens is equally annoyed by Taylor's obsession with her looks. 'Until you tone down your veneer, you'll never be an actress,' he tells her.

Their shared sense of directorial persecution may help forge a bond between Taylor and Dean: in time, the two stars grow to like each other. 'We were like brother and sister really; kidding all the time, whatever it was we were talking about. One felt he was a boy one had to take care of, but even that was probably his joke. I don't think he needed anybody or anything – except his acting.'

Both Dean and Taylor are reliant on drugs of one sort or another: he smokes marijuana, while Taylor takes medications for her plentiful ailments, which Stevens regards as psychosomatic. 'When Jimmy was eleven and his mother passed away, he began to be molested by his minister. I think that haunted him the rest of his life. In fact, I know it did. We talked about it a lot. During *Giant* we'd stay up nights and talk and talk and that was one of the things he confessed to me,' Taylor says forty-two years later.*

'He would tell me about his past life, some of the grief and unhappiness he had experienced, and some of his loves and tragedies. Then, the next day on set, I would say, "Hi, Jimmy," and he would give me a cursory nod of his head. It was almost as if he didn't want to recognise me, as if he was ashamed of having revealed so much of himself the night before. It would take maybe a day or two for him to become my friend again.'

One day in September, with only a few scenes left to shoot, the director, crew members and actors assemble in the screening room to view the day's rushes. In the middle of the screening, Stevens takes a call, then orders the lights up. James Dean, he announces, has been killed in a car crash.

The following day, Taylor is summoned to film reaction shots for a scene in which she acted with Dean a few days ago. She realises with a start that she is being asked to react to a young man whose corpse is now lying on a slab in a funeral home at Paso Robles, but she goes ahead with it just the same.

---

* To journalist Kevin Sessums when he interviews her in 1997 for a magazine for people living with AIDS, prefacing her remarks with, 'I'm going to tell you something, but it's off the record until I die. OK?'

JAMES DEAN

IS FOREWARNED BY

ALEC GUINNESS

The Villa Capri, Hollywood
September 23rd 1955

A week before he is due to die, James Dean is sitting at a table in his favourite little restaurant in Hollywood, the Villa Capri. He is very chummy with Nikkos, its maître d', from whom he has started renting a log house in Sherman Oaks.

Looking towards the entrance, he spots a familiar figure attempting to get a table, then being turned away. He recognises him as the English actor Alec Guinness, the star of so many of his favourite Ealing comedies, such as *Kind Hearts and Coronets*.

Guinness has always been more than a touch superstitious, and in a few minutes he will be applying his sixth sense to James Dean. He regularly visits fortune tellers, and has even indulged in a little table-turning. At one time in his life he became obsessed with tarot cards, until all of a sudden one evening, 'I got the horrors about them and impetuously threw cards and books on a blazing log fire.'

Guinness delights in recounting his psychic powers. On the afternoon of New Year's Eve, 1943, he was resting in the cabin of the naval ship of which he was a lieutenant, when he apparently heard a sinister voice saying, 'Tomorrow.' He became convinced that this was a premonition of death.

That night, sailing from Sicily to the Yugoslav island of Vis, his ship hit a hurricane. An electrical discharge caused ribbons of blue fluorescent light, 'until the whole ship was lit up like some dizzying fairground side-show'. Convinced that he was going to die, Guinness found the spectacle 'beautiful and strangely comforting'.

The ship was dashed against the rocks as it entered the small Italian port of Termoli, and he gave the order to abandon ship. He had, it seems, outwitted the sinister voice – or had it been delivering less of a judgement than a warning?

In March this year, he and his wife were on holiday in the Trossachs in Scotland when their car had a bad puncture. 'Couldn't get the wheel off,' he wrote in his diary. 'After nearly an hour's effort said a little prayer to St Anthony and the nuts came loose the very next time I tried – and with only a small effort.'

Six months later he arrives in Hollywood, thoroughly exhausted after a sixteen-hour flight from Copenhagen, in order to begin filming *The Swan* with Grace Kelly and Louis Jourdan.

The screenwriter of *Father Brown*, Thelma Moss, has invited him out to dinner, but they have difficulty finding a table because Thelma is wearing slacks. They finally settle for a small Italian restaurant, the Villa Capri, which has a much more casual dress-code, but when they get there they are told by the genial maître d' that it is full, and so they begin to walk away.

'I don't care where we eat or what. Just something, somewhere,' grumbles Guinness irritably, adding, 'I don't mind just a hamburger.'

At that moment, he becomes aware of the sound of feet running down the street behind him. He turns to see a young man in sneakers, a sweatshirt and blue jeans. 'You want a table?' he asks. 'Join me. My name's James Dean.'

'Yes, very kind of you,' replies Guinness with relief, and eagerly follows him back to the Villa Capri.

Before they go into the restaurant, James Dean says, 'I'd like to show you something,' and takes them into the courtyard of the restaurant. There, he proudly shows them his new racing car, one of only ninety Porsche 550 Spyders ever produced. He has had it customised: it now has tartan seating and two red stripes at the rear of its wheelwell, all designed by George Barris, the man who will go on to design the Batmobile. 'It's just been delivered,' Dean says, proudly. On the lower rear of the engine cover are the words 'Little Bastard'. The car is so brand new that it is still wrapped in cellophane, with a bunch of roses tied to its bonnet.

Alec Guinness is seized by one of his premonitions.

'How fast can you go in that?'

'I can do 150 in it.'

'Have you driven it?'

'I've never been in it at all.'

And then – 'exhausted, hungry, feeling a little ill-tempered in spite of Dean's kindness' – Guinness hears himself saying, in a voice he can hardly recognise as his own, 'Look, I won't join your table unless you want me to, but I must say something. Please do not get into that car.' He looks at his watch. 'I said, "It's now 10 o'clock, Friday the 23rd of September 1955. If you get in that car you will be found dead in it by this time next week."'

Despite this grim prognosis, Dean laughs. 'Oh, shucks!' he says. 'Don't be so mean!'

Guinness apologises, blaming his outburst on a lack of sleep and food. The three of them then have dinner together – 'a charming dinner' – before going their separate ways. Guinness makes no further reference to the car, 'but in my heart I was uneasy'.

Though Dean himself has an interest in morbid premonitions – passages about death and degradation are heavily underlined in his copy of Ernest Hemingway's *Death in the Afternoon* – he ignores Guinness's warning. A week later, on September 30th, he is driving his new Spyder across the junction of Route 46 and Route 41 near Cholame, California, when he collides head-on with a Ford Custom Tudor coupé driven by a student with the inappropriately comical name of Donald Turnupseed.

James Dean is taken by ambulance to Paso Robles War Memorial Hospital, where he is pronounced dead on arrival at 5.59 p.m. His last words, uttered just before impact, are, 'The guy's gotta stop … he'll see us.'

Fifty years after his death, this section of the road is renamed the James Dean Memorial Junction.

'It was a very odd, spooky experience,' recalls Alec Guinness of their strange meeting. 'I liked him very much. I would have liked to have known him more.'

ALEC GUINNESS

CRAWLS WITH

EVELYN WAUGH

The Church of the Immaculate Conception, Farm Street, London W1
August 4th 1955

On Tuesday, July 19th 1955, the postman delivers a parcel and a letter to Evelyn Waugh. The parcel contains his weekly box of cigars. He is put out when the postman tries to charge him almost £8 duty on it. The letter is from his sixty-seven-year-old goddaughter, Edith Sitwell. She says she is to be received into the Roman Catholic Church in just over a fortnight. The news makes Waugh uneasy. He is aware of her tendency to show off. 'She might be making an occasion of it,' he confides to his diary, adding that he has written to her confessor, Father Caraman, 'urging the example of St Helena'. This particular saint is noted for her piety.

August 4th is a bright, sunny day. Waugh wakes up in the Grand Hotel, Folkestone. The staff are civil and obliging, the food dull and lukewarm. 'If only the cook and the patrons were better it would be admirable,' he thinks. He keeps sending notes to the chef ('Don't put cornflour in the sauce'), who reacts badly. 'He comes up and glowers at me in his white hat from behind a screen in the dining room.'

Waugh catches the 9 a.m. train to Charing Cross. One of his fellow passengers is 'a ginger-whiskered giant who looked like a farmer and read the *Financial Times*'. Waugh's journey is enlivened by a cinder blowing in from the engine, landing on the giant's tweed coat and burning a hole in it.

From Charing Cross, Waugh walks to White's Club, stopping to buy a carnation on the way. At White's, he refreshes himself with a mug filled with stout, gin and ginger beer, before arriving at Farm Street at 11.45 a.m. He is wearing a loud black-and-white houndstooth tweed suit, a red tie and a boater from which stream red and blue ribbons. Waugh enters the Ignatius Chapel, which he finds empty save for 'a bald shy man' who introduces himself as Alec Guinness.

Getting dressed this morning, Alec Guinness found it hard to know what to wear. Eventually, he picked a navy-blue hopsack suit as 'suitably formal'. He felt a black or grey tie would be 'too severe', preferring a bright blue tie as 'more in keeping for what I assumed was a joyous event'. He has not yet become a Catholic himself.*

They are joined, in Waugh's words, by 'an old deaf woman with dyed red hair whose name I never learned'. Guinness, too, fails to catch her name, 'even when she barked at us'. She walks unsteadily with the aid of two sticks, and her bare arms are encased in metal bangles which give him the impression that she is some ancient warrior.†

Guinness watches as she attempts to sit down on a complicated seat she has brought with her – 'half prie-dieu and half collapsible deckchair'. Somehow, she manages to entangle herself in the mechanism, with disastrous results: 'The sticks slid from under her, the chair heaped itself on the floor and all the bangles rolled down her arms and sticks and propelled themselves in every direction around the room.'

'My jewels!' she cries. 'Please to bring back my jewels!'

Waugh and Guinness dutifully get down on all fours and wriggle their way under the pews and around the candle sconces, trying to retrieve 'everything round and glittering'.

'How many jewels were you wearing?' Waugh asks the old deaf woman.

'Seventy,' she replies.

Under the pews, Waugh whispers to Guinness, 'What nationality?'

'Russian, at a guess,' says Guinness, sliding on his stomach beneath a pew and dirtying his smart suit.

'Or Rumanian,' says Waugh. 'She crossed herself backwards. She may be a Maronite Christian, in which case beware.'

The two men start laughing, and soon, according to Guinness, get 'barely controllable hysterics'. They pick up all the bangles they can find. Guinness counts them into her hands, but the old deaf woman looks suspiciously at the pair of them, as if they might have pocketed a few.

'Is that all?' she asks.

---

* Guinness is received into the Catholic Church less than a year later, in April 1956.

† Victoria Glendinning identifies this lady as Evelyn Weil, and the Portuguese poet mentioned later as Alberto de Lacerda.

'Sixty-eight,' says Guinness.

'You are still wearing two,' observes Waugh.

At that moment, the organ strikes a deep note, and the other three witnesses enter. Waugh turns his unforgiving owlish stare upon 'Father D'Arcy … a little swarthy man who looked like a Jew but claimed to be Portuguese, and a blond youth who looked American but claimed to be English'. Guinness notes that the Portuguese man, a poet, looks 'a little peevishly atheistic'.

Then, up the aisle, 'swathed in black like a sixteenth-century infanta', glides Edith Sitwell, to be received into the Church by Father Caraman.*

The service concluded, they are driven in a Daimler from Farm Street to the Sesame Club, just two streets away. Waugh has heard bad things about it, but is pleasantly surprised by the 'gargantuan feast' that has been laid on: cold consommé, lobster Newberg, steak, strawberry flan and 'great quantities of wine'. All in all, he considers it 'a rich blow-out'.† Guinness notes, 'Edith presiding like a bride in black and Fr Caraman frequently casting his eyes heavenwards as if in ecstasy.'

An awkward moment comes when the old deaf woman suddenly says, 'Did I hear the word "whisky"?'

'Do you want one?' asks Waugh.

'More than anything in the world.'

'I'll get you some.'

But at this point the Portuguese poet steps in. He nudges Waugh and says, 'It would be disastrous.' So Waugh persuades her to stick with the white wine. Repeating the words of the Portuguese poet, he explains to Guinness that 'We couldn't face another disaster from that quarter.'

Over lunch, Guinness tipsily shares his few remaining theological anxieties with the blond English youth and the Portuguese poet. 'Would we

---

* Later, he writes to Edith Sitwell, thanking her for choosing him as her sponsor. 'I thought your circle of friends round the table remarkably typical of the Church in its variety and goodwill … I liked Alec Guinness so much and will try to see more of him. I have long admired his art.' He goes on to warn her that among her fellow Catholics she must expect to find 'bores and prigs and crooks and cads'.

† Waugh is always very particular about food. Before going to bed that night, he sends £2 to the chef at the Grand Hotel, along with a note demanding that all the dishes for him must be cooked specially, never just kept warm.

have to drink the Pope's health? If Edith died on the spot would she go straight to heaven? And would that be a case for ecclesiastical rejoicing or worldly and artistic distress?' A great deal is drunk; the following morning, try as he may, Guinness cannot recollect any of them leaving the table.

EVELYN WAUGH
WRONG-FOOTS
IGOR STRAVINSKY

The Ambassador Hotel, Park Avenue, New York
February 4th 1949

Evelyn Waugh claims to dislike all music, with the possible exception of plainchant. This does not bode well for Igor Stravinsky as he prepares to meet him in New York. He has already been warned by Aldous Huxley that Waugh can be 'prickly, pompous, and downright unpleasant'. But he is an admirer of Waugh's writing, particularly his talent for dialogue and the naming of characters (Dr Kakaphilos; Father Rothschild, S.J.), and is pleased when a friend arranges a meeting.

Stravinsky spent last night in the more congenial company of Vladimir Nabokov, W.H. Auden and George Balanchine, playing them his draft score of Act 1 of *The Rake's Progress*. As usual, he found himself a little irritated by Auden's tendency to talk during any performance, but this is small fry compared to what lies ahead: Waugh is, after all, notoriously prickly.

'Why does everybody except me find it so easy to be nice?' asks the distracted Gilbert Pinfold in Waugh's most autobiographical novel.* Tom Driberg identifies this as 'a true outcry' from Pinfold's creator. At the age of only forty-five, Waugh has somehow boxed himself into the character of a grumpy old curmudgeon. Penelope Fitzgerald sums up the social message he wishes to convey as: *I am bored, you are frightened.*

His rudeness has no age limit. When Ann Fleming brings her uninvited three-year-old son to tea at the Grand Hotel, Folkestone, Waugh is so annoyed that he puts 'his face close to the child's, dragging down the corners of eyes and mouth with forefingers and thumbs, producing an effect of such unbelievable malignity that the child shrieked with terror

---

* For Mr Pinfold, 'the tiny kindling of charity which came to him through his religion, sufficed only to temper his disgust and change it to boredom'.

and fell to the floor'. Fleming retaliates by giving Waugh's face a hard slap and overturning a plate of éclairs.

Observing him at Pratt's Club, Malcolm Muggeridge thinks Waugh presents a 'quite ludicrous figure in dinner jacket, silk shirt; extraordinarily like a loquacious woman, with dinner jacket cut like a maternity gown to hide his bulging stomach. He was very genial, probably pretty plastered – all the time playing this part of a crotchety old character rather deaf, cupping his ear – "Feller's a bit of a Socialist, I suspect." Amusing for about a quarter of an hour. Tony [Powell] and I agreed that an essential difference between Graham [Greene] and Waugh is that, whereas Graham tends to impose an agonized silence, Waugh demands agonized attention.'

Some of his rudest remarks are delivered in such a way that few, perhaps including himself, can tell whether they are intended. 'I spent two nights at Cap Ferrat with Mr Maugham (who has lost his fine cook) and made a great gaffe,' he writes to Harold Acton in April 1952. 'The first evening he asked me what someone was like and I said "A pansy with a stammer." All the Picassos on the walls blanched.'

He delights in wrong-footing one and all. When Feliks Topolski and Hugh Burnett arrive for lunch at Combe Florey to prepare for Waugh's appearance on *Face to Face*, he is at pains to point out that his house has no television set and a radio only in the servants' quarters. He then serves them a large tureen of green-tufted strawberries. 'Too late I saw the problem,' recalls Burnett. 'Put the strawberries on the plate, add the cream, take the spoon – and you were trapped with the strawberry tufts. My attempt to spear one shot it under the sideboard. That was the BBC disgraced. Topolski, seeing what had happened, did the socially unthinkable – dipped a strawberry into the cream with his fingers. "Ah, Mr Topolski," Waugh observed helpfully, "You need a spoon."' When the day for the recording comes, Burnett introduces him to his interviewer, John Freeman. 'How do you do, Mr Waugh,' said Freeman.

'The name is Waugh – not Wuff!' he replied.

'But I called you Mr Waugh.'

'No, no, I distinctly heard you say "Wuff".'

During the interview, Waugh confesses that his worst fault is irritability. What with? asks Freeman. 'Absolutely everything. Inanimate objects and people, animals, anything.'

The Stravinskys and the Waughs meet up at the Ambassador Hotel on Park Avenue. Waugh is never at his best in America: he finds the natives unappealing, and upsets them with observations such as, 'Of course the Americans are cowards. They are almost all the descendants of wretches who deserted their legitimate monarch for fear of military service.'

Stravinsky soon finds that the cutting edge in Waugh's work is even sharper in his person. 'Not an immediately endearing character,' he thinks. After they have introduced themselves, Stravinsky asks Waugh whether he would care for a whisky. 'I do not drink whisky before wine,' he replies, his tone suggesting faint horror at Stravinsky's ignorance.

Waugh seems to rejoice in causing all Stravinsky's remarks, polite, lively or anodyne, to bounce back in his face. At first, Stravinsky speaks to Waugh in French, but Waugh replies that he does not speak the language. Mrs Waugh contradicts him pleasantly, but is swiftly rebuked.

The conversation stutters on. Stravinsky says he admires the Constitution of the United States. Waugh replies that he deplores 'everything American, beginning with the Constitution'. They pause to study their menus. Stravinsky recommends the chicken; Waugh points out that it is a Friday.

'Whether Mr Waugh was disagreeable, or only preposterously arch, I cannot say,' Stravinsky recalls.* 'Horace Walpole remarks somewhere that the next worst thing to disagreeableness is too-agreeableness. I would reverse the order of preference myself while conceding that on short acquaintance disagreeableness is the greater strain.' Desperately trying to find common ground, Stravinsky attempts to relate his own recent sung Mass to the theme of Waugh's current lecture tour. 'All music is positively painful to me,' replies Waugh.

The only subject on which the two of them achieve a measure of agreement concerns the burial customs of the United States. Stravinsky is impressed by Waugh's knowledge. Waugh claims that he himself has 'arranged to be buried at sea', though this, it turns out, is just another of his little teases.

---

* 'If he was accused of some quality usually regarded as contemptible … he studied it, polished up his performance, and, treating it as both normal and admirable, made it his own' – Frances Donaldson.

IGOR STRAVINSKY

IS APPALLED BY

WALT DISNEY

Burbank Studios, Los Angeles
December 1939

Igor Stravinsky is himself not the easiest of folk, but Walt Disney is not to know this when the composer drops round to his studio.

Disney is at the height of his success. Mickey Mouse and Donald Duck are the most durable and biddable stars Hollywood will ever know, and his recent *Snow White and the Seven Dwarfs* will gross $8 million. He has just built himself a palatial studio in Burbank, the size of a modest town, complete with its own streets, electric system and telephone exchange.

Meeting Leopold Stokowski, the conductor of the Philadelphia Orchestra, at a dinner party, Disney mentions an idea he has had for a two-reel version of Dukas's *The Sorcerer's Apprentice*, starring Mickey Mouse. Stokowski grows tremendously excited at the idea of animating great works of music. He suggests other pieces Disney might transform into colour: Bach's Organ Toccata in D-minor, for instance. Disney sees it as orange. 'Oh, no, I see it as purple,' counters Stokowski.

Disney's modest idea balloons into a full-length film, with classical music galore. Both men become over-excited; no idea seems too preposterous. Stokowski suggests a Debussy prelude, '*Les Sons et les parfums tournent l'air du soir*', explaining that he has always craved perfume in theatres. Disney goes overboard for it. 'You've got something!' he says. 'You could get them to name a special perfume for this – create a perfume – you could get write-ups in the papers! It's a hot idea!'

Disney wants a sequence showing the creation of the world, full of volcanoes and dinosaurs. But what music to use? His researchers can only come up with Haydn's *Creation*, but Disney thinks it doesn't carry quite enough oomph. At this point, Stokowski alerts him to *Le Sacre du* *printemps* by Igor Stravinsky.* Disney listens to it, and is immediately gripped. He offers Stravinsky $5,000 for the rights, though Stravinsky will remember it as $10,000. According to Stravinsky, Disney hints that if permission is withheld he will use the music anyway: pre-Revolutionary Russian copyrights are no longer valid.

Stravinsky accepts; Disney steams ahead. Before long the human inhabitants of the Burbank studio find themselves working alongside animals in cages, including iguanas and baby alligators, with skilled animators studying their movements close-up. 'It should look as though the studio has sent an expedition back to the earth six million years ago,' enthuses Disney. He is so excited that he starts free-associating to the music: 'Something like that last WHAHUMMPH I feel is a volcano – yet it's on land. I get that UGHHWAHUMMPH! on land, but we can look out on the water before this and see water spouts.' As he listens to the music, he gets so worked up that he suddenly blurts, 'Stravinsky will say: "Jesus, I didn't know I wrote that music!"'

Which, as it turns out, is roughly what Stravinsky does say. In December 1939, he drops into the Burbank studio for a private screening of *Fantasia*. The experience leaves him with the most awful memories. 'I remember someone offering me a score, and when I said I had my own, that some-one saying, "But it is all changed." It was indeed. The instrumentation had been improved by such stunts as having the horns play their glissandi an octave higher in the *Danse de la terre*. The order of pieces had been shuf-fled, too, and the most difficult of them eliminated, though this did not save the musical performance, which was execrable.'

As Stravinsky remembers it, Disney tries to reassure him by saying, 'Think of the number of people who will now be able to hear your music.' To which Stravinsky replies, 'The numbers of people who consume music ... is of no interest to me. The mass adds nothing to art.'

But Disney's memories of the meeting are quite different. Stravinsky, he maintains, made an earlier visit to the studio, saw the original sketches for the *Fantasia* version of *Le Sacre* and declared how excited he was. Later,

---

* The story does the rounds of Stokowski saying, 'Why don't we do *Sacre*?', to which Disney replies, 'Sock? What's that?' But a correspondent to the *New York Times* in 1990 points out that a stenographer was present at the meeting between Stokowski and Disney on September 13th 1938, and this snippet of dialogue is nowhere in the transcript.

having seen the finished product, Stravinsky emerged from the projection room 'visibly moved'. Disney remembers the composer saying that prehistoric life was what he always had in mind when he wrote it. But Stravinsky disagrees. 'That I could have expressed approbation over the treatment of my own music seems to me highly improbable – though, of course, I should hope I was polite.'

Either way, he is much less polite twenty years later, when he and Disney clash in the pages of the *New York Times*. He dislikes what was done to his music, he writes, and furthermore, 'I will say nothing about the visual complement as I do not wish to criticise *unresisting imbecility*.'

Whose memory are we to trust? There may be a temptation to favour the highbrow over the lowbrow, the intellectual over the populist; but self-delusion rains on all, high and low. Many artists who took money from Hollywood felt able to absolve themselves by seeking a divorce from the finished product. For them, the prevailing myth of the philistine Hollywood producer offered a welcome escape hatch.

By and large, the evidence favours Disney. Less than a year after their supposed contretemps, Stravinsky cheerfully sells Disney two more options – one on the musical folk tale *Renard*, the other on *The Firebird*.* And his artistic halo always has a certain rubbery quality about it: he composes some hunting music for Orson Welles's *Jane Eyre*, and after contractual negotiations break down, uses the very same piece for a commission from the Boston Symphony Orchestra, transforming it into an ode to the memory of the wife of Serge Koussevitzky. On another occasion, he lifts the incidental music he has been commissioned to write for a film about the Nazi occupation of Norway, *Commandos Strike at Dawn*, straight from a collection of Norwegian folk tunes his wife has stumbled upon in a second-hand bookstore in Los Angeles. When this deal falls through, he further rejigs it into a piece for the Boston Symphony Orchestra, solemnly retitling it 'Four Norwegian Moods'.

---

* After the initial failure of *Fantasia*, Disney tells his studio chiefs, 'We're through with caviar. From now on it's mashed potatoes and gravy.' Yet no Hollywood studio ever entirely shook off the quest for respectability. Stravinsky likes to tell the story of Arnold Schoenberg, who turns down a fortune to supply music for Irving Thalberg's *The Good Earth* when it comes with impossible artistic conditions attached. Schoenberg refuses, declaring, 'You kill me to keep me from starving to death.'

WALT DISNEY

RESISTS

P.L. TRAVERS

Grauman's Chinese Theatre, Los Angeles
August 27th 1964

It is all smiles as Walt Disney and his most recent collaborator, P.L. Travers, pose with Julie Andrews at the world premiere of *Mary Poppins*. This, he tells reporters, is the movie he has been dreaming of making ever since 1944, when he first heard his wife and children laughing at a book and asked them what it was. At his side, Travers, aged sixty-five, appears equally thrilled. 'It's a splendid film and very well cast!' she enthuses.

The premiere is a lavish affair. A miniature train rolls down Hollywood Boulevard with Mickey Mouse, Snow White and the Seven Dwarfs, Peter Pan, Peter Rabbit, the Three Little Pigs, the Big Bad Wolf, Pluto, a skunk and four dancing penguins on board. At the cinema, the Disneyland staff are dressed as English bobbies; at the party afterwards, grinning chimney-sweeps frolic to music from a band of Pearly Kings and Queens.

The next day, Travers is over the moon, wiring her congratulations to 'Dear Walt'. The film is, she says, 'a splendid spectacle … true to the spirit of *Mary Poppins*'. Disney's response is a little more guarded. He is happy to have her reactions, he says, and appreciates her taking the time, but what a pity that 'the hectic activities before, during and after the premiere' prevented them from seeing more of each other.

Travers writes back, thanking Disney for thanking her for thanking him. The film is, she says, 'splendid, gay, generous and wonderfully pretty' – even if, for her, the real Mary Poppins remains within the covers of her books. On her copy, she adds a note saying that it is a letter 'with much between the lines'. The same month, she complains to her London publisher that the film is 'simply sad'.

Those smiles at the premiere are, in fact, the first and the last they will ever exchange. Pamela Travers is a long-time devotee of Gurdjieff,

Krishnamurti, Yeats and Blake. For her, the Mary Poppins books were never just children's stories, but intensely personal reflections of her Alphabetti Spaghetti blend of philosophy, mysticism, theosophy, Zen Buddhism, duality, and the oneness of everything. In the last year of her life, she will reveal to an interviewer that Mary Poppins is related to the mother of God. Disney's own conception of the finger-clicking nanny is rather more straightforward.

Nothing about the film of *Mary Poppins* has been easy. The contract alone took sixteen years to negotiate: Travers finally accepts 5 per cent of gross profits, with a guarantee of $100,000. But this is to prove inadequate compensation; she soon begins to complain that Disney is 'without subtlety and emasculates any character he touches, replacing truth with false sentimentality'.

Walt Disney's attitude to Travers is one of damage limitation. He wants to keep her on board, but positioned as far as possible from the driver's seat. This does not stop Travers making frequent lunges for the steering wheel, generally with a view to forcing the vehicle into reverse. She complains about everybody and everything, even stretching to the type of measuring tape Mary Poppins would use.*

She objects to all the Americanisms that seem to be creeping in – 'outing', 'freshen up', 'on schedule', 'Let's go fly a kite' – and considers the servants much too common and vulgar. Furthermore, the Banks home is much too grand, and any suggestion of a romance between Mary Poppins and the cockney chimneysweep Bert is utterly distasteful. Finally, she objects to Mrs Banks being portrayed as a suffragette, and considers the Christian name they impose on her – Cynthia – 'unlucky, cold and sexless', her own preference being Winifred.

---

* Recordings still exist of the daily conferences between the scriptwriters and P.L. Travers. On the first day, they start from the beginning: '17 Cherry Tree Lane, the Banks household is in uproar … The father comes home to find the children misbehaving. Mr Banks talks of his wife's job.'

'Just a minute,' says Travers. 'That's, that's, not job, ah, ah …'

'Domain?'

'Er, yes.'

'Responsibility?'

'Well, we can't have job.'

Travers even believes her responsibilities extend to the casting.* The day after Julie Andrews gives birth, she phones her in hospital. 'P.L. Travers here. Speak to me. I want to hear your voice.' When they finally meet, her first remark to the actress is, 'Well, you've got the nose for it.'

Mary Poppins is a worldwide success. Costing $5.2 million to make, it grosses $50 million. But the more the money rolls in, the more Travers' attitude to the film and its creator sours. She tells *Ladies' Home Journal* that she hated parts of the film, like the animated horse and pig, and disapproved of Mary Poppins kicking up her gown and showing her underwear, and disliked the billboards saying 'Walt Disney's *Mary Poppins*' when they should have said 'P.L. Travers' *Mary Poppins*'.

She writes to a friend that Disney wishes her dead, and is furious with her for not obliging. 'After all, until now, all his authors have been dead and out of copyright.' But there is always the promise of a sequel, and yet more money. It is only when Disney dies in December 1966† that her objections become more concentrated and vocal. In 1967, she says that the film was 'an emotional shock, which left me deeply disturbed', and in 1968 that she 'couldn't bear' it – 'all that smiling'. In 1972, she declares in a lecture that 'When I was doing the film with George Disney – that is his name, isn't it – George? – he kept insisting on a love affair between Mary Poppins and Bert. I had a terrible time with him.'

Her invitation to the world premiere is, it later emerges, not achieved without a struggle. Failing to receive an invitation, she instructs her lawyer, agent and publisher to demand one on her behalf. When it is still not forthcoming, she sends a telegram to Disney himself, informing him she is in the States, and plans on attending the premiere: she is sure somebody will find a seat for her, and will he let her know the details? Her attendance is, she adds, essential 'for the dignity of the books'.

---

* Somehow, Walt Disney manages to keep her from meeting Dick van Dyke. By mid-1963, with filming under way, Julie Andrews writes to Travers telling her not to worry about anything, adding that Dick van Dyke is good as Bert, but that 'he will be an "individual" cockney instead of a "regular type" cockney'. Disney originally wanted Cary Grant to play the part, but he turned down the role, as did Laurence Harvey and Anthony Newley.

† When Walt Disney is dying of lung cancer, he asks the film's composers, the Sherman brothers, to play his favourite song from the soundtrack when they drop by every Friday. Each time they play 'Feed the Birds', Disney goes over to the window and weeps.

Disney writes back saying that he has always been counting on her presence at the London premiere, but is now delighted to know she will also be able to come to the premiere in Los Angeles. And yes, they will happily hold a seat for her.

P.L. TRAVERS

WATCHES OVER

GEORGE IVANOVICH GURDJIEFF

The American Hospital of Paris, Neuilly-sur-Seine
October 30th 1949

Any meeting between the living and the dead is inevitably one-sided. Do they know something we don't know?

On October 30th 1949, P.L. Travers sits all night in a private room on the first floor of the American Hospital of Paris, gazing lovingly at the corpse of George Ivanovich Gurdjieff.

Pamela first encountered Gurdjieff thirteen years ago, in 1936, at his Institute for the Harmonious Development of Man, near Fontainebleau. After spending much of her life pursuing poets and mystics, she found in Gurdjieff what she had long been looking for, and was particularly drawn to his unusual emphasis on finding truth through dance. Back in London, she was to teach these Gurdjieffian dances before progressing to teaching the teachers; she spread his beliefs for the rest of her life.

Gurdjieff was a guru with an opaque past. Half Armenian, half Greek, he cultivated obscurity about many things, not least his age.* He tried his hand at many trades, dealing, in different places and at different times, in a range of products including carpets, antiques, oil, fish, caviar, false eyelashes, sparrows and corsets.

But around 1912, he found his calling as a guru, his core belief being that 'modern man lives in sleep, in sleep he is born and in sleep he dies'. Only by subscribing to Gurdjieff's special training could modern man snap out of it, rise to a higher level of consciousness, and find God, or, as Gurdjieff preferred to call Him, 'Our Almighty Omni-Loving Common Father Uni-Being Creator Endless'.

---

* He may have been born in 1866, or in 1877, in any year in between these two dates, or indeed either side of them.

Among his many other beliefs was that the moon lives off the energy of dead human beings, known as Askokin, and controls all man's actions. To guard against rebellion, the higher powers have implanted an organ at the base of man's spine called the Kundabuffer, which stops him becoming too intelligent.* Only those who follow Gurdjieff's path can break away from their fate as food for the moon, and thus attain immortality.

P.L. Travers' most famous creation, the flying nanny Mary Poppins, might be seen as Gurdjieff in a long dress, shorn of his handlebar moustache and propelled by an umbrella: in some of the stories, Poppins guides her charges to the secrets of the universe, with the planets all indulging in a great cosmic dance. In the chapter 'The New One' in *Mary Poppins Comes Back*, Mr and Mrs Banks give birth to a new baby, Annabel, who, it emerges, is formed from the sea, sky, stars and sun. Mary Poppins is, to all intents and purposes, one of the enlightened, aware of worlds beyond.

As Pamela Travers sits beside the corpse of Gurdjieff, she believes that the real Gurdjieff is somewhere else, somewhere on another plane, reunited with the being he used to call the Most Most [sic] Holy Sun Absolute. Alive, he was the most earthy of men, enjoying huge three-course meals, washed down with Armagnac, while his followers made do with bowls of thin soup. Some non-believers found his personal habits unseemly. In his palatial flat at his institute in Paris, he often didn't bother to visit the lavatory, preferring to defecate willy-nilly. 'There were times when I would have to use a ladder to clean the walls,' recalls one of the residents. He demanded unquestioning obedience from his wealthy followers, and enjoyed humiliating them; it was almost as though he relished the sight of grown men in tears. He was a stranger to celibacy, and loved to boast of all the babies he had fathered, peppering his pidgin English with the word 'fuck'. But for his devotees this only added to his air of other-worldliness: surely a guru so un-gurulike could not possibly be a fraud?

The Second World War separated the guru from his protégée. Stuck in Paris, Gurdjieff refused to let the Nazi occupation hinder his lifestyle, feasting on delicacies from local suppliers attained with promises – bogus, as it turned out – of massive wealth owed to him from a Texan oilfield.

---

* Today, these beliefs may seem a little far-fetched, but in their day they attracted a good many followers, among them Georgia O'Keeffe and Katherine Mansfield.

The moment the war was over, Pamela travelled to Paris on one of the first trains. She sat with Gurdjieff's other disciples and imbibed his latest thoughts and aphorisms such as 'Mathematic is useless. You cannot learn laws of world creation and world existence by mathematic,' and 'Useless study Freud or Jung. This only masturbation.' He advised Pamela and his other followers to have an enema every day, then donned a tasselled magenta fez to play his accordion in a minor key. 'This is temple music,' he assured them. 'Very ancient.'

Pamela sees Gurdjieff in Paris for one last time a little under a month before he dies. She brings her adopted son, Camillus, who tells Gurdjieff that he has no father. 'I will be your father,' says Gurdjieff. On October 25th 1949, Gurdjieff is taken to the American Hospital, carried into the ambulance in his bright pyjamas, smoking a Gauloise Bleue and exclaiming merrily, '*Au revoir, tout le monde!*'

He dies four days later. The next day, Pamela travels from Victoria Station to Paris with a group of his followers. She pays homage to his corpse first in his bedroom, and for the remainder of the week in the chapel. On November 2nd she sets eyes on him for the very last time. While she is there, the undertakers come to collect him, but the coffin is too small, and a fresh one has to be ordered.

She attends his funeral at the Alexandre Nevski Cathedral. Afterwards, she files up and kisses the coffin. He is buried at Avon near Fontainebleau; with the other mourners, she throws a handful of earth on his grave.

Travers dies aged ninety-five, in 1996, leaving £2,044,078 in her will, including a generous bequest to the Gurdjieff Society. At her funeral in Chelsea, her lawyers and accountants sit on one side of the aisle, her fellow Gurdjieffians on the other. As her coffin is carried away from Christ Church, these two sides of the congregation join together in a rendition of 'Lord of the Dance'.

GEORGE IVANOVICH GURDJIEFF

COOKS SAUERKRAUT FOR

FRANK LLOYD WRIGHT

Taliesin, Spring Green, Wisconsin
June 1934

Gurdjieff is no easy traveller. He arrives at Grand Central Station with seven suitcases, furious at the train driver for refusing to delay the departure of the midnight express until he is in a mood to board.

Cursing loudly, he bangs his way through thirteen Pullman cars, disturbing the sleeping passengers. Throughout the night, he moans and groans at theatrical volume. At breakfast, he refuses everything on the menu, informing the steward, at exhaustive length, about his complicated digestive processes and special dietary needs. For the rest of the journey he infuriates his fellow passengers with his chain smoking, drinks furiously and produces all sorts of smelly food, including an over-ripe Camembert. From Chicago, he travels to the Wrights' 1,000-acre architectural fellowship, Taliesin. 'Now must change, we are going to special place,' he informs his long-suffering assistant.

Gurdjieff and Frank Lloyd Wright have never met before. Both men are, by nature, leaders, not disciples; a clash of egos seems on the cards. Furthermore, there is a question of jealousy: Wright's wife Olgivanna was, for many years, one of Gurdjieff's sacred dancers. 'I wish for immortality,' she tells him on their first meeting, and Gurdjieff had agreed to organise it for her. Added to this, the Wrights' six-year marriage – his third, her second – is going through a stormy patch. Wright has taken to blaming Olgivanna for all his worst moods. One moment he will take an outlandish view, bulldozing her into agreeing with him, then he will change his mind and chastise her for letting him think like that. A few days ago, he dreamed that Olgivanna was in bed with a black man. When he woke up, he placed the blame on her. 'There must be something in you that led me to the conclusion of such a dream!' he said. Before the arrival of Gurdjieff, Olgivanna has been thinking of leaving Wright. 'I cannot bear this abuse any longer,' she tells her daughter.

Gurdjieff is no shrinking violet. The moment he sets foot in Taliesin he takes charge of the cooking, producing many little bags of hot spices and peppers from his various pockets. He takes control of the entertainment, too. After dinner, he supervises the playing of twenty-five or thirty of his own compositions on the piano: he is the self-proclaimed pioneer of a revolutionary new school of 'objective' music, the first ever to produce exactly the same reaction in all its listeners.

Without fuss, Wright becomes a willing disciple. Just twenty-four hours in the company of Gurdjieff have served to convince him of his genius. He compares him to 'some oriental buddha' who has 'come alive in our midst'; like Gandhi, though 'more robust, aggressive and venturesome ... Notwithstanding a superabundance of personal idiosyncrasy, George Gurdjieff seems to have the stuff in him of which genuine prophets have been made.' Wright sees him as ageless, like God. He is, he says, 'a man of perhaps eighty-five looking fifty-five'. In fact, though nobody knows for sure, most people reckon his year of birth to be 1866, which would in fact make him more like sixty-eight.

Gurdjieff loves to be in command, and is never happier than when a lot of people are doing exactly what he says. Before his stay is over, he has made everyone cook great quantities of sauerkraut from his own recipe, involving whole apples, including their skins, their stems and their cores. Even his most devoted disciples find it hard to swallow. On his departure from Taliesin, he leaves behind two fifty-gallon barrels of the stuff. In the first flush of discipleship, Frank Lloyd Wright will not hear a word against the sauerkraut. He insists the barrels must be transported to his Fellowship's desert camp in Arizona, watching attentively as they are loaded onto a truck.

The sauerkraut truck gets as far as Iowa before the crew decides to call it a day. 'We loosened the tailgate ropes,' one of them confesses years later, 'and dumped the barrels into a ditch.'

Even after such a brief meeting, Wright never loses his faith in Gurdjieff. Mysteriously, his rows with Olgivanna come to an end. 'I am sure Gurdjieff told Olgivanna to be devious, because it all changed,' notes a friend. Or was it something in the sauerkraut?

As time goes by, Taliesin comes increasingly to resemble Gurdjieff's Institute of Harmonious Development, particularly in its strictly pyramidical approach to harmony. 'Never have so many people spent so much time making a very few people comfortable,' remarks one disaffected disciple. By the late 1940s, the Wrights have taken to sitting on a dais, eating different meals to their followers, who are given fried eggs.*

The two men meet again from time to time. Whenever they clash, it is Wright who gives way: there is never any question as to which is the guru and which the disciple. When Gurdjieff returns to Taliesin in 1939, Wright suggests he sends some of his own pupils to Gurdjieff in Paris, 'Then they can come back to me and I'll finish them off.'

'YOU finish! You are IDIOT!' snaps Gurdjieff. 'YOU finish? No. YOU begin. I finish!'

In November 1948, Wright visits Gurdjieff in the Wellington Hotel, New York, where he is staying with his varied entourage. Gurdjieff places Wright beneath an enneagram constructed of large leaves, and listens attentively as Wright talks him through his problems with his gall bladder. 'I seven times doctor,' announces Gurdjieff, prescribing him a meal of mutton, avocado and peppered Armagnac. Oddly enough, it seems to do the trick. Gurdjieff then brings out his harmonium. 'The music I play you now came from monastery where Jesus Christ spent from eighteenth to thirtieth year,' he explains.

One of Gurdjieff's most striking pronouncements is, 'I am Gurdjieff. I will NOT die!' But die he does, just under a year later.† 'The greatest man in the world has recently died,' Wright announces to the audience as he is being presented with a medal in New York. 'His name was Gurdjieff.'

---

* Stalin's daughter Svetlana, who marries the husband of Olgivanna's late daughter (curiously also called Svetlana), compares her running of Taliesin to Stalin's running of the Soviet Union. 'This hierarchical system was appalling: the widow at the top, then the board of directors (a formality); then her own close inner circle, making all the real decisions; then working architects – the real working horses; at the bottom, students who paid high sums to be admitted, only to be sent the next day to work in the kitchen to peel potatoes ... Mrs Wright's word was law. She had to be adored and worshipped and flattered as often as possible.'

† In 1954, J. Edgar Hoover, the Director of the FBI, reports in a secret memorandum that Gurdjieff is brainwashing Frank Lloyd Wright. He is apparently unaware that Gurdjieff has been dead these past five years.

FRANK LLOYD WRIGHT

DESIGNS A HOUSE FOR

MARILYN MONROE

The Plaza Hotel, Fifth Avenue, New York
Autumn 1957

One afternoon in the autumn of 1957, the most venerated architect in America, Frank Lloyd Wright, now aged ninety, is working in his suite in the Plaza Hotel, New York, when the doorbell rings. It is Marilyn Monroe, come to ask him to design a house.

Since their marriage in June 1956, Arthur Miller and his bride Marilyn Monroe have been based at Miller's modest two-storey country house near Roxbury, Connecticut. Dating from 1783, it has 325 acres of land planted with fruit trees. A verandah at the back looks out across endless hills. A short walk from the house is a swimming pond, with clear spring water.

It is just right for Miller, who likes to live in the countryside, away from the flash world of celebrity, and is known to be careful with money. But Marilyn has other plans. She loves to spend, and has firm ideas about what is glamorous and what is not. Her self-esteem is bound up with her ability to splash out; she craves nothing but the best.

Like so many men, Frank Lloyd Wright is immediately taken with Marilyn.* He ushers her into a separate room, away from his wife and his staff, and listens intently as she describes the sort of home she has in mind. It is spectacularly lavish. Once she has left, Wright dips into his archives and digs out an abandoned plan for a building he drew up eight years earlier: a luxury manor house for a wealthy Texan couple.

The parsimonious Miller is taken aback when he hears of Marilyn's grandiose vision for their new home. 'That we could not really afford all of her ideas I did my best not to dramatize, but it was inevitable that some

---

* Later, when cheekily asked on a talk show, 'What do you think of Miss Monroe as architecture?' Wright replies, 'I think Miss Monroe's architecture is extremely good architecture.'

of my concern showed.' When she tells him the name of the architect, Miller's heart sinks. But he bites his lip, hoping good sense will prevail. 'It had to seem like ingratitude to question whether we could ever begin to finance any Wright design, since much like her, he had little interest in costs. I could only give him his day and let her judge whether it was beyond our means or not.'

One grey autumn morning, the Millers drive Frank Lloyd Wright to Roxbury. Wright is wearing a wide-brimmed cowboy hat. He curls up in the back seat and sleeps throughout the two-hour journey.

The three of them enter the old house together. Wright looks around the living room, and, in what Miller describes as 'a tone reminiscent of W.C. Fields's nasal drawl', says disparagingly, 'Ah, yes, the old house. Don't put a nickel in it.' They sit down to a lunch of smoked salmon. Wright refuses any pepper. 'Never eat pepper,' he says. 'The stuff will kill you before your time. Avoid it.'

After lunch, Marilyn remains in the house while the two men trudge half a mile up the steep hill to the crest on which the new house is to be built. Wright never stops to catch his breath: Miller is impressed. At the crest, Wright turns towards the magnificent view, unbuttons his fly and urinates, sighing, 'Yes. Yes indeed.' He glances about for a few seconds, then leads the way back down the hill. Before they go back into the house, Miller steals a quick private word with Wright. 'I thought the time had come to tell him something he had never bothered to ask, that we expected to live fairly simply and were not looking for some elaborate house with which to impress the world.'

The message is plural, but it should have been singular. An elaborate house with which to impress the world is, in a nutshell, just what Marilyn is after, which is why she hired Frank Lloyd Wright in the first place. But Wright affects not to hear. 'I saw that this news had not the slightest interest for him,' says Miller.

A few days later, Miller visits the Plaza Hotel alone. Wright shows him a watercolour of his extravagant plan: a circular living room with a dropped centre surrounded by five-foot-thick ovoid columns made of sandstone with a domed ceiling sixty feet in diameter, rounded off with a seventy-foot-long swimming pool with fieldstone sides jutting out from the incline of the hill. Miller looks at it in horror, mentally totting up the cost. He notes with indignation that Wright has added a final flourish to his painting – a huge limousine in the curved driveway, complete with a uniformed chauffeur.

Miller asks the cost. Wright mentions $250,000, but Miller doesn't believe him: it might cover the cost of the swimming pool, 'if that'. He also notes that Wright's 'pleasure dream of Marilyn allowed him to include in this monster of a structure only a single bedroom and a small guestroom, but he did provide a large "conference room" complete with a long board-room-type table flanked by a dozen high-backed chairs, the highest at the head, where he imagined she would sit like the reigning queen of a small country, Denmark, say'.*

The marriage goes from bad to worse. Miller and Monroe have nothing to say to each other. 'He makes me think I'm stupid. I'm afraid to bring things up, because maybe I am stupid.' Marilyn adds that 'I'm in a fucking prison and my jailer is named Arthur Miller … Every morning he goes into that goddamn study of his, and I don't see him for hours and hours. I mean, what the fuck is he doing in there? And there I am, just sitting around; I haven't a goddamn thing to do.'

Miller fails to give the go-ahead to Wright, who dies in April 1959. Miller and Monroe divorce in 1961; Monroe dies in August 1962.

Thirty years later, the plans are dusted off and enlarged. Marilyn's dream home finally emerges as a $35-million golf clubhouse in Hawaii, complete wtih banqueting rooms, a men's locker room and a Japanese *furo* bath with a soaking pool, not to mention seated showers.

---

* Wright also incorporates an elaborate nursery suite in his plans, but thirty years later Miller fails to mention this detail in his autobiography.

MARILYN MONROE
WEARS HER TIGHTEST, SEXIEST DRESS FOR
NIKITA KHRUSHCHEV

The Café de Paris, Hollywood
September 19th 1959

In her bungalow at the Beverly Hills Hotel, Marilyn Monroe is preparing to meet the Soviet Premier, Nikita Khrushchev. When she was first invited, his name hadn't rung a bell, and she wasn't keen to go. It was only when her studio told her that in Russia, America meant two things, Coca-Cola and Marilyn Monroe, that she changed her mind. 'She loved hearing that,' recalls Lena Pepitone, her maid. Marilyn tells Lena that the studio wants her to wear her tightest, sexiest dress. 'I guess there's not much sex in Russia,' she concludes.

Her preparations are lengthy and elaborate, involving a masseuse, a hairdresser and a make-up artist. When they are halfway through, the president of Twentieth Century-Fox, Spyros Skouras, arrives, just to make sure that, for once in her life, Marilyn will be on time. As agreed, she squeezes into a low-cut, skin-tight black lace dress. Her chauffeur drops her at the studio before noon. The parking lot is empty. 'We must be late! It must be over!' gasps Marilyn. In fact, they are far too early.*

Nikita Khrushchev's American tour has had more than its share of ups and downs. He is a temperamental character, apt to flair up at the slightest provocation. Perhaps because of this, the American media cannot get enough of him. 'It's Krush, Khrushy, Khrushchev!' writes a columnist for the *New York Daily News*. 'The fellow's all over the dials these days ... The pudgy Soviet dictator is smiling, laughing, scowling, shaking his forefinger or clenching his iron fist.' Others have been less generous. A rival columnist in the *New York Mirror* describes him as 'a rural dolt unwittingly proving a case against himself and his system'. The three main television

---

* Hearing this, Marilyn's long-suffering director Billy Wilder remarks that Khrushchev should direct her next picture.

networks show live coverage of his visit, repeating it every night in special thirty-minute bulletins. He is followed everywhere by 342 reporters and photographers, the largest travelling media group the world has ever known.

On the fifth day of his tour, Khrushchev arrives in Los Angeles, in time for lunch for four hundred people at Twentieth Century-Fox. There has been such demand for places that spouses have been banned unless they also happen to be stars. There are one or two couples – Elizabeth Taylor and Eddie Fisher, Tony Curtis and Janet Leigh – but they are few and far between.

Khrushchev enters a packed room. Everyone who is anyone is here: Edward G. Robinson, Judy Garland, Ginger Rogers, Kirk Douglas, Shelley Winters, Dean Martin, Debbie Reynolds, Nat 'King' Cole, Frank Sinatra, Maurice Chevalier, Zsa Zsa Gabor. Mrs Khrushchev is seated between Bob Hope and Gary Cooper. Conversation proves stilted.

'Why don't you move out here? You'll like the climate,' suggests Cooper.

'No,' replies Mrs Khrushchev. 'Moscow is all right for me.'

Khrushchev is on the top table, next to Skouras. Lunch has its awkward moments. When Khrushchev is told that his spur-of-the-moment request to visit Disneyland has been turned down, owing to security worries, he sends the American Ambassador to the UN a furious note. 'I understand you have cancelled the trip to Disneyland. I am most displeased.'

The after-lunch speeches are awkward. Khrushchev heckles Skouras during his speech of welcome, and further heckles Henry Cabot Lodge as he speaks of America's affection for Russian culture. 'Have you seen *They Fought for Their Homeland*?' he yells. 'It is based on a novel by Mikhail Sholokhov.'

'No.'

'Well, buy it. You should see it.'

In his own speech, Khrushchev grows very bullish. 'I have a question for you. Which country has the best ballet? Yours?! You do not even have a permanent opera and ballet theatre! Your theatres thrive on what is given to them by rich people! In our country, it is the state that gives the money! And the best ballet is in the Soviet Union! It is our pride!'

After going on like this for forty-five minutes, he suddenly seems to remember something. 'Just now, I was told that I could not go to

Disneyland. I asked, "Why not? What is it? Do you have rocket-launching pads there?" Just listen to what I was told: "We" – which means the American authorities – "cannot guarantee your security there." What is it? Is there an epidemic of cholera there? Have gangsters taken hold of the place?' He punches the air, and starts to look angry. 'That's the situation I find myself in. For me, such a situation is inconceivable. I cannot find words to explain this to my people!'

At last he sits down. The Hollywood audience applauds. As he is being shown to the sound stage to watch the movie *Can-Can* being filmed,* he recognises Marilyn Monroe and darts over to shake her hand. All wide-eyed, Marilyn delivers a line that Natalie Wood, a fluent Russian speaker, has coached her to say. For once, she gets it right first time: 'We the workers of Twentieth Century-Fox rejoice that you have come to visit our studio and country.'

Khrushchev seems to appreciate her effort. 'He looked at me the way a man looks on a woman,' she recalls.

'You're a very lovely young lady,' he says, squeezing her hand.

'My husband, Arthur Miller, sends you his greeting. There should be more of this kind of thing. It would help both our countries understand each other.'

Afterwards, Marilyn Monroe enthuses, 'This is about the biggest day in the history of the movie business.' But when she gets back home, she has changed her tune. 'He was fat and ugly and had warts on his face and he growled,' she tells Lena. 'Who would want to be a Communist with a President like that?'†

But she is pretty sure that the Premier enjoyed their meeting. 'I could tell Khrushchev liked me. He smiled more when he was introduced to me

---

* Throughout the racy can-can routine, involving a male dancer diving under the skirt of Shirley MacLaine and emerging holding her red knickers, the Russian Premier appears to be having a whale of a time, but he later denounces it as immoral, pornographic exploitation, adding that 'a person's face is more beautiful than his backside'.

† Her husband Arthur Miller, who was not invited, gives a rather diplomatic account of Marilyn's opinion of Khrushchev in his autobiography. 'The Soviet chairman was very obviously smitten with her, and she in turn liked him for his plainness,' he writes. Miller's achievements are in many ways overshadowed by his association with Marilyn. 'When Arthur Miller shook my hand I could only think that this was the hand that had once cupped the breasts of Marilyn Monroe,' recalls Barry Humphries in July 2010.

than for anybody else at the whole banquet. And everybody else was there. He squeezed my hand so long and so hard that I thought he would break it. I guess it was better than having to kiss him.'

NIKITA KHRUSHCHEV

LAMBASTS

GEORGE BROWN

Harcourt Room, Palace of Westminster, London
April 23rd 1956

A formal dinner is being held by the National Executive Committee of the Labour Party to honour Nikita Khrushchev, the leader of the Soviet Union, and Marshal Nikolai Bulganin, his Premier, both of whom are in Britain at the invitation of the Conservative government.

Khrushchev is never the easiest of guests.* Mrs Anthony Eden thinks his idea of dinner-table repartee is to declare that Soviet missiles 'could easily reach your island and quite a bit farther'.† Fortunately, dinner with the Queen earlier in the week passes without incident: she is not one to pick an argument. In fact, Khrushchev finds her 'completely unpretentious, completely without haughtiness … the sort of young woman you'd be likely to meet walking along Gorky Street on a balmy Sunday afternoon'.

During the Labour Party dinner, the Shadow Minister of Supply, George Brown, puffs away on his pipe, dutifully listening to a welcoming speech by the Chairman of the Labour Party, then to a speech by Bulganin. Before long, a few of his more left-wing colleagues, keen to demonstrate their friendliness towards the Soviet Union, start thumping the table and chanting, 'We – want – Khrush-chev,' over and over again.

Never short of things to say, Khrushchev leaps up with a great beam on his face to deliver an impromptu speech. The way Brown remembers it, Khrushchev 'just went on and on. He delivered a great denunciation of

---

* Harold Macmillan describes him as 'a kind of mixture between Peter the Great and Lord Beaverbrook'.

† Yet behind closed doors, his talk seems to be less about missiles than about his coiffure. When the British secret service bugs his room at Claridge's, they are, according to Peter Wright, surprised to hear nothing about the Cold War, 'just long monologues addressed to his valet on the subject of his attire. He was an extraordinarily vain man. He stood in front of the mirror preening himself for hours at a time, and fussing about his hair parting.'

Germany, put in a lot of stuff about the beginning of the war, and followed this with a particularly offensive passage about Britain's role in the war – how we had thrown the blood-thirsty Germans at the throat of the nice Russians, and so on.'

For Brown, enough is enough. He remembers muttering, 'May God forgive you,' but to his fellow guests the mutter emerges as more of a bark. Khrushchev stops speaking. He turns to Brown and asks him to repeat what he has just said. Brown does not reply, and those around him urge him to stay silent. But Khrushchev is spoiling for a fight, and announces to the room that Brown is clearly too afraid to repeat his remark.

Brown isn't going to take this lying down. 'I will gladly repeat my remark!' he announces. 'I said, "May God forgive you!" … What I meant was that it was you who signed the treaty with Ribbentrop, not us, and that if you hadn't signed your treaty with Ribbentrop, we wouldn't have been at war for a whole year before you even got started, that a lot of my comrades wouldn't now be dead, and that a lot of brave Poles wouldn't now be dead!'

At this, pandemonium breaks out, with Khrushchev launching a tirade against democratic socialists, against Britain, and, in Brown's words, against 'pretty well everybody'. Neither man is prepared to back down. Whenever Khrushchev pauses for breath, Brown puts his oar in, voicing his support for the Eastern European political prisoners whom the Labour Party has solemnly agreed, in a pre-dinner arrangement, not to mention. For good measure, he adds that Khrushchev's son Sergei, who is there at the meal, dares not disagree with his father. Khrushchev replies with a lengthy speech, delivered, thinks the mild-mannered Labour leader Hugh Gaitskell, 'with vehemence, even brutality', and ends by telling his hosts they should make an alliance with the Russians, because if not, they will be swatted 'off the face of the earth like a dirty old black beetle'.

At this point, the Welsh firebrand Aneurin Bevan leaps to Brown's aid, wagging his finger and repeating, 'But this is ridiculous, Mr Khrushchev, but this is ridiculous.' Gaitskell attempts a conciliatory speech, ending with a toast 'to our next meeting'.

'Not for me!' shouts Brown.*

---

* He is to omit this interjection from his memoirs, *In My Way*, perhaps thinking it insufficiently statesmanlike.

In Brown's memoir, he insists that 'I don't want to leave an impression that the events of this Khrushchev dinner were all either ludicrous, or bad-tempered, or bitchy ... It was not just a boorish evening with the hosts being discourteous to the guests.' He then rather ruins the impression of composure by adding a coda that might best be summarised as 'He started it': 'Khrushchev asked for what he got by the way he spoke to us – and it is just as important that a guest should not be rude to a host as that the host should be courteous to a guest.'*

The next day, the Speaker throws a lunch for the Soviet visitors at the House of Commons. Brown is once again invited. He decides to adopt a low profile, 'so when the drinks were being handed round before lunch I stayed in a corner with one or two of my own cronies and didn't go anywhere near where the Russians were being made much of by people who seemed to me a bit over-anxious to mollify their feelings'.

All goes fine until after they have finished eating. They are sipping coffee, 'when who should approach me but Bulganin. He looked closely at me with those lovely blue eyes and said something in Russian which clearly meant something like, "So you are the naughty fellow from last night!" ... and I said, "Oh yes."'

Bulganin invites Brown to come and see Russia for himself. Brown says he would be delighted. At this point, Khrushchev strides over to the two of them, and asks the interpreter what is going on. Brown doesn't want to get involved. 'I wished him a pleasant journey and said that I looked forward to seeing him in Moscow when I was able to take up Bulganin's invitation.'

---

* Brown has a knack for putting his foot in it. As Foreign Secretary in 1967, he conducts a European tour in pursuit of British membership of the European Economic Community. Arriving at the British Embassy in Brussels, he is greeted by the Ambassador.

'Secretary of State – welcome to my embassy.'

'It's not your bloody embassy – it's mine.'

At the end of a day of talks, the Belgian government throws a grand banquet in honour of Brown and his delegation. As the party is breaking up, Brown blocks the main door, waves his hands in the air and says, 'Wait! I have something to say!' He then says, 'While you have all been wining and dining here tonight, who has been defending Europe? I'll tell you who's been defending Europe – the British Army. And where, you may ask, are the soldiers of the Belgian Army tonight? I'll tell you where they are. They're in the brothels of Brussels!'

'We got him out of the room,' recalls an onlooker, 'but by that time the Belgians, who'd been shifting uncomfortably from one foot to another during this extraordinary outburst, were all absolutely frozen with embarrassment.'

Brown holds out his hand. Khrushchev refuses to shake it – '*Nyet, nyet!*' – and moves away. Brown leaves for his constituency. The Conservative politician and diarist Harold Nicolson is told all about it by a Labour contact. 'My friend told me that in a long experience of unsuccessful banquets, that will live in his memory as the most acid failure that he has ever witnessed.'

Khrushchev subsequently remarks that if he were British he would vote Conservative.*

Brown's invitation to Moscow fails to arrive.

---

* Though Harold Macmillan, the leader of the Conservative Party at the next general election, fails to reciprocate his admiration, at least in private. 'How can this fat, vulgar man with his pig eyes and ceaseless flow of talk be the head – the aspirant Tsar – for all those millions of people?' he asks.

GEORGE BROWN

BERATES

ELI WALLACH

Rediffusion TV Studios, Kingsway, London WC2
November 22nd 1963

Neither his temper nor his love of alcohol prevent George Brown from becoming deputy leader of the Labour Party.* This evening, he has been enjoying one or two drinks – a few at the Lebanese Embassy, followed by a few more at a mayoral reception at Shoreditch Town Hall – when he is called to the phone. It is Milton Shulman, from Rediffusion Television, with the news that President Kennedy has been shot. Will Brown come and appear on a special Kennedy Assassination edition of the current-affairs programme *This Week*? Realising he is already the worse for wear, Brown's wife attempts to dissuade him.

'George, you mustn't.'

---

* And, such is the unfairness of posterity, they have guaranteed that he is remembered long after his more sober colleagues have been forgotten. Stories illustrating both characteristics are legion. Presented to Princess Margaret at a reception, Brown kneels on the floor to kiss her hand, only to find himself unable to get up again. On another occasion, just as he is sitting down to a formal dinner, he makes what his biographer describes as 'a salacious suggestion' to the wife of an ambassador to the Court of St James's. '*Pas avant la soupe, Monsieur Brown,*' she replies.

An unverifiable story involves Brown's official visit to Brazil in his capacity as Foreign Secretary. He is said to have attended a glittering reception at the Palace of the Dawn. The military officers were in full dress uniform and the ambassadors in court dress. A member of his party takes up the story: 'As we entered, George made a bee-line for this gorgeously crimson-clad figure, and said, "Excuse me, but may I have the pleasure of this dance?" There was a terrible silence for a moment before the guest, who knew who he was, replied, "There are three reasons, Mr Brown, why I will not dance with you. The first, I fear, is that you've had a little too much to drink. The second is that this is not, as you suppose, a waltz that the orchestra is playing but the Peruvian national anthem, for which you should be standing to attention. And the third reason why we may not dance, Mr Brown, is that I am the Cardinal Archbishop of Lima."' The story is occasionally told of other notorious drinkers.

When the General Secretary of the Labour Party, Len Williams, is appointed Governor-General of Mauritius in 1968, Brown corners his old enemy in the House of Lords bar. 'Tell me, Len, when you're Governor-General, will you have to wear one of those plumed hats?' he asks.

'Yes,' replies Williams.

'Well, I hope your fucking feathers all fall out.'

'I must!' he replies.

Minutes later, Brown is driven from Shoreditch to the TV studios in Kingsway. He is a little early, so he helps himself to a couple more drinks in the green room. Before long, he is joined by two of the other guests – the historian Professor Sir Denis Brogan and John Crosby of the *New York Times*. Over another glass or two, he begins to hold forth about his close friendship with the late President and the future of the United States of America.

A third guest now puts his head round the door. It is the actor Eli Wallach, still clearly upset by the news of the assassination. Wallach is introduced to Brown, who tells him how much he admires his work. Wallach accepts Brown's compliments gracefully, but he is an unassuming man, so tries to steer the conversation away from himself.

Brown misinterprets his modesty. 'Why are American actors so conceited?' he asks loudly, adding, 'Someone like you always carries a newspaper sticking out of his pocket with his name in the headlines!' Wallach attempts to defend himself, saying that, on the contrary, he is always bumping into people who can't put a name to his face.

'Have you ever been in a play by Ted Willis?' asks Brown, randomly.

'No,' replies Wallach. 'Who's Ted Willis?'

'You've never heard of Ted Willis?!' exclaims Brown, as though this is further proof of Wallach's vanity.

Wallach moves away, and finds himself a place on a sofa, but Brown follows him, sits down nearby, and continues to make noisy remarks about the conceit of American actors. Suddenly, Wallach loses his temper, rises from the sofa, points at the deputy leader of the Labour Party, and yells, 'I didn't come here to be insulted! Is this bastard interviewing me on the programme? If so, I'm leaving now!'

Brown is in no mood to be conciliatory. He repeats his remark about the conceit of American actors. Wallach then takes off his jacket and says, 'Come outside! Come outside and I'll knock you off your can!'

Brown tells Wallach to shut up and sit down. Wallach rushes forward and is about to strike when Milton Shulman leaps between the two men, pushing Wallach back on the sofa. At this point, in comes Carl Foreman, the director of *The Guns of Navarone*, who imagines the dispute is between Wallach and Shulman, and attempts to intervene. Meanwhile, Shulman is trying to placate Wallach. 'He's not going to interview you! He's one of the guests!'

'I don't care who he is,' says Wallach. 'I'll still knock the shit out of him!' By now, Brown has been reduced to silence. The time has come to go downstairs to the studio, always a sobering moment. Brown goes over to Wallach. 'Brother, brother,' he says, 'I don't think we should go into the studio this way ... Let's shake hands.' They shake hands awkwardly. Wallach goes through the door first. As he advances along the corridor, Brown shouts after him, 'And now you'll know who Ted Willis is!'

The live broadcast begins. The urbane interviewer, Kenneth Harris, turns first to Brown. 'I know you met President Kennedy once or twice,' he says. 'Did you get to know him as a man?'

A look of intense irritation flashes across Brown's face. 'Now, you're talking about a man who was a very great friend of mine!' he barks. Tears welling in his eyes, he embarks on a slurred and rambling monologue, 'a compound', in his biographer's view, 'of maudlin sentimentality, name-dropping and aggression' about 'Jack' ('who I was very near to'), 'Jackie' and their children. Brown's colleague Richard Crossman is watching the programme at home. 'At the first moment I saw that he was pissed and he was pretty awful. He jumped up and down and claimed a very intimate relationship with Kennedy.'

In fact, the records show that Brown's acquaintance with Kennedy extended to three brief official meetings: on July 9th 1962, from 5.15 p.m. to 6.08 p.m.; on June 14th 1963, from 11 a.m. to 11.55 a.m.; and between 5.30 p.m. and 5.40 p.m. on October 24th 1963. Nevertheless, in his auto-biography he feels able to boast: 'Jack Kennedy was one of the two Presidents of the United States whom it has been my privilege to know well. I came to love and admire him ...' Who knows what the President thought of Brown? His initial briefing note on him from the American Embassy in London advises that 'certain character defects such as irascibility, impulsiveness and heavy drinking have left his future position in the Party in doubt'.

Brown's television appearance, and a subsequent, widely disseminated, report in the *New York Times* of his set-to with Eli Wallach, prompt many complaints from the general public, to all of which Brown dispatches the same printed reply: 'Thank you very much for your letter, and may I say how sorry I am that you felt that you had to write in those terms.'

Two months after the assassination, on January 23rd 1964, Brown finally gets down to writing a letter of condolence to Jackie Kennedy. 'You may remember vaguely that we caught sight of each other when your husband was showing my daughter around the garden as late as last October,' he begins, 'and we exchanged greetings across the garden when you were in the room upstairs.'

ELI WALLACH

FRANK SINATRA

Caesars Palace, Las Vegas
February 1974

The most belligerent people are sometimes unexpectedly warm-hearted. Even Frank Sinatra can disappoint onlookers who have been spoiling for a fight. Or is this just another example of his cruelty?

Ten years after his unfortunate contretemps with George Brown, Eli Wallach flies into Las Vegas. As he comes down the steps of the plane, he sees a huge billboard featuring two blue eyes. The caption states simply, 'HE'S HERE'.

Ol' Blue Eyes is back in Las Vegas, even though he promised four years ago never to return following a very public fight with the casino manager of Caesars Palace.

At that time, Sinatra had been under surveillance by the IRS. Their agents had noticed that he was cashing in his winnings at blackjack without paying for the chips – an easy way to pocket money tax-free. Leaned on by the IRS, the casino manager, Sanford Waterman, had confronted Sinatra, telling him, 'You don't get chips until I see your cash.'

Sinatra had called Waterman a kike; in turn, Waterman had called Sinatra a bitch guinea. Things had gone from bad to worse: Sinatra grabbed Waterman by the throat; Waterman pulled out a pistol and placed it between Sinatra's eyeballs; Sinatra laughed, called Waterman a crazy hebe and exited, declaring that he would never work at Caesars again. In the end, Waterman had been arrested for pulling a gun.

The next day, Waterman told the District Attorney he had heard Sinatra say, 'The mob will take care of you.' This caused the Sheriff to say, 'I'm tired of Sinatra intimidating waiters, waitresses, and starting fires and throwing pies. He gets away with too much. He's through picking on little people in this town. Why the owners of the hotels put up with this is what I plan to find out.'

The District Attorney's report indicated Waterman still had the finger-marks on his throat where Sinatra had grabbed him. 'There seems to be reasonable grounds for making the assumption that Sinatra was the aggressor all the way.' The charges against Waterman were dropped: he was judged to have acted in self-defence. It was at this point that Sinatra, denying he ever laid a finger on Waterman, vowed never to set foot in Nevada again. 'I've suffered enough indignities,' he said.

But four years later, things have changed. The casino manager has been arrested for racketeering, the District Attorney has been voted out, and the new management of Caesars Palace has tempted Sinatra back with the promise of $400,000 a week, plus full-time bodyguards 'to avoid any unpleasant incidents'.

The new Sheriff is delighted to welcome Sinatra back to Las Vegas. To celebrate his return, Caesars Palace is proud to present each member of the audience with a medallion inscribed, 'Hail Sinatra. The Noblest Roman Has Returned'.

But what of Eli Wallach? Ever since the publication of *The Godfather* in 1969, and its film adaptation in 1972, Wallach and Sinatra have been linked in the public mind as bitter rivals. The scene in which a studio boss wakes up to find the severed head of his favourite racehorse lying next to him in his bed has been the inspiration of an urban myth. In the film, it is the mafia's revenge for the studio boss's refusal to award a starring role to one of their own singers, Johnny Fontane. The horse's head helps him change his mind. He immediately drops the actor who has already been cast and replaces him with Fontane. Over time, word has got around that Johnny Fontane is really Frank Sinatra, and the dropped actor is really Eli Wallach. After all, twenty years ago, hadn't Harry Cohn offered Wallach a leading role in *From Here to Eternity* – and hadn't it unaccountably gone to the inexperienced Italian Frank Sinatra? Small wonder, then, that when Eli Wallach walks into the Frank Sinatra show at Caesars Palace, a frisson runs around the audience.

Halfway through his act, Sinatra stops singing, looks over to his wife in the audience and says, 'Barbara, did Eli get here?'

'He's sitting right beside me!' she replies.

'Ladies and gentlemen,' says Sinatra, 'I'd like to introduce a friend. Our paths have often crossed, and he played a big part in my career …'

The audience stirs. They all know what he is talking about. They sense a drama about to unfurl, perhaps even a fight. Sinatra pauses, looks over towards Wallach and says, '... Ah, the hell with that! It's an old story! I don't feel like telling it!'

Perhaps the audience is disappointed by this anti-climax, but Eli Wallach finds it hilarious. 'I fell out of my seat laughing. Every time Frank saw me after that, he'd say, "Hello, you crazy actor." And every time he came to New York, he'd send a limo for Anne and me. We'd sit in a box at the theater. He'd look up, smile at us, and afterward we'd have a late supper at 21.'

On the other hand, it may be worth adding that the author of *The Godfather*, Mario Puzo, does not get off so lightly. By chance, one night in 1970, after the book has become a bestseller, but before the film has been shot, he enters Chasen's restaurant in Beverly Hills and sees Sinatra dining there. 'I'm going to ask Frank for his autograph,' he tells his companion, the film's producer Al Ruddy.

'Forget it, Mario. He's suing to stop the movie,' replies Ruddy. But Puzo persists, and goes up to Sinatra's table. Sinatra loses his temper. 'I ought to break your legs,' he grunts. 'Did the FBI help you with your book?'

'Frank is freaking out, screaming at Mario,' Ruddy recalls thirty years later. As Puzo remembers it, Sinatra calls him 'a pimp', and threatens to 'beat the hell out of me'.

'I know what Frank was up to,' explains Al Martino, who eventually plays the part of Johnny Fontane.* 'You know how much Johnny Fontane was in the book? He was trying to *minimise the role*.'

---

* Martino has recently confirmed that the mafia put pressure on Francis Ford Coppola to cast him as Johnny Fontane. Coppola had originally cast Vic Damone. 'There was no horse's head, but I had ammunition ... I had to step on some toes to get people to realise that I was in the effing movie. I went to my godfather, Russ Bufalino,' he says, referring to the East Coast crime boss. When word got around that Martino had obtained the part, he claims to have been 'completely ostracised on the set ... Brando was the only one who didn't ignore me'.

FRANK SINATRA

DEALS WITH

DOMINICK DUNNE

The Daisy, Rodeo Drive, Los Angeles
September 1966

On a normal day, Frank Sinatra is not slow to take umbrage, nor to accompany it with the promise of revenge, a promise he enjoys keeping. 'Make yourself comfortable, Frank! Hit somebody!' the fearless comedian Don Rickles once greeted Sinatra as he strode into his cabaret lounge.

The TV producer Dominick Dunne has never been able to fathom why Sinatra has taken against him. 'I wish I knew, but he took a major dislike to my wife and me.' One moment, he was part of Sinatra's wider circle, the next the object of abuse. 'You're a no-talent hack,' Sinatra says to Dunne as he passes him at a party; whenever Sinatra sees Dunne's wife Lenny, he tells her she married a loser. Why this change of heart? Dunne can only imagine that Sinatra bears him some sort of grudge for a TV show on which they worked together some years ago.

Sinatra's ire appears to increase with their every encounter. Last year, Dunne was having dinner at the Bistro in Los Angeles when Sinatra, clearly drunk, abused him loudly from a neighbouring table. Sinatra then turned his venom on Lenny, before continuing around the table, going for Lauren Bacall, Maureen O'Sullivan and Swifty Lazar, in rapid succession. Finally, he grabbed the tablecloth and pulled it from beneath all their plates and glasses, threw a plate of food over Lazar, and stomped out.

This year, Sinatra has been involved in any number of fights. In June, for instance, a businessman called Frank Weissman asked him and his party in the Polo Lounge of the Beverly Hills Hotel if they wouldn't mind piping down. Weissman ended the night in a coma at the emergency hospital.

Tonight, Dominick Dunne is out for dinner at the Daisy with his wife and a small group of friends after attending a wedding. He often eats here, and knows the staff. By chance, Frank Sinatra is sitting at the next table, along with his two daughters, Nancy and Tina, and his new wife, Mia Farrow, who at twenty-one years old is younger than each of them. Over the past months, Sinatra has come in for a good deal of ribbing about his child bride, which perhaps explains his bad mood. 'Frank soaks his dentures and Mia brushes her braces …' one of his most vocal tormentors, the comedian Jackie Mason, joked in his stage act a few months ago, 'then she takes off her roller skates and puts them next to his cane … he peels off his toupee and she braids her hair …'

It probably wasn't a wise move. The next day, Mason received an anonymous call telling him that if he valued his life, he should consider changing his material. When he failed to follow this advice, three shots were fired through the glass door of his Las Vegas hotel room. But the police saw no reason to pursue an investigation. 'I knew that Sinatra owned Las Vegas when the detectives there made me the prime suspect and asked that I take a lie detector test,' said Mason, adding, 'I have no idea who it was who tried to shoot me. After the shots were fired, all I heard was someone singing, "Doobie, doobie, doo".' Over the following year, Mason will have his nose and cheekbones broken, again by a complete stranger.

But, in the meantime, we must return to Dunne and his party as they sit there enjoying their dinner. All of a sudden, Dunne feels a tap on his shoulder. He looks up. The maître d' of the Daisy is looking down at him, 'very nice guy called George, Italian, we all knew him, gave him Christmas presents, wonderful man'.

George says, 'Oh, Mr Dunne, I'm so sorry about this, but Mr Sinatra made me do it.' So saying, he leans back, clenches his fist, and hits Dunne smack in the face. 'It wasn't a hit to knock me out, but it was embarrassing,' recalls Dunne. The crowded restaurant falls silent.

Dunne looks across at Sinatra, who is looking back at him with a smile on his face. Dunne and his wife leave the restaurant. As they wait for their car to be brought around by the concierge, George runs out. He is sobbing, and afraid.

'I'm sorry, so sorry. Mr Sinatra made me do it,' he says. He tells the Dunnes that Sinatra tipped him $50. 'It was the social talk of the town,' Dunne recalls. 'I was the amusement for Sinatra. My humiliation was his fun.'

Sinatra's reputation for violence follows him not only to his own grave, but to the graves of others. On two occasions, he sets his men onto the same newspaper columnist, Lee Mortimer, because Mortimer has written unflattering remarks about him. After Mortimer's death, Sinatra is travelling with his friend Brad Dexter when he insists they drive to his grave. As he stands on the grave, Sinatra unzips his trousers and urinates on it. When Dexter asks him why, he replies, 'This cocksucker made my life miserable. He talked against me, wrote articles, caused me a lot of grief. I got back at him.'

'Frank always had to settle the score,' explains Dexter.

But Jackie Mason refuses to be silenced. 'I love Frank Sinatra. You love Frank Sinatra. We all love Frank Sinatra,' he says in his stage act for many years to come. 'And why do we love Frank Sinatra? Because *he'd kill us if we didn't*.'

Like Mason, Dominick Dunne outlives Sinatra, enjoying a highly successful second career as a newspaper columnist and author with a particular interest in seeing that the guilty are brought to book. He never forgives Sinatra for his behaviour that night. 'It showed the kind of power Sinatra had, to make a decent man do an indecent act. And you know, I am aware totally that his voice is one of the great voices of his era, if not the greatest. And to this day, I can't stand the sound of it.'

DOMINICK DUNNE

URINATES WITH

PHIL SPECTOR

The Clara Shortridge Foltz Criminal Justice Center, Los Angeles
April 2007

Forty-one years later, *Vanity Fair* magazine's star columnist Dominick Dunne is covering the trial of Phil Spector, who is charged with the murder of the actress Lana Clarkson.

Short of acting jobs, Clarkson had been working as a hostess in the VIP room of the House of Blues, a nightclub on Sunset Boulevard. She hadn't recognised Spector when he entered, even addressing him as 'Miss', perhaps misled by his size – he is only five feet five inches – and by his voluminous candy-floss wig, only marginally smaller. 'Mister,' he had corrected her.

This man, a fellow waitress had told her, was the famous 1960s record producer, 'the tycoon of teen', as Tom Wolfe once called him. He was known, she added, for his generous tips.

After a drink (he left $450 for a $13.50 bar bill), Spector persuaded the reluctant Lana back to his Castle. 'Just for one drink,' she insisted. Travelling back in his chauffeur-driven Mercedes, they watched a James Cagney movie called *Kiss Tomorrow Goodbye*.

They had only been in the Castle a short time before Spector's chauffeur, waiting outside in the car, heard a gunshot. After some delay, Spector came out and said, 'I think I killed somebody.' The chauffeur called the police, who discovered Clarkson's corpse on a white French bergère chair.

'The gun went off accidentally! She works at the House of Blues! It was a mistake! I don't understand what the fuck is wrong with you people! I don't know how it happened. It scared the shit out of me!' Spector screamed, as a policeman held him down. Later, he claimed Clarkson had picked up one of his guns and shot herself in the face.

Ever since the man who murdered his daughter Dominique was given what he describes as 'a slap on the wrist', Dunne has had an abiding interest in reporting the murder trials of the rich and famous, among them O.J. Simpson, Claus von Bulow and the Menendez brothers. He is fuelled by outrage at the idea that money may buy an acquittal.

He is already convinced of Spector's guilt,* and listens impatiently as Spector's defence attorney complains, 'The police had murder on their minds!' He is unimpressed. 'I should hope to God that the police had murder on their minds, with a woman less than an hour dead, shot in the face, bleeding from the mouth, her teeth all over the floor, life over, in a French bergère chair in the foyer of a castle, and an arrogant man in a house full of guns who had to be Tasered by police. I think that's cause for having murder on your mind.'

The trial has been going for just a few days when the court takes a break, and Dunne heads for the men's room. It is empty but for a single man standing at the central urinal, which is lower than the other two, as though designed for little boys.

Spector is wearing the Edwardian frock-coat in which he arrived at the court this morning. He has opened it wide to urinate, so that it billows out and blocks the remaining two urinals, one on either side. Dunne doesn't quite know what to do, but decides to remain where he is. 'I didn't have the nerve to ask him to move his coat and free up a urinal, and I also didn't really want to pee next to him, considering that he was on trial for murder just down the hall, and I was there to write about him. So I waited my turn in silence in the back by the sinks.'

After he has finished peeing, Spector, who is today sporting a blond pageboy toupee, goes over to the basins, carefully rolls up his sleeves and elaborately soaps and scrubs his hands in hot water. Dunne is reminded of the way germophobes wash obsessively after shaking hands.

As he dries his hands with a paper towel, Spector turns and notices Dunne. 'Hi, Dominick,' he says.

'Hi, Phil,' says Dunne. The last time the two men met was after Spector asked their mutual friend Ahmet Ertegun to arrange a get-together so he

---

* Others take a more easy-going attitude. On the night before Dunne flies out to LA, he bumps into Yoko Ono at a party in New York, and tells her he is going to be covering the trial of Phil Spector. 'She smiled sweetly and said, "Oh, Phil," in the most affectionate manner. I said, "What do you mean, 'Oh, Phil'? He pulled a gun on your husband." Yoko said, "Oh, that story has become so exaggerated. He took out the gun and shot it in the ceiling."'

could pick Dunne's brains about the O.J. Simpson murder trial, by which, like so many people, he was riveted.

Dunne is not sure what to say next, particularly as Spector must know that he is not on his side: he is, in his own words, 'a longtime victims' advocate'. Yet Dunne still feels there is something likeable about Spector. Finally, it occurs to him what to say.

'I went to Ahmet's memorial service in New York at Lincoln Center last week.'

'You went? Oh my God, this is the first I've heard about it from someone who went. I owe everything to Ahmet. He started me in the business!'

Spector wants to know everything about it. Dunne runs through the famous names present: Eric Clapton, Bette Midler, Mayor Michael Bloomberg, Oscar de la Renta, Henry Kissinger. 'Mick Jagger mentioned you in his eulogy.'

'Mick mentioned me?'

'Nothing about this. It was about you and Ahmet and your friendship.'

The two men return to the courtroom, Dunne to the public gallery, Spector to the accused's chair. From their different vantage points, they watch as a woman testifies about how Spector held her at gunpoint; she is the first of four such witnesses.

The two men never speak again, but a few days later, Dunne is handed a note thanking him for the programme from Ertegun's memorial service. 'Dear Dominick ... I did so enjoy reading the words about our dear friend; and the pictures were a treasure. Thanks for thinking of me. Love, Phillip.'

The trial comes to an end five months later, with the jury unable to agree on a verdict.

At the retrial, Spector is found guilty and sentenced to a minimum of nineteen years in prison. He is sixty-nine years old. Three months later, Dominick Dunne dies of cancer, at home in Manhattan, at the age of eighty-three.

PHIL SPECTOR

LEONARD COHEN

Whitney Recording Studios, Los Angeles
June 1977

It has been three years since Leonard Cohen's last album, *New Skin for the Old Ceremony*. His record company is getting twitchy. He is forty-two years old, and his career has hit the doldrums. When he made his first album ten years ago, there was quite a vogue for his mellow, introspective, wordy songs, but now the circus has moved on. The music scene no longer has a use for him; it prefers things brash, youthful, rhythmic, punky.

Cohen's home life is not going all that well either. He is drinking heavily, interspersing his binges with visits to a Zen retreat in California. His sharp-suited manager, Marty Machat, who used to represent the boxer Sugar Ray Robinson, tells Cohen he has come up with a brilliant way to revitalise his career. How about he puts him together with another of his clients who has been bypassed by fashion: the legendary Phil Spector?

Machat drives the sceptical Cohen to a party at Spector's mansion on La Collina, Los Angeles. Attached to the front gates are numerous 'No Entry' signs, drawing attention to a medley of guard dogs and armed guards, and warning trespassers that they will be putting their lives at risk. In the courtyard, chain-link fences and barbed wire block the entrance. Further warning signs point out that the wire is high-voltage.

Cohen finds the party tedious, and the mansion dark and dreary. He dislikes the way Spector shouts at his servants. But he makes the mistake of not leaving. When the other guests have gone, Spector locks the front door and informs Cohen that he is not allowed to leave. Spector hates being by himself even more than he hates being with people.

To lighten the atmosphere, and with a view to his eventual release, Cohen suggests they try writing songs together. Spector is primarily known as a producer,* but he has also written many popular songs. Oddly enough, his first, 'To Know Him is to Love Him', a hit made famous by the Teddy Bears, comes from the inscription on the grave of his father, who committed suicide when Spector was nine years old. Phil's mother, Bertha, used to scream, 'Your father killed himself because you were a bad child,' as she chased him around the kitchen with a carving knife, but Cohen does not know this.

The two men sit at the piano. Their session goes unexpectedly well. Over the course of the next three weeks, they write fifteen songs together. They also drink a great deal of alcohol. They are, says one observer, 'like two drunks staggerin' around'.

In June 1977 they enter the studio. Spector is more moody than ever, by turns batey and matey. 'Somebody would say something and he'd just get in a mood and stalk off …' says Cohen's former girlfriend Devra Tobitaille. 'He'd disappear into the bathroom for hours at a time, fixing his hair.'

As time goes by, Cohen finds that he and Spector disagree on virtually everything. 'I was flipped out at the time and he certainly was flipped out. For me, the expression was withdrawal and melancholy, and for him megalomania and insanity and devotion to armaments that was really intolerable. In the state that he found himself, which was post-Wagnerian, I would say Hitlerian, the atmosphere was one of guns. I mean that's what was really going on, guns. The music was subsidiary, an enterprise. People were armed to the teeth, all his friends, his bodyguards, and everybody was drunk, or intoxicated on other items, so you were slipping over bullets, and you were biting into revolvers in your hamburger. There were guns everywhere.'

One evening, Phil Spector enters the studio and approaches Leonard Cohen with a bottle of his favourite Manischewitz sweet white wine in one hand and a pistol in the other. He puts an arm around Cohen, thrusts the pistol to his neck, and says, 'Leonard, I love you.'

---

* 'He was demonic,' writes Nik Cohn, prophetically, in his landmark 1970 history of pop, *Awopbopaloobop Alopbamboom*. 'He'd take one good song and add one good group, and then he'd blow it all up sky-high into a huge mock-symphony, bloated and bombasted into Wagnerian proportions. Magnificent, chaotic din … huge outpourings of spite and paranoia, rage and frustration and visioned apocalypse. And if you were teenage, you probably felt exactly the same way, and you loved it.'

Cohen reacts in his most mellow fashion, calmly pushing away the pistol. 'I hope you do, Phil,' he says, tentatively.

The recording goes from bad to worse. At one point, Phil pulls out his pistol again, this time on a violin player. 'Phil, I know you don't mean anything, but accidents happen,' says the engineer, who threatens to go home. Eventually, Cohen and Spector stop speaking to one another. Spector refuses to allow Cohen to be present at the mixes, or even to hear the album before it is released.

The album, *Death of a Ladies' Man*, comes out the following year to disastrous reviews. Spector's overblown, soupy arrangements drown out Cohen's poetic murmurings. The cranky musical marriage proves a mess, and it is Cohen's worst-selling record ever. 'He couldn't resist annihilating me,' concludes Cohen. 'I don't think he can tolerate any other shadows in his own darkness.'

When Spector is found guilty of murder some thirty years later, the roster of those on whom he has pulled a gun seems to increase by the day. It includes Michelle Phillips of the Mamas and the Papas, Ronnie Spector, Dee Dee Ramone and even Twiggy.

But at least Phil Spector has learned his lesson about taking greater care when choosing his collaborators. In July 2009, the *New York Post* reports that Charles Manson, Spector's fellow inmate at Corcoran State Prison, has dispatched a guard to Spector with a note suggesting that the two of them start writing songs together. It seems that Spector has failed to get back to him. 'Phil's like, "I used to pick up the phone and it was John Lennon or Celine Dion or Tina Turner, and now Charles Manson is trying to get hold of me!"' reports his publicist, Hal Lifson. Manson's only recorded composition is the B-side to the Beach Boys' 'Bluebirds Over the Mountain' (1968). Originally it was called 'Cease to Exist', but the group thought this too bleak, changed the key phrase to 'cease to resist', and issued it under the more upbeat title 'Never Learn Not to Love'.

LEONARD COHEN

SHARES A LIFT WITH

JANIS JOPLIN

The Chelsea Hotel, 222 West 23rd Street, New York
Winter 1967

At the age of thirty-three, the Canadian singer-songwriter Leonard Cohen has just released his first album. He is in New York, staying in the Chelsea Hotel, which is his kind of place. 'I love hotels to which, at 4 a.m., you can bring along a midget, a bear and four ladies, drag them to your room and no one cares about it at all.'

At three in the morning, Cohen returns to the Chelsea. So far, it has been a dismal evening. He ate a cheeseburger at the Bronco Burger, but found it 'no help at all'. Then he wasted time in the White Horse Tavern.

He presses the button to summon the unusually small lift, and gets in. But before he has had time to pull the door closed, a young lady with wild hair has entered.

It is Janis Joplin, who is resident in Suite 411. Aged twenty-four, she too has just released her first album, and her career is taking off. 'I never ever thought things could be so wonderful!' she wrote to her mother some months ago, adding, '... Guess who was in town last week – Paul McCartney!!! (he's a Beatle). And he came to see us!!!! SIGH ... Gawd, I was so thrilled – I still am! Imagine – Paul!!! ... Why, if I'd known that he was out there, I would have jumped right off the stage and made a fool of myself.'

In fact, the naïve tone she reserves for her mother belies her wild life-style: so far this autumn she has enjoyed a range of one-night stands, some with stars like Jimi Hendrix and Jim Morrison (who she hit over the head with a whisky bottle), but others with lesser-known figures. 'Before she was famous, people didn't think Janis was attractive,' observes Peggy Caserta, one of her long-time lovers. 'She could barely get laid, and now she had all these admirers.'

Travelling up in the lift with Janis Joplin, Leonard Cohen asks her if she is looking for someone.

'Yes,' she replies. 'I am looking for Kris Kristofferson.'

'Little lady,' says Cohen, making his voice gruffer, 'you're in luck. I am Kris Kristofferson.'

'I thought he was bigger.'

'I used to be bigger, but I've been sick.'

By the time the lift reaches the fourth floor, it is clear to both of them that they will be spending the night together. In fact, it is not uncommon for women to offer themselves to Cohen as he rides in the lift: this is, after all, the Chelsea Hotel,* and, as he observes some decades later, 'Those were generous times.'

Three years later, Cohen hears that Janis Joplin has died from a heroin overdose in the Landmark Hotel in Los Angeles.† The following year, he is sitting in a bar in a Polynesian restaurant in Miami Beach, sipping a 'particularly lethal and sinister' coconut drink, and thinking of their encounter. He feels inspired, so he picks up a napkin and writes down the words, 'I remember you well at the Chelsea Hotel'; they are to become the first line of one of his most famous songs.

'We spent a little time together,' Cohen reminisces, coyly, nearly thirty years later, to a packed concert hall in Prague. He then sings 'Chelsea Hotel' for the umpteenth time:

> *I remember you well in the Chelsea Hotel,*
> *you were talking so brave and so sweet;*
> *giving me head on the unmade bed,*
> *while the limousines wait in the street.* [...]

For some years now, the song has had a new verse, which Cohen added just before he came to record it:

---

* The Chelsea is the setting for many songs, among them 'Chelsea Girl' by Nico, 'Chelsea Morning' by Joni Mitchell (which, in turn, gave Chelsea Clinton her name), 'Third Week in Chelsea' by Jefferson Airplane, 'Hotel Chelsea Nights' by Ryan Adams, and 'Sara' by Bob Dylan, which includes the line 'Staying up for days in the Chelsea Hotel, writing "Sad Eyed Lady of the Lowlands" for you'.

† 'I hoped that Janis might have been in for a long haul the way that Bob Dylan or Joni Mitchell have been but you kind of knew that the candle was burning at both ends and she probably wouldn't make it. Just in the way that she sang and the way that she lived. But at the time we didn't know that you couldn't do that forever. It's like now they say that cigarettes and sugar and even white bread can kill. But we didn't even know that heroin could kill you,' Leonard Cohen says in an interview with Q magazine in 1991.

I remember you well in the Chelsea Hotel,
you were famous, your heart was a legend.
You told me again you preferred handsome men,
but for me you would make an exception.
And clenching your fist for the ones like us
who are oppressed by the figures of beauty,
you fixed yourself, you said: 'Well, never mind,
we are ugly, but we have the music.' […]

His introduction to the song varies slightly from concert to concert, according to whim. In Tel Aviv in 1972, he says only that 'It's for a brave woman who put an end to it all.' But as time passes, he grows more candid, more loquacious. 'One evening, about three in the morning, I met a young woman in that hotel. I didn't know who she was. Turned out she was a very great singer. It was a very *dismal* evening in New York City. I'd been to the Bronco Burger; I had a cheeseburger; it didn't help at all. Went to the White Horse Tavern, looking for Dylan Thomas, but Dylan Thomas was dead … I got back in the elevator, and there she was. She wasn't looking for me either. She was looking for Kris Kristofferson. "Lay your head upon the pillow." I wasn't looking for her, I was looking for Lili Marlene. Forgive me for these circumlocutions. I later found out she was Janis Joplin and we fell into each other's arms through some divine process of elimination which makes a compassion out of indifference, and after she died, I wrote this song for her. It's called the Chelsea Hotel.' In the sleeve notes to his 1975 *Greatest Hits*, he is more discreet, writing only that 'I wrote this for an American singer who died a while ago. She used to stay at the Chelsea too.' But in 1976 he is publicly admitting, or boasting, that the singer in question was Janis Joplin. 'It was very indiscreet of me to let that news out. I don't know when I did. Looking back, I'm sorry I did because there are some lines in it that are extremely intimate.'

He repeats the apology to the late singer almost as often as he delivers his introduction to the song. 'I'm very sorry, and if there is some way of apologising to the ghost, I want to apologise now, for having committed that indiscretion,' he is still telling BBC viewers in 1994.

JANIS JOPLIN

BEFRIENDS

PATTI SMITH

The Chelsea Hotel, 222 West 23rd Street, New York
August 1970

Three years on, Janis Joplin is hanging out with her band in El Quixote, the bar attached to the Chelsea Hotel. She is the toast of hippy America. She doesn't seem to notice the young girl who has just strolled in.

Patti and her friend Robert Mapplethorpe have recently moved into Room 1017, the smallest bedroom in the hotel. Aged twenty-three, Patti is a bookstore assistant who yearns to be an artist of one kind or another. The Chelsea represents her aspirations. She enters it as a novice might enter a convent.

Dressed in a long rayon polkadot dress and straw hat, she puts her head round the door of the bar. The scene that greets her is almost absurdly characteristic of its era, scattered in roughly equal proportions with musicians and bottles of tequila. Jimi Hendrix is there in his big hat, slumped over a table at the far end; to the right of him, Grace Slick and Jefferson Airplane are sitting around a table with Country Joe and the Fish; and to the left, Janis Joplin is hanging out with her band. They are all here for the Woodstock Festival.

Grace Slick brushes past her.

'Hello,' says Patti.

'Hello yourself,' replies Grace Slick. But Patti stubbornly persists in feeling at home. Returning to her room, she feels 'an inexplicable sense of kinship with these people'.

Over the next few months, she walks around the hotel in awe, an autograph hunter too cool to hunt for autographs. 'I wandered the halls seeking its spirits, dead or alive.' She loiters outside Arthur C. Clarke's rooms, but fails to catch a glimpse; she nudges Virgil Thompson's door ajar, and spots his grand piano. The composer George Kleinsinger invites her into his suite; it is filled with ferns, palms, caged nightingales and a twelve-foot python. Someone points out the room in which Edie Sedgwick set herself on fire while glueing on false eyelashes by candlelight.

One night, the beat poet Gregory Corso drops by, and falls asleep while reading Patti's poems. His cigarette makes a burn-mark on her chair, and she is thrilled. When he leaves, she runs her fingers lovingly over the burn-mark, 'a fresh scar left by one of our greatest poets'.

Smith remains unsure of her particular vocation: is she a poet or a singer or a songwriter or a playwright? She can't quite place herself, and no one else can either. 'You don't shoot up and you're not a lesbian. What do you actually do?' asks a fellow guest. But she continues to make inroads into bohemia. It is the golden age of the hanger-on: even the hangers-on's hangers-on have hangers-on. Recently, Bobby Neuwirth became top dog after he popped up as a friend of Bob Dylan in *Don't Look Back*.* Now Neuwirth takes Patti under his wing, introducing her to Tom Paxton, Kris Kristofferson and Roger McGuinn. One day, he introduces her to Janis Joplin with the words, 'This is the poet Patti Smith.' From that moment, Joplin always calls her 'the Poet'.

Over the coming year, Patti Smith is allowed to join those drifting in and out of Joplin's suite. Joplin sits on an easy chair in the centre, 'the queen of the radiating wheel', brandishing a bottle of Southern Comfort, even in the afternoon. One day, Patti sits at the feet of Kris Kristofferson and Janis Joplin as Kristofferson sings his new song, 'Me and Bobby McGee'.† In her rasping, wailing voice, Janis Joplin joins in the chorus. This is later deemed a moment of rock history, but Patti's mind is elsewhere, preoccupied with the poem she is trying to write. That is the way with these moments: at twenty-three, Patti is 'so young and preoccupied with my own thoughts that I hardly recognised them as moments'.

In August 1970, when Janis Joplin plays in Central Park, Neuwirth finds Patti a place at the side of the stage. Patti is mesmerised by Joplin, but suddenly there is a downpour, then a thunderstorm, and Joplin is forced to leave the stage. As the roadies clear the equipment away, the crowd

---

* He co-writes Joplin's song 'Mercedes Benz'.

† Janis Joplin also covers the song for inclusion on her *Pearl* album a few days before her death in October 1970. Kristofferson does not find out that she has covered it until after her death (the first time he hears it is the day after she dies).

boos. Joplin is distraught. 'They're booing me, man,' she tells Neuwirth. 'No, they're booing the rain,' he assures her.

After another concert, Joplin's vast entourage troops off to an after-show party at the Remington, near Lower Broadway. Among the guests are the girl in the red dress from the cover of Dylan's *Bringing it All Back Home*, and the actress Tuesday Weld. Patti notes that Janis – in magenta and pink, with a purple feather boa – spends most of the evening with a good-looking man to whom she is obviously attracted. But just before closing time, the man leaves with someone else, someone prettier.

Joplin bursts into tears. 'This always happens to me, man. Just another night alone.'

Neuwirth tells Patti to take Janis back to the Chelsea Hotel and keep an eye on her. Patti sits with Janis and listens while she talks about how unhappy she is. Patti has written a song for her, and, never backward in coming forward, seizes the opportunity to sing it. It is on the theme, not wholly original, of the star adored by the public but lonely offstage.

'That's me, man! That's my song!' says Joplin.

Before Patti sets off for her own room, Joplin adjusts her boa in the mirror. 'How do I look, man?' she asks.

'Like a pearl. A pearl of a girl,' replies Patti.

A few weeks later, on October 4th 1970, Patti is hanging out with the guitarist Johnny Winter when the news comes through that Janis Joplin has died of a heroin overdose in the Landmark Motel, Los Angeles, aged twenty-seven. Winter, who is highly superstitious, thinks of two other musicians who have recently died, Brian Jones and Jimi Hendrix, and starts fretting that he too has a 'J' in his name.* Patti Smith offers to read his tarot cards, and predicts – accurately, as it turns out – that he is in no immediate danger.

---

* Perhaps odder than their shared 'J's is the fact that all three of them died at the age of twenty-seven.

PATTI SMITH

IS TREATED TO A SANDWICH BY

ALLEN GINSBERG

Horn and Hardart automat, West 23rd Street, New York
November 1969

Who can fathom the consequences that may hang on the raising of the price of a cheese roll by ten cents?

On November 1st, Patti Smith and Robert Mapplethorpe gather their belongings and move several flights downstairs in the Chelsea Hotel. Their new room, 204, is next to the one in which Dylan Thomas was resident when he died. Like the British upper classes, the bohemian inhabitants of the Chelsea Hotel thrive on these ghostly connections to grandees of the past.

Patti has always disliked using the lift, and feels a sense of release at being able to nip up and down the stairs. 'Because it was only the second floor I could fly up and down the stairs … It gave me a sense that the lobby was an extension of the room.' Together in their slightly larger room she and Mapplethorpe work at making necklaces from ribbons, string and old rosary beads. Sometimes the beads get lost in the folds of the bedcovers, or slip through the cracks of the wooden floor. But these are early days. Within a few months, they will both have branched out from this comparatively traditional activity. Soon they will stage a 'happening' called 'Robert Getting his Nipple Pierced'. It consists of Mapplethorpe having a gold ring inserted in a nipple while Patti intones a meandering monologue about her love life. This will be followed by 'Patti Getting her Knee Tattooed', in which Patti has a small lightning flash tattooed on her knee by an Australian artist called Vali Meyers.

Their fellow residents express their approval. 'We who were watching certainly suffered vicariously … The result was wholly satisfactory in the idiom of the day,' reports one of them. The 'happening' is filmed by another Chelsea resident and screened at the Museum of Modern Art, before an appreciative audience also formed largely of residents of the Chelsea Hotel.

But while they are still engaged in jewellery, Smith and Mapplethorpe develop a routine of picking up lobster claws (ideal for spray painting) from the El Quixote restaurant next door, then off to the Capitol Fishing Tackle Shop two doors down for feathered bait and lead weights for the necklaces, ending up at the Horn and Hardart automat down the street. At the automat, their usual procedure is to get a seat and a tray, go to the back wall, where there are rows of little windows, put a coin in a slot, open a glass hatch, and pick out a sandwich or a fresh apple pie. Patti's favourite dish is cheese and mustard with lettuce on a poppyseed roll; Robert prefers macaroni cheese. Patti drinks coffee, Robert chocolate milk.

One wet afternoon, Patti is overcome by a craving for a cheese and lettuce sandwich. She searches their room high and low for the necessary fifty-five cents, puts on her grey trenchcoat and her Mayakovsky cap, rushes down to the automat, finds a seat, picks up a tray, goes to the back wall and puts her fifty-five cents in the slot.

The hatch won't open, so she pulls it again. But still it won't open; only now does she notice a sign that says the price has risen by ten cents, to sixty-five cents.

'Can I help?'

She turns around. It is a portly man with a dark curly beard. She recognises him: 'no mistaking the face of one of our great poets and activists'. It is Allen Ginsberg, the author of 'Howl', the man described in an FBI report, not altogether inaccurately, as 'an entertainer with a fuzzy beard who chants unintelligible poems'. He is also a hobby nudist* and a vociferous advocate of drugs.†

Ginsberg has just returned from the funeral of his old lover and fellow beat writer Jack Kerouac, who collapsed while watching *The Galloping Gourmet* on television, then died in hospital of cirrhosis of the liver. 'So he drank himself to death, which is only another way of living, of handling the pain and foolishness that it's all a dream, a great baffling silly

---

* At a party in London in the mid-1960s, Ginsberg is wearing nothing but a 'Do Not Disturb' sign attached to himself when John Lennon arrives with his first wife. 'You don't do that in front of birds,' complains Lennon, and leaves the room.

† Though when Ginsberg offered Dame Edith Sitwell heroin she declined, saying, 'It brings me out in spots.'

emptiness, after all,' Ginsberg concluded in a speech at Yale University the day before yesterday.

'Can I help?' he asks.

Patti nods her consent. Ginsberg adds the extra ten cents, and also treats her to a cup of coffee. She follows him to his table and starts eating her sandwich. Ginsberg introduces himself, and begins talking about Walt Whitman. In her deep voice, Patti mentions that she was brought up near Camden, New Jersey, where Whitman is buried. At this point, something strikes Ginsberg. He leans forward in his chair and looks at her quizzically.

'Are you a girl?' he asks.

'Yeah. Is that a problem?'

Ginsberg laughs. 'I'm sorry. I took you for a very pretty boy.'

Patti senses a misunderstanding.

'Well, does this mean I return the sandwich?'

'No, enjoy it. It was my mistake.'

Thus, on the strength of an unexpected hike in the price of a cheese roll, Ginsberg and Patti Smith meet and form a lifelong friendship. Keen self-mythologisers, as the years roll by they take to reminiscing about this chance encounter. Once, Ginsberg asks her, 'How would you describe how we met?'

'I would say you fed me when I was hungry,' she replies.

In his latter years, Ginsberg is inspired by Patti to write rock lyrics, though with limited success: he is just too *wordy*. Always a generous man, he takes to introducing her concerts with lengthy preambles. 'Patti Smith was one of the pioneers of spoken poetry music,' he tells an audience in Michigan on April 5th 1996. '... She pioneered that combination of music and poetry which has caught fire among the younger generation to the point where a lot of older folks including myself learned from her how to put the two together.'

Exactly a year after this particular concert, Ginsberg dies. At his memorial service at St Mark's church, Patti dresses in a white T-shirt with Rimbaud's face on it and sings 'I'm So Lonesome I Could Cry'.

ALLEN GINSBERG

PRESSES NUDE PHOTOGRAPHS OF HIMSELF ONTO

FRANCIS BACON

Room 9, The Villa Muniriya, 1, rue Magellan, Tangier
May 1957

For a gay Western man in the 1950s, there is nowhere quite like Tangier.*
In March 1957, Allen Ginsberg and his boyfriend Peter Orlovsky arrive
there to stay with Ginsberg's old lover, William Burroughs.

On the first night, Burroughs, still pining for Ginsberg, grows very
drunk, and starts waving a machete around. But over the next few days,
things settle down. They soon establish a nightly routine of chewing
majoun, a sort of hashish candy heated into what Ginsberg describes,
unappealingly, as 'the consistency of sticky shit', and arguing about the
nature of art until the early hours. Sometimes they come to blows – one
night Ginsberg rips open Burroughs' shirt with a hunting knife – but, by
and large, everything goes swimmingly. Early each morning, Ginsberg
retreats to the patio to edit the rambling manuscript of Burroughs' *The
Naked Lunch*.

If the English expatriates have a leader, it is David Herbert, who rules
them with what someone calls 'a whip of knotted floss silk'. They gather
in the louche Dean's Bar, described by Ian Fleming as 'a sort of mixture
between Wiltons and the porter's lodge at White's'. In a letter home,
Fleming adds, 'There's nothing but pansies, and I have been fresh meat for
them ... Francis Bacon is due next week to live with his pansy pianist
friend.'

The pansy pianist in question is Peter Lacy, the former Battle of Britain
pilot with whom Bacon is desperately in love. To settle a drinking debt,
Lacy plays piano in Dean's Bar, but drinks so much that the debt escalates
nightly. In the early hours, he tends to snap and resorts to violence. One

---

* Joe Orton, Kenneth Williams, Noël Coward, Tennessee Williams, Paul Bowles, William
Burroughs and Ronald Kray are among those who take advantage of its charms.

night, Bacon's face is so damaged it must be repaired with stitches around the right eye, but at the end of it all, notes a friend, 'Bacon loved Lacy even more.'

Some blame the repetitive violence on muggers. 'Francis was always being beaten up,' recalls Herbert. 'Our consul general was very upset and got hold of the chief of police and told him he had to do something about it. He impressed on him that Francis was a very distinguished painter. A few days later, the chief of police returned, patently embarrassed. "*Pardon, mais il n'y a rien à faire. Le peintre adore ça!*"'

The sex and violence in Tangier also provide perverse tourist must-sees for Burroughs' gloating prose: 'The City is visited by epidemics of violence, and the untended dead are eaten by vultures in the streets. Albinos blink in the sun. Boys sit in trees, languidly masturbate. People eaten by unknown diseases watch the passer-by with evil, knowing eyes.' During his annual visits, Bacon spends time with Burroughs, though he prefers alcohol to drugs: when Burroughs gives him *kif*, his face blows up like a balloon, so he never tries it again.

Burroughs introduces Bacon to his guests. For Ginsberg, Bacon is 'an English schoolboy with the soul of a satyr, wearing sneakers & tight dungarees and black silk shirts & always looks like going to tennis … who paints mad gorillas in grey hotel rooms dressed in evening dress with deathly black umbrellas'. Ginsberg thinks the Beat writers have much in common with Bacon, and that Bacon paints the way Burroughs writes, in 'a sort of dangerous bullfight of the mind'. For him, Bacon is just like Burroughs, placing himself in psychic danger with his art, jeopardising the very foundations of his being, and so forth. But Bacon has no time for such claptrap. His own reputation is, he says, 'a lot of chic shit'. His real love, he boasts, is gambling: he once won $4,000 at Monte Carlo, and was offered a larger stake for letting himself be whipped, plus a bonus for every stroke that drew blood.

Ginsberg likes to shock convention, but Bacon prefers to go one step further, and shock the shockers. He bashes away at the halo of sanctity that hovers over artists, and takes to goading Ginsberg and Burroughs with provocative statements about abstract art. 'It's never meant anything to me. To me, even the best of it is just decoration. Jackson Pollock's paintings might be very pretty but they're just decoration. They look like old lace ... I always think marvellous painting will come out of America, because it should, a country with an enormous mixed race. But it doesn't, it's so *dreary*, those super realists, the abstract expressionists, all so very *dreary*.'

'What about Jasper Johns?' asks Burroughs, when they recreate their Tangier discussions years later.

'I try never to think about Jasper Johns. I hate the stuff and don't like him either.'*

Bacon plays the philistine, *pour épater les beats*, sticking pins into anything that smacks of the self-indulgent and the self-important. Ginsberg, on the other hand, sees art as a sacred calling. Still searching for common ground, he talks about editing *The Naked Lunch*: how, he wonders, can Bacon tell when a painting is complete? Bacon says that he can't orchestrate or predict it – he simply finishes with a chance brush-stroke that locks in the magic. In a gesture of friendship, Ginsberg offers Bacon a drink out of an old tin can he has picked out of the garbage. This is a further misjudgement; Bacon, horrified, refuses it.

Ginsberg hopes to be immortalised on canvas by Bacon, preferably in the nude; he has never been slow to strip off. Perhaps by way of an advertisement, he hands Bacon some photographs of himself and Orlovsky naked in bed. Would Francis like them to sit for him?

'That might be awkward, Allen. How long can you hold it?' asks Bacon, saucily.

Bacon pockets the photographs, though he has no interest in the naked Ginsberg or his boyfriend. Something else has caught his eye: the clapped-out old mattress. 'Those photos were terribly useful,' he explains later. 'The lovers weren't interesting, but there was something about the way the mattress spilled over the metal spindles of the bed that was so *despairing*. So I decided to keep them and use them.'

---

* The conversation continues:
  Burroughs: Do you remember the alligator that Paul and Janie Bowles had in Tangier? Such a delicate little thing.
  Bacon: She died there, you know, Janie.
  Burroughs: Didn't she die in Malaga?
  Bacon: Died in a madhouse in Malaga, it must have been the worst thing in the world. Looked after by nuns, can you imagine anything more horrible?

FRANCIS BACON

HECKLES

HRH PRINCESS MARGARET

Warwick House, St James's Place, London SW1
1977

Brought along by his fellow painter Lucian Freud to a ball thrown by Lady Rothermere, Francis Bacon clings to the champagne bar. He is not one for mingling, and would certainly never dance. At the furthest corner of the ballroom, Princess Margaret, emboldened by champagne and egged on by her fellow party-goers, decides to put on a bit of a performance.

Traditionally, members of the royal family are granted a special licence as entertainers. Their efforts at sparkling, however dim, are greeted with enthusiasm; their repartee, however pedestrian, sets tables aroar; their musical forays, however painful, are hailed as delightful. This conspiracy of sycophancy has, over the years, led one or two of them to gain an inflated notion of their own talents.

From an early age, Princess Margaret has been encouraged to believe that she is blessed with a heaven-sent knack for playing the piano, singing and mimicry. 'She has an impeccable ear, her piano playing is simple but has perfect rhythm and her method of singing is really very funny,' swoons Noël Coward in 1948.

Occasionally, a guest might come a cropper, misdirecting the gush. The biographer Michael Holroyd was once placed on the right of Princess Margaret at dinner. The Princess began a series of terrible impersonations, adopting a heavy Irish brogue for the author Edna O'Brien, who was also present. Holroyd laughed dutifully at the first two, which he vaguely recognised, then continued to laugh at a third – a high-pitched, nasal squeak – which he did not. 'If I may say so, ma'am, that's your funniest yet!' he remarked. The moment he did so, it occurred to him that the Princess had, in fact, reverted to her own voice.

'What happened next?' the Princess's biographer asks him some years later.

'I seem to remember,' Holroyd recalls, 'that she spent rather a lot of time talking to the person on her left.'

As a house-guest, Princess Margaret is allowed exceptional leeway. Hosts bend over backwards to satisfy her every whim. One hostess has the guest bedroom rewired so that the Princess can employ her Carmen rollers. Another swims out to her in a pool, fully clothed, bearing the glass of gin-and-tonic she has ordered. Lights in dining rooms are always kept bright, in accordance with the Princess's professed belief that 'a dark dining room upsets my tummy. I can't see what I'm eating.' When the Princess finally departs, her hosts invariably take a masochistic pleasure in recounting her more outrageous demands to their friends and acquaintances. If the Princess were aware of the pleasure afforded by her haughtiness, she might feel less inclined to make such a display of it.*

On this particular evening at Warwick House, she has the wind behind her. She strides up to the stage, adroitly removes the microphone from the hand of the singer and instructs the band to strike up some Cole Porter. 'All the guests who had been waltzing under the vast chandeliers instantly stopped dancing,' recalls Lady Caroline Blackwood, the former wife of Lucian Freud. 'They stood like Buckingham Palace sentries called to attention to watch the royal performance.' Francis Bacon, however, stays rooted to the bar.

Princess Margaret bursts into song. She sings off-key, but with ever-increasing gusto, egged on, as always, by her jubilant fellow guests, who shout and roar and beg for more. Consequently, she grows fearfully over-excited and starts, in the words of one observer, 'wiggling around in her crinoline and tiara as she tried to mimic the sexual movements of the professional entertainer. Her dress with its petticoats bolstered by the wooden hoops that ballooned her skirts was unsuitable for the slinky act but all the rapturous applause seemed to make her forget this.'

---

* Servants, too, find Princess Margaret a trial, but they also take pleasure in transforming misdemeanour into anecdote. The former royal butler Guy Hunting recalls the uphill task faced by the Princess's dresser, Isobel Mathieson, each morning. 'During her many years with Princess Margaret, the biggest challenge Isobel faced each day was separating the royal body from its bed. On a non-engagement day (and there were many) the 10 o'clock tray of tea seldom did the trick. Opening the curtains produced a moan but no serious improvement. Only after the teapot was replenished two or three times was the order likely to be given for the bath to be run.'

She has just embarked on 'Let's Do It' when 'a very menacing and unexpected sound came from the back of the crowded ballroom. It grew louder and louder until it eclipsed Princess Margaret's singing. It was the sound of jeering and hissing, of prolonged and thunderous booing.'

Everyone looks round aghast, as though drawn by H.M. Bateman. It is Francis Bacon, barracking the Princess from the bar. As Lucian Freud remembers it, 'People became extraordinarily angry about it. Binkie Beaumont, the promoter, was one of the angriest. Because I was the one who had brought him, they turned on me, blaming me. Of course, in response I was fiercely defensive of Francis.'

Princess Margaret falters and screeches to a halt mid-song. 'Mortification turned her face scarlet and then it went ashen. Because she looked close to tears, her smallness of stature suddenly made her look rather pitiful.'

The Princess rushes offstage. The band stops playing, unsure what to do next. A furious red-faced man comes up to Caroline Blackwood and splutters, 'It's that dreadful Francis Bacon! He calls himself a painter but he does the most frightful paintings. I just don't understand how a creature like him was allowed to get in here. It's really quite disgraceful!'

Bacon complains afterwards: 'Her singing was really too awful. Someone had to stop her. If you're going to do something, you shouldn't do it as badly as that.'

Caroline Blackwood is one of the few present to be impressed by Bacon's refusal to kowtow. 'I can think of no one else who would have dared to boo a member of the royal family in a private house. Among all the guests assembled in Lady Rothermere's ballroom, more than a few were secretly suffering from Princess Margaret's singing, but they suffered in silence, gagged by their snobbery. Francis could not be gagged. If he found a performance shoddy, no conventional trepidation prevented him from expressing his reactions. Sometimes his opinions could be biased and perverse and unfair, but he never cared if they created outrage ... He had an anarchic fearlessness which was unique.'

Thirteen years later, Lord Rothermere is introduced to Francis Bacon at a *Daily Mail* party, but fails to recognise him. 'And what do you do?' he asks.

'I'm a nancy boy,' replies Bacon.

HRH PRINCESS MARGARET

WATCHES A BLUE MOVIE WITH

KENNETH TYNAN

20 Thurloe Square, London SW7
Spring 1968

Princess Margaret is a regular guest at Kenneth and Kathleen Tynan's risqué parties. Tynan, who has made his name as an iconoclastic theatre critic, is one of the most flamboyant figures in town. His parties are formed from a combustible mix of pornography, snobbery and revolution. 'A new kind of man is being evolved in Castro's Cuba,' is just one of his beliefs, yet at the same time he has been known to upbraid guests for failing to curtsey to the Princess. He is at the cutting edge of both left-wing politics and high society, and refuses to acknowledge any contradiction. Swanning around his own party in a deep purple suit, he causes a gatecrashing member of the Workers Revolutionary Party to ask, 'Who's the antiques dealer?'

The Tynans' guests dress in the latest beads and bobbles, consuming Kathleen's turbot *monegasque* or lamb *Casa Botin*, drinking fine wine and, when they feel like it, taking drugs. Tynan runs his parties as though they were theatrical productions, with Kathleen as his stage manager. His choice of cast members is determined by their capacity for friction. He grows bored if no row is brewing or in progress, and fills any vacuum by plotting ever more outlandish diversions.

'I remember very clearly at one of our parties somebody suggesting a Pee-In at Buckingham Palace,' Kathleen recalls. 'On another occasion, to emulate the students who had occupied the Beaux Arts, we planned to take over Covent Garden opera house. An argument started among the prospective occupiers over what we would present on stage. Was it to be propaganda or art? Readings from Shelley or from Freud? And on that note of aesthetic discord the plan was dropped. Instead we wondered whether it would not be better to burn down the Old Vic.'

Mary McCarthy, Germaine Greer, Mike Nichols and Vanessa Redgrave are regular attenders. One evening John Lennon is sitting on their stone stairs in a white suit, talking about his idea for a sketch in Tynan's forth-coming production, *Oh! Calcutta!*: 'You know the idea, four fellas wanking – giving each other images – descriptions – it should be ad-libbed anyway. They should even really wank, which would be great!' Meanwhile, Sharon Tate, newly married to Roman Polanski, is sitting cross-legged, doling out hash brownies she has just baked.

Tynan is forever on the lookout for new forms of sexual adventure. In July 1961, after Jonathan Miller tells him of a group of motorcyclists who wear masks, drive at breakneck speeds, have orgasms and then throw themselves off their bikes to their deaths, he takes his guests in a taxi ('costing fortunes') to the spot where the ritual is supposed to take place, but they find nothing happening. 'It was deadly respectable and the only crazy people around were us,' remembers Christopher Isherwood.

On this particular evening, Ken has decided to show avant-garde films as an after-dinner entertainment. There are just eight for dinner: the play-wright Harold Pinter and his actress wife Vivien Merchant, the comedian Peter Cook and his wife Wendy, and Lord Snowdon and Princess Margaret. Within the next few years, all their marriages will end in divorce.

The dinner starts badly – or perhaps well, given Tynan's preference for fireworks – when Ken attempts to present Vivien Merchant to Princess Margaret, and Merchant cocks a snook by simply carrying on talking to Peter Cook. 'I put out my hand which was refused,' recalls Princess Margaret, 'so I sort of drew it up as if it were meant for another direction.'

At dinner, Merchant is placed next to Lord Snowdon, who recently photographed her playing Lady Macbeth at Stratford. 'Of course, the only reason we *artistes* let you take our pictures is because you are married to *her*,' she informs him, stabbing a finger in the general direction of the Princess.

At this point, 'everyone began to drink steadily', observes Kathleen Tynan.

After dinner, they settle down to watch the pornographic films. Tynan prides himself on being at the forefront of the permissive society. Nevertheless, he has taken the precaution of warning Lord Snowdon that there will be 'some pretty blue material'. But Snowdon is relaxed, even excited. 'It would be good for M,' he replies.

The films start. 'The English bits were amateurish and charming, with odd flashes of nipple and pubic bush,' writes Tynan in his diary, 'and the American stuff with fish-eye lens and zoom was so technically self-conscious that the occasional bits of explicit sex passed almost unnoticed – eg a fast zoom along an erect prick looked like a flash zoom up a factory chimney.' The atmosphere, hopelessly awkward over dinner, is settling down into something more relaxed and playful.

But then a film by Jean Genet, *Chant d'amour*, begins. It is set in a prison, and features male prisoners getting up to all sorts of adventures. 'It contained many quite unmistakeable shots of cocks – cocks limp and stiff, cocks being waved, brandished, massaged or just waggled – intercut with lyrical fantasy sequences as the convicts imagine themselves frolicking in vernal undergrowth,' reveals Tynan.

Silence descends on the party. It is as though the sixties had just reverted to the fifties. Society suddenly seems a lot less permissive. But Peter Cook saves the day by starting to speak over the images. Tynan is thankful: 'He supplied a commentary, treating the movie as if it were a long commercial for Cadbury's Milk Flake chocolate and brilliantly seizing on the similarity between Genet's woodland fantasies and the sylvan capering that inevitably accompanies, on TV, the sale of anything from cigarettes to Rolls-Royces. Within five minutes we were all helplessly rocking with laughter, Princess M. included. It was a performance of genius ... I hugged Peter for one of the funniest improvisations I have ever heard in my life.'

Sex has been skilfully filtered for comedy, relieving everyone of embarrassment. The Tynans' guests all leave content, except, perhaps, for Harold Pinter. He is so drunk that 'having solemnly taken his leave', he falls all the way down the stairs.

KENNETH TYNAN

IS CUT INTO LITTLE PIECES BY

TRUMAN CAPOTE

United Nations Plaza, New York

1970

Kenneth Tynan and Truman Capote have much – perhaps a little too much – in common. They share an epigrammatic style of writing and a love of high society, and are both a combustible mix of affectations and afflictions, Capote with his high-pitched baby voice, rolling eyes, tiny stature (just over five foot two inches) and effeminate hand gestures, and Tynan with his stammer and facial contortions (lips puckering, eyes squinting shut). Tynan has also developed a louche way of holding his cigarette between his two middle fingers.

Both men have been dandies since their youth. At Oxford, Kenneth Tynan – middle name Peacock – wears a purple doeskin suit and gold satin shirt. At the same age, Truman Capote – middle name Streckfus – dresses, according to one friend, 'as though he were going to a costume ball'. Both have offbeat sexual preferences – Tynan is a sado-masochist with a love of pornography, Capote a homosexual attracted almost exclusively to heterosexuals. Both are iconoclasts, favouring artistic overstatement.* Furthermore, the two are born – and due to die – within four years of one another.†

For a time, they are distant friends, each amused by the other's bravura. But then in 1965, Capote writes *In Cold Blood*, a so-called 'non-fiction novel' about the murder of a Kansas farming family six years ago. Before publishing his book, Capote has been forced to wait for the execution of the two murderers, as the tale needs a suitably dramatic ending. Published

---

* 'I doubt I could love anyone who did not wish to see *Look Back in Anger*' – Kenneth Tynan. 'Finishing a book is just like you took a child out in the back yard and shot it' – Truman Capote.

† Capote aged fifty-nine, from drinking too much; and Tynan, aged fifty-three, from smoking too much.

in 1966, it becomes an instant bestseller, extravagantly praised on both sides of the Atlantic.

But not by Kenneth Tynan: early signs of his disapproval emerge when he encounters Capote a year earlier, in the spring of '65. According to Tynan, Capote has just heard that the execution day has been set and is hopping up and down with glee, clapping his hands, saying, 'I'm beside myself! Beside myself! Beside myself with joy!' Tynan is shocked. They have an argument, and Tynan ends up calling Capote's behaviour 'outrageous'.*

The following autumn, Capote is staying at Claridge's in London, and asks to drop in on the Tynans, just around the corner in Mount Street. The Tynans suspect that Capote, knowing Ken is planning to review his book, is intent on buttering him up. He is notably deferential and effusive. The next day, Capote sends Tynan 'a small, rather miserable little plant'.

The review is printed in the *Observer*. It is a stinker. Tynan suggests that, by refusing to testify in support of the murderers' pleas of insanity, Capote let them die, just to give his book a dramatic ending. It is a view corroborated, he says, by a 'prominent Manhattan lawyer'. He adds, 'Where lives are threatened, observers and recorders who shrink from participation may be said to betray their species. No piece of prose, however deathless, is worth a human life … In cold cash, it has been estimated that *In Cold Blood* is likely to earn him between two and three million dollars. It seems to me that the blood in which his book is written is as cold as any in recent literature.'

Capote goes berserk, complaining to the *Observer* that Tynan has 'the morals of a baboon and the guts of a butterfly'. He challenges Tynan, offering him $500 if he can produce a 'prominent Manhattan lawyer' willing to sign an affidavit saying that a successful appeal might have been made on the grounds of insanity. Tynan wins the bet, producing a lawyer who not only does so, but adds that it is unlikely the book could have been published at all had the murderers not been executed. A triumphant Tynan pins Capote's $500 cheque to his study wall.

---

* On the other hand, Tynan's first wife, Elaine Dundy, considers the cause of Tynan's outrage less principled. 'His pique at Truman was just jealousy. He wanted to write that book *In Cold Blood* himself. What was *he* doing – *Oh! Calcutta!*' she tells Capote's biographer, George Plimpton. 'Oh, no, it was just jealousy.'

This makes Capote hate Tynan all the more. The two men avoid one another for several years. Then, one day they find themselves walking towards each other along a lengthy corridor at the UN Plaza.

'Coming in the opposite direction toward us was his tiny figure,' recalls Kathleen. 'It was a wonderful theatrical moment because of the length and the height and width of those corridors and wondering what the heck Capote was going to do. Was he going to hit him? Was he going to spit on him?'

The two men approach each other from this great distance, like a pair of dandy gunfighters. As they draw level, Tynan simply nods at Capote. In return, Capote drops a curtsey, pipes, 'Mr Tynan, I presume,' in his high-pitched voice, and walks on.

But Capote's anger does not subside, nor do his dreams of retribution. One day, he shares with his friend George Plimpton the very particular revenge he has cooked up.

It kicks off with a kidnapping. Tynan is to be blindfolded, gagged and bundled into a Rolls-Royce, then deposited in a hospital room.

'Truman was very careful with the details,' says Plimpton. 'He described how pleasant the nurses were, what a nice view there was out the window, and that the meals were excellent. Then his voice took on an edge as he described how Tynan would be wheeled off somewhere in the clinic into surgery to have a limb or an organ removed.

'Truman announced this last chilling detail quite cheerily, followed by a burst of laughter. In that oddly deep voice he used for dramatic effect, he then went on to describe the extensive postoperative procedure, the careful diets, a complex exercise programme to get Tynan back into good shape ... at which point he would be carried off to the operating room yet again to have something *else* removed, until finally, after months of surgery and recuperation, everything had been removed except one eye and the genitalia. Truman cried out, "Everything else goes!"

'Then he leaned back in his chair and delivered the dénouement. He said, "What they do then is to wheel into his hospital room a motion-picture projector, a screen, along with an attendant in a white smock who sets everything up, and what they do is show *pornographic* films, very high-grade, enticing ones, absolutely *non-stop!*"'

TRUMAN CAPOTE

PEGGY LEE

Le Restaurant, Bel Air, Los Angeles
1979

Truman Capote loves to mix with famous people. Among the five hundred guests at his black-and-white ball at the Plaza Hotel in 1966 were Frank Sinatra, Mia Farrow, J.K. Galbraith, Tallulah Bankhead, Henry Ford, Douglas Fairbanks Jr, Norman Mailer, Candice Bergen, Gianni Agnelli, Andy Warhol and Lauren Bacall.*

A devoted jazz fan, he has long admired Peggy Lee, but has never met her. Luckily, Peggy Lee also likes to name-drop. In Los Angeles, their mutual friend Dotson Rader resolves to introduce them. He telephones Peggy Lee. 'I'm here with Truman and we'd love to take you to dinner. Are you free tomorrow?'

Peggy Lee sends a car for the two men. They are taken through to what Rader describes as 'the biggest living room I ever saw in my life and the longest sofa … It's an enormous, dramatic theatrical Hollywood kind of place.' The house has beige carpeting throughout, so deep that you can see your footprints in it. The living room is very sparse, and gives the impression that no one has been there for a very long time. The house has two storeys, but Peggy tells friends that she hasn't been upstairs in a decade. 'There's no reason to,' she explains.

At the end of the room is Peggy Lee, clad in a thin white chiffon gown. She moves very slowly, as she has an oxygen tent attached to her. She is

---

* Also Claudette Colbert, the Maharajah and Maharani of Jaipur, Rose Kennedy, Virgil Thomson, Irving Berlin and Anita Loos. It is the hottest ticket in town. On the big night, a bellboy at the nearby Regency Hotel is overheard saying, 'Boy, is this town full of phonies! Do you know, there are people hanging around here in black and white clothes who ain't even going to Truman's party.'

Cecil Beaton writes in his diary: 'It seems such a terrible waste of money to spend so much on one evening … What is Truman trying to prove?' But he then cheerfully flies across the Atlantic, just to be there.

prone to illness, and to offbeat diagnoses and cures: she once spent the afternoon hanging head-down on a slanted board, explaining to concerned onlookers that she was experiencing extreme pain in her stomach because her liver had turned upside down; by going topsy-turvy, she sought to realign it.

Capote introduces himself by taking her hand and kissing it. 'Oh, my God,' he says, 'I'm in the presence of an angel.'

'Can I get you something to drink?' asks Peggy, buzzing for her butler. Her two visitors ask for vodka, but the butler informs them that they don't have any alcohol in the house, so they reluctantly settle for Perrier water. As a result, Capote grows irritable.

'Well, Truman, can I show you the gardens?' asks Peggy.

'All right. Show me the gardens, but then we've got to go,' he snaps.

Peggy tries to open the sliding doors into the garden, but cannot budge them. Truman tries to help. Together, they tug and pull, but the doors remain firmly closed. After a while, Peggy abandons the idea of going into the garden.

Instead, they set off for dinner at Le Restaurant. At last Truman and Dotson can have their vodkas. Peggy settles for a bottle of Evian water, which arrives in a silver ice-bucket, and is charged at $50 a bottle. The restaurant has a tin roof, and it is raining hard. They have to shout in order to be heard. 'You felt like you were on the Western Front in World War I and the Germans are machine-gunning your lines,' recalls Dotson.

Suddenly, Peggy asks Truman, 'Do you believe in reincarnation?'

'I don't know. Do you?'

'Oh, yes. I've been reincarnated many times. In my other lives I've been a prostitute, a princess, an Abyssinian queen ...'

Truman asks her how she knows.

'I can prove it!' she shouts. 'I remember being a prostitute in Jerusalem when Jesus was alive.'

'Oh, really? What else do you remember?'

'I remember the crucifixion very well.'

'Oh?'

'Yes, I'll never forget picking up the *Jerusalem Times* and seeing the headline "Jesus Christ Crucified".'

Peggy Lee departs for the lavatory. The two men look at each other. 'She's totally bonkers,' hisses Truman.*

(Some might say he has hit the nail on the head: she once got in contact with Albert Einstein, seeking his imprimatur for an invention of hers which involved singing in front of a chemically-treated screen so that the sound waves would conjure up different colours, and somehow heal the sick. As it happens, Einstein never accepted her invitation to dinner, though he did post her a book inscribed, 'To my favourite girl singer'.)

When Peggy returns from the lavatory, Truman changes the subject. He asks about her childhood, and how she started singing. She tells him her mother died when she was four. Six months later, the family home burned down. Her father, an alcoholic, had married a very large, aggressive woman, who used to beat her. 'Florid face, bulging thyroid eyes, long black hair to her waist pulled back in a bun, heavy breathing. Obese and strong as a horse, she beat everyone into a fright,' is the way Peggy Lee describes her stepmother in her autobiography. She accompanied her beating with verbal abuse, telling the five-year-old Peggy that she was too fat, and her hands were too big.

Peggy Lee confesses to remaining self-conscious about her hands for many years. 'I would hold them behind me … fold them up, never present them flat to view but edge-wise only. I was one of the quickest handshakers you ever saw.' Today, she tells Truman that her stepmother once stabbed her in the stomach with a butcher's knife; she still has the scar.

Truman Capote is touched. He has always possessed an uncanny instinct for the vulnerability of others. People open up to him. 'He would meet someone, make fun of them, although they weren't aware of it, and then they would say something that would reveal a vulnerability, some heartache or pain, and suddenly Truman's attitude would change,' says Rader. '… Unless he knew a vulnerability of yours, he never felt safe around you.'

---

* Though he is not without his own superstitions. 'I have to add up all numbers: there are some people I never telephone because their number adds up to an unlucky figure,' he tells the *Paris Review* in 1957. 'I won't accept a hotel room for the same reason. I will not tolerate the presence of yellow roses – which is sad because they're my favourite flower. I can't allow three cigarette butts in the same ashtray. Won't travel on a plane with two nuns. Won't begin or end anything on a Friday.'

The mood has changed. Truman asks Peggy if she will sing a song. She sings 'Bye-Bye Blackbird' and 'I'll Be Seeing You', and Truman joins in. For the next forty minutes they sing old standards together, heedless of the other diners in Le Restaurant.

'All the way back in the car, they talked about music and every once in a while the two of them would start singing,' says Rader. 'It was a lovely evening.'

PEGGY LEE

PLANTS A SMACKER ON

PRESIDENT RICHARD M. NIXON

The East Room, the White House, Washington DC
February 24th 1970

'Our artist tonight, Miss Peggy Lee, comes from the heartland of America ...' begins President Richard Nixon. 'From the farm in North Dakota she went to Hollywood, and then to New York, and then finally to the pinnacle of success in the musical world.'

The President has been enjoying his social life as never before, and never again. In the space of a single week, he has toasted the artist Andrew Wyeth with 1962 Dom Perignon at the unveiling of a collection of his paintings in the East Room, he has hosted his daughter Tricia's twenty-fourth birthday party at Camp David and he has attended a special performance of the Broadway production of *1776* at the White House.

Now, for the state visit of the President of France, Georges Pompidou, he is really pushing the boat out. Bands on the South Lawn are followed by a dinner of *Contre-Filet de Boeuf aux Cèpes* served with Château Ausone 1962. After dinner, the President takes to the stage to introduce the evening's star performer.

But behind the scenes, there had been problems. Other performers have dropped out in protest at Pompidou's decision to sell 110 Mirage fighter jets to Libya while refusing to sell fifty to Israel. Peggy Lee is asked to step in only at the last minute.*

She takes to the stage and launches into the up-tempo 'Almost Like Being in Love'. She follows it with 'Watch What Happens' and a medley of

---

* Peggy Lee has performed for a president before. In May 1962, she sings at the birthday party for President Kennedy at Madison Square Garden, but the evening is chiefly remembered for the act that followed her – Marilyn Monroe singing a breathy 'Happy Birthday' wearing a dress Adlai Stevenson described as 'skin and beads'. Other performers outshone by Monroe that night include Jack Benny, Jimmy Durante, Ella Fitzgerald and Maria Callas.

'Some Day My Prince Will Come' and 'The Most Beautiful Man in the World'. But the applause is muted: by her usual standards, this audience is very stuffy. After the first few songs, she nips offstage and downs a stiff drink, all in one. 'You can't believe how much cognac she just had!' whispers her make-up lady to her press agent.

Peggy Lee returns. In defiance of White House protocol, she starts speaking directly to the President and his guests. 'I want to thank you so very much for making me feel so very welcome here. Do you realise I've tried to be here a number of times? And, uh … it's a very kind of wonderfully warm feeling, and Mr President and Mrs Nixon … you have a lovely house.'

She doesn't stop there. She puts on a Mae West accent. 'I'm very fond of poetry … *among other things*,' she says, saucily. She pauses for laughter, but it fails to arrive, so she tries to make a joke about it.

'One of my favourite humorous verses is by Samuel Hoffenstein from his book *Pencil in the Air* and it's very short. And it goes like this:

> *Everywhere I go*
> *I go, too.*
> *And spoil ever-thang.'*

The audience shifts uneasily in their seats. President Nixon, a little sweaty, adopts a fixed smile. Peggy Lee remains undeterred, quoting a poem by the fourteen-year-old Grace Kelly in the high-pitched, lisping voice of a little girl:

> *I hate to see the sun go down*
> *And squeeze itself into the ground*
> *'Cos some warm night it might get stuck*
> *And in the morning not get up.*

'Isn't that divine? Do you like her poem? I love it. I really wish she'd kept on writing, but I know she's happier now.'

There is silence in the room while Peggy Lee giggles.

'You know, more serious poetry isn't that well accepted. In fact, to quote one writer, "To publish a book of verse is like dropping a rose petal down the Grand Canyon and waiting for the echo." And I know. I wrote a book of verse and dropped it into the Grand Canyon.'

The audience tries to laugh, but it sounds effortful. There is widespread relief as she signals to the orchestra to start the next song – her current hit 'Is That All There Is?', a bleak ramble through the various disappointments in her life. It begins, as usual, with a spoken reminiscence from her childhood in North Dakota: 'I remember when I was a little girl, our house caught on fire.' But she adds, 'And it did, Mr Nixon.' She manages to finish the song, but her mind is clearly elsewhere.

The applause is muted. 'Well, I don't want to sing goodnight right now, if you don't mind. Do you? You've all been to Disneyland, I presume. No? Well, you must go. I am going to be Tinker Bell someday. I don't think *any* of you have been to Disneyland. Don't you know what Tinker Bell does? She hits that peanut-butter jar and flies over the Matterhorn. I think she's about seventy-five. So that's my next job.'

Her next song is her signature 'Fever'. But she swaps her usual cool, laid-back delivery for something more crazed, and, halfway through, slips into a stream of consciousness, free-associating the words:

'Fee-verr! Fee-vah! I boin. I boin? I burn? I bin. Oh, look out for the Indians ... Fee-verr! What a lovely way to learn. You know what you learn? You learn not to kiss chickens! You know why? Ask me why?'

Someone in the audience yells, 'Why?'

'Because they have such funny lips.' She puts on a funny face and performs a noisy, slurpy imitation of kissing a chicken.

At the end of her act, she zigzags up to a fearful President Nixon and, without warning, plants her lips smack on his.* The next day, the *Chicago Daily News* carries the headline 'PEGGY "BOMBS" AT WHITE HOUSE FETE'.†

---

* Not all presidents are so standoffish. On June 20th 1983, Tammy Wynette sings for President Reagan at a catfish dinner in Jackson, Mississippi. After her performance, the President is photographed kissing her. 'Ronald Reagan definitely had a thing for Tammy,' says her hairdresser, Jan Smith. 'After it was over, Tammy said to me, "Oh, my God, Jan, that was so embarrassing! He swabbed my tonsils!" Well, Nancy Reagan got real out of joint about it.'

† It is another eighteen years before Peggy Lee is invited to perform again at the White House, this time at dinner for another French President, François Mitterrand. The thirty guests include Jerry Lewis, Oscar de la Renta, Rudolf Nureyev and Jacques Cousteau. It all goes fine.

Two months later, a report in the *New York Times* suggests that 'the only way you can make Peggy angry these days is to mention "the White House dinner" ... "I don't really wish to discuss it," she says, her moist pink lips drawing together tightly. "Those reports were totally inaccurate, and therefore deserve no comment. If I'm sexy, I can't help it ... Mrs Nixon gave me a warm embrace and I returned it. I would never kiss the President. I just leaned forward as he spoke to me, and it may have looked like it, but I didn't kiss him."'

PRESIDENT RICHARD M. NIXON

AWARDS A BUREAU OF NARCOTICS AND DANGEROUS DRUGS SPECIAL AGENT BADGE TO

ELVIS PRESLEY

The White House, Washington DC
December 20th 1970

As 1970 nears its end, Elvis Presley is riddled with worries about assassinations, anti-war protests, a lack of respect for authority, and the prevalence of drugs. His paranoia about the abuse of drugs by young people is exacerbated by the quantity of drugs he himself consumes.

Shopping proves a reasonably effective method of allaying his fears about everything else. He particularly enjoys buying guns, cars and jewellery, not just for himself, but for friends and employees, and sometimes total strangers. Over the course of three nights he spends $20,000 on guns at Kerr's Sporting Goods in Memphis; the following week, he buys two Mercedes, one for himself and another for a girlfriend; the week after, he buys a third Mercedes for an aide, plus a new Cadillac as a wedding present for a Palm Springs patrolman with whom he has struck up a friendship.

When his father first warned him that he was spending too much, Elvis tried to calm him down by buying him a Mercedes. But on December 19th, his father and his wife Priscilla confront him: his spending is getting out of hand.

Presley takes it badly; it is his money, he says, and he can do with it what he likes. 'I'm getting out of here,' he shouts. Without telling anyone where he is going, he flies from Memphis to Washington, from Washington to Dallas, then on to Los Angeles, where he has arranged to be met by his new driver, an Englishman called Gerald Peters.*

He then takes the next flight back to Washington. In flight, he writes the following letter:

---

* Who, incidentally, was once chauffeur to Sir Winston Churchill.

Dear Mr President,

First, I would like to introduce myself. I am Elvis Presley and admire you and Have Great Respect for your office. I talked to Vice President Agnew in Palm Springs three weeks ago and expressed my concern for our country. The Drug Culture, the Hippie Elements, the SDS, Black Panthers, etc. do not consider me as their enemy or as they call it The Establishment. I call it America and I love it. Sir I can and will be of any service that I can to help the country out …

He asks to be made a Federal Agent at Large. 'First and foremost I am an entertainer but all I need is the Federal credentials.' He has, he adds, pursued 'an in depth study of Drug Abuse and Communist brainwashing techniques … I would love to meet you just to say hello if you're not too busy.' On another piece of paper, marked 'Private and Confidential', he lists his various phone numbers.

At 6.30 a.m., Presley drops off his letter at the White House. Later that morning, he receives a phone call at his Washington hotel. It is Egil 'Bud' Krogh, deputy counsel to the President, wondering if he would drop by in forty-five minutes.*

The senior staff at the White House, including the President's chief of staff, Bob Haldeman, feel that, in view of Nixon's poor standing among the young, it would be 'extremely beneficial for the President to build some rapport with Presley'.

Elvis Presley arrives at the White House in full make-up, wearing a large brass-buttoned Edwardian jacket over a purple velvet tunic with matching trousers, held up by a vast gold belt. A necklace and a gold pendant hang from his neck. Though slightly put out when asked to hand over the chrome-plated World War II Colt .45 he has brought as a gift for the President, he strides confidently into the Oval Office at 12.30 p.m. and proceeds to present President Nixon with two signed photographs. He then spreads his collection of police badges over the Oval Office desk for him to admire. The two men speak about Las Vegas and young people.

---

* Presley misses an earlier opportunity to meet the President. He has been invited to perform at the White House, but on hearing that no payment is involved, his manager, Colonel Parker, refuses on his behalf.

Elvis launches into a passionate diatribe against the Beatles: they have come to America and taken American money, then gone back to England to foster anti-American feeling.

'The President nodded in agreement and expressed some surprise,' reads Bud Krogh's official memo of the meeting. 'The President then indicated that those who use drugs are also in the vanguard of anti-American protest … Presley indicated to the President in a very emotional manner that he was "on your side". Presley kept repeating that he wanted to be helpful, that he wanted to restore some respect for the flag.'

'I'm just a poor boy from Tennessee. I've gotten a lot from my country. And I'd like to do something to repay for what I've gotten,' says Elvis.

'That will be very helpful,' replies Nixon, cautiously.

Elvis senses the moment is right to ask the President for a Bureau of Narcotics and Dangerous Drugs special agent badge.* The President looks a little uncertain, turns to Krogh and says, 'Bud, can we get him a badge?' Krogh is unsure of the correct response. Does the President want him to bluff it out? 'Well, sir,' he answers, 'if you want to give him a badge, I think we can get him one.'

The President nods. 'I'd like to do that. See that he gets one.'

Presley is overcome. 'This means a lot to me,' he says. He pulls Nixon to him and hugs this least tactile of presidents to his chest. Nixon pats Presley briskly on the shoulder. 'Well, I appreciate your willingness to help, Mr Presley.'

Managing to extricate himself from Elvis Presley's embrace, he takes a step back.

'You dress kind of strange, don't you?' he says.

'You have your show and I have mine,' explains Elvis.

Elvis Presley returns home, badge in hand, in such a state of triumph that he buys a further four Mercedes as Christmas presents. His wife later

---

* The lead singer of Jefferson Airplane, Grace Slick, is denied admission to a tea party at the White House for alumni of Tricia Nixon's alma mater, Finch College, where she has also been a pupil. It is perhaps just as well: before setting off, she calls Abbie Hoffman. 'We decided Nixon needed about 600 micrograms of acid. It's very small so I could have put it into his teacup, and it's tasteless. But I never got in, not because I wasn't invited but because they recognised Grace Slick unfortunately, and they said you can't come in because you're on the FBI list, I guess because of some of my lyrics.'

claims he only wanted the badge so he could transport all his prescription drugs and guns without being arrested. But he will use it for other purposes, too: as a fully-fledged FBI special agent, he sometimes flashes the blue light on his car to pull motorists over for speeding, or to offer assistance at road accidents.

ELVIS PRESLEY

RECEIVES

PAUL McCARTNEY

Perugia Way, Beverly Hills, Los Angeles
August 27th 1965

The negotiations have been fraught. The Beatles idolise Elvis, and long to meet him.* In turn, Elvis resents the Beatles, and blames them for stealing his thunder.

Over the past year, Elvis's manager, Colonel Tom Parker, has been trying to orchestrate a meeting, but his client has been dragging his heels. Until last April, Elvis had not achieved a Top 10 single since 1963, the very same year the Beatles took off. The Beatles' only two movies, *A Hard Day's Night* and *Help!*, have been huge successes, while Elvis's movie career is in the doldrums: his last, *Tickle Me*, set in a beauty parlour, made no impact at all.

Beatlemania, on the other hand, seems to know no bounds. On their last American tour, tins of Beatles' breath sold like hot cakes in New York. After the Beatles have passed through Denver, dirty linen from their hotel beds is cut into three-inch squares, each square mounted on parchment, to be sold for $10 a square inch. The Beatles are the talk of the country, even the world. 'I like your advance guard,' President Johnson greets the British Prime Minister Sir Alec Douglas-Home on his arrival at the White House on February 12th 1964. 'But don't you think they need haircuts?'

In the spring of 1965 things begin to perk up for Elvis. His old recording of 'Crying in the Chapel' climbs to No. 3 in the charts in America and No. 1 in Britain. With the playing field levelled, negotiations can recommence.† In early August, Colonel Parker and Brian Epstein sit in the

---

* 'We all wanted to be Elvis,' Lennon recalls. 'Before Elvis, there was nothing.'

† Colonel Parker has secretly been keeping the Beatles sweet, sending them a congratulatory telegram after their Madison Square Garden show, and a consignment of four cowboy suits, complete with real six-shooters and holsters.

Colonel's office in New York on chairs made from elephants' feet, and, over pastrami sandwiches and root beer, they reach an agreement: Elvis will meet the Beatles, but only on condition that they come to him.

Elvis is staying in a Frank Lloyd Wright house he rents from the Shah of Iran. On their way there in a Cadillac, the Beatles quell their nerves by smoking a couple of joints. They arrive giggling. 'We all fell out of the car like a Beatle cartoon, in hysterics, trying to pretend we weren't silly,' says George. They are led into the presence of Elvis, who is sitting on a sofa, playing a Fender bass, watching the television with the sound turned down. He is dressed in tight grey trousers and a bright red shirt, surrounded by bodyguards and hangers-on. On the jukebox is 'Mohair Sam' by Charlie Rich. 'He just played it endlessly. It was the record of the moment for him,' says Paul. On the mantelpiece there is a sign saying 'All the Way with LBJ'.

The wives and girlfriends in his entourage have taken care to hide their excitement at the prospect of meeting the Beatles. They have no wish to upset Elvis. After a while, the two managers peel off: the Colonel has uncovered a roulette wheel inside a cocktail table, and Brian Epstein is a keen gambler.

The Beatles can't think of a word to say. They just look straight ahead, finding it hard to adjust to being in the same room as the King. 'Wow! That's Elvis!' is all Paul can think. They are impressed, however, by the way Elvis can change channels on his television without moving from his seat. They have never seen a television remote control before.

'Look, if you guys are gonna sit here and stare at me all night, Ah'm gonna go to bed!' says Elvis. 'Ah didn't mean for this to be like the subjects calling on the King. Ah jist thought we'd sit and talk about music and maybe jam a little.'

John Lennon asks if he is preparing for his next film. 'Ah sure am,' says Elvis. 'Ah play a country boy with a guitar who meets a few gals along the way, and ah sing a few songs.' The Beatles are not sure how to respond, but Elvis breaks the ice by laughing. This is, after all, the plot of all his films.*

---

* Other than *Wild in the Country* (1962), in which he plays a troubled young man from a dysfunctional family who hopes to become a writer. It loses money.

Ringo goes off to play pool with Elvis's friends. Later, he describes them as sycophants. 'Elvis would say, "I'm going to the loo now," and they'd say, "We'll all go to the loo with you."'

George shares a joint with Elvis's spiritual adviser and hairdresser; the same man combines both roles. They discuss Eastern philosophy. Some members of the entourage find it hard to distinguish one Beatle from another. One of them solves the problem by addressing each of them as 'Hey, Beatle!'

Meanwhile, guitars are produced for John and Paul, who strum their way through some of the Elvis numbers they used to play in their Cavern days. Elvis continues to lounge on the sofa, playing his bass. 'Coming along quite promising on the bass, Elvis,' jokes Paul. In a break from the music, John performs a medley of Peter Sellers voices, which Elvis appears to enjoy. But he seems to bristle when John asks him why he no longer plays rock-and-roll. 'I loved those Sun records,' John adds.

After a couple of hours, the meeting draws to a close. Elvis sees them to the door. They invite him over to their house in Benedict Canyon, and he appears to accept. The Colonel gives the four Beatles souvenirs of their meeting, little covered wagons that light up when you push a button. As the Beatles leave, John shouts, 'Long live the King!'*

The following evening, Elvis's security guards come over to Benedict Canyon to check out the house. John Lennon asks one of them to tell Elvis, 'If it hadn't been for you, I would have been nothing.' He tells another, 'Last night was the greatest night of my life.' Perhaps he senses that they have failed to make a good impression, and Elvis will not be making a return visit. Sure enough, he never arrives, and none of the Beatles ever meets Elvis again.†

'It was great, one of the great meetings of my life,' recalls Paul, forty years on.

---

* In the long run, this meeting does little to lessen Elvis's natural suspicion towards the Beatles. An official memo of a tour by Elvis of the FBI building in Washington on December 30th 1970 notes that 'Presley indicated that he is of the opinion that the Beatles laid the groundwork for many of the problems we are having with young people by their filthy unkempt appearances and suggestive music while entertaining in this country during the early and middle 1960s.'

† Except for George, who briefly meets him backstage at Madison Square Garden in the early seventies. 'He had all them squawking girl singers and trumpet players and all that stuff … I just wanted to say to him, "Just get your jeans on and get your guitar and do 'That's All Right Mama' and bugger all that other crap,"'

PAUL McCARTNEY

IS CONGRATULATED BY

NOËL COWARD

The Adriana Hotel, Rome
June 27th 1965

John Lennon and Paul McCartney enjoy the parties thrown by Alma Cogan* in her flat at 44 Stafford Court, Kensington High Street. This flat has become something of a refuge since they first struck up a friendship with the archetypal 1950s singer when they appeared with her at the London Palladium eighteen months ago.

'They needed to relax and get away from crowds,' Alma's sister Sandra remembers. 'Our flat gave them refuge for many months to come, with Mum – Mrs Macogie, as they called her – making pots of tea and sandwiches, and playing charades.' Fellow contestants in these games might include actors like Stanley Baker (whose new film *Zulu* has been such a huge hit) and all-round family entertainers like Lionel Blair and Bruce Forsyth.

For McCartney, the parties at Stafford Court become part of the experience of growing up. 'One of the things that it's hard for people to realise is that we were on the cusp of the change-over between showbiz styles … They were all a little older than us, probably ten, twelve years older than us, but they were great fun, very confident showbiz people who welcomed us into their circle. It was exciting for us, we could hear all the showbizzy gossip and meet people that we hadn't met before. We'd known Alma as the big singing star … She was old-school showbiz. She invited us round to her mum's place in Kensington, she and her sister lived with her mum,

---

* Cogan is famous for her bouffant hairdo, her glittery dresses – she sometimes changes costumes eleven times over the course of a show – and her novelty records like 'I Can't Tell a Waltz from a Tango'. Her song 'Never do a Tango with an Eskimo' is a huge hit in Iceland. Paul McCartney is to be heard playing tambourine on her single 'I Knew Right Away'. After writing 'Yesterday', McCartney is worried that the tune is so simple that it must already exist, but when he plays it to Alma Cogan, she assures him it is original.

and her mum was an old Jewish lady. They were very nice, Alma and her sister Sandra … I saw a documentary about John Betjeman, who said that when he got out of college there was a country house to which he was invited. And he said, "There I learned to be a guest," and that's what was happening to us at Alma's flat. There we learned to play charades, and we started to do it at our own parties. it was just a little learning curve.'

Alma Cogan is to become part of John Lennon's growing up, too: over this summer, they conduct an affair.* Nor is Brian Epstein immune to her charms, taking her to meet his parents in Liverpool, and even talking of marrying her.

Alma Cogan's other guests are drawn largely from mainstream, old-fashioned showbiz: Danny Kaye, Ethel Merman, Cary Grant, Sammy Davis Junior, Frankie Vaughan, Tommy Steele. And it is here that John Lennon and Paul McCartney are first introduced to Noël Coward. Now in his sixties, for Coward the pair represent everything he detests about the modern age, with its emphasis on the working class, and its seemingly inexorable drift away from his own particular area of interest, the upper class. 'Duchesses are quite capable of suffering too,' he complains after seeing *Look Back in Anger* in 1956. 'I wonder how long this trend of dreariness for dreariness' sake will last?' But he does not voice these qualms to the two young Liverpudlians; instead, he is charm itself.

Afterwards, in an offhand moment, Coward mentions their meeting to David Lewin of the *Daily Mail*. 'The Beatles, those two I met, seemed nice, pleasant young men, quite well behaved and with an amusing way of speaking,' he begins. But he does not stop there. He cannot resist adding, 'Of course, they are totally devoid of talent. There is a great deal of noise. In my day, the young were taught to be seen but not heard – which is no bad thing.' Lewin prints his comments in full.

Coward is greatly upset when, on June 12th, the Queen's Birthday Honours list includes MBEs for the Beatles. 'A tactless and major blunder on the part of the Prime Minister,' he writes in his diary, 'and also I don't think the Queen should have agreed. Some other decoration should have been selected to reward them for their talentless but considerable contributions to the Exchequer.'

---

* In West End hotels, generally registering as 'Mr and Mrs Winston'.

On June 27th, Coward goes to see them in concert in Rome. 'I had never seen them play in the flesh before. The noise was deafening throughout and I couldn't hear a word they sang or a note they played, just one long, ear-splitting din. It was like a mass masturbation orgy, although apparently mild compared with what it usually is. The whole thing is to me an unpleasant phenomenon. Mob hysteria when commercially promoted, or in whatever way promoted, always sickens me. To realise that the majority of the modern adolescent world goes ritualistically mad over those four innocuous, rather silly-looking young men is a disturbing thought. Perhaps we are whirling more swiftly into extinction than we know. Personally I should have liked to take some of those squealing young maniacs and cracked their heads together. I am all for audiences going mad with enthusiasm after a performance, but *not* incessantly *during* the performance so that there ceases to be a performance.' Nevertheless, he concedes that though 'it is still impossible to judge from their public performance whether they have talent or not ... They were professional, had a certain guileless charm, and stayed on mercifully for not too long.'

After the concert, Coward goes backstage, where he is greeted by Brian Epstein, who gives him a drink. An embarrassed Epstein is obliged to inform him that the Beatles were not amused by the unflattering remarks he made about them to the *Daily Mail*, and so do not wish to see him.

Coward bridles, but stands firm. 'I thought this graceless in the extreme but decided to play it with firmness and dignity.' He asks Epstein's personal assistant to go and fetch one of the Beatles. 'She finally reappeared with Paul McCartney and I explained gently but firmly that one did NOT pay much attention to the statements of newspaper reporters.'*

This seems to break the ice somewhat. 'The poor boy was quite amiable and I sent messages of congratulations to his colleagues,' Coward continues, 'although the message I would have liked to send them was that they were bad-mannered little shits.'

---

* Or perhaps one should: six months later, Coward's rage has not abated: 'I am INFURIATED by those bloody little Beatles going to Buckingham Palace and all those "Teenagers" knocking policemen's hats off and Paul Macartney [sic] saying the Queen was just a "Mum". I DO know what the younger generation is coming to *non mi piace* at all, at all.'

NOËL COWARD

IS SERENADED BY

PRINCE FELIX YOUSSOUPOFF

Biarritz
July 29th 1946

Noël Coward and his friend Graham Payn are enjoying a summer holiday
in post-war France. Their few weeks in Paris pass 'in a whirl of pleasure
and Alka-Seltzer' as they spend time in the company of Sir Duff and Lady
Diana Cooper. Coward pops into the British Embassy and finds 'nobody
about but Winston Churchill. He was very amiable and we talked for
about forty minutes and I played him some of the operette tunes.' From
Paris, they motor down to Biarritz in Noël's MG to stay with his old
friend, the fashion designer Edward Molyneux.

On their first sunny day in Biarritz, they spend the morning sunbathing
on the beach, followed by a light lunch and then back to the beach. In the
early evening, Coward catches up on his correspondence and then dresses
for dinner; he is a little excited, because one of Molyneux's guests is none
other than Prince Felix Youssoupoff, famous, or infamous, for the murder
of Rasputin.

The gothic demise of Rasputin continues to hold an almost mesmeric
appeal for high society. As with Lord Lucan's murder of his children's
nanny some sixty years later, everyone likes to claim inside knowledge. A
few days after the death of Rasputin, Duff Cooper writes in his diary, 'We
have had at the Foreign Office such thrilling telegrams about the murder
of Rasputin. It appears to have been done by Felix Elston* [Youssoupoff]
whom I used to know intimately at Oxford. It took place at a supper party
in his palace. The telegrams read like pages from Italian renaissance
history.' Later the same year, on December 6th 1917, Cooper records being
driven home from a dinner party in Upper Berkeley Street by Bertie

---

* Youssoupoff was known as Count Felix Elston while he was an undergraduate at Oxford
University.

Stopford. Perhaps inevitably, they gossip about Rasputin. '[Stopford] is a notorious bugger and was very attentive to me, saying I looked younger than when he last saw me which was in Venice before the war. He has been in Russia for some time and talked to me about the murder of Rasputin. After Rasputin was dead, Felix Elston fell on the body and beat it. Felix told Stopford this himself. He suspects there had been some relationship between Felix and Rasputin. The great charm of the latter for women was that when he had them he never came and so could go on forever. Also he had three large warts on his cock.'

Until his death at the age of eighty in 1967, Youssoupoff knows full well that his murder of Rasputin is the signature tune that accompanies his entrance into any gathering. He embraces his notoriety. In his Knightsbridge home in the 1920s, he regularly entertains guests with increasingly melodramatic renditions of that fateful night in 1916. He even submits paintings of bearded men with evil grimaces to an art exhibition. So identified are he and his wife Irina with the death of Rasputin that a New York hostess mistakenly introduces them as the Prince and Princess Rasputin. Around the same time, Helen Izvolsky, the daughter of the Tsar's former ambassador to France, visits Youssoupoff and notices 'something Satanic about his twisted smile. He talked for several hours about the assassination, and seemed quite pleased to reminisce, going over all the horrifying details. In conclusion, he showed me a ring he was wearing, with a bullet mounted in silver. He explained that this was the bullet that had killed Rasputin.'

The murder not only defines Youssoupoff's life, but finances it too: in 1932, he gains between $2 million and $2.5 million, in today's terms, in compensation from MGM, who in their movie *Rasputin and the Empress* suggested that Princess Irina was hypnotised and raped by the Mad Monk. This windfall allows the couple to live the high life.

By the time they enter the Molyneux house, ready to meet Noël Coward, the Youssoupoffs are resident in France, and mixing in a curious circle of the wealthy and the exiled that includes J. Paul Getty, Philippe de Rothschild, Sir Oswald and Lady Diana Mosley and the Duke and Duchess of Windsor. Felix, born in 1887, is now in late middle age. His youthful lustre has long gone, but he does his best to counterfeit it. Every morning, he prepares for the day ahead by spending hours at his dressing table, applying eyeliner, mascara and rouge to his face, and combing his thinning hair into a latticework that very nearly covers his scalp.

The dinner party goes as planned. 'Dinner very chic,' Coward writes in his diary. 'Felix Youssoupoff sang really quite sweetly with a guitar. He is made up to the teeth. I looked at him: a face that must, when young, have been very beautiful but now it is cracking with effort and age. I imagined him luring Rasputin to his doom with that guitar and "dem rollin' eyes". It was all a little macabre. I sang but not very well. Graham was really wonderful. He was not only socially vital and attractive, but he suddenly proceeded to sing in Russian so much better than Youssoupoff and his friend that the whole party was astonished. It went on far too long. Home about three o'clock.'

Twenty-one years later, on October 15th 1967, less than a month after the death of Felix Youssoupoff, Coward finishes reading *Nicholas and Alexandra* by Robert K. Massie. 'It really is such an appalling story,' he writes in his diary. 'The Tsar amiable, kindly and stupid, and the Tsarina, a hysterical ass. The most fascinating character to emerge is, as usual, Rasputin. What an extraordinary phenomenon! His murder is brilliantly described and coincides in every detail with what Dmitri told me years ago. The only thing I query is that Youssoupoff lured Rasputin to his house to meet his wife Irina, who was in the Crimea. Rasputin would have known this perfectly well. The truth, I think, is that Rasputin had a tiny little lech on Youssoupoff himself.'

Oddly enough, this accords with what Duff Cooper first suspected, fifty years earlier.

PRINCE FELIX YOUSSOUPOFF

MURDERS

GRIGORI RASPUTIN

The Moika Palace, St Petersburg
December 29th 1916

If, as Noël Coward suspects, Rasputin has a tiny little lech on Prince Felix Youssoupoff, it is a lech that backfires.

At their first meeting, in 1909, Youssoupoff draws back in horror. 'There was something about him which disgusted me … He had a low, common face, framed by a shaggy beard, coarse features and a long nose, with small shifty grey eyes … He was not in the least like a holy man: on the contrary he looked like a lascivious, malicious satyr. There was something base in his unctuous countenance; something wicked, crafty and sensual.'

But others are captivated. By 1916, Rasputin's hold over the Tsarina is more powerful than ever, so much so that some think it threatens the very stability of the state. Youssoupoff and his aristocratic friends decide to do away with him. They plan to gain his trust, then lure him to his death.

By chance, only a few days later, a mutual friend tells Youssoupoff that Rasputin wants to see him again. The two men meet. Even though Rasputin has spruced himself up in his smartest blue-silk blouse and velvet breeches, Youssoupoff continues to find him offputting. 'His offensive familiarity and insolent assurance made him seem still more obnoxious.' He feigns intense fatigue, which Rasputin, as if on cue, offers to cure. They meet for several surgeries, Rasputin attempting to cure the bogus fatigue through hypnosis.

The day of reckoning finally arrives. Rasputin accepts Youssoupoff's invitation to spend an evening at his home. 'The simple way in which he consented to everything, and even went out of his way to make things easier for me, horrified and surprised me.'

Youssoupoff plans to murder Rasputin in the cellar. To make Rasputin feel at home, he decorates it with curtains, carpets, ancient embroideries and a selection of charming knick-knacks. His fellow conspirators drop round. The doctor among them, Lazovert, puts on rubber gloves, grinds the cyanide to powder, and places poison on each cake 'sufficient to kill several men instantly', and into several glasses as well. Rasputin arrives, smartly dressed for the evening's entertainment in a silk blouse embroidered in cornflowers, a thick, raspberry-coloured belt and his velvet breeches. He has even gone to the trouble of brushing his hair and combing his beard. Youssoupoff notes, too, the smell of cheap soap.

As he helps him off with his overcoat, a feeling of great pity sweeps over Youssoupoff, who has accompanied Rasputin to the house. 'I was ashamed of the despicable deceit, the horrible trickery to which I was obliged to resort … I looked at my victim with dread, as he stood before me, quiet and trusting. What had become of his second sight?'

From upstairs comes the sound of his co-conspirators chatting while 'Yankee Doodle Went to Town' plays on the gramophone. 'Is there a party going on?' asks Rasputin. Youssoupoff explains that his wife is entertaining a few friends: she will be down soon. 'Meanwhile, let's have a cup of tea in the dining room.'

They go downstairs. Youssoupoff offers Rasputin wine, but he refuses. They gossip about mutual friends. Youssoupoff offers him some cake. He refuses, but then he changes his mind. He has another, but the poison does not seem to be working.

Rasputin accepts a glass of wine, then asks for some Madeira. He holds out the same glass, but Youssoupoff contrives to drop it, allowing him to pour the Madeira into a glass containing extra cyanide. Rasputin accepts a second glass of Madeira. He complains of a tickle in his throat and puts his head in his hands. Things are looking up. He asks for another cup of tea. 'I'm very thirsty.'

He seems to rally. Spotting a guitar, he asks Youssoupoff to play a tune. By now, two hours have passed since his arrival at the palace. Youssoupoff finds an excuse to nip upstairs, where he consults with his friends. They are impatient: why can't they just come down and strangle him? Youssoupoff urges discretion: he will return to the basement alone, with a revolver.

On his return, Rasputin is complaining of a headache and stomach pains, and suggests that another glass of wine might do the trick. He drinks it in a single gulp; it seems to revive him. He starts to admire a crystal crucifix: how much did it cost? Enough is enough. Youssoupoff produces his revolver, tells Rasputin to say a prayer, and pulls the trigger. Rasputin lets out a wild scream and crumples to the floor.

The conspirators rush in. They watch Rasputin's fingers twitch as blood spreads over his silk blouse. His body goes still. The doctor declares Rasputin dead. They all go upstairs, leaving Rasputin's body below. But before long, Youssoupoff is filled with 'an irresistible impulse' to go back downstairs. 'Rasputin lay exactly where we had left him. I felt his pulse: not a beat.'

For some reason, Youssoupoff seizes the corpse and shakes it violently. Without warning, the left eyelid quivers, and slight tremors contract the face. The left eye pops open, and a few seconds later the right eye too. 'I then saw both eyes – the green eyes of a viper – staring at me with an expression of diabolical hatred.'

Rasputin leaps to his feet, foaming at the mouth. With a wild roar, he makes a grab for Youssoupoff. 'His eyes were bursting from their sockets, blood oozed from his lips … it was the reincarnation of Satan himself who held me in his clutches.' They struggle. Youssoupoff breaks free. Rasputin falls on his back, gasping horribly.

Youssoupoff rushes upstairs, shouting for help. Rasputin follows him, 'gasping and roaring like a wounded animal'. He manages to stumble out to the courtyard, and is struggling in the direction of the entrance when Youssoupoff's co-conspirator Pourichkevitch shoots him four times at close quarters. Rasputin is dead at last.*

Towards the end of his long life, Youssoupoff is asked if he has any regrets over the murder of Rasputin. 'No,' he replies, 'I shot a dog.'

---

* There are many different accounts of Rasputin's assassination, most by those who were not there to witness it. Sixty years later, his daughter Maria claims that prior to her father's murder, Youssoupoff 'used him sexually', and that after it 'with the skill of a surgeon three elegant young members of the nobility castrated Gregory Rasputin and flung the severed penis across the room'. Maria's co-author, Patte Barham, claims to have been shown the penis in question on a visit to Paris, preserved in a velvet case and guarded by a group of White Russian ladies.

Of this notably long-winded murder, Leon Trotsky later priggishly observes that, 'It was carried out in the manner of a scenario designed for people of bad taste.' Maria Rasputin agrees. After reading Youssoupoff's account of the murder, she complains, 'To me it is atrocious, and I do not believe that any decent person could help feeling a sentiment of disgust in reading the savage ferocity of this story.' She condemns Youssoupoff, saying that he 'vomited forth the vilest calumnies against my father'. In an unexpected move, this cabaret-singer-turned-lion-tamer is to name her two pet dogs Youssou and Pov.

GRIGORI RASPUTIN

TESTS THE PATIENCE OF

TSAR NICHOLAS II

Tsarskoye Selo, nr St Petersburg
June 21st 1915

Eighteen months before he dies, Rasputin receives a rap over the knuckles from Tsar Nicholas II himself.

As Rasputin's influence on the Tsarina has grown, so has his reputation for drunken debauchery. In 1911, an editorial in an Orthodox periodical describes him as a 'sex maniac and a charlatan', and by 1915 this is pretty much the view of the country at large. The Tsar, on the other hand, tries to think of him as 'a good, simple-minded religious Russian', while the Tsarina goes much further, addressing him as 'My beloved, unforgettable teacher, redeemer and mentor', and adding, 'I am asking for your Holy Blessing and I am kissing your blessed hands. I love you for ever.'

She reveres his wisdom. 'When he says not to do a thing and one does not listen, one sees one's fault always afterwards.'

Meanwhile, the secret police have been keeping close tabs on Rasputin's daily routine:

February 12th
Rasputin and an unknown woman went to house 15/17 on Troitskaya Street … at 4.30 in the morning he came back with six drunken men and a guitar. They remained till six, singing and dancing.

March 11th
At 10.15 a.m. Rasputin was seen on Gorokhovaya Street and followed to No. 8 Pushkin Street, home of the prostitute Tregubova, from there he went to the bathhouse.

14 May

At 5.00 p.m. he drove to No. 15 Malaya Dvoryanskaya St. At 10.00 p.m. one
of the windows in the flat was unlit, but one of the detectives could see a
woman leave the lighted room to look into the dark one, she quickly ran
back. Then Rasputin could be seen running out of the dark room, he grabbed
his hat and coat and ran out on to the street with two men chasing him.
They just ran out, called out, 'There he goes,' and went back inside. Rasputin
jumped in to a cab at a run and went down Liteiny Prospekt looking
anxiously over his shoulder.

And so forth. It is the job of the police both to keep track of Rasputin's behaviour and to keep it under wraps. But one day he goes too far. After praying at the tombs of the saints, he visits his favourite restaurant, the Villa Rhode, with a boisterous group of followers. They drink heavily, particularly Rasputin himself, who starts to brag about his relationship with the Tsarina. He points to his embroidered blouse and says that 'the old woman' sewed it for him, and goes on to make increasingly lewd comments about her.

A fellow diner questions whether he is really Rasputin: can he prove it? In reply, Rasputin unbuttons his fly and waves his penis around.* This, he boasts, is the way he behaves in the presence of the Tsar. He adds that he has often had his way with 'the old girl'. He then hands out a series of notes with mottoes such as 'Love Unselfishly'.

By chance, the British Ambassador to Moscow, Robert Bruce Lockhart, is present in the same restaurant that evening. 'A violent fracas in one of the private rooms. Wild shrieks of a woman, a man's curses, broken glass and the banging of doors. Headwaiters rushed upstairs. The manager sent for the police ... But the row and roaring continued ... The cause of the disturbance was Rasputin – drunk and lecherous ...' Eventually, Rasputin is dragged away by the police, snarling and vowing revenge.

The news reaches the Governor of Moscow, who makes a report to the assistant minister of internal affairs, Vladimir Dzhunkovsky, who submits

---

* Apparently this was not the only trick he kept up his sleeve. 'I remember his strange ability to transform himself instantaneously, like a magician of old: strike the ground and up jumps a grey wolf, roll over and up flies a black raven, fall like a stone to the ground – and away creeps a green wood goblin,' recalls V.A. Jukovskaya, a devoted member of Rasputin's circle.

a bowdlerised report to the Tsar, who in turn places it, unread, to one side. But then a new minister of internal affairs, no friend to Rasputin, commissions a re-investigation by Dzhunkovsky, incorporating it into a much more detailed report on Rasputin's way of life. This final report is once again submitted to the Tsar, who this time reads it all the way through. What is to be done?

On June 21st, the Tsar sends for Rasputin and demands an explanation. Rasputin says that he is only human, and as much a sinner as the next man, but he would never have exposed himself or referred in any way disrespectfully to the Imperial Family. The Tsar is far from convinced, and orders him to leave the capital. As he departs, Rasputin mutters to one of the guards, 'Your Dzhunkovksy is finished.' Leaving Moscow with, as it were, his tail between his legs, Rasputin nevertheless remarks to his escort that 'life for seekers after truth and righteousness can sometimes be very hard'. On the steamer home, he gets into a fight with two fellow passengers, accuses the steward of theft, and falls into a drunken stupor.

The Tsarina is handed Dzhunkovsky's report and immediately bursts into tears. She calls it a pack of lies, and breathlessly urges the Tsar to sack its author. 'I long knew Dzhunkovsky hates Grigory … If we let our Friend be persecuted we and our country shall suffer for it … I am so weary such heartache and pain fr. all this – the idea of dirt being spread about one we venerate is more than horrible.

'If Dzhunkovsky is with you, call him, tell him you order him to tear it up and not to dare to speak of Grigory as he does and that he acts as a traitor.

'Ah my love when *at last* will you thump with your hand upon the table and scream at Dzhunkovsky and others when they act wrongly – one does not fear you – and one *must* – they must be frightened of you otherwise all sit upon us.'

Once again, the Tsar changes tack, and acts on his wife's advice. In September, he dismisses Dzhunkovsky, allowing Rasputin to re-establish his place at court. The Tsarina pens a letter to her husband reminding him to hold Rasputin's holy trinkets for good luck: 'Remember to keep the Image in your hand again and several times to comb your hair with His comb before the sitting of the ministers …'

TSAR NICHOLAS II

IS TRICKED BY

HARRY HOUDINI

Kremlin Square, Moscow
May 23rd 1903

The Tsar and Tsarina believe in magic. Séances and table-tappings are *de rigueur* among their court, and no palace is complete without its domestic ghost, ready to play a suitably eerie tune on the piano whenever a member of the family is dying.

Over the years, Nicholas and Alexandra have allowed themselves to be guided by a succession of *wolshebniks*, or miracle men, the more outlandish the better. The roster includes Matronushka Bosoposhka, 'Matrona, the barefooted one', who, it is thought, can tell the future; Vasili Tkatchenko, an elderly soothsayer much given to grave pronouncements on foreign policy; and Philippe Vachot, a former butcher's assistant from Lyons, who offers the full range of spiritualism, hypnotism and faith healing. M. Philippe, as he styles himself, is a dab hand at conjuring up the spirits of the Tsar's predecessors, who encourage the Tsar to be vigorous in his suppression of dissent. But M. Philippe's reputation for determining the sex of unborn children takes a tumble when the Tsar's next child turns out to be not a son, as predicted, but a girl, Anastasia. Two years later, M. Philippe declares once again that the Tsarina is pregnant with a son, but this prediction too proves faulty: she isn't pregnant after all. Vachot is paid off, and booted back to Paris.

In May of the same year, Harry Houdini, the greatest magician the world has ever seen, sets off from Berlin for Russia on the next stage of his European tour. 'We leave for Moscow this evening, and I hope they will not send me to Siberia,' he writes in his American newspaper column.

His welcome is decidedly lukewarm. At the border town of Alexandrowo, patrolmen ransack his luggage. When they find a selection of burglary tools, they cut up rough until Houdini produces the necessary permit.

Houdini does not like travelling in Russia. 'I think that a butcher in America would hesitate before he would ship his cattle in one of these third-class trains. There is nothing that I have ever witnessed that has equalled it,' he tells his readers.

But the Russians are soon captivated by him. In Moscow, he manages to escape from a Siberian Transport Cell in the old Butirskaya prison, even after a full body-search that is supervised by the head of the secret police. The newspapers say it can only be explained by Houdini's extraordinary ability to dematerialise. In fact, he wears a false finger, in which he stores a miniature metal-cutting tool and a coil of wire with sawed teeth, of the type used by surgeons for cutting through skulls. The wonders never cease. After a private performance, a Moscow newspaper gasps, 'Mr Houdini, in front of a serious committee, was able to turn into a woman, then turn into a baby, then come back to his regular appearance.' People believe what they want to believe.

Small wonder, then, that Houdini is soon summoned to entertain the royal household. On the evening of May 23rd, the Tsar and Tsarina attend a performance at the home of the Tsar's uncle, the Grand Duke Sergei, which overlooks Kremlin Square. After a few mind-reading tricks, Houdini asks each guest to jot down on a piece of paper an impossible task. The papers are gathered and placed into a hat. Houdini then asks the Grand Duke to fish one out and read it to him. The Grand Duke looks at the piece of paper he has picked, and shakes his head.

'I am afraid that this task will be impossible for even such a wonder-worker as you,' he says.

'To make the impossible possible is my job,' replies Houdini.

The Tsar is impatient to know what the task is.

'Can you ring the bells of the Kremlin?' reads the Grand Duke. The women in the room start to giggle. They all know that the bells of the Kremlin have not pealed for over a century, and the ropes have all rotted to dust.

But Houdini remains unabashed. He walks over to the large window overlooking Kremlin Square and beckons his audience to gather around him. He pulls a handkerchief from one pocket and a container full of purple powder from another and proceeds to sprinkle the powder onto the handkerchief. Then he waves his handkerchief in solemn arcs, and recites this mysterious incantation:

> *Powder travel through the night,*
> *Your assignation before dawn's light,*
> *From Seventh Heaven to deepest Hell,*
> *Do your bidding and ring the bell!*

With that, he throws open one of the great windows. There is a pause, and suddenly the bells of the Kremlin begin to ring. Everyone is amazed. It is, they declare, a miracle.

Oh no it isn't. Unbeknownst to them, Houdini's new assistant, Franz Kukol, was standing on a balcony of the hotel across the square. At the sight of the prearranged signal of the handkerchief being waved, he aimed an air rifle at the bells and fired a volley of shots, causing them to ring.

After it is all over, the Tsar is particularly impressed by the way Houdini refuses any sort of payment. What he does not know is that the magician has been tipped off by Grand Duke Sergei's wife that the royal family regards anyone who accepts payment as a menial. Instead, Houdini accepts a variety of gifts for these private shows: an antique champagne ladle, expensive rings, a fluffy white Pomeranian called Charlie.

Houdini performs again for the Tsar. On his return to America, he boasts that the Tsar wanted him to become an official adviser, but that he refused, saying his art was not for one family, or even one country, but for the world. Grigori Rasputin soon steps in to fill this void. Before very long, the Tsarina grows convinced that he has been sent by God. In 1912 Houdini is contacted by suspicious Russian court officials, who want him to come and expose Rasputin. Houdini, who enjoys unmasking charlatans, considers making the trip, but decides to stay put.

HARRY HOUDINI

BAFFLES

THEODORE ROOSEVELT

SS *Imperator*
June 23rd 1914

Houdini is finding it very hard to recover from the death of his mother last year. It has affected him deeply. Spending Christmas in Monte Carlo, he tries to assuage his grief in the casinos. He wins 2,000 francs, but feels no sense of elation. Instead, he is drawn to a special graveyard in Monte Carlo, filled with the corpses of those who committed suicide after losing their fortunes to roulette and cards.

'A terrible feeling pervades the first time one sees the graves, and thinks of the human beings who finish their lives in this manner,' he writes in his diary. He has heard that the casino workers place money in the pockets of suicide victims so as to suggest that penury has played no part in their deaths; the casino pays for the shipping of the corpses back home in order to keep things quiet. Sometimes it seems that all human life is full of such dirty tricks.

Harry and Beatrice Houdini celebrate their twentieth wedding anniversary by taking a cruise back across the Atlantic on the SS *Imperator*. The ship sets sail from Hamburg on June 17th, stopping en route at Southampton to pick up more passengers. On the night of June 23rd, two days before they are due to dock in New York, Houdini tops the bill of a charity benefit being staged for the German Sailors' Home and the Magicians' Club of London.

Among the audience is Theodore Roosevelt, the rumbustious former President of the United States.* The onboard entertainment kicks off with

---

* Colonel Roosevelt, as he likes to be styled, knows all about miraculous escapes. Campaigning two years earlier in Milwaukee for his own Progressive Party, he is shot at by a saloonkeeper by the name of John Schrank. The bullet passes through his steel spectacle case, and then through a folded fifty-page speech he is carrying in his jacket, before lodging in his chest wall. A keen big-game hunter, Roosevelt correctly determines that, as he isn't coughing blood, the bullet hasn't reached his lung, and so decides to carry on with his speech before calling in at a hospital. The speech lasts ninety minutes, during which blood pours down his shirt. The bullet remains buried in Roosevelt's chest muscle for the rest of his life.

the Ritz Carlton Orchestra playing selections from *La Bohème*. They are joined by the celebrated soprano Madame Cortesao, who sings an aria from *Madame Butterfly*. Finally, amidst much excitement, the great Houdini takes to the stage.

He warms up his audience with a couple of tricks involving silk handkerchiefs and playing cards, before announcing that he will now be performing a séance. 'I was asked to give an entertainment,' he later recalls, 'and the subject of spirit writing came up. A number of other well-known men were present, all of them having intelligence of a high order. Certainly it was not a credulous audience. I offered to summon the spirits and have them answer any question that might be asked.'

He tells the audience, 'As we all know, mediums do their work in the darkened séance room, but tonight, for the first time anywhere, I propose to conduct a spiritualistic slate test in the full glare of the light!' A hum of anticipation ripples through the audience as Houdini distributes paper, envelopes and pencils. 'If you will be so kind as to write upon the blank paper a question that you would like the spirit world to answer … then fold the paper and seal it in the envelope so there is no chance whatsoever of my seeing the particular query,' he says.

Houdini approaches President Roosevelt's table and asks him to write down his question on the piece of paper, then to fold the paper over, place it in the envelope and seal it. Returning to the stage, he says to the audience, 'I am sure there will be no objection if we use the Colonel's question.' The audience murmurs its consent.

Houdini now shows Colonel Roosevelt a small wooden frame containing two double-sided chalkboards. 'Can you confirm to the audience that there is absolutely nothing written on these slates?' he asks.

'They are blank,' confirms Roosevelt.

Houdini asks him to place his envelope between the two slates.

'Can you please tell the audience what your question was?' he says.

'Where was I last Christmas?' states the Colonel.

Houdini opens the slates, and holds them up for the audience to see. On one slate there is a map of Brazil: the River of Doubt in the Amazon is highlighted. The other slate carries the message: 'Near the Andes'. It is signed by the committed spiritualist W. T. Stead, a campaigning British journalist who met his death two years ago, on another cruise liner, the *Titanic*.

'By George, that proves it!' shouts Roosevelt, jumping up and waving his arms. Last Christmas, he had indeed spent his time exploring the River of Doubt in Brazil. He laughs until tears run down his cheeks.* The audience gasps and screams in amazement.†

Houdini's extraordinary success is the talk of the ship. An account of the evening is transmitted by the radio operator of the *Imperator* to Newfoundland, and from there to New York. Before the ship docks, Houdini's extraordinary feat is all over the American newspapers.

The following morning, Houdini and Roosevelt walk around the upper deck of the ship together. Halfway round, Roosevelt stops and looks Houdini straight in the eye.

'Houdini, tell me the truth, man to man,' he says. 'Was that genuine spiritualism or legerdemain last night?'

Houdini is surprised that someone so clear-headed could be so gullible.

'No, Colonel,' he replies, shaking his head. 'It was hocus pocus.'

Only much later, as a way of undermining the growing craze for spiritualism, does Houdini reveal how he pulled it off. Like so many of his tricks, it had taken elaborate preparation. Some time before, he had been tipped off by a ticket clerk that Roosevelt was to be on board, giving him time to research Roosevelt's recent voyage up the Amazon. Coming across a map of this trip, Houdini copied it onto a chalk slate, which he then hid behind the blank slate, first signing it with a copy of W.T. Stead's signature. As the audience was full of Roosevelt's friends, he was confident that

---

* 'You must always remember that the President is about six,' says the British Ambassador to the United States, Cecil Spring Rice, who was Roosevelt's best man at his wedding to Edith Carrow. Spring Rice is today best known as the author of the poem 'I Vow to Thee My Country', later set to music by Gustav Holst.

† His escapology, in particular, baffles everyone at the time, but years later an onlooker seems to have cracked it. Before any death-defying stunt, Houdini would insist on being kissed by his wife, just in case he never saw her again. Having been manacled, handcuffed, wrapped in chains and then in a sheet, and searched by police, he would kiss his wife before being lowered into a pit. Earth was then shovelled on top of him. For two minutes, the crowd stared at the ground, and then suddenly two hands would appear, followed by the rest of Harry Houdini.

'It took me years to work that one out,' says the bystander, who in 1941 had been sitting in a cinema watching *You're in the Army Now*, the film in which Regis Toomey gives Jane Wyman a three-minute kiss – the longest in cinematic history. 'Halfway through that scene the answer hit me. I found myself thinking, "With all that kissing time, Mrs Houdini could have slipped Harry an entire bunch of keys."'

someone – possibly Roosevelt himself – would ask a question about the trip. Nevertheless, he had earlier insured himself by filling the hat with pieces of paper in envelopes, all asking the same question. But by looking at the indentations on the book on which Roosevelt placed his piece of paper, he could see that, by good fortune, Roosevelt had asked the very question he wanted him to ask. Hey presto!

THEODORE ROOSEVELT

FINDS IT HARD TO GET A WORD IN EDGEWAYS WITH

H.G. WELLS

The White House, Washington DC
May 6th 1906

One is the most literary of politicians; the other, the most political of novelists. Together, they sit down to lunch in the White House.

President Theodore Roosevelt – ebullient, big-game-hunting, boyishly unrefined, wildly gesticulative, a Republican at war with big business – has been in the White House for five years. *The Works of Theodore Roosevelt* – history, biography, criticism, political philosophy, natural history, memoir – now stretch to fifteen volumes, published in a seemingly limit-less variety of editions. His pen shows no sign of running out of steam: he has just written two magazine articles – 'Wolf-Coursing' and 'A Colorado Bear Hunt' – and his new book *Outdoor Pastimes of an American Hunter* is due out in the Fall. He is an unstoppable force, or, as H.G. Wells puts it, 'the Big Noise of America'.

Since the publication of his first book, *The Time Machine*, eleven years ago, H.G. Wells has enjoyed success after success, particularly with his science fiction: *The Invisible Man*, *The War of the Worlds*, *The First Men in the Moon*. His work is futuristic, but always with a present purpose: by constructing an imaginary future, he hopes to alert the world to the potential consequences of current attitudes.*

Wells has been lionised throughout this, his first tour of America. He has come to lecture, but also to listen; he is writing a series of pieces for the *Tribune* as well as an instant book, to be called, characteristically, *The Future in America*.

From the moment he enters the White House, he feels at home; he appreciates its classlessness, its absence of livery and flummery. As the

---

* In 1941, five years before his death, Wells suggests his own epitaph should be: 'I told you so. You damned fools.'

President enters, Wells, never immune to hero-worship, feels all his preconceptions evaporate. The President, he notes, is not larger-than-life, but 'of a quite reasonable size, with a face far more thoughtful and perplexed than strenuous, with a clenched hand that does indeed gesticulate'. He also has 'friendly screwed-up eyes behind the glasses ... like a man with the sun in his eyes'.

Wells is struck by Roosevelt's candour; unlike other politicians, he does not check himself, or worry about being misquoted. His talk floods out, 'provisional and speculative': he thinks aloud. Other politicians have closed minds, 'but any spark may fire the mind of President Roosevelt; he seems to be echoing all the thought of the time, he has receptivity to the pitch of genius ... He is the seeking mind of America displayed.'

By this H.G.Wells may really mean that the President listens to what he has to say, as it is the interviewer who monopolises the conversation. Wells tells Roosevelt about the creation of a World State, a society driven by science and eugenics, free from nationalism, a world whose citizens advance according to their merit.

He finds the President receptive to his ideas, if not quite so convinced as he is himself. Roosevelt believes in a loose alliance of nations rather than one single nation, and shies away from socialism. Rather, he is 'a hearty individualist, convinced that no man who sought work could fail to find it ... and that all that was needed to keep the world going was strenuous "go" with big business and monopolies the only barrier'.

After lunch, the two men take a walk in the garden. Wells continues to hold forth about the World State, and worries about the future of America. 'Does this magnificent appearance of beginnings, which is America, convey any clear and certain promise of permanence and fulfilment whatever? Is America a giant childhood or a gigantic futility?' In short, is the great American experiment doomed to come to nothing?

The President says he has no way of disproving this pessimistic view of the future. If someone says America will lose the impetus of her ascent, that she and all mankind must pass, then, in truth, he cannot conclusively deny it. On the other hand, it is his choice to carry on living as if this were not so.

Roosevelt now reveals that he has read Wells's first novel *The Time Machine*, a bleak voyage into a future (AD 802701) in which the world is divided between the Eloi, who live effete, carefree lives, and the grim Morlocks, who toil below ground, and, it gradually emerges, feed on the Eloi. Roosevelt's voice grows higher and more strained, his arms ever more wildly gesticulating, as he argues against the book as a template for man's destiny.

'Suppose, after all, that should prove to be right, and it all ends in your butterflies and morlocks. *That doesn't matter now*. The effort's real. It's worth going on with. It's worth it. It's worth it even so. The effort – the effort's worth it!'

So saying, the President kneels on a garden chair, embracing it to his chest as he argues for optimism. The scene could be from an opera. President and argument are one: he has become Hope. For Wells, he symbolises man's creative will, his determination to persist. 'Never did a President before so reflect the quality of his time. The trend is altogether away from the anarchistic individualism of the nineteenth century, that much is sure, and towards some constructive scheme which, if not exactly socialism, as socialism is defined, will be, at any rate, closely analogous to socialism.'

Twenty-eight years on, Wells is not so sure about his meeting with the late President Roosevelt.* It is now 1934. The world has advanced. Did his admiration for the President's swashbuckling character get the better of him? After all, Roosevelt's plan for America was 'by our modern standards … scarcely a plan at all'. Instead, it was 'a jumble of "progressive" organisation and "little man" democracy'. Looking back, and 'when one comes to think it over', he suspects Roosevelt's belief in the splendour of strenuous effort was, 'on the intellectual side, not so very strenuous after all'.

How much more enlightened the world is now, how infinitely more benevolent and progressive! And, looking around the world, which man could be said to personify these advances more perfectly than Josef Stalin?

---

* Wells is to meet three further US presidents: Harding ('all loud geniality and hand-shaking'), Hoover ('a sickly overworked and overwhelmed man') and FDR ('something more than open-minded … the most effective transmitting instrument for the coming of the new world order').

H.G. WELLS

HAS NEVER MET A MORE CANDID,
FAIR AND HONEST MAN THAN

JOSEF STALIN

The Kremlin, Moscow
July 22nd 1934

H.G. Wells has come to the Kremlin to interview Stalin for the *New Statesman*. A few years ago, he had high hopes for the Soviet Union. 'I had talked of it, dreamt of it and, if it were possible, even prayed for it.' Since then, he may have lowered these hopes just a little, but his faith in the communist ideal remains unshaken.

Perhaps to placate the sceptics, he claims to be approaching Stalin with 'a certain amount of suspicion and prejudice'. Might there perhaps be something in Trotsky's view of the General Secretary as 'a very reserved and self-centred fanatic ... a ruthless, hard – possibly doctrinaire – and self-sufficient man'? Wells fears that his hero may be flawed, and 'this lonely overbearing man ... may be damned disagreeable'.

He is led into Stalin's large, bare office. Stalin is staring out of the window, wearing a baggy, embroidered white smock, black trousers and knee-boots, a kind of designer-version of proletarian garb. As if by magic, Wells's doubts disappear. 'All lingering anticipations of a dour sinister Highlander vanished at the sight of him.' Stalin does not look him in the eye, but Wells puts it down to shyness – the Soviet leader evidently has 'a dread of self-importance'.

Stalin speaks no English and Wells no Russian, so a Mr Umansky sits in on their meeting, dutifully jotting down what each man says before translating it out loud. It makes for cumbersome conversation. The interview begins awkwardly.

'I am very much obliged to you, Mr Stalin, for agreeing to see me. I was in the United States recently. I had a long conversation with President [F.D.] Roosevelt and tried to ascertain what his leading ideas were. Now I have come to ask you what you are doing to change the world.'

'Not so very much,' replies Stalin.

'I wander around the world as a common man and, as a common man, observe what is going on around me.'

'Important public men like yourself are not "common men",' retorts Stalin, '... at all events you do not look at the world as a "common man".'

Wells says he is not feigning humility, but simply trying to see the world through the eyes of the common man. Once again, he hogs the conversation, and wants to promote his enduring belief in an imminent World State. 'It seems to me that what is taking place in the United States is a profound reorganisation, the creation of planned, that is, socialist economy. You and Roosevelt begin from two different starting points, but is there not a relation in ideas, a kinship of ideas and needs, between Washington and Moscow?'

Stalin replies, not unreasonably, that the aims of the two nations are entirely different. 'They are trying to reduce to a minimum the ruin, the losses caused by the existing economic system ... Even if the Americans partly achieve their aim, i.e., reduce their losses to a minimum, they will not destroy the roots of the anarchy which is inherent in the existing capitalist system ... Without getting rid of capitalists, without abolishing the principle of private property in the means of production, it is impossible to create planned economy.'

He goes on to talk of the contrast between 'the propertied class, the capitalist class, and the toiling class, the proletarian class'. Wells objects, saying this is an over-simplification: 'Are there not plenty of people in the West, for whom profit is not an end, who own a certain amount of wealth, who want to invest and obtain an income from this investment, but who do not regard this as their main object?'

Stalin counters that though there are some in the middle – 'the technical intelligentsia' – they are a distraction from the essential divide between rich and poor.

And so it goes on, though, like circus riders, the two keep switching horses as they pass, Wells attacking capitalism and Stalin defending it. At one point, Wells calls the wealthy financier J. Pierpont Morgan 'a parasite on society', adding, 'It seems to me that I am more to the Left than you, Mr Stalin. I think the old system is nearer to its end than you think.' To which Stalin counters: 'We Soviet people learn a great deal from the capitalists. And Morgan, whom you characterise so unfavourably, was undoubtedly a good, capable organiser.'

Later, Stalin declares that 'of all the ruling classes, the ruling classes of England … proved to be the cleverest'.

'You have a higher opinion of the ruling classes of my country than I have,' replies Wells.

Presently, they get bogged down in metaphor. Stalin compares the proletariat to a ship: 'Big ships go on long voyages.'

But, says Wells, ships need navigators.

'What is a navigator without a ship? An idle man!' says Stalin. 'You, Mr Wells, evidently start out with the assumption that all men are good. I, however, do not forget that there are many wicked men. I do not believe in the goodness of the bourgeoisie.'

Their conversation, scheduled for forty minutes, lasts over three hours.* Wells's faith is renewed. 'I have never met a man more candid, fair and honest. I had thought before I saw him that he might be where he was because men were afraid of him, but I realise that he owes his position to the fact that no one is afraid of him and everybody trusts him.'

He thanks Stalin for their talk, 'which has meant a great deal to me'. Though he only arrived in Russia yesterday, 'I have already seen the happy faces of healthy men and women and I know that something very considerable is being done here.' He ends by mentioning his hope that Soviet writers will join the PEN club, of which he is president. PEN, he explains, 'insists on the free expression of opinion – even of opposition opinion … I do not know if you are prepared yet for that much freedom.'

'We Bolsheviks call it "self-criticism",' Stalin reassures him. 'It is widely used in the USSR.'

---

* George Bernard Shaw is scornful of this interview, believing that Wells is too keen on the sound of his own voice, and insufficiently reverential. 'Wells trots into the Kremlin and tells Stalin that his head is over-stuffed with some absurd nonsense called class warfare … Wells does not listen to Stalin: he only waits with suffering patience to begin again when Stalin stops. He has not come to be instructed by Stalin, but to instruct him.' Stalin is, he adds, 'a first-rate listener', while Wells is 'the worst listener in the world'.

Shaw's enthusiasm for Stalin is both more cold-blooded and more realistic than Wells's. 'We cannot afford to give ourselves moral airs when our most enterprising neighbour [the USSR] humanely and judiciously liquidates a handful of exploiters and speculators to make the world safe for honest men,' he declares, at the height of Stalin's purges.

JOSEF STALIN

GIVES CANDY TO

MAXIM GORKY

6 Malaya Nikitskaya Street, Moscow
Early June 1936

In the first week of June, Comrade Stalin sends Maxim Gorky a chummy letter: 'How do you feel? Healthy? How's your work? Me and my friends are fine.'

Maxim Gorky is dying. The only copy of *Pravda* that does not carry daily news of his impending death is his own; the authorities have tactfully censored it, just for him.

Following his return from exile, eight years ago, Gorky has overcome any previous misgivings he had about Stalin. 'I must tell you in all honesty that the party is truly your brain, your strength, your actual leader – a leader that the Western proletariat, to its great regret and misfortune, does not yet have!' he tells workers in the industrial town of Sormovo.

Aged sixty-eight, he is the most decorated writer in the Soviet Union, but he has had to work for it. 'Long live Stalin, the man with an immense heart and mind!' he exclaimed last year. He sees virtue in turning a blind eye. 'You are used to keeping quiet about things you find revolting,' he writes dismissively to one reproachful exile.* 'As for me, not only do I feel I have a right to keep quiet about them, but I even regard that ability as one of my best qualities. Immoral, you say? ... The fact is that I have a sincere and implacable hatred of truth when it is an abomination and a lie for 90 per cent of the population.'

In the realm of the arts, he sought to promote a new, improved optimism. Visiting an exhibition in 1933, he declared, 'Our painters must not be afraid of a certain idealisation of Soviet reality ... I'd like to see more children's faces, more smiles, more spontaneous joy.'

---

* Ekaterina Kuskova.

In return, Stalin has given Gorky as much spontaneous joy as he could possibly need, awarding him every prize known to Soviet authors, and many more besides, among them the Order of Lenin, the highest civilian distinction in the USSR. He has even had the film *Our Gorky* produced in his honour. Gorky has a mansion in Moscow, a dacha a few miles from it, and a palatial villa in the Crimea. He is president of the Union of Soviet Writers. In Moscow, a literary institute has been founded in his name, Tverskaya Street has been renamed Gorky Street, and the city of his birth, Nizhni Novgorod, has been renamed Gorky.* Just under a year ago, Gorky paid a visit to Gorky in a ship named *Maxim Gorky*. Who could ask for anything more?

While the fellow idealists of his youth disappeared into jail, Gorky was writing Stalin letters urging him to commission Socialist Realist writers to 'rewrite the world's books anew'. 'What was going on inside him?' wonders his former colleague Victor Serge, many years later.

Every morning, the dying writer is visited by his friend Genrikh Yagoda on his way to the Lubianka, where he serves as head of the NKVD, Stalin's secret police. Yagoda, the mastermind of the gulags, has supplied Gorky with a secretary and a doctor, both of whom are, naturally, agents of the NKVD.

In early June, Gorky receives his chummy card from Stalin, who adds that he'd like to drop round with some old friends. 'Let them come – if they can get here in time,' says Gorky.

Stalin arrives at his bedside with Molotov and Voroshilov† in tow. The doctors have given Gorky an injection of camphor to ensure he stays awake. Stalin immediately takes charge. 'Why are there so many people here?' he asks. He points at Gorky's mistress Baroness Moura Budberg, dressed all in black. 'Who's that sitting beside Alexei Maximovich? A nun, is she? The only thing she lacks is a candle in her hands!' He shoos them away. 'Get them all out of here!' He is determined, once again, to force through the triumph of optimism. 'Why is there such a funeral mood here? A healthy person might die in such an atmosphere!' He spots Yagoda

---

* In 1990 it is renamed Nizhni Novgorod.

† Respectively, Chairman of the Council of People's Commissars and Defence Commissar.

in the dining room. 'And what's that creature hanging around here for? Get rid of him!'

Once the others have departed, Gorky attempts to discuss literature with Stalin, who is an unexpectedly bookish man.* But Stalin hushes him, calls for some wine, and toasts Gorky. The two men embrace.

The next day, Stalin drops by again. The doctors tells him that Gorky is too ill to see him, so he leaves him a note. 'Alexei Maximovich,' he writes, 'we visited you at two in the morning. Your pulse was they say 82. The doctors did not allow us to come in to you. We submitted. Hello from all of us, a big hello. Stalin.' Molotov and Voroshilov add their signatures. Of all the Get Well cards in history, this must surely be the most sinister.

Gorky dies in the morning of June 18th. His doctors list the causes as TB, pneumonia and heart failure. He is given a full state funeral, with orchestras and troops. Stalin leads the mourning, wearing a black armband.

Twenty months later, Yagoda is put on trial on a multitude of charges, including high treason, espionage, conspiracy and acts of terrorism. Listed among the offences is the murder of Maxim Gorky. Gorky's doctors and his secretary are also charged with his murder. At their trial, they all confess to the crime. The doctors declare that they conspired to make Gorky catch a cold in his garden in the Crimea. The state prosecutor describes the defendants as 'stinking piles of human garbage'.

The secretary and one doctor are executed; another doctor, Pletnev, is given a twenty-five-year prison sentence. In 1948, he tells a fellow prisoner that Stalin himself killed Gorky with a box of poisoned candy. 'We doctors kept quiet,' he adds. According to him, Stalin was worried that Gorky was planning to tell the world that his show trials were a sham. In 1963, ten years after Stalin's death and twenty-seven years after her husband's, Gorky's widow backs up his chilling claim.

---

* He has a library of some 20,000 volumes, and a particular liking for Zola, Chekhov and Galsworthy. It also includes *The Last of the Mohicans*. In an unusually carefree mood, he once greeted a young translator with the words, 'Big chief greets paleface.'

MAXIM GORKY

IS IN TWO MINDS ABOUT

LEO TOLSTOY

21 Ulitsa Lva Tolstogo, Moscow
January 13th 1900

Aged thirty-one, Maxim Gorky, the bright-eyed author and Marxist activist, eager for revolution, permanently clad in a black peasant's smock, finally manages to meet his hero, Count Leo Tolstoy.

He first tried to meet him eleven years ago, when he was still a struggling railway worker. He travelled five hundred miles on foot, hitching lifts on freight trains, only to be told that Tolstoy was not at home. He then went a further 124 miles to Moscow, to find Tolstoy too ill to receive visitors. He returned home in a cattle truck, spending thirty-four hours with eight cows.

But now that Gorky has made a name for himself,* Tolstoy's curiosity is piqued, and he invites him to his home. Gorky's first impression of the seventy-two-year-old is one often heard in encounters with the illustrious: how small he is! 'I'd pictured him quite differently – taller and bigger-boned. But he turned out to be a small old man.'

It is only when Tolstoy speaks that his grandeur reveals itself. 'Everything he said was simple and profound.' On the other hand, the great man is not always consistent. 'When it comes down to it, he's a complete orchestra in himself, it's just that not all the trumpets are playing in tune. And this is also very good, for it's very human, i.e. typical of a man. In essence, it's terribly stupid to call a man a genius. It's totally incomprehensible what a genius is. It's far simpler and clearer to say "Leo Tolstoy".'

The disciple and his master sit and talk for three hours or more in Tolstoy's study. Tolstoy is everything Gorky has hoped – simple, gentle,

---

* In both senses: he is born Aleksey Maximovich Peshkov. He considers his surname, Peshkov, meaning 'pawn', inappropriate, and so in 1892 he reverts to the nickname his father was given: Gorky, meaning 'bitter'.

tactful, profound – but also, in a funny way, everything he would rather he wasn't. 'There were times when it was hard and unpleasant to listen to him. I never liked what he had to say about women; in that area he was excessively crude. There was something artificial about it, something at the same time insincere and very personal. It was as if he'd been hurt once in a way that he could neither forget nor forgive.'

Gorky is disconcerted by how Tolstoy can be at the same time both more and less than he had imagined. 'I do not consider him a miracle of nature in any respect. When you look at him it's terribly nice to feel that one is also a man, to realise that a man can be Leo Tolstoy.'

Tolstoy talks about two of Gorky's short stories, but Gorky is upset by his tone. Tolstoy is vehement that chastity is not natural in a healthy young girl: 'If the girl is over fifteen and healthy, she wants to be hugged and squeezed. Her mind fears what it doesn't yet know or understand – that is what people mean when they talk about chastity and modesty. But her flesh already knows that what is incomprehensible is nevertheless inevitable and legitimate, and that it demands fulfilment, her mind's fears notwithstanding. You describe Varenka Olesova as being healthy, but her feelings are anaemic and that is false!'

Tolstoy then starts talking about the girl in Gorky's story 'Twenty-Six Men and a Girl'. He utters 'a stream of "indecent" words with a casualness that struck me as unseemly and even somewhat offensive'. But Gorky says nothing, and suddenly Tolstoy changes the subject, becoming kind and considerate, asking him about his life, his education, and his reading.

Their talk turns to other writers. Tolstoy likes Veltman. 'He's good, isn't he? Lively, exact, no exaggeration. At times he's better than Gogol. He knew Balzac. Whereas Gogol imitated Marlinsky.' Gorky notes that Tolstoy, like so many authors, would rather talk about his fellow authors' personalities than their works.

For some days after this meeting, Gorky bubbles with enthusiasm. 'Everything that was said, his manner of speaking, of sitting and watching you. It was all of a piece, powerful and beautiful,' he tells his friend Anton Chekhov. But as time passes, he begins to count more flaws in Tolstoy's character. Wasn't he a little condescending? To put his lowborn guest at his ease, didn't he talk in a bogusly folksy manner?

The two men meet again on a number of occasions, and they get along fine, but Gorky is unable to sustain his initial adoration. They disagree on important issues: Tolstoy preaches non-violence, while Gorky is prepared for violent revolution; Gorky trusts the workers, Tolstoy the peasants; Tolstoy believes in people living free, as brothers; Gorky thinks this wishy-washy, and wants workers' control; Tolstoy is Christian, Gorky atheist. 'Why don't you believe in God?' demands Tolstoy.

'I don't have faith.'

'That's not true; you're a believer by nature, and you can't do without God. If you don't believe, it's out of stubbornness, and out of resentment that the world isn't as you'd like it to be.'

Gorky stares at Tolstoy. 'And though I don't believe in God, I looked at him, I don't know why, with great wariness, and a little fear too. I looked at him and I thought, "This man is like God."'

A year after this first meeting, Gorky is arrested for revolutionary activities, but Tolstoy intercedes on his behalf, and he is released from prison.

For the rest of his life, Gorky remains in two minds about Tolstoy, prefacing his abuse with praise, and his praise with abuse. He exhibits the disciple's opposing needs: to revere and to surpass. 'Count Leo Tolstoy is an artistic genius, perhaps our Shakespeare,' he writes, two years before Tolstoy's death,* before immediately backtracking: 'but although I admire him, I do not like him. He is an insincere man; inordinately enamoured of himself, he sees and knows nothing except himself. His humility is hypocritical and his desire for suffering is repulsive. Such a desire comes from a sick, perverted mind, but in this case the arrogant Tolstoy wants to be put in prison only to strengthen his authority ... No, that man is foreign to me, in spite of his great beauty.'

---

* After Tolstoy's death, Gorky writes a long and detailed memoir of him, but he leaves out various incidents he has mentioned to others. For instance, he once told Victor Shklovsky of the time when 'Tolstoy's daughters brought a rabbit with a broken leg up to the balcony. "Oh, the poor little rabbit!" Leo Nikolaievich came down the stairs. Almost without stopping, he took the rabbit's head in his big hand and, with the practised movement of a professional hunter, throttled it with two fingers.'

LEO TOLSTOY

RUMBLES, AND IS RUMBLED BY

PYOTR IL'ICH TCHAIKOVSKY

Moscow Conservatory, Bolshaya Nikitskaya
December 1876

The fear of being found out afflicts even the greatest; or perhaps the greatest most of all.

Tchaikovsky is upstairs at the Moscow Conservatory when he hears that Leo Tolstoy is downstairs. Apparently he is refusing to leave until he has made his acquaintance.

But Tchaikovsky is reluctant to go down. In the past, whenever he has encountered one of his heroes, 'I invariably just felt disillusioned, saddened, and worn out afterwards.' He worries, too, that Tolstoy will see through him. 'It seemed to me that this supreme student of human nature would, with one glance, be able to penetrate into all the recesses of my soul.' But there is no way out, so, reluctantly, he goes downstairs to greet him.

As they shake hands, Tchaikovsky is 'overcome by fear and a sense of awkwardness ... I said that I was awfully glad, that I was ever so grateful – well, in short, a whole string of inevitable but false words.'

'I would like to get to know you better,' says Tolstoy. 'I would like to talk to you about music.'

'And then and there, after our first handshake,' recalls Tchaikovsky, 'he expounded his musical opinions to me.'

Alas, Tolstoy's musical opinions clash with Tchaikovsky's. Tolstoy considers Beethoven untalented. 'What a fine start!' thinks Tchaikovsky, taken aback by the way in which Tolstoy, 'this writer of genius, this great student of human nature', should be so crass in person as to say 'in a tone of complete certainty, something quite stupid and offensive for any musician'.*

---

* He has an element of the wind-up merchant. 'Tolstoy would spend many years of his life trying to persuade people that Shakespeare was no good; that Jesus wasn't a Christian; that folk songs were better than Beethoven and that property is theft' – A.N. Wilson.

He is uncertain how to react. 'Argue? Well, yes, I did start arguing with him … Properly speaking, I should have read him a whole lecture! Perhaps someone else in my place would have done that. All I did, though, was to supress my inner sufferings and continue to act out this comedy, i.e. I pretended to be an earnest and good-humoured fellow.' But secretly, he thinks that 'bringing down to the level of one's ignorance a genius who has been recognised as such by all, is typical of narrow-minded people'.

At least his key fear has not been realised: Tolstoy hasn't penetrated the inner recesses of his soul. Though in his writings Tolstoy seems to have reached the highest summit of human wisdom, in person he demonstrates 'very little of that all-knowingness which I had been afraid of'.

Tchaikovksy persuades Nikolai Rubinstein to present a piano recital simply for Tolstoy's benefit. When his Andante in D Major is being played, Tchaikovsky sees tears running down Tolstoy's cheeks. 'Probably never in my life have I been so moved by the pride of authorship as when Leo Tolstoy, sitting by me and listening to the Andante of my quartet, burst into tears,' he writes in his diary. In a letter to his brother Modest, he is rather more bullish: 'Before the holidays, old chap, I became great friends with the writer Count Tolstoy and I liked him very much … and yes sir, he heard my First Quartet and during the Andante he really started crying … I am quite a top dog now!'

They part on the best of terms, and exchange thank-you letters. Tolstoy writes to Tchaikovsky: 'I have never received such a cherished reward for my literary endeavours as this wonderful soirée.' Tchaikovsky writes to Tolstoy that, 'As for me, I cannot describe to you how happy and proud I was to see that my music could move and captivate you.'

But their mutual admiration proves jittery. Might it be that, when the dust has settled, each man suspects he has been rumbled by the other? At the end of the month, Tolstoy sends Tchaikovsky some Russian folk songs to arrange, but Tchaikovsky considers them bogus: how surprising that the man who sets himself up as an expert in folk music should be so easily taken in! On this occasion, he is only partly able to button his lip. 'I must tell you frankly that they have been recorded in a very clumsy manner, and they display no more than a few traces of their primitive beauty,' he writes to Tolstoy.

The two men never meet again, even though they have plenty of opportunities. Tchaikovsky's brother Modest thinks Pyotr goes out of his way to avoid Tolstoy. 'He himself told me that in spite of all the pride and joy which he felt on making this acquaintance, the beloved works of Tolstoy temporarily lost their charm for him.' On a couple of occasions, Tchaikovsky is spotted ducking into a courtyard as he sees Tolstoy approaching along the street.

A year later, Tchaikovsky feels even less in awe of Tolstoy. 'You ought to be ashamed of being so enthusiastic about this disgracefully banal nonsense, camouflaged with pretensions to depth of psychological analysis!' he writes to Modest, who has been going on about Tolstoy's new novel, *Anna Karenina*.* As the years go by, he grows increasingly irritated by Tolstoy's preachiness. In 1886, he writes in his diary: 'I am inwardly angry at him; I almost hate him ... all this scribbling he is doing now exudes coldness; one can sense fear and one feels vaguely that he, too, is *human* ... that is a being who, in the sphere of questions about the purpose and meaning of life, about God and religion, is as insanely arrogant and at the same time as insignificant as any ephemeral insect which appears at noon on a hot July day and has already terminated its existence by night fall.'

When Tolstoy hears of Tchaikovsky's death in November 1893, he writes to his widow expressing his regret, and wondering why they never quite clicked. 'It really is a pity, since there seems to have been some misunderstanding between us. I visited him once and invited him here but he seems to have been offended because I did not attend *Evgenii Onegin*.'

But a year later, Tolstoy has lost sympathy with the man whose music once made him cry. 'What an obvious artistic falsehood Tchaikovsky is!' he reflects.

---

* Five years later, he has changed his mind, writing to another brother, Anatolii, that he has recently read *Anna Karenina* all the way through for the first time 'with an enthusiasm bordering on the fanatic'.

PYOTR IL'ICH TCHAIKOVSKY

EXAMINES

SERGEI RACHMANINOFF

Moscow Conservatory, Bolshaya Nikitskaya
May 1888

Twelve years later, Pyotr Il'ich Tchaikovsky is the most renowned composer in Russia. Aged forty-eight, he has just returned from months abroad, and is settling down at his country retreat to begin work on his new symphony, the 5th. But he has a keen sense of obligation, so has agreed to spend two days sitting on the Conservatory's examining board.

The examination begins smartly at 9 a.m. The pupils are set two tasks: to harmonise a theme by Haydn in four parts, and to write a prelude of sixteen to thirty bars, in a given key and with a specified modulation, to include pedal points on both the dominant and the tonic. They are not permitted the use of a piano. As examinations go, it is notoriously arduous, but this year it is made even more so by the presence of the great Tchaikovsky.

One by one, the candidates hand in their work. As their teacher Arensky surveys each paper, a frown forms on his face. He is clearly dissatisfied. The last candidate to hand in his work is the fifteen-year-old Sergei Rachmaninoff; over the course of the day, his prelude has become more and more complicated, defying any sort of speedy solution. Eventually, after eight hours, he manages to complete it, and hands in his two pages to Arensky. For the first time that day, he fails to frown. This gives Rachmaninoff hope.

The next day, the board hears the students play their own work. When Rachmaninoff finishes, Arensky turns to Tchaikovsky and says that this pupil has written some piano pieces in ternary song form for his class. Would he care to hear them?

Tchaikovsky nods his assent. Rachmaninoff remains at the piano, and starts to play; he knows them by heart.

When he comes to an end, the board holds a secret discussion, each writing his mark in the examination book. Afterwards, Rachmaninoff watches as Tchaikovsky goes over to the examination book and writes something else in it. Rachmaninoff has no idea what he has written, good or bad. It is a full two weeks before Arensky tells him that the board has granted him a 5+, the highest rating, and that Tchaikovsky himself added three further plus signs to this mark, one above it, one below it, and one beside it.

The excitement runs both ways. Tchaikovsky's sister-in-law, Anatol, remembers him arriving back from the Conservatory with a spring in his step. 'For Rachmaninoff,' he proclaims, 'I predict a great future.'

Rachmaninoff's success in the examination remains the talk of the Conservatory for some time. 'We all heard of his success, we know what an extraordinary sight reader he is, what a perfect ear he has, and we are infected by his love for Tchaikovsky,' writes a fellow student.

As Rachmaninoff prepares to graduate, Tchaikovsky further encourages him by commissioning an arrangement of *The Sleeping Beauty* for piano duet from him. Rachmaninoff is known as a diligent student with a sure sense of purpose, and it is apparent to everyone that he has the makings of a composer. Yet he shies away from this task. 'I am burdened with work, but to tell you the truth, I do little, and scarcely practise the piano at all. I simply can't get down to work. My laziness is *gigantic*,' he writes to his sister Natalia in September 1890.

He eventually sends his transcription of *The Sleeping Beauty* to Tchaikovsky in June 1891, but it is no good. Tchaikovsky can scarcely believe its incompetence. 'We made a great mistake in entrusting this work to a boy, no matter how talented,' he writes to Rachmaninoff's tutor, complaining of his pupil's 'lack of courage, skill and initiative' and declaring that 'in general, inexperience and lack of boldness can be sensed at every step ... these proofs have so upset me that I haven't been able to sleep – I feel a sickness approaching ...'

Rachmaninoff recognises the truth of these criticisms. 'Tchaikovsky swears terribly at me for the transcription. And quite reasonably and justly. Of all transcriptions mine is undoubtedly the worst.'

In fact, he has been diverted by his own compositions, among them the opera *Aleko*, his first piano concerto, and the Prelude in C-Sharp Minor. When he hears them, Tchaikovsky, always generous, brushes aside his earlier irritations and celebrates the advent of a new composer. Attending the last rehearsals of *Aleko*, he timidly asks Rachmaninoff if he would object to having his work produced alongside one of his own. Rachmaninoff is overjoyed. 'To be on the poster with Tchaikovsky was about the greatest honour that could be paid to a composer, and I would not have dared to suggest such a thing. Tchaikovsky knew this. He wanted to help me but was anxious not to offend or humiliate me ... He literally said – "Would you object?" – he was fifty-three, a famous composer – and I was only a twenty-year-old beginner!'

Tchaikovsky sits alongside Rachmaninoff during rehearsals. Rachmaninoff is upset by some of the conductor's ideas, but is too frightened to say anything. Sensing this, Tchaikovsky leans over and says, 'Do you like this tempo?'

'No.'

'Then why don't you say so?'

'I'm afraid.'

During a break, Tchaikovsky says to the conductor, 'Sergei Vasilyevich and I think that the tempo in that part might be taken a little faster.'

Aleko is premiered at the Imperial Theatre on April 27th 1893. Rachmaninoff's father and grandmother are in the audience. As it draws to its close, Tchaikovsky leans far out, so that the audience can see him applauding the new work.

In October of that year, the two men set off in opposite directions. 'You see, Seryozha, we're famous composers now!' jokes Tchaikovsky. 'One goes to Kiev to conduct his opera and the other to Petersburg to conduct his symphony!'

On November 6th, Tchaikovsky dies of cholera. When he hears the news later the same day, Rachmaninoff immediately starts composing his *Trio Élégiaque* for piano, violin and cello. He dedicates it 'to the memory of a great artist'.

SERGEI RACHMANINOFF

IS DROWNED OUT BY

HARPO MARX

The Garden of Allah, Los Angeles
Summer 1931

Forty-three years later, Rachmaninoff's youthful Prelude in C-Sharp Minor remains by far his most popular piece. 'One day the Prelude simply came and I put it down,' he recalls. 'It came with such force that I could not shake it off even though I tried to do so. It had to be there – so it was.'

And so it remains, his albatross. Now devoting himself exclusively to his career as a concert pianist, it exasperates him that it is the only piece of his that audiences ever want to hear him play: they seem to think he has never composed anything else. Consequently, he has grown to detest it, and prefers all his other preludes. 'I think them far better music than my first, but the public has shown no disposition to share my belief,' he complains. The piece pursues him everywhere, an obligation he can never shake off. When he played it in London a few months ago, one critic detected a certain grudging quality about it, complaining that he 'flung it at the audience like a bone to a dog'.

If it is a bone, it doubles as a boomerang. 'The big annoyance of my concert life is my C sharp minor Prelude. I'm not sorry I wrote it. It has helped me. But people ALWAYS make me play it. By now I play it without feeling – like a machine!'

Between concerts in Texas and Chicago, the elderly Rachmaninoff is taking a break in a bungalow at The Garden of Allah. Sometimes known as 'the Uterus of Flickerland', the Garden of Allah consists of twenty-five bungalows set around a main hotel, in lush grounds full of orange, grape-fruit, banana and palm trees. Built in 1927 by Alla Nazimova, a star of the silent movies, its vast swimming pool is shaped like the Black Sea, to remind Nazimova of her childhood in Yalta.

It is, in a way, the Los Angeles precursor of New York's Chelsea Hotel, a refuge for transients from the East Coast like Scott Fitzgerald and

Dorothy Parker.* Alexander Woollcott describes it as 'the kind of village you might look for down the rabbit-hole'. Over the years, it has certainly been populated by some outlandish figures. The switchboard was once taken over by an operator who believed he could read character from voices, and refused to put through calls from anyone whose voice he disliked. Many residents drink to excess, regularly losing their footing and tumbling headlong into the pool. 'I used to wait for them to come home and fall in,' says the playwright Arthur Kober. 'It was like waiting for a shoe to drop. I'd hear the splashes and then I'd go to sleep.' Tallulah Bankhead used to like strolling naked around the pool by moonlight. Less seductively, while filming *The Hunchback of Notre Dame*, Charles Laughton loved to swim in it with his hump still on.

Perhaps Sergei Rachmaninoff should have guessed from its reputation that the Garden of Allah would not offer the necessary respite from his busy concert schedule. But, then again, how was he to know who his next-door neighbour would turn out to be?

For three years, the Marx Brothers have been on the road, performing their stage show *Animal Crackers* across America. But in 1931 they are offered a film contract by Paramount, and move to Los Angeles. Harpo, the brother who never speaks, chooses to rent a bungalow at the Garden of Allah. He thinks that his bungalow – a little distance from the main hubbub – will let him exercise both sides of his character, extrovert comedian and introvert harpist.† He takes to the Garden of Allah like a duck to water. It is, he says, 'the best place to practise I ever had'.

---

* It is at the Garden of Allah that a friend of Robert Benchley tells him that drink is a slow poison, prompting Benchley to reply, 'That's all right. I'm in no hurry.' Humorists are attracted by the irreverent atmosphere of the Garden of Allah, among them Arthur Sheekman, one of the Marx Brothers' scriptwriters, who plays Cecil B. DeMille's *The Crusades* over and over again in his bungalow simply so that he can hear Loretta Young say to her husband, Richard the Lionheart, 'Ya gotta save Christianity, Richard, ya gotta!'

† 'There is a character who goes by the same name I do who *is* kind of a celebrity,' he writes in *Harpo Speaks!*. 'He wears a ratty red wig and a shredded raincoat. He can't talk, but he makes idiotic faces, honks a horn, whistles, blows bubbles, ogles and leaps after blondes and acts out all kinds of hokey charades. I don't begrudge this character his fame and fortune. He worked damn hard for every cent and every curtain call he ever got. I don't begrudge him anything – because he started out with no talent at all. If you've ever seen a Marx Brothers picture, you know the difference between him and me. When he's chasing a girl across the screen it's Him. When he sits down to play the harp, it's Me. Whenever I touched the strings of the harp, I stopped being an actor.'

But one day while he is practising his harp, the sound of a piano shatters the peace.

'I was looking forward to a solid weekend of practice, without interruptions, when my new neighbor started to bang away. I couldn't hear anything below a *forte* on the harp. There were no signs the piano banging was going to stop. It only got more overpowering. This character was warming up for a solid weekend of practice too.'

He storms over to the office to register a complaint. 'One of us has to go,' he says, 'and it's not going to be me because I was here first.'

But the management prevaricates. When he discovers that the neighbour 'whose playing was driving me nuts' is none other than Sergei Rachmaninoff, it occurs to him that they will never ask such an illustrious guest to move. He has only one weapon left in his armoury: his harp. 'I was flattered to have such a distinguished neighbor, but I still had to practise. So I got rid of him my own way. I opened the door and all the windows in my place and began to play the first four bars of Rachmaninov's Prelude in C-Sharp Minor, over and over, *fortissimo*. He wished he'd never written it. After playing it for two hours I knew exactly how he felt … My fingers were getting numb. But I didn't let up, not until I heard a thunderous crash of notes from across the way, like the keyboard had been attacked with a pair of sledgehammers. Then there was silence. This time it was Rachmaninov who went to complain. He asked to be moved to another bungalow immediately, the farthest possible from that dreadful harpist. Peace returned to the Garden.'

Six years later, Harpo exacts further revenge. In *A Day at the Races*, he appears in a battered top hat playing the piano with increasing ferocity. The more he plays the piano, the more he wrecks it; by the end, he has reduced it to smithereens, leaving only the plate, which he then picks up and plays as a harp.

Is it really a coincidence that the piece he destroys in this memorable scene is the Prelude in C-Sharp Minor by Sergei Rachmaninoff?

HARPO MARX

IS DENUDED BY

GEORGE BERNARD SHAW

Villa Galanon, Cap d'Antibes
Summer 1928

Harpo Marx is cheery by nature. 'I am the most fortunate self-taught harpist and non-speaking actor who has ever lived,' he claims. But nothing has ever proved so much fun as the French Riviera in summer. 'The living was easy in 1928. Life was mostly fun and games and the world was our private, million-dollar playground.'

Staying in the Villa Galanon with his friend from the Algonquin Circle, Alexander Woollcott, Harpo spends his days swimming, feasting, visiting the casinos and playing badminton. While they are playing badminton one afternoon, the postman cycles up the drive with a special-delivery letter. When Woollcott spots the return address, he utters a joyful little gasp, and tears it open, recalls Harpo, 'like it was money from home'.

'Harpo,' he says. 'He's coming to have lunch with us next Wednesday. Bernard Shaw!'

'Bernard Shaw?' replies Harpo, who likes to make a play of his lack of education.* 'Didn't his name used to be Bernie Schwartz? Ran the cigar stand in the Hotel Belvedere?'

The coming of Mr and Mrs George Bernard Shaw to Villa Galanon is, in Harpo's words, 'Woollcott's supreme coup of the season'. For days, Woollcott fusses about the menu he should roll out. He knows Shaw is a vegetarian, but does not know to what extent. One guest thinks Shaw would eat bacon, but Woollcott finds this hard to believe. He finally settles on an omelette with truffles, broiled tomatoes and eggplants, asparagus, artichokes, green salad, hot breads, aspics, mousses, ices, cheeses and wild strawberries with thick cream. Harpo senses that Woollcott thinks him

---

* He left school aged eight.

unsophisticated and would rather he made himself scarce until their honoured guest has been and gone.

On the Monday before Shaw's arrival, Woollcott and his French chef spend the day deciding which wines to serve. On the Tuesday, they shuttle from the village market to the villa all day long, with load after load of groceries.

When Wednesday finally comes, Woollcott seems 'as jittery as a girl getting ready for her first date', and can't decide what to wear. At last, he sets off in his car to collect the Shaws from their hotel in Antibes wearing an Italian straw hat and a linen cape. The other guests go upstairs to change, while the French chef remains down in the kitchen 'screaming at the aspic to gell'.

Finding himself alone, Harpo walks down the cliff to a sheltered cove. He takes off his clothes, goes for a swim, and stretches out his towel on the sand in order to sunbathe. He plans to get dressed and go back up to the villa in his own time, 'maybe in time for lunch, maybe not'.

He is dozing in the nude stretched out on his towel when he hears an Irish voice blaring from the top of the cliff, 'Halloo! Halloo! Is there nobody home?'

Harpo wraps the towel around himself and scrambles up the rocks to see who it is. There he finds 'a tall, skinny, red-faced old geezer with a beard, decked out in a sporty cap and a knicker suit', with a woman at his side.

'Where the devil's Woollcott?' asks the bearded man. 'And who the devil are you?'

Harpo Marx introduces himself. The man grins.

'Ah yes, of course. I'm Bernard Shaw.'

Shaw puts out his hand, but instead of shaking hands he makes a sudden lunge for Harpo's towel and snatches it away, leaving Harpo 'naked to the world'.

'And this,' says Shaw, 'is Mrs Shaw.'

At this point, Woollcott arrives back, 'wild-eyed and wringing wet with flop sweat'. He breathlessly explains that he had driven to the hotel, to find that the Shaws had not checked in. He had then gone to the railway station, where he learned that a couple answering to their description had already hired a driver to take them to Villa Galanon. He is in the midst of this long-drawn-out apology when Shaw interrupts him.

'Nonsense, my boy,' says Shaw. 'We had a grand reception here. We were met by a naked jackanapes, your immodest Mr Marx. A bit shocking, but quite grand!'

The lunch goes well. It is a dazzling one-man show, with Shaw excelling himself, flinging himself in and out of doorways, performing Chaplin's shuffle, dashing around like Douglas Fairbanks, and mounting full-scale impersonations of some of the famous characters he has known 'from Disraeli and Lenin to Darwin and Huxley, from Gilbert and Sullivan to Liszt and Debussy, from Oscar Wilde to Henrik Ibsen', as Harpo remembers it.

Throughout the performance, Harpo has been trying to work out whether or not Shaw is wearing a tie beneath his famous long beard. At one point, Shaw throws back his head and laughs. Harpo spots not only that he is not wearing a tie, but he has no collar either.

Shaw breaks from his anecdotes to ask him why he is staring at him so oddly.

'I just discovered,' says Harpo, 'that you couldn't have sat downstairs at Loew's Delancey Street Theatre.'

'What do you mean? Why not?'

'The downstairs seats are strictly high class at Delancey Street. A man has to be wearing a tie to sit downstairs. Otherwise he must sit in the balcony.' He explains to Shaw that the assistant manager used to stand by the entrance, lifting up each beard as it passed, saying, 'Upstairs … Downstairs … Upstairs … Downstairs …'

Shaw replies that he would be flattered to go upstairs 'with the sensible crowd who know what a beard is for'.

Woollcott is delighted at his bringing together George Bernard Shaw and Harpo Marx. 'He loved playing the game of Strange Bedfellows,' recalls Harpo. '"Harpo Marx and Bernard Shaw," he used to say, with that smirking chuckle of his. "Corned beef and roses!"'*

---

* Later that same week, Harpo drives Shaw in his open jalopy to Cannes, where a friend of Shaw called Rex Ingraham is directing a movie called *The Three Passions*. Ingraham sets Shaw and Harpo to work as extras, playing billiards together. Alas, the scene is cut from the final movie. 'No audience could ever mistake us for extras, lost in the crowd. The way we shot pool we could only be taken for what we were – a couple of ringers, a couple of sharpies.'

For the Shaws' farewell dinner at Villa Galanon, Harpo Marx adds to the game of Strange Bedfellows when he secretly invites another pair of guests. At the appointed time, in walk Peggy Hopkins Joyce, the raunchy, multi-husbanded American actress, together with Oswald Mosley.

GEORGE BERNARD SHAW

CRASHES HIS BICYCLE INTO

BERTRAND RUSSELL

Penallt, Monmouthshire
September 12th 1895

How many intellectuals does it take to crash two bicycles?

George Bernard Shaw is staying with the socialists Sidney and Beatrice Webb* at their house in Monmouthshire. Though aged twenty-nine, he is still learning to ride a bicycle, and is doing so with a recklessness at odds with his usual physical timidity. He regularly falls off at corners, simply because no one has satisfactorily convinced him of the need to lean into them. Faced with a steep downhill slope, he places his feet on the handle-bars, and is then unable to steady himself when he hits a bump. Whenever he falls off his bicycle, which is often, he never admits to a mistake, behaving as though it had always been his intention.

'Many of his falls, from which he would prance away crying "I am not hurt," with black eyes, violet lips and a red face, acted as trials for his optimism,' notes his biographer, Michael Holroyd. 'The surgery afterwards was an education in itself. Each toss he took was a point scored for one or more of his fads. After one appalling smash (hills, clouds and farm-houses tumbling around drunkenly), he wrote: "Still I am not thoroughly convinced yet that I was not killed. Anybody but a vegetarian would have been. Nobody but a teetotaller would have faced a bicycle again for six months." After four years of intrepid pedalling, he could claim: "If I had taken to the ring I should, on the whole, have suffered less than I have, physically."'

But his incompetence on bicycles never deters him from employing them in intellectual propositions. 'The man who is learning how to ride a bicycle has no advantage over the non-cyclist in the struggle for existence; quite the contrary,' he writes in *Back to Methuselah*. 'He has acquired a new

---

* Founders of the London School of Economics (1895) and the *New Statesman* (1913).

habit, an automatic unconscious habit, solely because he wanted to, and kept trying until it was added unto him. But when your son tries to skate or bicycle in his turn, he does not pick up the accomplishment where you left it, any more than he is born six feet high with a beard and a tall hat.'

The Webbs' other house guest is the twenty-three-year-old Bertrand Russell, an up-and-coming young philosopher, recently married to the American heiress Alys Pearsall Smith. He too will, in years to come, employ the example of a bicycle in all manner of philosophical propositions. In *On Education* (1926), he argues that learning to ride a bicycle allows one to pass from fear to skill, which is, he adds, 'a valuable experience'; in *An Outline of Philosophy* (1927), he compares the acquisition of speech to learning to ride a bicycle; and in *The Analysis of the Mind* (1921), he uses the bicycle to highlight the broad distinction between instinct and habit, observing that while every animal eats food by instinct, 'no one can ride a bicycle by instinct, though, after learning, the necessary movements become just as automatic as if they were instinctive'.

But do they? On this bright September day, fate seems determined to prove the antithesis: that the necessary movements for riding a bicycle will always remain, for at least one of the two men, just out of reach.

The two spindly intellectuals set off on their bicycles through the rolling hills of Monmouthshire. Before long, Bertrand Russell, slightly out in front, stops his bike in the middle of the road in order to read a direction sign and work out which way they should head. Shaw whizzes towards him, fails to keep his eyes on the road, and crashes right into the stationary Russell.

Shaw is hurled through the air and lands flat on his back 'twenty feet from the place of the collision', in Russell's empirical estimation. Following his normal practice, Shaw picks himself up, behaves as though nothing is wrong, and gets back on his bicycle, which is, like him, miraculously undamaged.

But for Russell, it is a different story. 'Russell, fortunately, was not even scratched,' Shaw tells a friend, adding mischievously, 'But his knickerbockers were demolished.' Russell's bicycle is also in a frightful state, and is no longer fit to ride. Russell says of his assailant: 'He got up completely unhurt and continued his ride. Whereas my bicycle was smashed, and I had to return by train.'

The train is extremely slow, so Shaw is easily able to outpace it. Never one to let tact get in the way of comedy, he pops up with his bicycle on the platform of every station along the way, putting his head into the carriage to jeer at Russell. 'I suspect that he regarded the whole incident as proof of the virtues of vegetarianarianism,' suggests Russell sixty years later.

Their relationship never fully recovers, though it bumbles on for half a century or so.* Russell concludes that, 'When I was young, we all made a show of thinking no better of ourselves than of our neighbours. Shaw found this effort wearisome, and had already given it up when he first burst upon the world. My admiration had limits ... it used to be the custom among clever people to say that Shaw was not unusually vain, but unusually candid. I came to think later on that this was a mistake.'

For Russell, the bicycle is to remain a source of sometimes uncomfortable inspiration for years to come. In the spring of 1902, he is cycling from Cambridge to Grantchester, when 'suddenly, as I was riding along a country road, I realised that I no longer loved Alys'. He finally agrees to a divorce in 1921, threatening to commit suicide if Alys drags the name of his lover, Lady Ottoline Morrell, into the proceedings. 'Thereupon her rage became unbearable. After she had stormed for some hours, I gave a lesson in Locke's philosophy to her niece, Karin Costelloe, who was about to take her Tripos. I then rode away on my bicycle, and with that my first marriage came to an end.'

---

* At lunch with the Shaws, Russell would be filled with envy of Shaw's delicious vegetarian meal, compared with the drabber meat dish set before his guests. He would also notice the 'look of unutterable boredom' that used to appear on the face of Mrs Shaw as she found herself having to sit through one of her husband's well-trodden anecdotes.

Shaw's insensitivity and heightened sense of competition, evidenced on those Monmouthshire railway stations, is never to wane. At a lunch held in honour of the French philosopher Henri Bergson, Russell witnesses Shaw explaining Bergson's philosophy to Bergson, and brooking no interruption from Bergson himself. When Bergson mildly interjects, 'Ah, no-o! It is not quite zat!' Shaw is unabashed, replying, 'Oh, my dear fellow, I understand your philosophy much better than you do.'

Bergson, recalls Russell, 'clenched his fists and nearly exploded with rage, but, with a great effort, he controlled himself, and Shaw's expository monologue continued'.

BERTRAND RUSSELL

BUTTERS BREAD FOR

SARAH MILES

43 Hasker Street, London SW3
October 1964

Sixty-nine years later, Bertrand Russell befriends a huge white Pyrenean mountain dog which has taken to prowling past his front door in Chelsea.

The dog's name is Addo. He is owned by Sarah Miles, the sexy young actress who lives at number 18. Addo has recently been the subject of a petition from various other residents of Hasker Street, who want to stop him roaming around unaccompanied. If his roaming continues, dog and owner may both face eviction.

Sarah thinks this most unfair. 'If Addo had been ferocious, I would have understood, but except for lusting after cleaning fluid and window-cleaners, he'd never put a foot wrong. How could I hold up my head coming home to Addo, knowing he was chained up in a dark, smelly patio? Simply too cruel after almost two years of front-doorstep heaven.'

One morning, she looks out of her drawing-room window and notices Addo walking along the street with an old man in carpet slippers. 'They were so deep in conversation that I thought I'd leave them to it.' Over the course of the summer, she often spots the two of them out together. 'Off they'd set on their meander in harmless rhythmic contemplation.'

One afternoon, opening the window, she notices the old man, still in his carpet slippers, sitting with Addo on the doorstep in the sunshine. She surmises that the old man and the dog are locked in silence, 'as if mutually having discovered the secrets of the universe'. But the sound of the window opening breaks the spell. The old man turns round to look at her. 'And in that instant,' she recalls, 'I knew he was a flirt.'

'What a day we're having!' he exclaims.

'Splendid. You and Addo certainly hit it off.'

'We have ... how shall I put it? ... an affiliation.'

The other-worldly Sarah Miles is surely the only person in the street not to know that the old man at number 43 is the most famous philosopher in the world. Two years ago, his ninetieth birthday was celebrated with a *festschrift* with contributions from, among others, Dr Martin Luther King, Leonard Bernstein, Jawaharlal Nehru, Kenneth Kaunda, U Thant, Albert Schweitzer and David Ben-Gurion. But Sarah mixes in different circles: Robert Morley, Eric Sykes, Terry-Thomas, Flora Robson and Benny Hill are all in her next film.*

For a few minutes, the three of them – the philosopher and the actress and the dog – let their minds drift through the mellowness of the Indian summer. 'Care to come over one afternoon for tea?' asks Russell.

'I'd love to.'

'When?'

'At the moment, I'm here most of the time.'

'Good, tomorrow afternoon. Five o'clock.'

He says goodbye to Addo, rises and crosses the street without looking back; but Sarah can feel his mischief brewing. The next day, she knocks on the door of number 43 sharply at five.

'Right on the dot. I am impressed. Come on in and make yourself at home.'

For Sarah, 'his eyes dazzled with a friendly foxiness'. She is captivated by his house, its dusty old furniture and fraying carpets. She sits down on a wobbly chair that topples over.

'Sorry. We're all a bit dilapidated in here.'

He goes into the kitchen, and bids her follow him. 'Don't leave me to make tea all on my own!'

The sunlight spotlights his silky silvery hair. 'Holding his head sideways, he reminded me of a remarkably alert mottled hawk, scrutinising my every move.'

'I trust you'll take cucumber sandwiches with your tea?' He starts cutting a loaf of brown bread. 'Each slice has to be paper thin, enough to see daylight through.' He places his hand between a slice of bread and the

---

* 'And there was I topping the bill for merely being the Fuckable Object,' she observes about the film in question, *Those Magnificent Men in Their Flying Machines*.

window. 'Hopeless,' he says, throwing it in the bin. He cuts another; it too fails the test, so he chucks it in the bin too. And another.

Sarah realises they have not introduced themselves.* 'What's your name?' she asks.

'Someone told me you were a film star,' he replies, 'yet I don't need to know your name.'

By now, he has assembled six acceptably thin slices of bread from a whole loaf. They are ready to be buttered. Sarah tells him that she has never been able to butter bread without tearing it.

'Ha! It's all in the butter texture. Easy when you know how.'

He beckons her over to watch. 'No fun to be had in a mean sandwich.'

He gives her a funny look, as if they are talking about much more private things. Dirty old man, thinks Sarah, who then catches him peering up at her breasts.

'Essential that everything be paper thin except the quantity. Now for the cucumber. Here again, there must be plenty of daylight.'

Again, he raises his hand between the slice of bread and the sunlight. 'Ample,' says Sarah. 'Three sandwiches each.'

'Incorrect.' Obviously no mathematician, thinks Sarah. But he piles them on top of one another and slices them diagonally down the middle. 'Six each.'

They sit down to eat the cucumber sandwiches off Russell's porcelain peacock tea-set. As they eat, he keeps squeezing her knee under the table, 'not half-heartedly, either'. Sarah is thankful Addo is nearby, asleep beneath the table. Russell asks all the questions, so she leaves his house knowing nothing about him at all.

A week later, he invites her back. Again, he asks all the questions. She thinks it is a way of distracting her attention from the tweaks he is giving her knees. She doesn't know how to tell him to stop, so lets him carry on.

---

* As a child, Bertrand Russell met Gladstone, so Sarah Miles, born in 1941, is just one meeting away from Gladstone, born in 1809. Gladstone himself used to breakfast with the elderly William Wordsworth, who was born in 1770. On the BBC programme *Face to Face* on March 4th 1959, Russell reads out an obituary of himself that he wrote in 1937. It begins, 'By the death of the 3rd Earl Russell, or Bertrand Russell, as he preferred to call himself, at the age of ninety, a link with the very distant past has been severed. His grandfather, Lord John Russell, the Victorian Prime Minister, visited Napoleon on Elba. His maternal grandmother was a friend of the Young Pretender's widow ...'

'You didn't tell me you were Bertrand Russell.'

'You never asked.'

She might have to leave the street, she says, because of their neighbours' attitude to Addo.

'What utter nonsense. Addo wouldn't hurt a fly.'

'Tell them that, will you?'

By now, his hand has moved from her knee to her thigh.

'Worry not. Consider it done.'

From that moment on, Sarah Miles doesn't hear another peep from the other residents of Hasker Street.

SARAH MILES

TERENCE STAMP

Bray, the Republic of Ireland
January 1961

Aged nineteen and fresh out of RADA, Sarah Miles has landed a part in a film, *Term of Trial*, opposite the fifty-three-year-old Laurence Olivier. She has had a crush on him ever since she was eleven years old and on a rainy Sunday-afternoon outing from Roedean School saw him as Heathcliff in *Wuthering Heights*. 'The moment he stood at the window, looking out across the misty moor, searching for his soulmate and crying, "Cathy! Cathy! Cathy!" I was a goner.'

From then on, she kept his photograph under her dormitory pillow, 'sometimes dreaming he would come galloping towards me on his white charger, scoop me up into his arms and carry me off. He had brought my first glimmer of sexual awakening, and here I was about to star opposite him.'

As her plane descends into Dublin, where the film is to be shot, she hums the song 'Once I had a secret love, that lived within the heart of me', and wonders whether her love for Olivier will blossom, though he is, she estimates, 'almost old enough to be my grandfather ...'

Terence Stamp is twenty-two, and bound for stardom. He has just finished shooting his first major feature film, *Billy Budd*, and has already spent the £900 fee. His agent phones to tell him that he has been offered an audition for a role in a new film, *Term of Trial*. He reads through the script with mounting disappointment: his role is so small that he can barely find it.

'Blimey,' he says to his agent. 'It's about as big as No Smoking in the Auditorium.'

'I know, but it will be distinguished.'

'Yeah, maybe, but I won't. The part is a yobbo schoolboy, strictly one-dimensional stuff.'

'Just go and see them, all right?'

Grudgingly, he agrees. At the audition, the director wants him to put on a Northern accent. He has recently watched Albert Finney in an interview, so he mimics him saying 'I can read, but I'm not an avid reader,' in a broad Mancunian accent. With no intention of taking the part, he plays it for laughs, 'clenching my teeth and rolling my eyes like an Albert's brother who was completely off his rocker'. He is immediately given the job. 'You'd better speak to my agent,' he says.

They offer £2,000 for ten days' work, but Stamp turns them down. Peter Ustinov has advised him only to take on good work, and he doesn't think *Term of Trial* falls into that category. They raise the fee to £4,000. Reluctantly, he agrees.

It takes a whole day to film the scene in which Terence Stamp gets his gang to hold Sarah Miles down as he attempts to rape her and fails. He doesn't enjoy it, and neither does Sarah, who is wishing fervently that it was Laurence Olivier who was attempting to rape her.

Both Stamp and Sarah Miles are having second thoughts about the film. Sarah has already lost confidence in the director, Peter Glenville. She thinks him too cultured and 'soft' to capture the true horror of the action: what should be a violent gang rape is, she thinks, going to end up as a polite, late-fifties-style simulation. 'It was cold and uncomfortable lying there in the unyielding schoolyard hour after hour, knowing none of it tasted of truth ... Although this was my first film, I realised, lying there with my skirt up, that *Term of Trial* wasn't going to turn out the winner that I felt it could have.'

Whenever she lifts her performance so as to capture the true terror of rape, Glenville says, 'Cut! That's too much, Sarah – we'll have them fleeing the cinema scared to death.' Eventually, with more experience, she will be able to judge within the first two days of any shoot whether or not the film will be a success.

She is also put out by the figure of Terence Stamp. For most people he is, she can quite understand, a tremendous sex symbol, 'a startling creature: dark brown glossy locks and piercing bue eyes, with a virgin complexion and rosebud lips. So striking were his features, within such a pale and sullen countenance, that any healthy young maiden would have been struck right between the eyes – before being quickly struck somewhere else. But not me.'

All day, Stamp simulates raping her, and she simulates being raped; but, in truth, their minds are elsewhere. Stamp is regretting taking the money for an unsuitable part in a film in which he has no interest; Sarah is thinking of her boyfriend back home, James Fox, and, more especially, her leading man here, Laurence Olivier, with whom she has already started to flirt, and is shortly to embark on an affair.*

And what of Olivier?

He, too, is preoccupied by other things. He is already sleeping with Simone Signoret, who is playing his on-screen wife, but Signoret is distracted by the fact that her husband, Yves Montand, is sleeping with Marilyn Monroe. On top of all this, Olivier's new wife, Joan Plowright, has recently given birth to a baby boy. To complicate matters still further, Olivier has suggested to Sarah Miles that 'You should make a play for Simone. She has lovely breasts.'

Later on in the film, Sarah Miles attempts to seduce her alcoholic schoolteacher, played by Olivier, but he rejects her. 'Listen,' says Olivier's character, 'think how young you are. I'm more than twice your age. I have a wife. I love her ... You're a beautiful young creature, but I can't allow myself to think of you like that.' These eerie cross-currents between real life and the drama make everything terribly complicated, particularly as real life seems so much the more dramatic.

Having finally completed his filming, Terence Stamp leaves them all to it. On his return to London, 'to celebrate my release from bondage', he buys himself a lovat-green Mercedes 220SE convertible with antique red leather seats, and rides around in it with the top down, freezing to death.

---

* Throughout their affair, Olivier gets her to call him 'Lionel Kerr'. He explains that Lionel means 'Lionheart'. Decades later, Miles dedicates the middle of her three volumes of memoirs to 'Lionel Kerr'.

TERENCE STAMP

ADVISES

EDWARD HEATH

F2, Albany, Piccadilly, London W1
February 1968

Albany is the grandest apartment block in London. It is sometimes called The Albany by those not in the know. In another of those linguistic booby-traps employed by the upper classes to keep outsiders at bay, the flats in Albany are referred to not as flats or apartments but as 'sets'. There are sixty-nine sets in Albany.

As a teenage messenger boy, Terence Stamp peeked through the back entrance in Burlington Street and looked in awe at the arcade entrance, lined with rhododendrons. Ever since then, he has dreamed of living there; now, with the success of *Billy Budd* and *The Collector*, he can afford to. He sees himself as 'a new kind of Englishman ... very swinging, very aware, well-dressed and all that but with great phsyical and mental strength ... the working-class boy with a few bob as opposed to the chin-less wonder'.

The interior decorator Geoffrey Bennison is the first person to take Stamp inside, having invited the actor and his famous girlfriend, the model Jean Shrimpton, to tea with the art critic John Richardson, whose set is on the ground floor. 'I took in the high ceilings, the walls festooned with paintings and prints, all surfaces scattered with objets d'art ... I was under a spell.'

Richardson informs him that, until recently, residents were obliged to sign a covenant declaring that they won't 'behave in an unacceptable manner, keep pets, or entertain ladies overnight in their chambers'.

'Ladies?' replies Stamp, addressing Richardson and Bennison. 'D'you mean I'd have to dress the lovely Shrimpton up as a chap?'

Richardson explains that the rule has now been repealed.

'So girls live here now?'

'Oh, yes, thin end of the wedge. Changed the whole tone. Chaps moved out, wasn't top drawer any more.'

But Stamp is reassured, and asks Bennison to let him know if ever he hears of a set coming onto the market. Sure enough, a month later Bennison passes on the news that a Mr Timewell, who leases D1, is moving to Morocco, and wants to sell.

'He knows it's me?' Stamp asks Bennison.

'Oh, yes, dear, he knows it's you. He's seen that butch photo in the supplement. Quite curious to meet you in the flesh, he is.'

Stamp snaps it up. Bennison takes on the decoration, stripping D1 to its bare bones, painting the floorboards of the two main rooms white, and placing a fashionable polar-bear skin in front of the specially widened Empire bed. He covers the bed with a black, biscuit and cream overlay, with matching sausage bolsters at each end. A Goan ebony chest inlaid with flowers and clouds completes the picture. Stamp is delighted. 'That first afternoon I rolled around on the carpet in front of the fireplace, hugging myself in reassurance it was true.'

Before long, he has developed a daily routine around Piccadilly: morning coffee at Fortnum's, tea at the Ritz, dinner at Wilton's. A pivotal figure in Swinging London, he lives the life of a Regency dandy. 'There's a timelessness here,' he says. 'It wouldn't really surprise me to find the streets crowded with carriages.'

Albany has long possessed an almost collegiate feel, standoffish yet distantly familiar, with a suggestion of louche goings-on behind closed doors. Lord Byron once lived here, and so too did Edgar Lustgarten.* The first act of Oscar Wilde's *The Importance of Being Earnest* is thought to be based in B1, while the fictitious gentleman burglar Raffles also lives in Albany. Marmion Savage in *The Bachelor of the Albany* (1848) describes it, not inaccurately, as 'the hospital for incurable oddities, the home of homeless gentlemen'.

When Stamp moves in, he finds that another set is occupied by the leader of the Conservative Party, Edward Heath, a solitary bachelor,

---

* Byron lived in Albany with a macaw and a maid called Mrs Mule. Other past and future residents include Lord Snowdon, Terence Rattigan, Graham Greene, Thomas Beecham, Bruce Chatwin, T.S. Eliot, Dame Edith Evans, Alan Clark MP and William Gladstone.

guarded and prickly, the complete opposite of swinging.

Heath took over F2 in 1963, on a seven-year lease at £670 a year, following the death of Clifford Bax, the brother of the composer Arnold. He was then aged forty-seven. Employing the interior designer Jo Pattrick, he set about redecorating it in a style described by his official biographer as 'assertively modern yet classically restrained', with cream walls, orange curtains, a chocolate carpet, and black leather Scandinavian armchairs. The walls are decorated with prints of uniformed soldiers, two landscapes by Winston Churchill (presented to him by the artist) and a lithograph by Picasso. On the mantelpiece stands a variety of white porcelain horses from the Spanish Riding School. Photographs of Heath with the Queen, Khrushchev and the Pope are on display on a special shelf. A Steinway grand piano* dominates the drawing room.

One day, the stiff, awkward, virginal leader of the opposition takes the unusual step of inviting his relaxed, fashionable, sexually charged neighbour to lunch. A few days later, Stamp describes their three-hour meeting to his friend, the author John Fowles, who duly records it in his diary:

'He could have learnt a lot, but he just couldn't get the groove, didn't seem to hear what I said.' Apparently Heath said that Wilson† frightened him and hurt him in the House. Terry's remedy was this: 'OK, you're sitting on the Opposition Front Bench, old Wilson gets up. As soon as he starts annoying you, you just think, This morning Harold got up at Number Ten, he went downstairs to the kitchen, got out the best tea, warmed the pot, did it all perfect, took it upstairs to the old woman, thinking, Maybe this is it, this time, she'll open her arms and we'll have a lovely screw. Instead of which the old bag just says, Oh gawd, and turns over and goes to sleep again. You just think, It's not me he's trying to hurt, it's his missus or whatever. All I got to do is work out what it is in Wilson's life that makes him have to hurt me. Then I can handle him.'

---

* On which Heath will one day trot out 'The Red Flag' in response to a request from Vic Feather, at a supper party in Albany for trade union leaders. 'It put the seal on a jolly evening, although I must say that Ted did not play "The Red Flag" very well,' remembers Jack Jones.

† Prime Minister Harold Wilson.

Fowles asks Stamp whether Edward Heath has taken this advice to heart.*

'He didn't understand,' complains Stamp. 'He's forgotten how to listen.'

---

* In his autobiography, written forty years later, Heath fails to record this meeting, or the advice he was once offered by London's most fashionable young actor. As a young man, he yearned to be someone different, someone rather more like Terence Stamp. 'I have a desire, perhaps when analysed not very rational or even sane, to get "hard" like other men,' he confided to his diary while he was awaiting his army call-up in March 1940, 'to take the knocks they can take, to go wining and whoring with them. Yet whenever I meet them I feel repelled by their lack of intelligence and concern only with things like pay, leave and food. Perhaps my nature's different.'

EDWARD HEATH

SINGS TO

WALTER SICKERT

Hauteville, St Peters, Kent
December 1934

The eighteen-year-old Edward Heath has always been known to his family (though never beyond it) as Teddy. It is a nickname which belies his character. He is aloof, unsmiling and exceptionally diligent, so much so that his doting parents sometimes urge young Teddy to work a little less and play a little more. Not long ago, when his mother entered his room to suggest he might be working too hard, he snapped back: 'Mother, sometimes I think you don't WANT me to get on!'

Born and brought up in Broadstairs in Kent, he attends St Peters Primary School until the age of ten, then gains a scholarship to Chatham House, the fee-paying county grammar school in Ramsgate, three miles down the coast. Though never an outstanding pupil – in classes of thirty, he tends to hover somewhere between fifth and sixteenth – he is a hard worker. He is always immaculately dressed, his hair neat and tidy. But he is not matey, and never joins a gang.*

He rises to become a conscientious – some would say over-conscientious – prefect. 'He was very down on kids who had their hands in their trouser pockets, or weren't behaving well in the street in their school cap and blazer,' notes one of his teachers.

His achievements are rife. He wins prizes for his piano playing, and conducts the school orchestra. He is secretary of the debating society – opposing, on different occasions, sweepstakes, Sunday cinemas and

---

* He remains standoffish for the rest of his life. 'He has no social graces whatever. He is not faintly interested in women, probably not men either,' complains James Lees-Milne to his diary in July 1974, after attending a dinner party at which Heath talked across his female neighbour for the entire meal. Four years later, Lees-Milne encounters him again. 'He looked like a figure cut from a turnip, as it were for All Hallows E'en, quite square and pointed, his profile, nose and mouth sharp gashes.'

co-education – and keeps the score for the first cricket XI. He never steps out of line, or breaks a school rule. In the school nativity play, he is given the part of the Archangel Gabriel.

In the summer of 1934, he sits the scholarship exam for Balliol College, Oxford. At his interview, he says that his ambition is to be a professional politician, the only time the Tutor for Admissions has ever heard such a reply from a schoolboy. With poor marks in French and in the general paper, he fails to get in, but decides to stay on at school in order to try again next year.

A keen bicyclist, young Teddy often cycles past a large house in the village of St Peters, near Broadstairs. It used to be called Hopeville, but its new owner has renamed it Hauteville. Sometimes as he bicycles past, Teddy spies paintings hanging out to dry on a clothes line in the garden. Someone tells him that it is the home of the painter Walter Sickert.

At the age of seventy-four, Walter Sickert is as frisky and freewheeling as young Teddy is dogged and dutiful. He recently flung himself into an affair with the twenty-seven-year-old Peggy Ashcroft, fresh from her success in *Romeo and Juliet* at the Old Vic.*

'As we get older, we get *worse!*' he once said. It is an aphorism as fit for his accounting as for his love life. Famously spendthrift – he can never resist taxis, telegrams, clothes, leaseholds or bric-à-brac – Sickert has been on the verge of bankruptcy, owing well over £2,000 to land-lords, art dealers, tradesmen and, not least, the Inland Revenue. Some of his friends suspect that, for him, impecunity is the badge of the true artist.

A group of friends rode to his rescue by launching an appeal, raising £2,050; they then persuaded him to move from London to Kent. This was how he ended up in this large old red-brick house. It has a big garden with an orchard and outbuildings. Local rumour has it that as a child Queen Victoria was out donkey riding in Broadstairs when the animal bolted and carried her all the way to this very garden.

---

* Sickert never loses his interest in the sexual act. At a Henry Moore exhibition at the Leicester Galleries, Moore gestures to one of his nudes – a large stone with a hole in the middle – and tells Sickert earnestly that he 'had to use a very special tool to do her'. Sickert considers the sculpture before replying, 'I think I would need one too.'

Among the many improvements Sickert has made to the house are the conversion of the Georgian stable block into a studio and the erection of a hutch-like construction on the east side, where he hangs his paintings out to dry. There is nothing quite like an east wind for drying paint on canvas, he tells his students: it can cut the process down from a fortnight to twenty-four hours.

Few people in the village know who on earth he is, though his flowing opera cloak, wide-brimmed hat and collarless shirt all serve to flame the suspicion that he might well be an artist. His friendliness further unnerves the inhabitants; he has even been known to invite total strangers into his house for tea and bananas. He is fond of children, and values their opinions. His garden borders on the playground of St Peters Primary School; Sickert sometimes places his canvases outside so that he can hear the comments of the pupils. He advises other artists to do the same. 'Children always know.' But, like many artists, he has periods of *ennui*, and there are times when he is gruff towards unexpected visitors.

The eighteen-year-old Teddy Heath is a keen choral singer, and one December evening he leads a procession of carol singers up the gravel path to the front door of Hauteville with music sheets in hand. The group sing two carols and then wait expectantly outside the front door, collecting box at the ready.

But no one emerges. 'Neither pressing the bell nor using the knocker elicited any response,' Heath recalls forty years later, 'but eventually the curtain at the window was drawn aside and through the chink we saw a small, wizened, grey-bearded face.* Almost immediately the curtain slipped back again. We waited. Then the door, on a chain, was opened a fraction.

'"Go away!" said Sickert, and we left.'

---

* Three years later, he is to set eyes on two other famous men. Travelling in Germany in the summer of 1937, he receives a chance invitation to attend a Nazi rally in Nuremberg. He is placed in a gangway seat, so that when Adolf Hitler marches alone up the centre aisle, he almost brushes Heath's shoulder. 'He looked much smaller than I had imagined and very ordinary. His face had little colour and the uniform seemed more important than the man.' The next day, Heath is invited to a party given by Heinrich Himmler, who he describes as 'peering rather short-sightedly through his pince-nez. I remember him for his soft, wet, flabby handshake.' He also meets Goebbels, 'his pinched face white and sweating – evil personified'.

On his death in 2005, Sir Edward Heath leaves virtually all of his £5.4 million fortune to ensure that his Salisbury home is open to the public.* The only other twentieth-century British Prime Minister to achieve this distinction is Sir Winston Churchill.

Among the pictures on display in the house is a study in brooding disappointment which Heath managed to pick up for £19 from the Leicester Gallery shortly after the Second World War, a signed etching called *Ennui* by Walter Sickert.

---

* Though he only serves as Prime Minister for four years, Heath has some of the qualities of an apparition, popping up where you least expect him. Both Graham Greene and Kenneth Williams confess to dreams of meeting him. On Saturday, March 9th 1974, Williams writes in his diary, 'Went to bed & dreamed that I was attending a political meeting addressed by Harold Wilson: I was talking to him & he was complaining of the sparse attendance, and I saw Heath in the front row smiling and wearing a ridiculous square-shouldered ladies' musquash coat. it was absurd.'

In his posthumously published dream diary, Greene recounts a dream in which Heath offered him the post of Ambassador to Scotland, 'and I refused. However, when I read in the paper that no one else would accept, I went to him and told him that I was ready to be appointed after all.

'He looked exhausted and a little suspicious of me, so I explained that the only reason I had at first refused was that I felt incapable. But I would do my best. Perhaps as a mark of friendship we went swimming together in a muddy river, and to show my keenness for my job I suggested we should hold a World Textile Fair in Scotland. He replied that David Selznick had once told him that such fairs might possibly do good in the long run, but that the last one had ruined many local industries.'

WALTER SICKERT

INSTRUCTS

WINSTON CHURCHILL

11 Downing Street
June 1927

As Walter Sickert is reading his newspaper, a story catches his eye. It concerns someone he knew when she was a girl of sixteen, over a quarter of a century ago. Clementine Churchill, now married to the Chancellor of the Exchequer, Mr Winston Churchill, has, it seems, been knocked down by an omnibus while crossing the road in Knightsbridge.

The two of them first met when Clementine, then aged fourteen, was holidaying in Dieppe in 1899. Sickert was a friend of her mother, and in the habit of dropping round. Clementine was instantly taken with this bohemian figure with his thick fair hair and piercing green eyes. 'Clementine was deeply struck by him, and thought he was the most handsome and compelling man she had ever seen,' writes her daughter Mary, eighty years later.

Out on shopping errands for her mother, Clementine often bumped into Sickert at work in the streets. One day, she stopped to look at his new painting.

'Do you like my work?' he asked.

Clementine paused for just a little too long.

'… Yes,' she replied.

'What is it you don't like?'

Clementine paused again. 'Well, Mr Sickert, you seem to see everything through dirty eyes.'

Sickert asked her mother if Clementine could come to tea with him. She climbed the hill to his house in Neuville-lès-Dieppe and was let in by his housekeeper and mistress, the doughty Madame Villain. Sickert was out, so Clementine waited in his bedroom, which she considered 'very dirty'. 'I was profoundly shocked and thought, "Perhaps Mother can find Mr Sickert a better housekeeper."' When Sickert failed to materialise, she made herself useful by tidying the room. First she made the bed, then swept the floor. Next she picked up the skeleton of a herring from a plate and flung it out of the window, before washing the plate and putting it away.

At this point, Sickert entered. 'Where's my herring?' he barked.

'I threw it away.'

'You interfering wretch! I was just going to paint it! And where, pray, is the handsome plate it was sitting on?'

'I have washed it and put it on the shelf.'

But Sickert forgave her, and that winter engraved a portrait of her on her hockey stick with a red-hot poker. Two years later, in Paris, he entertained her for a whole day, introducing her to Camille Pissarro and taking her round the Luxembourg Gallery. During lunch, she asked him who was the greatest living painter. He looked astonished, and replied, 'I am, of course.'

Twenty-six years later, Sickert goes to visit the invalid Clementine at Number 11 Downing Street. She introduces him to her husband; the two men hit it off straight away. Churchill is an enthusiastic painter, ever keen to improve. But he is also impatient. Sickert encourages him to slow down, advising him to work from drawings and under-paintings rather than plunging headlong into 'a riot of colour', which is Churchill's usual method.

In return, the Chancellor of the Exchequer advises the feckless painter on sound financial management. Alas, it goes in one ear and out the other. Sickert has no head for sums, or any inclination for restraint.*

Over the summer, the Churchills regularly invite Sickert to Chartwell. He arrives in bright red socks, and entertains his hosts after dinner with a selection of music-hall songs. During the day, Churchill sits in the sun, transfixed by his canvas, while Sickert spends most of his time inside the house with the curtains drawn, reading novels. Every now and then, he ventures outside in his opera hat. Churchill begs him to divulge the secret of how to 'transfer the marvellous greens and purples' he can see all around him onto the canvas, but Sickert long ago gave up any interest in painting *en plein air*.

---

* In 1940, when Sickert is facing bankruptcy, Churchill arranges for his Civil List pension to be supplemented by the Royal Bounty fund. He dies in relative poverty on January 22nd 1942.

Some suggest that Sickert has a corrupting influence on Churchill, as he teaches him the advantages of painting from photographs rather than real life. But Churchill thinks differently. 'I am really thrilled by the field he is opening to me,' he writes to Clementine. 'I see my way to paint far better pictures than I ever thought possible before. He is really giving me a new lease of life as a painter.'

Churchill buys himself a 'beautiful camera', and then takes Sickert's process one stage further, acquiring a projector, too, and tracing the photographic image straight onto the canvas, pioneering a method later taken up by artists like Andy Warhol and David Hockney.

Painting is Churchill's most constant source of pleasure, his great escape from the pressures of office.* 'With his brushes and paint, he forgot everything, like a child does who has been given a box of paints,' writes another of his tutors, the painter Paul Maz, adding, 'Knowing that Winston painted only between crises, it was a refuge for him, and all I ever attempted was to simplify his method and reduce his means and insatiable appetite for colour. He would have eaten a tube of white, he loved the smell of it so.'

Over the course of this summer, Churchill and Sickert paint portraits of each other. Churchill uses a photograph to paint a small, charming group portrait of himself, Sickert, Randolph Churchill, Diana Mitford and others, all sitting around the tea table at Chartwell. Sickert's portrait of Churchill proves more controversial. When it is first shown at the Saville Gallery early in 1935, the *Sunday Times* declares it 'the most brilliant portrait Mr Sickert has yet executed'. On the other hand, Clementine's sister Nellie thinks it so unrealistic that she loses her self-control and attacks the manager of the gallery, who, not recognising her, retorts that he doesn't suppose she has ever even *seen* Mr Churchill. At this point, reports one observer, 'much fur flew'.

Unaware of the fracas, Sickert presents Clementine with one of his studies for the portrait of her husband. At a later date, she somehow contrives to put her foot through it, and the painting is never seen again.

---

* Francis Bacon tells Churchill's biographer Martin Gilbert that Churchill's technique is 'not to be scorned'.

WINSTON CHURCHILL

BARGES IN ON

LAURENCE OLIVIER

St James's Theatre, London SW1
Summer 1951

Winston Churchill has long been an admirer of Laurence Olivier, and is keen on two of his films in particular. When *Lady Hamilton* is released in 1941, he watches it over and over again – perhaps as many as a hundred times, according to one author. He also loves *Henry V*. 'We saw the film of Henry V in Technicolor, with Laurence Olivier,' writes his Private Secretary, Jock Colville, in his diary on November 25th 1944. 'The P.M. went into ecstasies about it. To bed at 2.30.'

He admires Olivier as a stage actor, too. During one lengthy speech in his performance of *Richard III*, Olivier grows aware of another voice speaking his lines. He looks out, and spots Mr Churchill in the fourth row, reciting all the lines in unison.

The influence runs in both directions, though Olivier is inspired by Churchill in a less predictable way. On holiday in the South of France in 1949, he and his wife Vivien Leigh take up painting, having just read Churchill's book *Painting as a Pastime*.

In 1951, the Oliviers are starring in *Caesar and Cleopatra*. During one performance, Olivier is informed that Churchill is in the audience. In the interval, Olivier is hovering about in his dressing room, wondering how his performance is going down with 'the great man', when the door swings open, and there he is. Olivier is too taken aback to say anything.

'Oh, I'm so sorry,' says Churchill. 'I was looking for a corner.'

Olivier escorts Churchill back, and points him in the right direction. At the same time, he makes sure there will be someone waiting to take him back to his seats in the auditorium.*

---

* On visits to the theatre, Churchill always books three seats: one for himself, one for his companion – generally his daughter Mary – and a third for his hat and coat. 'I thought this one of the most sensible extravagances I had ever heard of,' enthuses Olivier.

Churchill goes about his business, returning in time for the second half. As he sits down, he jokes to Mary, 'I was looking for Loo-Loo, and who do you think I ran into? Ju-Lu!'

A few weeks later, the actor and the world statesman are introduced in more formal circumstances, when the Duchess of Buccleuch takes Churchill to see *Antony and Cleopatra*. Olivier is entranced. 'Adoring him as of course we already did, we found his sweetly polite, unforced kindness, and the courteous generosity of his conversation an unforgettable example,' he records in his convoluted prose. In his encounters with other politicians, Olivier, who prides himself on reading faces, has always found them furtive, with 'a certain guardedness, obviously caused by a fear of being caught out ... only detectable in the slightly hooded look around the eyes'. But not Churchill.

Over dinner, Olivier reminds Churchill of the time he joined in with *Richard III*, adding, 'I can't tell you how envious I am of such a wonderful memory.'

'Oh, but you – so many myriads of words packed into your brain,' replies Churchill. 'It must be a great burden.'

Olivier confesses that, three weeks after he has finished playing a part, he is unable to quote a single word from it.

'Aaah,' replies Churchill. 'That must be a great mercy to you.'

To celebrate Olivier's birthday, Churchill invites the Oliviers to Sunday lunch at Chartwell. Churchill is smitten by Vivien Leigh, and presses one of his paintings onto her; later, they are told that this is the only painting Churchill has ever given away. (He has an eye for a pretty face: at a later dinner, when the women have left the room, Churchill turns to Olivier and says, 'By Jove, she's a clinker!')

After lunch, Churchill stays indoors while Churchill's son-in-law, Christopher Soames, shows the visitors around the farm. On their way round, they hear a bull issuing 'a groan of agonised pain and grief; his head was pressed tightly against the wall and his wild eyes rolling'. Soames explains that the bull has already killed a man, and the only way to get him out of his stall to clean it is to entice him into another stall with a cow in season.

When they return to the house, Olivier tells Churchill that he is worried about his bull. 'Oh, he's all right,' says Churchill. 'And even if he does lead a life of unparalleled dreariness, it is punctuated …' – he pauses for dramatic effect – 'by moments of intense excitement.'

Years later, on January 30th 1965, Olivier speaks the commentary for the ITV broadcast of the funeral of Winston Churchill. It is, he believes, 'more than a day of national mourning'. Rather, it is 'a celebration of a nation's overwhelming gratitude for the life of their "Valiant Man", to whom they owed so incalculably much'. In his memoirs, he boasts that he was 'proudly informed' that of the broadcasts on BBC and ITV his own 'gained the greater viewing audience of the two'.

But the story of the two men does not end there. In 1968, Olivier, by now Director of the National Theatre, is enveloped in a debate over whether a play called *Soldiers* by Rolf Hochhuth should be staged there. The play is highly critical of Churchill's saturation bombing of German cities, and accuses him of complicity in the assassination of the Polish leader Władysław Sikorski.

Kenneth Tynan is determined to stage it; the Chairman of the National Theatre, Lord Chandos, a member of Churchill's war cabinet, is equally determined to prevent it being staged. Olivier, confessing himself 'deeply distressed and torn about', flounders around in the middle. He is torn, he explains to the board, between his prejudices as an Englishman and his wishes for the National Theatre. His position is further complicated by the fact that Tynan is keen for him to play the part of Churchill.

Tynan detects much in common between the actor and the statesman. 'My god how like you the old bastard is!' he writes to Olivier. 'The passionate maddening love of detail; the concentration that can wither people by simply ignoring their presence; the sudden changes of subject; the sudden focusing on apparent irrelevancies; the love of anecdote and quotation … the brutally realistic assessment of human motives; the impatience; and the patience.'

LAURENCE OLIVIER
BRINGS OUT THE PHONY IN
J.D. SALINGER

4 Christchurch Street, London SW3
May 21st 1951

In the same season, Laurence Olivier performs before the up-and-coming American novelist J.D. Salinger.

On May 8th 1951, Salinger sets sail for Britain on the *Queen Elizabeth*, hoping to avoid the hoo-ha surrounding the American publication of *The Catcher in the Rye*. There have already been requests for a rewrite and a change to the title,* along with a succession of misunderstandings involving publicity.† The *New Yorker* has refused to serialise the novel, complaining that the characters lack credibility, but his British publisher, Hamish Hamilton, has proved far more sympathetic. On Salinger's arrival, Hamilton presents him with the British edition; as requested, it has a subdued cover, no author photograph and no biographical details.

Salinger's entertainment in London is orchestrated by Hamish Hamilton, who Salinger calls 'a professional get-together boy'. Hamilton treats his author to a series of nights out involving what Salinger describes as 'tearing around to theater, supper parties'.

Among the plays they attend are two on the theme of Cleopatra – *Antony and Cleopatra* by Shakespeare, and *Caesar and Cleopatra* by George Bernard Shaw – both starring Sir Laurence Olivier and Vivien Leigh. 'Very good, very pure,' Salinger observes appreciatively, adding that,

---

* When the Book of the Month club asks him to change the title, Salinger explains that Holden Caulfield won't agree to it.

† 'J.D. Salinger wrote a masterpiece, *The Catcher in the Rye*, recommending that readers who enjoy a book call up the author; then he spent his next twenty years avoiding the telephone' – John Updike.

'Publishing is a terrible invasion of my privacy,' Salinger writes to a friend many years later. 'There is a marvelous peace in not publishing.' Some estimates suggest that by the time of his death he may have written as many as fifteen full-length novels, unread by anyone but himself.

'The audiences here are just as stupid as they are in New York, but the productions are much, much better.' Afterwards, Hamish Hamilton is particularly buoyed up to have secured an invitation for himself and his author to dinner with the Oliviers at their house in Chelsea.

It all goes well; Salinger enthuses to a friend* about 'a marvelous little house, very posh evening – formal clothes and all that'. Olivier, he says, is a 'very nice guy, very bright. He's knocked out about his wife, which was nice to see. She's a charmer. Naturally, while we were having drinks in the living room, some gin went up my nose. I damn near left by the window.'

On the other hand, Salinger can't help feeling a bit of a phony. When Hamilton arranged the invitation, he had apparently overlooked a passage in *Catcher in the Rye* in which the protagonist, Holden Caulfield, rants against the phoniness of actors in general, and one actor in particular:

> *I don't like shows very much, if you want to know the truth. They're not as bad as movies, but they're certainly nothing to rave about. In the first place, I hate actors. They never act like people. They just think they do. Some of the good ones do, in a very slight way, but not in a way that's fun to watch. And if any actor's really good, you can always tell he knows he's good, and that spoils it. You take Sir Laurence Olivier, for example. I saw him in* Hamlet. *D.B. took Phoebe and I to see it last year … But I didn't enjoy it much. I just don't see what's so marvelous about Sir Laurence Olivier, that's all. He has a terrific voice, and he's a helluva handsome guy, and he's very nice to watch when he's walking or dueling or something, but he wasn't at all the way D.B. said Hamlet was. He was too much like a goddam general, instead of a sad, screwed-up type guy … The only thing old Phoebe liked was when Hamlet patted this dog on the head. She thought that was funny and nice, and it was. What I'll have to do is, I'll have to read that play. The trouble with me is, I always have to read that stuff by myself. If an actor acts it out, I hardly listen. I keep worrying about whether he's going to do something phony every minute.*

---

* The commercial artist E. Michael Mitchell, who created the final cover of *The Catcher in the Rye*.

However, none of these qualms is evident during his dinner with Olivier. In fact, Salinger gives every appearance of having countermanded the suspicions of Caulfield, exchanging lively conversation with the actor his creation considers to be teetering on the phony.

A few days later, Salinger sets off around England in a Hillman car he has bought, driving to Stratford-upon-Avon, where he rows a young lady on the river instead of going to the theatre, to Oxford, where he attends Evensong at Christchurch, and to Yorkshire, where he thinks he may have spotted the Brontë sisters running across the moors. He then travels to Ireland and then on to Scotland, where he thinks of settling. From London, he goes back to New York, taking his new Hillman with him.

It is only on his return to New York* that Salinger entertains second thoughts about whether he was entirely genuine with the Oliviers. Had they read Caulfield's views on Olivier? Salinger's worries are possibly exacerbated by the news that the Oliviers are planning a trip to New York, and have asked to see him again. He writes Hamilton a panicky letter, explaining that Caulfield's opinion of Olivier's acting is not necessarily his own, and asks him to explain all this to Olivier, and to apologise for any hurt caused.

Hamilton does so, and in turn Olivier sends Salinger a sympathetic letter. On September 1st, Salinger writes back: 'At risk of sounding terribly oracular, not to say presumptuous as hell, I'd like – in fact I'd love – to tell you what I personally think of your acting … I think you're the only actor in the world who plays in a Shakespeare play with a special, tender familiarity – as if you were keeping it in the family. Almost as if you were appearing in a play written by an older brother whom you understand completely and love to distraction. It's an almost insuperably beautiful

---

* Salinger returns to London with his children in 1969, taking them to see the Changing of the Guard at Buckingham Palace, Hampton Court, Harrods Food Hall and Carnaby Street. One afternoon they visit Edna O'Brien. Salinger tells his daughter Margaret with a wink that she is a good writer, and a hell of a nice girl, but that she writes some *really* dirty stuff. They also go to see Engelbert Humperdinck starring as Robinson Crusoe at the London Palladium. 'Awful, but we all sort of enjoyed it, and the main idea was to see the Palladium itself, because that's where the last scene of *The 39 Steps* was set,' he writes to his friend Lillian Ross. In January 2011, newly released letters to an English friend reveal more of his unexpectedly prosaic pleasures, including Whoppers chocolates ('better than just edible'), the TV series *Upstairs Downstairs*, the Three Tenors, Tim Henman and Burger King.

thing to watch, and I certainly think you're the only actor who can bring it off.'

Nevertheless, two years later when Olivier asks, through Hamilton, for his permission to adapt 'For Esmé – with Love and Squalor' into a radio drama, Salinger refuses. As time goes by, his doubts about Olivier increase. In 1983, thirty-two years after his 'very posh evening' in Chelsea, Salinger writes a letter to a friend unfavourably comparing Olivier's acting with John Wayne's performance in *The Shootist*.

J.D. SALINGER

SEEKS OUT

ERNEST HEMINGWAY

The Ritz Hotel, 15 place Vendôme, Paris
Late August 1944

The twenty-five-year-old Jerry Salinger is experiencing a terrible war. Of the 3,080 men of the 12th US Infantry who disembarked with him at Normandy on D-Day, only a third are still alive.

His regiment is the first to enter Paris. They are mobbed by happy crowds. Salinger's job as an officer in the Counter-Intelligence Corps entails weeding out and interrogating Nazi collaborators. As they go through Paris, he and a fellow officer arrest a collaborator, but a crowd wrests their prisoner away and beats him to death.

Salinger has heard that Ernest Hemingway is in town. A writer himself, with a growing reputation for his short stories, he is determined to seek out America's most famous living novelist. He feels sure he will find him at the Ritz, so he drives the jeep there. Sure enough, Hemingway is installed in the small bar,* already bragging that he alone liberated Paris in general and the Ritz in particular.

To this latter claim, there is a slight smidgin of truth. 'It was all he could talk about,' remembers a fellow member of the press corps. 'It was more than just being the first American in Paris. He said, "I will be the first American at the Ritz. And I will liberate the Ritz."' In fact, by the time he arrives, the Germans have already abandoned the hotel, and the manager has come out to welcome him, boasting, 'We saved the Cheval Blanc!'

'Well, go get it,' snaps Hemingway, who then begins slugging it down.

Hemingway proceeds to make the Ritz his home. From then on, he can't be bothered to cover the liberation of Paris, though he lends his typewriter to someone who can. Instead, he spends most of his time drinking Perrier-Jouet in the bar.

---

* Since named the Hemingway Bar.

Over brandy after lunch on liberation day, a female guest says she wants to go and watch the victory parade.

'What for?' says Hemingway. 'Daughter, sit still and drink this good brandy. You can always see a parade, but you'll never again lunch at the Ritz the day after Paris was liberated.'

As the days go by, he continues to hold court in the Ritz, boasting how many Germans he has killed, though no one with him can remember him killing a single one.*

Upon Salinger's arrival, Hemingway greets him like an old friend, saying that he recognises him from his photograph in *Esquire* and has read all his short stories. Does he have any new work with him?† Salinger produces a recent copy of the *Saturday Evening Post* containing one of his stories. Hemingway reads it and congratulates him. The two writers sit and talk for hours. Salinger (who secretly prefers Fitzgerald's writing) is pleasantly surprised by the difference between Hemingway's public and private personas; he finds him 'a really good guy'.

A few days later, Hemingway tells a friend about meeting 'a kid in the 4th Division named Jerry Salinger'. He notes his disdain for the war, and his urge to write. He is also impressed by the way Salinger's family contin- ues to post him the *New Yorker*.

The two men never meet again,§ but they correspond. Hemingway is a generous mentor. 'First you have a marvelous ear and you write tenderly and lovingly without getting wet … how happy it makes me to read the stories and what a god damned fine writer I think you are.'

---

* 'I know my father claimed to have killed 122 "krauts" as he called them but I think that's what he probably wished he had done,' his son John tells Hemingway's biographer Denis Brian, who concludes, 'There's no hard evidence that he killed even one.'

† Throughout the war, Salinger never stops writing. He has written eight stories since landing in Europe in mid-January, and a further three between D-Day and September 9th. 'He tugged that little portable type-writer all over Europe … Even during the hottest campaigns, he was writing, sending off to magazines,' recalls a fellow soldier.

§ Later, the legend grows that Hemingway visits Salinger in his unit, and the two men argue about the relative merits of Hemingway's German Luger and Salinger's US .45. To prove his point, Hemingway is meant to have aimed his gun at a chicken and blasted its head off, making Salinger very upset. But there is no evidence this ever happened. Rather, it shows that readers like their writers to behave in person as they would in print: Hemingway tough and blood- thirsty, Salinger sensitive and fearful.

The chumminess of their single meeting is captured in a letter Salinger writes to Hemingway the following year from the military hospital in Nuremberg where he is being treated for combat stress:

Nothing was wrong with me except that I've been in an almost constant state of despondency and I thought it would be good to talk to somebody sane. They asked me about my sex life (which couldn't be normaler – gracious!) and about my childhood (Normal) ... I've always liked the Army ... There are very few arrests left to be made in our section. We're now picking up children under ten if their attitudes are snotty. Gotta get those ole arrest forms up to Army, gotta fatten up the Report.

... I've written a couple more of my incestuous stories, and several poems, and part of a play. If I ever get out of the Army I might finish the play and invite Margaret O'Brien to play with me in it. With a crew-cut and a Max Factor dimple over my navel, I could play Holden Caulfield myself. I once gave a very sensitive performance as Raleigh in 'Journey's End'.

I'd give my right arm to get out of the Army, but not on a psychiatric, this-man-is-not-fit-for-the-Army-life ticket. I have a very sensitive novel in mind, and I won't have the author called a jerk in 1950. I am a jerk, but the wrong people mustn't know it.

I wish you'd drop me a line if you can manage it. Removed from this scene, is it much easier to think clearly? I mean with your work.

Around this time, Salinger experiences some sort of nervous breakdown fuelled by the horrors he has endured.* His biographer Ian Hamilton suggests his chummy letter to Hemingway cannot be taken at face value. It is, he believes, 'almost manically cheerful'. He is probably right. Years later, Salinger tells his daughter: 'You never really get the smell of burning flesh out of your nose entirely, no matter how long you live.' In Greenwich Village in 1946, Jerry Salinger has regained some of his old bravado. To his poker-playing friends he speaks disparagingly of many well-known writers, Hemingway among them. 'In fact, he was quite

---

* After Paris, his regiment is trapped in the notorious Hürtgen Forest; five hundred of his comrades die in five days, many of them freezing to death.

convinced that no really good American writers existed after Melville –
that is, until the advent of J.D. Salinger,' recalls one.

Hemingway, on the other hand, is happy to name Salinger one of his
three favourite contemporary authors; when he dies, a copy of *The Catcher
in the Rye* is found in his library. He is neither the first writer with a disciple who turns against him, nor the last.

ERNEST HEMINGWAY

TURNS AGAINST

FORD MADOX FORD

La Closerie des Lilas, 171, boulevard du Montparnasse, Paris
Autumn 1924

Twenty years earlier, Ernest Hemingway is himself a young man of twenty-five. He is sitting outside his favourite bar in Paris, when he hears the words, 'Oh, here you are. May I sit with you?' His mentor, Ford Madox Ford, twenty-five years his senior, joins him at the table.

Eighteen months ago, Ford, novelist and editor, launched *transatlantic review*, largely as an outlet for younger writers. He is Hemingway's keenest supporter: 'I did not read more than six words of his before I decided to publish everything that he sent me.' He has also taken him on as his assistant editor, published his stories, and introduced him to Paris literary society. But the familiar tale of discipleship is soon to unwind: the more Ford helps Hemingway, the more Hemingway despises him.

Encouragement is repaid with irritation. 'The thing to do with Ford is kill him,' Hemingway complains to Ezra Pound. '... I am fond of Ford. This ain't personal. It's literary. You see Ford's running the whole damn thing as a compromise.' He believes Ford has reneged on his promise to favour young writers, and has settled for the old and the mainstream, 'except Tzara and such shit in French. That's the hell of it.'

Hemingway's claim to be fond of Ford grows shakier and shakier. He is irritated by Ford's mannerisms, his walrus moustache and his war reminiscences ('I'm going to start denying I was in the war for fear I will get like Ford'). Nor does he trust him. 'He is an absolute liar and crook and always motivated by the finest synthetic English gentility.'

Hemingway is scooped up by the burly *grande dame* of Parisian literary life, Gertrude Stein. Bypassing Ford, he assures her that *transatlantic review* will publish her vast novel *The Making of Americans*, all 925 pages of it. It is, he says, 'one of the very greatest books I've ever read', and 'a remarkable scoop for his magazine'. Stein shares his high opinion, and is delighted.*

In fact, Hemingway has told Ford that *The Making of Americans* is merely a long short story, not a six-volume novel, which leaves Ford in the awkward position of having to tell Stein he can't publish it in its entirety. Consequently, Stein is furious with Ford. Is this all part of Hemingway's plan?

Soon he is undermining Ford's authority with almost systematic rigour. The moment Ford leaves for America to rustle up funds for his ailing magazine, Hemingway changes the July and August issues. He prints an attack on Ford's beloved Dadaists, as well as writing an unsigned editorial against three of Ford's favourite authors: Jean Cocteau, Tristan Tzara and Gilbert Seldes. He also drops the scheduled serialisation of Ford's own novel, replacing it with terrible poems already rejected by Ford.†

Ford is a very forgiving man, so doesn't sack him. Hemingway regards such magnanimity as a sign of weakness. When his old friend and collaborator Joseph Conrad dies on August 3rd, Ford persuades Hemingway to contribute to a special memorial issue. Hemingway writes in it that he could never reread Conrad, and is even ruder about another friend of Ford: 'if I knew that by grinding T.S. Eliot into a fine dry powder and sprinkling that powder on Mr Conrad's grave Mr Conrad would shortly appear ... I would leave for London early tomorrow morning with a sausage grinder'. Ford apologises to Eliot for this insult; his apology further annoys Hemingway.

'Oh, here you are. May I sit with you?'

This is the beginning of Hemingway's description of having a drink with Ford, written thirty-five years later, when Ford is safely dead. He describes him as resembling an 'up-ended hogshead' with a 'heavy, stained mustache'. He is a 'heavy, wheezing, ignoble presence'.§

---

* Though she too counts the cost. When she later writes that Scott Fitzgerald 'will be read when many of his well-known contemporaries are forgotten', and that Hemingway is the creation of herself and Sherwood Anderson, and that they are 'both a little proud and a little ashamed of the work of their minds', Hemingway sends her a copy of *Death in the Afternoon* inscribed, 'A Bitch is a Bitch is a Bitch is a Bitch. From her pal Ernest Hemingway.'

† They are written in pidgin English by Elsa von Freytag von Loringhoven, a German poetess who wears an inverted coal scuttle on her head and ice-cream spoons for earrings.

§ Others share Hemingway's distaste for Ford's physique. Rebecca West describes being embraced by him as like 'being the toast under the poached egg'.

And smelly, too: 'I had always avoided looking at Ford when I could and I always held my breath when I was near him in a closed room, but this was the open air … I took a drink to see if his coming had fouled it, but it still tasted good.'

According to Hemingway, during their drink together Ford sees Hilaire Belloc passing, and cuts him dead. Hemingway gets on his high horse: 'The afternoon had been spoiled by seeing Ford but I thought Belloc might have made it better.'

As Hemingway relates it, Ford insists that 'A gentleman will always cut a cad,' then starts telling him which of their acquaintances is a gentleman, and which is not: Ezra Pound is not ('he's an American'), Ford himself is ('naturally – I have held His Majesty's commission'), Henry James was 'very nearly', Trollope was not ('of course not'), nor was Marlowe, and Donne was clearly not ('he was a parson'). Thus, Hemingway sets out to portray Ford as a ludicrous snob.

But did this particular meeting take place in the way described? Friends of both men doubt it. Basil Bunting, who worked on the magazine, suggests Hemingway's sketch of Ford is 'deliberately assembled to damage the reputation of a dead man who had left no skilled close friend to take vengeance; a lie cunningly adjusted to seem plausible to simple people who had never known either Ford or Hemingway and to load his memory with qualities disgusting to all men and despicable to many'. Ford's loyal biographer, Alan Judd, sees it as an act of revenge against Ford for being Hemingway's 'superior in age, status, experience, knowledge of his craft, sensitivity and ability'.

When he first employs Hemingway, Ford seems to have an intimation that his protégé is set to betray him. 'He comes and sits at my feet and praises me,' he confides. 'It makes me nervous.' But why does Hemingway feel such antagonism towards a man who treats him so generously? Might it date back to the time Hemingway asked Ford for his truthful opinion of his novels? Ford replied that, for all their undoubted virtues, they were weak on construction, and that this was something he should work on. Is this honesty his unforgivable mistake?

FORD MADOX FORD

EITHER HELPS, OR FAILS TO HELP

OSCAR WILDE

Montmartre, Paris
November 1899

In 1944, the twenty-five-year-old J.D. Salinger meets the fifty-year-old Ernest Hemingway in Paris; in 1924, the twenty-five-year-old Hemingway meets the fifty-year-old Ford Madox Ford in Paris. Leap a further quarter of a century back, and the twenty-five-year-old Ford Madox Ford is meeting the forty-five-year-old Oscar Wilde, also in Paris. Each encounter carries peculiar echoes of the others.

Ruined and almost penniless, Wilde is drinking alone in a cabaret bar in Montmartre. He is presently living as a guest of the patron in the Hôtel d'Alsace, having been kicked out of the Hôtel Marsollier for not paying his bills. He can no longer find a reason to live. 'I have lost the mainspring of life and art, *la joie de vivre*; it is dreadful,' he writes to Frank Harris, in one of many begging letters. 'I have pleasures, and passions, but the joy of life is gone. I am going under: the morgue yawns for me.' He means to write something wonderful, but he doubts he ever will.* 'The cruelty of a prison sentence starts when you come out,' he observes.

He never rises before noon, and drinks throughout his waking hours, first advocaat, then brandy, and finally absinthe, which, he writes to a friend, 'has a wonderful colour, green. A glass of absinthe is as poetical as anything in the world. What difference is there between a glass of absinthe and a sunset?' To another friend, he says, 'I have discovered that alcohol taken in sufficient quantity produces all the effects of drunkenness.' There is still humour in him, though it sometimes comes close to drowning.

---

* John Fothergill, part of Wilde's circle in his youth, later a famously irritable innkeeper, recalls: 'Oscar Wilde once told me that when he went to heaven, Peter would meet him at the gate with a pile of richly bound books saying, "These, Mr Wilde, are your unwritten books."'

He is often to be seen drinking in the boulevards. His front teeth have fallen out, and he has no plate with which to replace them. 'Like dear St Francis of Assisi I am wedded to poverty, but in my case the marriage is not a success. I hate the bride that has been given to me.'

The writer Frédéric Boutet remembers coming across him sitting outside a café on the boulevard Saint-Germain. The pouring rain has turned his straw hat into a candle-snuffer and his coat into a sponge. The waiter, desperate to get rid of this last customer, has piled up all the chairs and wound up the awning, but Wilde is unable to leave because he has run out of money to settle his bill.

There are countless stories of old friends crossing the street to avoid him. But one night, the palmist Cheiro spots him in a restaurant and goes over to him. 'How good of you, my dear friend,' says Wilde. 'Everyone cuts me now.' They have met only once before, at a society party back in 1893; Cheiro had been performing blind readings of guests' palms.

'The left hand is the hand of a king, but the right that of a king who will send himself into exile,' he told Wilde.

'At what date?' asked Wilde.

'A few years from now, at about your fortieth year.' Wilde, ever superstitious, left the party without another word. Six years on, Wilde tells Cheiro that he has often reflected on the truth of his remarkable prediction.

Ford writes two wildly differing accounts of his youthful meeting with Wilde in Paris, one in 1911, the other in 1931. In the first, he portrays him as a tragic figure, sitting at a table at a cabaret, 'lachrymosely drunk, and being tormented by an abominable gang of young students of the four arts'. Though impoverished, Wilde has managed to keep an ivory walking stick from his days of prosperity. Prowling about the club is a man Ford describes as 'a harmless, parasitic imbecile' called Bibi Labouche. The students convince the sozzled Wilde that Labouche is in fact a dangerous criminal who is planning to murder him for his walking stick while he is on his way back to his hotel.

In this version, Wilde cries and protests; Ford is so disgusted by the casual cruelty of the scene that he leaves the café at once, 'permanently cured of any taste for Bohemianism that I may ever have possessed. Indeed, I have never since been able to see a student ... without a feeling of aversion.' He adds, by way of an afterthought, 'I do not know that I acted any heroic part in the matter.'

But in his second version, written twenty years after the first, Ford has expanded his own role, injecting it with heroism. In this one, he encounters Oscar Wilde not once but 'several times' in Paris, and each time Wilde is the butt of these merciless students, their pranks still centring around his walking stick, which is now not only 'of ebony with ivory insertions, the handle representing an elephant', but a gift from Lady Mount Temple.

In this version, the tearful Wilde continually surrenders his stick to the students, who keep returning it to his hotel the next morning, by which time he has forgotten everything that happened the night before. Instead of simply skulking off in a fury, Ford rushes to Wilde's aid. 'I once or perhaps twice rescued his stick for him and saw him home ... He did not have a penny and I, as a student, had very little more. I would walk him down the miserably lit Montmartrois streets, he completely silent or muttering things that I did not understand. He walked always as if his feet hurt him, leaning forward on his precious cane ...'

The accounts are linked by Ford's visceral dislike of Wilde. In 1911, it is confined to Wilde's writing: 'His works seemed to me derivative and of no importance, his humour thin and mechanical.' But by 1931, Ford has extended it to the man: 'It was humiliating to dislike so much one so unfortunate. But the feeling of dislike for that shabby and incoherent immensity was unavoidable.' In his elaboration of the revulsion youth feels towards age, is Ford Madox Ford rehearsing his own imminent destruction at the hands of Ernest Hemingway?

OSCAR WILDE

LOSES HIS NERVE WITH

MARCEL PROUST

9, boulevard Malesherbes, Paris
November 1891

When the much-fêted Oscar Wilde arrives in Paris, he is preceded by his reputation as a wit and dandy.* Now aged thirty-seven, he has come for two months to brush up his first play, *Salome*, which he is writing in French. 'French by sympathy, I am Irish by race, and the English have condemned me to speak the language of Shakespeare,' he complains to Edmond de Goncourt. He speaks the language fluently, with a prodigious vocabulary, though he makes no attempt at an accent.

He makes his mark straight away, aphorisms spraying from his blubbery lips in all the most fashionable salons. Everyone is held spellbound. At one lunch party, guests weep to think words can achieve such splendour. 'I have put all my talent into my works,' he announces. 'I have put all my genius into my life.'

He is adept at conquering all conversational obstacles, brushing aside contradiction as pedantry. When he tells a dinner party about Salome, and a professor points out that he is confusing two Salomes – one the daughter of Herod, the other the dancer – Wilde retorts that this is the drab truth of an academic: 'I prefer the other truth, my own, which is that of a dream. Between the two truths, the falser is the truer.'

L'Echo de Paris describes Wilde's arrival in the city as '*le "great event" des salons littéraires parisiennes*' of the season. His principal guide is a young literary lion called Marcel Schwob, who also translates his story 'The Selfish Giant'. After Wilde's departure, Schwob describes him as 'A big man, with a large pasty face, red cheeks, an ironic eye, bad and protrusive teeth, a vicious childlike mouth with lips soft with milk ready to suck

---

* Though he has gained his reputation as much through his children's stories and his poems: his major plays are yet to be written, and *The Picture of Dorian Gray*, which was the talk of London last year, has yet to be published in France.

some more. While he ate – and he ate little – he never stopped smoking opium-tainted Egyptian cigarettes. A terrible absinthe-drinker, through which he got his visions and desires.'

Schwob often entertains Wilde at his apartment. Léon Daudet, who meets him there, finds him both attractive and revolting, words tumbling out of his slack mouth 'like a fat, gossipy woman'. Sensing this ambivalence, at their third meeting Wilde asks Daudet what he thinks of him: Daudet hedges with a few words about his complexity, and his possible guile. The next day, he receives a letter from Wilde, insisting he is 'the simplest and most candid of mortals, just like a tiny, tiny child'.

A glimpse of Wilde's manner of speaking is offered by Ernest Raynaud, who bumps into him on a sunny day in the boulevard des Capucines: 'We must let our instincts laugh and frolic in the sun like a troop of laughing children. I love life. It is so beautiful and –' at this point, Wilde surveys his surroundings, lit by the sun '– How all this outdoes the languishing beauty of the countryside! The solitude of the country stifles and crushes me … I am not really myself except in the midst of elegant crowds, in the exploits of capitals, at the heart of rich districts or amid the sumptuous ornamentation of palace-hotels, seated by all the desirable objects and with an army of servants, the warm caress of a plush carpet under my feet … I detest nature where man has not intervened with his artifice! When Benvenuto Cellini crucified a living man to study the play of muscles in his death agony, a pope was right to grant him absolution. What is the death of a vague individual if it enables an immortal world to blossom and to create, in Keats's words, an eternal source of ecstasy?'

But, just occasionally, language fails him.

Wilde is first introduced to the twenty-year-old Marcel Proust at the home of Madame Arthur Baignères on rue du Général Foy. He is impressed by Proust's extraordinary knowledge of English literature, and when Proust asks him to dinner at his home in boulevard Malesherbes he immediately accepts.

On the evening in question, Proust is delayed, so arrives puffing and panting, several minutes late. 'Is the English gentleman here?' he asks his servant.

'Yes, sir, he arrived five minutes ago. He had barely entered the drawing room when he asked for the bathroom, and he has not come out of it.'

Proust runs to the end of the passage, and shouts through the door of the bathroom, 'Monsieur Wilde, are you ill?' Wilde unlocks the door and peers out. 'Ah, there you are, Monsieur Proust. No, I am not in the least ill.'

It emerges that he has suffered an unprecedented attack of shyness, and is now overcome by embarrassment. 'I thought I was to have the pleasure of dining with you alone, but they showed me into the drawing room. I looked at the drawing room and at the end of it were your parents. My courage failed me. Goodbye, dear Monsieur Proust, goodbye …'

With that, he departs in a flurry. Baffled, Proust goes into the drawing room and greets his parents, who inform him that Wilde burst into the room, took one look at the interior decoration, exclaimed, 'How ugly your house is!' and rushed out.*

It is an odd sequence of events, somehow out of character. Wilde may be bombastic, but he is seldom rude, and his retreat into the bathroom seems additionally strange.

Could this be the most likely explanation? On first entering the drawing room, Wilde fails to notice anybody else. He exclaims, 'How ugly your house is!' out loud, but to himself; only then does he catch sight of Proust's parents, sitting quietly in the corner. Horribly embarrassed, he rushes out of the room, and can then think of no way of returning with his dignity intact.

Wilde returns to Paris in the summer of 1894, the year before his downfall, and again encounters Marcel Proust. Might it be some subliminal imprint of his past mistake that makes him come out with another rude remark† about Proust's furnishings? 'I don't think Mr Wilde has been well brought-up,' comments Monsieur Proust as soon as he has departed.§

---

* Proust puts these same words into the mouth of Baron Charlus in *La Prisonnière*. Charlus speaks them, we are told, 'with a mixture of insolence, wit and world-weariness'.

† Alas, unrecorded.

§ Proust does not like Wilde – in a letter to Cocteau in 1919, he even goes so far as to say 'I detest Wilde' – but he maintains some sympathy for him after his downfall, chiding André Gide for his lack of charity towards him. 'You were very patronising towards Wilde. I don't much admire him. But I don't understand reticence and harsh words towards a person who is down on his luck.' In *Sodome et Gomorrhe*, he writes of the instability of the homosexual life: 'Their honour precarious, their liberty provisional, their position unstable, like the poet once fêted in all the drawing rooms, and applauded in every theatre in London, and the next day driven out of every lodging house, unable to find a pillow on which to lay his head.'

MARCEL PROUST

GETS RID OF

JAMES JOYCE

Hôtel Majestic, avenue Kléber, Paris
May 19th 1922

Marcel Proust, once so social, is nowadays very picky about going out, preferring to stay in his bedroom. He has developed a particular distaste for exclusive, intimate parties. 'Nothing amuses me less than what was called, twenty years ago, "select", he observes.

The British art patrons Sydney and Violet Schiff are obliged to employ stealth to attract him to the dinner party of their dreams, which they are holding in a private room at the Hôtel Majestic, in celebration of Diaghilev's Ballets Russes.

For some time, they have been plotting to gather the four men they consider the world's greatest living artists – Igor Stravinsky, Pablo Picasso, James Joyce and Marcel Proust – together in the same room. Proust is perhaps their greatest catch, being both the most lionised and the most elusive; since the publication of *Sodome et Gomorrhe* the week before last, he has been the talk of the town. Knowing his aversion to select gatherings, Sydney Schiff does not send him a formal invitation, but craftily slips a reference to it into a letter a few days before: might he perhaps drop by after dinner?

Picasso and Stravinsky arrive in good time. The less dependable James Joyce arrives after coffee, drunk and shabby, swaying from side to side. 'I cannot enter the social order except as a vagabond,' he admits. He sits to the right of his host, places his head in his hands, and says nothing.

Their fellow guest Clive Bell remembers the entry at 2.30 a.m. of 'a small, dapper figure clad in exquisite black with white kid gloves ... looking for all the world as though he had seen a light in a friend's window and had just come up on the chance of finding him awake. Physically he did not please me, being altogether too sleek and dank and plastered: his eyes were glorious however.' This otherwise elegant entrance of Marcel Proust gets off to a bad start when another guest, Princesse Violette Murat, looks daggers at him and flounces out of the party, furious at being depicted as a skinflint in his recent volume.

Proust, flustered by this rebuff, is placed between Igor Stravinsky and Sydney Schiff. Stravinsky notes he is 'as pale as a mid-afternoon moon'. Proust tries to pay Stravinsky a compliment by comparing him to Beethoven.

'Doubtless you admire Beethoven,' he adds.

'I detest Beethoven.'

'But, *cher maître*, surely those late sonatas and quartets ...?'

'Worse than the others.'

Around this time, James Joyce emits a loud snore ('I *hope* it was a snore,' adds Bell), then wakes with a jolt. Proust – looking ten years younger than he is, or so Joyce thinks – introduces himself.* The two are widely regarded as rivals; their works are often compared, generally to Joyce's disadvantage.

Encounters at parties are subject to the vagaries of memory, and further obscured by layers of gossip and hearsay and inaudibility, the whole mix invariably transformed even more by alcohol. So it is unsurprising that the Proust/Joyce exchange should be related in at least seven different ways:

1) As told by Joyce's friend Arthur Power:
PROUST: Do you like truffles?
JOYCE: Yes, I do.

2) As told by the Duchesse de Clermont-Tonnerre:
PROUST: I have never read your works, Mr Joyce.
JOYCE: I have never read your works, Mr Proust.†

---

* Proust's handshake lacks vigour. 'There are many ways of shaking hands. It is not too much to say that it is an art. He was not good at it. His hand was soft and drooping ... There was nothing pleasant about the way he performed the action,' writes his friend Prince Antoine Bibesco.

Joyce's right hand is another matter. When a young man comes up to him in Zürich and says, 'May I kiss the hand that wrote *Ulysses*?' Joyce replies, 'No – it did a lot of other things too.'

† Some maintain this dialogue cannot be accurate, as Joyce tells a friend in 1920 that he has read 'some pages' of Proust, adding, 'I cannot see any special merit but I am a bad critic.' But Joyce can be perverse like this: on meeting Wyndham Lewis, he pretends not to have read his work, though he definitely has.

3) As told by James Joyce many years later to Jacques Mercanton:
'Proust would talk only of duchesses, while I was more concerned with their chambermaids.'

4) As told by James Joyce to his close friend Frank Budgen:
'Our talk consisted solely of the word "No". Proust asked me if I knew the duc de so-and-so. I said, "No." Our hostess asked Proust if he had read such and such a piece of *Ulysses*. Proust said, "No." And so on. Of course the situation was impossible. Proust's day was just beginning. Mine was at an end.'

5) According to another friend of Joyce, Padraic Clum, Joyce wants to undermine the Schiffs' hopes for a legendary occasion, so tries to stay as silent as possible:
PROUST: Ah, Monsieur Joyce, you know the Princess …
JOYCE: No, Monsieur.
PROUST: Ah, you know the Countess …
JOYCE: No, Monsieur.
PROUST: Then you know Madame …
JOYCE: No, Monsieur.
However, in this version, Joyce clearly wrong-foots himself, as his silence becomes part of the legend.

6) As told by William Carlos Williams:
JOYCE: I've had headaches every day. My eyes are terrible.
PROUST: My poor stomach. What am I going to do? It's killing me. In fact, I must leave at once.
JOYCE: I'm in the same situation. If I can find someone to take me by the arm. Goodbye!
PROUST: *Charmé.* Oh, my stomach.

7) As told by Ford Madox Ford:
PROUST: As I say, Monsieur, in *Du Côté de chez Swann*, which without doubt you have –
JOYCE: No, Monsieur.
(PAUSE)

JOYCE: As Mr Bloom says in my *Ulysses*, which, Monsieur, you
    have doubtless read …
PROUST: But, no, Monsieur.
(PAUSE)
Proust apologises for his late arrival, ascribing it to malady, before
going into the symptoms in some detail.
JOYCE: Well, Monsieur, I have almost exactly the same symptoms.
    Only in my case, the analysis …

And from then on, for a number of hours, the two men discuss their various illnesses.

According to Schiff, who has a leaning towards accuracy, the party ends with Proust inviting the Schiffs back to his apartment, and with Joyce squeezing into the taxi too. Joyce then starts smoking, and opens the window, causing upset to Proust, an asthmatic who hates fresh air. In the brief journey, Proust talks incessantly, but addresses none of his remarks to Joyce.

When the four of them alight in rue Hamelin, Joyce tries to join the others in Proust's apartment, but they do their best to divert him. 'Let my taxi take you home,' insists Proust, before disappearing upstairs with Violet Schiff, leaving Sydney Schiff to bundle Joyce back into the taxi. Free of Joyce's company at last, Proust and the Schiffs drink champagne and talk merrily until daybreak.

JAMES JOYCE

FINDS LITTLE TO SAY TO

HAROLD NICOLSON

31 Hyde Park Gardens, London W2
July 30th 1931

A small group of guests has gathered in the drawing room of the Chairman of Putnam, the publishers, ready for a lunch in honour of James Joyce. The air is heavy with Madonna lilies, their scent intensifying an already nervy and oppressive atmosphere.

The Chairman's wife, Gladys Huntington, is perhaps the most agitated of all. Any lunch is made all the more daunting for a hostess if her chief guest has an almost militant devotion to silence. Though the characters in Joyce's novels are known for talking – internally, externally, both at the same time, for pages on end – the author himself is more likely to translate his thoughts into long sighs. Joyce is seldom prepared to break his silence unless a topic really interests him: at his meeting with Le Corbusier, he only really got going when the architect asked after his parakeets, Pierre and Pepi.

Those sitting in the drawing room upstairs – the Chairman, Constant Huntington; his wife Gladys; Lady Gosford, a former Lady of the Bedchamber to Queen Alexandra; the critic Desmond MacCarthy; and the author and diarist Harold Nicolson, who has recently joined Oswald Mosley's New Party – are making polite conversation when they hear a sound on the staircase. They rise apprehensively.

In walks Nora Barnacle, who married Joyce at the beginning of this month, having been with him, on and off, for twenty-seven years. (Up until then, their twenty-three-year-old daughter had assumed they were already married.) Nora is, observes Nicolson, 'a young-looking woman with the remains of beauty and an Irish accent so marked that she might have been a Belgian. Well dressed in the clothes of a young French bourgeoise.' He also notices that she is wearing an art nouveau brooch.

She is followed by James Joyce himself, 'aloof and blind'. Harold Nicolson, the most beady-eyed of diarists, offers his first impression of Joyce as 'a slightly bearded spinster'. He wears huge concave spectacles which flick reflections of light onto the walls as he moves his head. Threatened by glaucoma, Joyce is to undergo eleven operations on his eyes in his lifetime, and sometimes wears an eyepatch, which causes his eyes to have, according to one friend, 'the same paleness seen in plants long hidden from the sun'. Nicolson thinks of him as 'some thin little bird, peeking, crooked, reserved, violent and timid. Little claw hands. So blind that he stares away from one at a tangent, like a very thin owl.'

The party troops downstairs to the dining room while Gladys Huntington talks to Joyce nervously, in a very shrill voice, on the subject of the late Italo Svevo, the author of *Confessions of Zeno*, whom Joyce once taught. A tremor goes around the group as Lady Huntington suddenly bursts into Italian. At the table, Harold Nicolson is placed next to Lady Gosford. Their conversation is on the dull side – Eton College, and whether boys under twenty should be allowed to go flying – but Nicolson keeps his left ear tuned in to the neighbouring conversation between Huntington and Joyce. Joyce is apparently already contradicting his hostess pretty sharply, and with a sort of bored indifference. Nevertheless, Nicolson notes that he has a very beautiful voice. 'The most lovely voice I know,' he notes at a later date, '– liquid and soft with undercurrents of gurgle.'

The two conversations peter out at about the same time, at which point Desmond MacCarthy starts talking about last month's murder of a lieutenant in the British Army. Hubert Chevis ate a poisoned partridge and died; soon afterwards, his father, Sir William Chevis, was sent an anonymous telegram saying simply, 'Hooray Hooray Hooray.'* Nicolson and MacCarthy join in an animated discussion of the case with great verve and enthusiasm. Nicolson politely tries to draw Joyce in. 'Are you interested in murders?' he asks.

'Not in the very least,' he replies, flattening his hands towards the ground, with, in Nicolson's view, the gesture of 'a governess shutting the piano'. Joyce says no more; he has never been nervous of silence, and takes

---

* The murder is never solved.

great pride in any silence he himself has created. He likes to punctuate his silences with sighs; Nora has warned him time and again that he could destroy his heart with his excessive sighing.

Nicolson and MacCarthy swiftly try to change the subject. MacCarthy starts talking of Sir Richard Burton, mentioning that Burton was once the consul in Trieste, where Joyce lived for some time. Later, Nicolson thinks that he may have noticed this topic sending 'a pallid but very fleeting light of interest across the pinched features of Joyce'.

'Are you interested in Burton?' asks MacCarthy.

'Not,' replies Joyce, 'in the very least.'

Again, they speedily switch the subject. Nicolson says that he has been allowed to mention Joyce's novel *Ulysses* in his wireless talks. At last, Joyce perks up. 'What talks?'

Nicolson tells him. Joyce says he will send him a book about *Ulysses* – he pronounces it 'Oolissays' – for him to read and quote. Now that he is safely on the subject of himself, he is full of enthusiasm. 'He is not a rude man,' concludes Nicolson. 'He manages to hide his dislike of the English in general and of the literary English in particular. But he is a difficult man to talk to.' And also to read: eight years later, Nicolson is faced with the prospect of having to review *Finnegans Wake*. 'I try very hard indeed to understand that book but fail completely. It is almost impossible to decipher, and when one or two lines of understanding emerge like telegraph poles above a flood, they are at once countered by other poles going in the opposite direction ... I truly believe that Joyce has this time gone too far in breaking all communication between himself and his reader. It is a very selfish book,' he concludes.

As their awkward luncheon at the Huntingtons' comes to an end, Desmond MacCarthy makes this observation to Harold Nicolson. 'Joyce,' he says, 'is not a very *convenient* guest at luncheon.'

HAROLD NICOLSON

IS DIARISED BY

CECIL BEATON

Sissinghurst Castle, Cranbrook, Kent
August 1967

'Your purple border is wonderful,' says one diarist to the other. 'Congratulations.'

The relationship between the fashionable photographer and designer Cecil Beaton and Harold Nicolson is edgy, though whenever they meet they are impeccably polite. It is, in its way, a clash of diarists. Both keep diaries with a view to publication, so that when they are together in the same room they inevitably feel a sense of competition. Who will have the last word?

Nicolson, eighteen years Beaton's senior, refuses to take Beaton seriously, either as a person or as an artist. He has always had a stern, puritanical side to him, and disapproves of Beaton's natural flamboyance, his addiction to glamour. He pigeonholes him in the jet-set, a modish group for whom he maintains a natural aversion. In the opinion of his friend James Lees-Milne, 'Harold loathed what he considered spurious people. He was inclined to be critical of actors, stage producers, scene designers, no matter how talented they might be, because he associated them with the meretricious.'

When the first of Harold Nicolson's three volumes of diaries is published in 1966, three decades after being written, Beaton records in his own diary that he has been reading them with 'enormous pleasure. I can really hardly fault the book –' But he then adds a testy, almost rabid cavil: '– although I have been on the lookout to do so on every page, for I have never liked Harold Nicolson, have always mistrusted him, considered him a phoney. I don't know whether I've resented his "getting away" with *so* much, being a fairly successful politician, at any rate respected by Churchill, Eden and group, a worthy critic, a figure in contemporary literature, a personality in the glittering world, a father, a loving husband, a gardener, and all the time a man with a most greedy lust for young men.'

Beaton is passionate in his denunciation, not of the diaries, which he so keenly enjoys, but of the diarist, who repels him. He disapproves of the essential contradiction at the heart of Harold Nicolson: so straight in his diaries, yet so unbuttoned in real life. 'Perhaps it is more the greed than the lust that irritates me. Perhaps it is just that I dislike his obvious lusting. Although furtive of eye, no one shows his feelings more nakedly than Harold. He digs into a second helping of suet pudding, his double chins pucker. As he looks at a hefty schooboy bicycling by, Harold's fly buttons pop through the air like rockets. Physically he is repellent to me, the pig features in a fat bladder, the awful remains of schoolboyishness, the pink cheeks, the crinkly hair, the offensive pipe … Yet here is a book full of very frank self-revelations. He comes out of it with enormous charm, a man of great perceptiveness, fairness and sincerity, altogether admirable.'

Nine months later, Beaton reads the just-published second volume of the diaries. 'Again I wonder why it has been that, in spite of being told again and again by his friends, James P[ope]-H[ennessy] and others what a fine fellow he is, I've never liked the man.'

Once more, he is struck by the contradiction between the real-life hedonist and the 'unvulgar, noble-minded' voice in the diaries. But there is something more visceral in his distaste: 'When scrutinising the photographs I again see that I am as put off by his physical appearance as I was in life. How unfair this is, especially as he is the first to denigrate himself in all respects. But the Cupid doll mouth, the paradoxical moustache, the corpulence of hands and stomach all give me a *frissant* [sic] and there is no getting over the fact that I could never become a friend of his.'

Cecil Beaton has long been transfixed by the horrors that come with age. His diaries are full of grim descriptions of lines and sags: the furriness of Greta Garbo's skin, the 'fat, coarse hands' of Elizabeth Taylor, the Queen Mother 'fatter than ever, but yet wrinkled'. He is equally horrified by his own decrepitude: 'The mouth is a slit, the head on top baldly bullet-like, and the wild hair sticking cockatoo fashion out above the ears is that of King Lear.'

Three months after reading the second volume of Nicolson's diaries, Beaton visits Nicolson's gardens at Sissinghurst, which are open to the public. Having gloried in this 'triumph of horticultural knowledge and imagination', he spots Nicolson sitting in the sun outside his home, now eighty years old, and a widower. He has suffered a stroke and is in decline: he no longer reads or writes, and has virtually stopped speaking. He is indifferent to the acclaim that has greeted the publication of his diaries; how odd, he remarks to his son Nigel, to publish three books one does not realise one has written. On summer evenings, Nicholson sits beneath a bundle of coats by his cottage door, 'like a venerable buddha gazing into space', according to his biographer.

Beaton walks over to what he calls 'the remains of Harold N'. After his stroke, 'he is really just a clockwork dummy'. He sees him smile. 'His eyes are bright, but he is clothed in the anonymous vestments of old age, scraggy white moustache, bald white hair, pendulous stomach. But his brain does not work any more, just vague automatic answers in reply to something he doesn't understand,' Beaton will jot down in his diary on his return home.

'Your purple border is wonderful,' he tells Nicolson. 'Congratulations.'

This too he will jot down.

'I haven't been out much lately. I haven't seen it,' replies Nicolson. To other questions, he responds with 'a good-humoured low benevolent growl'.

Beaton bids farewell to his fellow diarist. 'He seems contented in his animal state of relaxation and inactivity, which could presumably continue for another fifteen years,' he concludes. As it happens, Harold Nicolson dies nine months later, while undressing for bed, thus handing the last word to Cecil Beaton.

CECIL BEATON

IS OFFERED LSD BY

MICK JAGGER

La Mamounia Hotel, Marrakesh
Early March 1967

Cecil Beaton is exhausted. 'I feel stiff and terribly old ... with aching eyes, neck and back ... I face up to the horrible realities. My body is misformed, my head a mess, my brain a morass.'

He has come to Marrakesh to recuperate. He was tempted to stay with the fashionable art dealer Robert Fraser, as he knows his fellow house-guests would include Mick Jagger ('At last an opportunity to photograph one of the most elusive people, whom I admire and am fascinated by, not determined whether he is beautiful or hideous'). But he is feeling anti-social, so he checks into the Mamounia Hotel.

It offers him no respite from his weary introspection. 'Extremely displeased with myself' and 'hating all that I saw of myself in the nude', he spends four days alone, but one evening when he goes down to dinner he is buoyed* to discover 'sitting in the hall ... Mick Jagger and a sleepy-looking band of gypsies'. Robert Fraser, who is coughing by the swimming pool ('he had swallowed something the wrong way'), invites him to join them for the evening.

Mick Jagger and Keith Richards have come to Marrakesh to escape the furore surrounding their forthcoming drugs trial, and are using the opportunity to consume more drugs. The local hash is a particular favour-ite. 'I heard that a way of collecting it was to cover children in honey and run them naked through a field of herbs, and they came out the other end and they scraped 'em off,' Keith recalls.

Beaton has eyes only for Jagger, though he does his best to conceal it. 'His skin is chicken breast white, and of a fine quality. He has enormous inborn elegance.' Over drinks, Jagger rambles on about how England is a

---

* Cyril Connolly nicknames him Rip Van With-It.

police state; he plans to sue the *News of the World* for saying he has depraved the youth of the country.

Off to a restaurant, they jump into a Bentley filled with Pop Art cushions, scarlet fur rugs, pornography and 'the most deafening volume of pop music'. Mick and Brian Jones start jigging around, while Anita Pallenberg fills Beaton in on her role in a new film:* she plays a woman who shoots her boyfriend dead after he tries to beat her up. Coincidentally, Brian has recently been beating her up, suspecting her – rightly, as it happens – of conducting an affair with Keith.

Over dinner, Beaton finds Jagger 'very gentle, with perfect manners'. A black woman starts singing. 'What marvellous authority she has,' says Mick, who takes to the dance floor. Beaton is 'fascinated with the thin concave lines of his body, legs, arms. Mouth almost too large, but he is beautiful and ugly, feminine and masculine, a "sport", a rare phenomenon.'

As the evening unwinds, their conversation blossoms. 'Have you ever taken LSD?' asks Mick. He thinks Cecil should: being a painter, he would never forget the colours; one's brain works on 4,000 cylinders, not just four. 'You saw everything glow. The colours of his red velvet trousers, the black shiny satin, the maroon scarf. You saw yourself beautiful and ugly, and saw other people as if for the first time.' Jagger insists it has no bad effects. 'It's only people who hate themselves who suffer.'

He offers Beaton a pill. 'They can't stamp it out. It's like the atom bomb. Once it's been discovered, it can never be forgotten.' He adds that he doesn't take LSD often, just when he is with people he likes.

They walk through the decorated midnight souks in the old town. Beaton is struck by how Jagger appreciates everything: the archways, the mysterious alleyways. They bundle back into their cars. The chauffeur is drunk, and drives on the wrong side of the road. Beaton worries that they won't get home safely, but they do. At 3 a.m. he goes to bed, while the Rolling Stones and their entourage hang about. 'Where do we go now?' 'To a nightclub.' 'It's closed.' 'Well, let's go somewhere and have a drink.'

While Beaton is sound asleep, the Stones retreat to the tenth floor to take LSD. Trays of food are brought up; they use them as toboggans. Brian

---

* *Mord und Totschlag* (A Degree of Murder), directed by Volker Schlöndorff.

and Anita start fighting, and Anita locks herself in their bedroom. Brian goes into town, returns with two prostitutes, and tries to force Anita to have sex with them. When she refuses, he beats her up and flings food at her. Anita takes refuge in Keith's room. Keith says, 'I can't take this shit any more. I can't listen to you getting beaten up and fighting and all this crap. Let's get the hell out of here.'

The next morning, Beaton is up bright and breezy, unaware of all this unpleasantness. At 11 a.m., Jagger appears. Beaton notes that the bright Moroccan sunshine does not suit him: the light makes his face 'a white, podgy, shapeless mess, eyes very small, nose very pink and spreading, hair sandy dark ... like a self-conscious suburban young lady. All morning he looked awful.'

Jagger agrees to pose for photographs. Beaton takes him to a shady spot, and finds him transformed: 'A Tarzan of Piero di Cosimo. Lips of a fantastic roundness, body white and almost hairless. He is sexy, yet completely sexless. He could nearly be a eunuch.'

Gradually, the others appear. Beaton notes their 'marvellously flat, tight, compact figures', but fails to detect the underlying tension. Out of his hearing, Jagger says, 'It's getting fucking heavy,' and leaves for London. Beaton is left alone with the rest of the group. Conversation around the pool is conducted largely in grunts. Beaton examines their wardrobe, and finds it wanting. 'Keith himself had sewn his trousers, lavender, dull rose, with a band of badly stitched leather dividing the two colours.'*

Late for lunch, they get into a row with the elderly waiter, who retorts, 'You're a lot of pigs.' For Beaton, the Rolling Stones lack glamour without Jagger. 'Gosh, they are a messy group ... One can only wonder as to their future.'

---

* Reading Beaton's published diary of their time in Morocco, Keith notes: 'I used to spend hours stitching old pants together to give them a different look. I'd get four pairs of sailor pants, I'd cut them off at the knee, get a band of leather and then put another colour from the other pants and stitch them in. Lavender and dull rose, as Cecil Beaton says. I didn't realize he was keeping an eye on that shit.'

MICK JAGGER

TALKS POLITICS WITH

TOM DRIBERG

Harley House, Marylebone, London NW1
Spring 1967

Mick Jagger is wearing a jerkin and tights when the Labour MP Tom Driberg drops round to his flat accompanied by their mutual friend, the poet Allen Ginsberg.

Ginsberg has arranged the meeting; Jagger is interested in politics, while Driberg is interested in youth. Two years ago, after a magistrate described the Rolling Stones as 'complete morons who wear their hair down to the shoulders and wear filthy clothes', Driberg introduced a motion deploring 'the action of a Glasgow magistrate ... in using his privileged position to make irrelevant, snobbish and insulting personal comments on the appearance and performance of a "pop" group, the Rolling Stones, who are making a substantial contribution to public entertainment and the export drive'.

Driberg is on a mission to persuade Jagger to enter politics. Since he was busted for drugs in Keith Richard's house in Wittering, Jagger has been issuing semi-political pronouncements such as, 'Teenagers the world over are being pushed around by half-witted politicians who attempt to dominate their way of thinking and set a code for their living.' Jagger's girlfriend Marianne Faithfull thinks that, though he is not particularly interested in politics ('certainly not left-wing politics'), if anyone can persuade him to become a politician it is Driberg, who she describes as 'utterly charming and beautifully dressed. Such a perfect model for Mick, too, because he had a lot of money. He had a country house, he was homosexual, and he was a Labour MP. A real socialist of the old school, with ideals and all that. All these apparently contradictory things in one person ... a shining example.'

The four of them – Driberg and Ginsberg, Jagger and Faithfull – sit on cushions discussing art and politics. Ginsberg unveils an idea for turning

William Blake's poems into rock lyrics. They talk of drugs, and of the Establishment's suppression of youthful rebellion.

'Why don't you try politics, Mick?' suggests Driberg. Jagger asks him where a man with his anarchistic feelings would fit in. 'The Labour Party, of course,' replies Driberg. 'Labour is the only hope.'

Britain is on the brink of revolution, he adds. 'I know that's the view of some of the Trotskyites, that it is all breaking up and loosening up. And the Labour Party is where a young man should be when it happens.' He later confesses his surprise at hearing himself say this, as he doesn't believe a word of it. 'But one begins to share that revolutionary hope when one is in the company of someone like Mick,' he explains.

Mick takes the idea perfectly seriously, at least for a while. 'What about touring and that?' he asks. 'My first commitment is to my music, so I wouldn't want to have to give any of that up to sit behind a desk.'

'Oh, that wouldn't be a problem. You could carry on with your music the same as you always have and still do something very important for the party.'

'I mean, I don't exactly see myself scrutinising the Water Works Bill inch by inch, if you know what I mean.'

'Dear boy, we wouldn't expect you to attend to the day-to-day ephemera of the House. Not at all. We see you more as, uh, a figurehead, like, you know …'

'The Queen?' says Jagger, completing the sentence.

'Precisely!' exclaims Driberg.

The meeting has got off to a flying start, with, in Faithfull's words, 'lots of funny chat and zinging questions', when Driberg's eyes stray towards Jagger's tights, causing his attention to wander. There is an awkward moment of silence as Driberg looks at Jagger's crotch. 'Oh my, Mick, WHAT a big basket you have!' he says.*

Jagger blushes, the conversation founders; even Ginsberg feels 'slightly embarrassed, as Driberg was my guest. I was also astounded at his

---

* He makes a practice of this type of comment. Driving with the future Prime Minister James Callaghan, the two men stop to urinate at the verge of the road. 'While I was peeing, Tom came up to me and took hold of my penis,' Callaghan confides to their colleague Woodrow Wyatt. '"You've got a very pretty one there," he said.' But Callaghan is not that way inclined. 'I got away as quick as I could.'

boldness. I had eyes for Jagger myself, but I was very circumspect about Jagger's body. Yet here was Driberg coming on crude. There was a kind of Zen directness about it that was interesting: I suddenly realised that with directness like that you could score many times.'

But the moment passes, and the talk returns to politics. Marianne Faithfull thinks Driberg 'very clever ... because he could see exactly what Mick wanted, which was a form of respectability'.

In June, Jagger is found guilty of possessing a potentially harmful drug, and sentenced to three months' imprisonment. The case goes to appeal. Meanwhile, Driberg argues in Parliament for the legalisation of cannabis. When a Home Office minister asks, 'What sort of society will we create if everyone wants to escape from reality?' Driberg rises to his feet: 'They want to escape from this horrible society we have created.'

Over the next year, Driberg and Jagger enjoy regular lunches together, often at the Gay Hussar. A pattern emerges: Jagger, buoyed, returns home telling Marianne Faithfull he is going into politics. She grows excited – 'Mick Jagger, leader of the Labour Party! And me, the little anarchist in the background, pushing the great man further into folly!' – but by the next day he has invariably changed his mind.

Driberg is not easily dissuaded; he even hatches an idea of a breakaway party, headed by Jagger and himself. On February 4th 1969 he writes to Sir Richard Acland, who formed the doomed Common Wealth Party during the Second World War. 'I have been discussing the electoral possibilities, and the problems of revolution (and the difficulty of founding a new party) with two people, friends of mine, who could have some influence among the young: Mick Jagger and his lady, Marianne Faithfull – both more intelligent than you might suppose from their public *personae*. They would like to meet you. Would you?'

The meeting never takes place, and Jagger's interest in a career in politics wanes, largely because, as Marianne Faithfull recalls, 'It would be unbelievably dull.'* It is Keith Richard who finally puts a stop to it. When

---

* Driberg keeps in touch with Faithfull for some time after she has split up with Jagger. In 1972, he invites her to dinner at the Gay Hussar with W.H. Auden. 'In the middle of the evening Auden turned to me and, in a gesture I assume was intended to shock me, said, "Tell me, when you travel with drugs, Marianne, do you pack them up your arse?"

'"Oh no, Wystan," I said. "I stash them in my pussy."'

Jagger asks him for his opinion as to whether he should become an MP, Richard says it's the worst idea he has ever heard.

TOM DRIBERG

TAKES HIS EYES OFF

CHRISTOPHER HITCHENS

601 Mountjoy House, the Barbican, London EC2
June 1976

Now aged seventy-one, and recently ennobled,* Tom Driberg – socialist, gossip columnist, High Churchman, suspected spy, sexual predator[†] – is beginning to feel his age. 'I wish I were sixteen again,' he announced at a party to celebrate his seventieth birthday. 'No I don't. I wish I were dead.'

He is, in the words of his swashbuckling young journalist friend Christopher Hitchens, 'at the fag-end of his career … tending to live off his store of anecdotes and acquaintances'. He occupies much of his time dropping names from the past. Whenever he dines in an Indian restaurant, he makes a point of drinking milk simply so that he can say, 'Aleister Crowley – the Beast, you know – always advised it.'

He is particularly proud of his private collection of dirty limericks by W.H. Auden and Constant Lambert;[§] he likes to recite them whenever there is a lull in a conversation.

---

* As Lord Bradwell. The occasion is celebrated in verse by his old friend John Betjeman:

> *The first and last Lord Bradwell is to me*
> *The norm of socialist integrity;*
> *He makes no secret of his taste in sex;*
> *Preferring the lower to the upper decks.*

[†] 'From first to last, Driberg was a homosexual philanderer of a most pertinacious and indefatigable kind, wholly shameless, without the smallest scruple or remorse, utterly regardless of the feelings of or consequences to his partners, determined on the crudest and most frequent form of carnal satisfaction to the exclusion of any other consideration whatever: a Queers' Casanova,' observes Paul Johnson, a little ungenerously, in the *Daily Telegraph*.

[§] Lambert possessed other talents, even more hidden: 'When the weather is right, I can play "God Save the King" by ear,' he would say. 'Literally.' Lambert was deaf in his right ear, having sustained a punctured eardrum as a child. He was able to hold his nose, take a breath through his mouth, and blow the tune through his ear. Anthony Powell testified to the truth of this: when he leaned close, faintly from the ear in question he heard the recognisable notes 'God save our gracious King …'

'That will do!' said the Lady Maude Hoare.
'I can't concentrate any more.
You're perspiring like hell,
There's that terrible smell –
And look at the time – half-past four!'

But he still makes space in his diary for his old pursuits. 'In only one respect did he keep his old life up to speed,' says Hitchens, indiscreetly. 'He would go anywhere and do anything for the chance to suck somebody off.' But what was once a pleasure has now become more of a chore, and he claims to do it on doctor's orders ('the potassium ingredient is frightfully good for one'). His twenty-five-year marriage to Ena Binfield has done nothing to convert him to the joys of heterosexuality. 'She tried to seduce me! On our HONEYMOON!' he tells his friends in horror.

The novelist Kingsley Amis is compiling *The New Oxford Book of Light Verse*, and has heard of Driberg's colourful collection. Amis asks Hitchens to ask Driberg if he might be induced to share it. If so, he will treat him to a meal at a restaurant of his choice with Hitchens and Amis's son Martin. Hitchens duly telephones the friend he calls 'the old cocksucker' and puts the proposition to him.

'I'd be most interested to meet the senior Amis,' drawls Driberg. 'But do tell me, is he by any chance as attractive as his lovely young son?'

'Yes, Tom, absolutely,' replies Hitchens. 'But – how shall I put it? Kingsley is old enough to be Martin's father.'

'Oh, dear, yes, I suppose he must be,' sighs Driberg.

In return for his saucy limericks, Driberg proposes lunch at the Neal Street Restaurant. The four are escorted to a table halfway down the room. Kingsley Amis, no stranger to irritation, is perfectly satisfied with it, but both he and Hitchens note Driberg's dissatisfied glances.

'Complaint coming up,' mutters Hitchens to Amis.

'Eh?'

'He has to find fault with something to feel properly settled in.'

At that very moment, Driberg summons the manager and demands to be moved to a quieter area of the restaurant. He is a stickler for prompt service and fine food. In his new role as a peer of the realm, he tells Hitchens he disapproves of the 'abysmal' food served in the dining room of the House of Lords. 'The white wine is warmer than the food,' he complains.

The lunch never really gets going. In Kingsley's view, Martin does not exert himself. While Kingsley and Hitchens gabble away, Driberg remains very quiet. 'I have since thought he might have been ill,' Kingsley reflects in his memoirs, 'since he was to die within months of our meeting.'

Driberg announces that his poetic trove is back in his flat in the Barbican, and so off the four of them set, a little unwillingly. Over whisky, he produces a bundle of the famous Constant Lambert limericks and proudly presents them to Kingsley Amis, who eagerly starts to read them. Meanwhile Martin asks Driberg if he can ring for a mini-cab. Driberg leads him to the phone in the bedroom.

As he reads on, Kingsley grows vaguely aware that he is sitting alone in the room with Hitchens: the other two have disappeared. After a while, Driberg reappears, followed a little later by Martin.

The limericks are not to Kingsley's liking. 'Written out in an unattractive hand, they featured one at a time all or many of the diocesan bishops of probably England and Wales. Each limerick had e.g. the Bishop of Truro in its first line, a limited amount of technical ingenuity and an obscenity of some kind, usually mild. Nothing else of significance, for example humour, was anywhere present.'

> The Bishop of Central Japan
> Used to bugger himself with a fan;
> When taxed with his acts
> He explained: 'It contracts
> And expands so much more than a man.'

There is only one poem by Auden, and it rules itself out even faster 'by being a long and detailed account of an act of fellatio told by the fellator in the first person. This too I politely kept my eyes on for some time.' Amis reads them all through 'with simulated care and interest' before announcing 'with pretended regret and real evasiveness' that he is afraid they won't quite do for the Oxford University Press.

The three of them make their excuses and leave. The next morning, Martin telephones Kingsley. 'A fine fucking father you are. The slag at the cab firm told me to hold on a moment, please, caller, and in no time bloody caller was holding on with one hand and beating Driberg off with the other. We must have gone round the bed about five times before he clapped me on the shoulder, said, "Fair enough, youngster," in a sort of bluff style and buggered off.'

'That was sporting of him,' replies Kingsley. 'Anyway, you should have taken the Hitch into the bedroom with you.'

'Maybe. And maybe not.'

Reflecting on the incident later, Kingsley Amis wonders whether exhaustion from chasing his son around the bed might have hastened Driberg's demise.

'The idea does not displease me much,' he adds.

CHRISTOPHER HITCHENS

TRADES ABUSE WITH

GEORGE GALLOWAY

Baruch College, 55 Lexington Avenue, New York
September 14th 2005

Nearly thirty years on, Christopher Hitchens is living in America. A celebrated iconoclast, contrarian and master of what Auberon Waugh termed the vituperative arts, he is a vociferous supporter of the allied invasion of Iraq. For all these reasons, he holds the radical politician George Galloway in particular contempt.

There is no one more radical than Galloway. A throwback to an earlier, more revolutionary era, he has been expelled from the Labour Party for bringing it into disrepute, and now heads his own party, 'Respect', or 'Respect (The George Galloway Party)', as he calls it on the ballot papers. Like Hitchens, he stalwartly refuses to hide his light under a bushel.

The two men have much else in common: a passion for smoking (cigarettes for Hitchens, cigars for Galloway), a roguish theatricality, an instinctive command of rhetoric, a simple delight in their own capacity for holding the strongest opinions. Only a few years ago, Galloway viewed Hitchens as a comrade, praising him as 'that great British man of letters' and 'the greatest polemicist'. But things have soured. Now Galloway includes him in his list of the damned. 'The people who invaded and destroyed Iraq and have murdered a million Iraqi people by sanctions and war will burn in Hell in the hell fires, and their name in history will be branded as killers and war criminals for all time,' he says.*

The two men met for the first time on the steps of the Senate building in Washington a few months ago, as Galloway prepared to defend himself before a Senate committee against its allegation that he had traded in oil.

---

* Later, he tells the viewers of Al Jazeera that the 'globalised capitalist economic system ... is the biggest killer the world has ever known. It has killed far more people than Adolf Hitler.'

With television cameras whirring, Hitchens approached him and questioned a few of his claims.

GALLOWAY: This is a bloated, drink-sodden former Trotskyist popinjay, who is just walking around as a sort of bag lady in Washington.

HITCHENS: Just enquiring ... I just wondered. You said you'd contacted the committee by letter, by email. Did you bring copies of the letters with you?

GALLOWAY: Has anyone got any sensible questions?

HITCHENS: Or the email?

GALLOWAY: You're a drink-soaked, bloated –

AMERICAN REPORTER: Are you going to answer his question? The substance of his question?

GALLOWAY: I'm here to talk to the Senate.

Hitchens followed him inside the building, and continued to barrack him with questions. Perhaps unsurprisingly, 'a fresh hose of abuse was turned on me'.

GALLOWAY: Your hands are shaking. You badly need another drink.

HITCHENS: And you're a real thug, aren't you?

Soon afterwards, Galloway accepts Hitchens' invitation to a public debate. Meanwhile, Hitchens accelerates his personal attacks. 'Study the photographs of Galloway from Syrian state television and you will see how unwise and incautious it is for such a hideous person to resort to personal remarks,' he writes in one of his many columns. 'Unkind nature, which could have made a perfectly good butt out of his face, has spoiled the whole effect by taking an asshole and studding it with ill-brushed fangs.'*

Hitchens announces the ground rules for their forthcoming confrontation. 'There'll be no courtesies and no handshakes.' On the evening of

---

* Hitchens has always been free with his abuse. In his memoir, *Hitch-22*, he describes Bill Clinton as 'loathsome', Henry Kissinger as 'indescribably loathsome', Jimmy Carter as a 'pious born-again creep', Alexander Haig as 'vain, preposterous' and Ronald Reagan as 'appallingly facile'. Elsewhere, he calls Mother Teresa 'a fanatic, a fundamentalist and a fraud'.

their debate on the motion 'The March 2003 war in Iraq was necessary and just', Hitchens stands outside Baruch College distributing leaflets listing some of his opponent's more outlandish remarks, among them his greeting to Saddam Hussein in 1994: *Your Excellency, Mr President ... I salute your courage, your strength, your indefatigability.'*

Galloway remains undeterred. Aptly, he picks an analogy from the world of heavyweight boxing. 'He's all washed up, like Sonny Liston,' he says.

At their separate podia, Galloway, spruce, tanned and besuited, resembles a prosperous capitalist, while the bearded Hitchens, sweat stains inching along his purple shirt, his jacket tossed any-old-how to the floor, looks the very model of a modern rebel socialist. Over the next two hours, they exchange insults, with Iraq as the backdrop. Galloway attacks Hitchens for his 'crazed shifts of opinion' and asks, 'How can anybody take you seriously?'

Hitchens congratulates Galloway on being 'absolutely 100 per cent consistent in your support for unmentionable thugs and bastards'. Galloway calls Hitchens a hypocrite, 'a jester at the court of the Bourbon Bushes', and speaks of his voyage from left to right as 'something unique in natural history ... the first metamorphosis of a butterfly back into a slug'. Hitchens counters by saying that Galloway's 'vile and cheap guttersnipe abuse is a disgrace ... beneath each gutter there's another gutter gurgling away'. To which Galloway replies, 'You've fallen out of the gutter into the sewer.'

And so it goes on. In the heat of the moment, both debaters grow intemperate. At one point, Hitchens praises the Bush administration's handling of the flooding in New Orleans. 'This is where it ends,' retorts Galloway, '– you end up a mouthpiece and apologist for these miserable malevolent incompetents who cannot even pick up the bodies of their own citizens in New Orleans.'

In turn, Galloway appears to excuse the 9/11 terrorists. 'Some believe that those aeroplanes on September 11 came out of a clear blue sky,' he says. 'I believe they came out of a swamp of hatred created by us.'

'Mr Galloway,' replies Hitchens, 'you picked the wrong city to say that ... Our fault? No, this is masochism. And it is masochism being offered to you by sadists.'

America has grown used to its political elite wanting to be loved, or at least respected. It is fresh to the pleasures of mutual vituperation.

'That is the end of my *pro bono* bit,' Hitchens says at the end of his summing-up. 'From now on, if you want to speak to me, you'll need a receipt, and I'll be selling books, because this is, after all, America.' There is no vote taken, so no way to judge the winner. The opponents refuse to exchange another word: each stays in his own corner, busily signing copies of his latest book.* The debate's mediator also has a book to sign. After a tiring day, they stand united behind the cause of self-promotion.

---

* Respectively *Mr Galloway Goes to Washington* and *Love, Poverty and War*.

GEORGE GALLOWAY

FACES THE POPULAR VOTE AGAINST

MICHAEL BARRYMORE

Elstree Studios, Borehamwood, Hertfordshire
January 23rd 2006

The Respect Party MP enters the television *Big Brother* house on January 5th. He is doing so, he maintains, because it is good for politics: 'I believe that politicians should use every opportunity to communicate with people. I'm a great believer in the democratic process.' As he enters the house, he shouts, 'Stop the war!'

His fellow housemates are: Dennis Rodman, a retired American basketball player; Faria Alam, a former secretary at the Football Association, infamous for her kiss-and-tell affairs with the England football manager and the Football Association chief executive; Jodie Marsh, a former 'glamour model'; Pete Burns, a transvestite singer with the group Dead or Alive; Preston, lead singer with the group the Ordinary Boys; Rula Lenska, an actress; Traci Bingham, the first black actress on *Baywatch*; Chantelle Houghton, a part-time Paris Hilton lookalike; Maggot, a Welsh rapper; and finally Michael Barrymore, the all-round family entertainer whose career nosedived five years ago, following the discovery of a corpse in his swimming pool.

Their first task is to line up in order of fame. In fact, Chantelle is not remotely famous, but has been secretly tasked with convincing the others that she is. Within the short time allotted, the housemates decide that Michael Barrymore is the most famous and Maggot the least. George Galloway comes fourth, between the *Baywatch* actress and the transvestite singer.

During the first few days, Galloway is chummy with Barrymore, and tells everyone he wants him to win. Barrymore is so moved by this unexpected show of support that he starts to cry. Galloway kisses him on the head. After a week, they have become firm friends, with Galloway defending Barrymore from an attack by Jodie Marsh, who is upset that he has eaten her food. He calls Marsh 'a wicked person'.*

Outside the *Big Brother* house, his fellow MPs criticise Galloway for neglecting his duties. He has, they argue, become a national laughing stock after going down on all fours and pretending to be a cat, then cavorting about in a red leotard.

Inside the house, his bonhomie is beginning to fray. He rounds on Chantelle and Preston for going into a secret room and eating luxury food denied to other housemates. 'If I had been called in there I would have stood ramrod straight, refused to sit down, refused to eat, refused to drink, refused to smoke. I would have said, "You brought me here under duress, but I will refuse to partake in things that others are not allowed!"'

'We were playing a game,' replies Chantelle, reasonably. Galloway then attacks Preston: 'You're a sneak and a liar and you're exposed to the world as a sneak and a liar ... We'll see what the viewers thought of your double standards, your indignation about me and the aplomb with which you become a lying plutocrat in your gentleman's club.'

He then turns his rhetoric on Barrymore for failing to support him when *Big Brother* removed his right to nominate people for eviction.

'I was close to you, and Dennis was close to you and you stabbed both of us because of your mania about hoarding cigarettes ... Despite all the support I had given you, despite all the efforts I had made for you, when it came to a problem that I was facing, you were silent. You know why? Because you care about nobody except yourself. You're the most selfish, self-obsessed person I have ever met in my entire life! ... You're the only person you've talked about in here.'

At this point, Preston steps in.

PRESTON: He's talked about everyone non-stop!

GALLOWAY: You haven't even talked about your partner in here ...

---

* For this he earns the ire of Germaine Greer. After assuring *Guardian* readers that she cannot watch *Celebrity Big Brother*, she goes on to say that 'Anyone who can remember what a thoroughly supercilious and nasty performer Barrymore always was, must watch unmoved as he dissolves in snot and tears.' She adds that 'For Galloway to blame Barrymore's pathetic condition on Jodie Marsh is outrageous.'

PRESTON: He's talked about him non-stop! I can tell you
everything he's said about him! ...

GALLOWAY: You're self-obsessed!

BARRYMORE: Oh, come on, George. George, you're in this frame of
mind because you've been nominated again, and you take it as a
personal slight ... I'm an easy target ... You're playing to the
outside world.

GALLOWAY: Poor me, poor me, pour me a drink!

PRESTON: Oh, don't fucking bring that into it, that is low!

GALLOWAY: Poor me, poor me, pour me a drink!

BARRYMORE: You are out of order ... you are out of order!

PRESTON (POINTING AT GALLOWAY): You are a fucking wanker!
You are fucking low!

BARRYMORE: You are out of order!

PRESTON: Wanker!

GALLOWAY: Poor me, poor me.

BARRYMORE: And you're doing it with a smile!

GALLOWAY: Poor me, poor me.

BARRYMORE: You want to play around with an addict?

GALLOWAY: Poor me, poor me.

BARRYMORE: Is that what you want to do?

GALLOWAY: Poor me, poor me.

BARRYMORE: That's how caring you are, you care so much about
everybody! ... George, I feel really sorry for you. You're that sad,
no wonder Tony Blair threw you out!

GALLOWAY: Keep on talking, keep on talking.

BARRYMORE: No wonder Blair threw you out.

GALLOWAY: Keep on talking!

BARRYMORE: You can do that smile, George, it don't work, you
need a bigger smile than that for the camera! ... You can do
what you like to me, you can tear me down and rip me apart.
But one thing you can't have is my sobriety. When you've
been to where I have been to, some of you may know what
it's like. Then stand up and have a go at me, until you reach
that spot in your life, if ever you reach that spot in your life
... I beg you, please, to keep your opinions to yourself. And

I'll do what I've done all the way through here and keep mine
to myself.

(LONG PAUSE)

BARRYMORE: Coffee, anyone?

The argument rages for twenty minutes. The next day, Galloway becomes
the second housemate to be evicted from the house, with 65 per cent of
the popular vote. The eventual winner is Chantelle Houghton. Barrymore
comes second, emerging from the house to a chorus of cheers. But his
career fails to revive; three years later he is spotted working part-time at a
vehicle bodyworks business in Epping.

MICHAEL BARRYMORE

IS BEFRIENDED BY

DIANA, PRINCESS OF WALES

Bayswater, London W2
May 1996

The chief psychiatrist at the Marchwood Priory mental-health hospital looks over his half-moon glasses. 'I have something for you which I think may cheer you up,' he says to his patient, Michael Barrymore. He is holding a letter from someone his patient has never met.

My dearest Michael,

I was so sad to hear that once again you had had to be re-admitted to The Priory … You have given so much happiness and pleasure to me and my family over the years, as you have millions of others. The least we can do is to be there for you when you need all the love and care you can get.

At the moment I am writing this to you from Majorca, where I am on holiday with the boys. As soon as I return and you are well I would love to meet up and have some time together. The boys send you their very best wishes. Much love from me, and please let me know when we can meet.

Love, Diana

The psychiatrist gives his patient a broad smile. 'It wasn't every day that one of his patients received a letter from the Princess of Wales, and I guess he couldn't hide his excitement,' reflects Barrymore.

A few weeks later, Barrymore, fresh out of rehabilitation, receives a letter from Diana asking why he hasn't phoned. He sends a letter back saying, 'I didn't want to bother you.' The reply comes: 'Well, bother me!'

Their first meeting is, in Barrymore's view, 'all very cloak and dagger'. It is arranged through courtiers: Barrymore's agent deals with the journalist Martin Bashir, who has become something of a fixer for the Princess.

It was in his *Panorama* interview with her that she spoke of her betrayal by her husband, her bulimia, and her affair with James Hewitt. It was also in this interview that she announced her intention to be the 'Queen of Hearts', helping 'other people in distress'.

The Princess stipulates that they should meet at Barrymore's house, and that no one else should be there, not even Barrymore's wife Cheryl. On the day itself, Bashir rings twice more, to make sure that Cheryl will not be present.

At the back of Barrymore's mind is the idea that it is all a hoax. 'Then in walked the Princess of Wales as large as life. Up until then, I was extremely nervous, but the moment she walked in she had this amazing ability to put you at ease.'

'Hello,' she says, kissing him. 'How are you feeling?'

They sit together on a sofa and talk about Barrymore's shows. Barrymore is impressed by how many the Princess remembers. 'It was as if we'd known each other all our lives.'

'So, what do I call you? Princess Diana?'

'Just Diana. I'm not a princess any more.'

Diana looks around the room. She points at a framed photograph of Cheryl, Barrymore's wife of twenty years.

'Oh, is this wifey?'

'Yes.'

Cheryl is at that moment alone at the top of the house, four floors above them.

'I want you to know that you can come through all this – you just have to be strong.' The Princess tells the entertainer that she really wants to be there for him.

'It was pretty strange really, hearing that the Princess of Wales wanted to be there for me,' he says some years later. 'I keep asking myself *Why? Why me?* … I think she truly believed that we were both very similar in personality.'

She is right. Both are adored by the public but uncomfortable with those close to them. They have the gift of empathy, but largely with people they don't know. They possess unstable, addictive personalities but have become popular through their capacity to appear 'down to earth'. And they both like to retreat into the spotlight.

After several hours, the door opens. It is Cheryl, interrupting them. 'Diana, your car is waiting.'

Diana gives Barrymore her telephone number, and leaves. He feels a huge weight lifting from his shoulders, 'I felt I was getting advice and immense support from the highest level possible. I will always remember those eyes … she was able to show every emotion through them.'

From then on, they talk almost every day. She sends him handwritten notes, delivered by her butler Paul Burrell, asking him to call her whenever he has a problem. It is a bad year for Barrymore: he has a nervous breakdown, his new television series is cancelled, he is readmitted to a clinic and his next television show, *Barrymore in Hollywood*, is shelved.

He begins seeing Diana at Kensington Palace. One day, she ticks him off for parking his Bentley in Princess Margaret's parking space. He thinks of her as a counsellor. She tells him they are so alike, so unique, and nobody must ever control them again.

He starts to rebel, falling over at awards ceremonies and slurring inappropriate jokes at charity shows. Cheryl thinks of Diana as a destructive force, and blames her for mesmerising him: 'He would often have a distant look in his eyes, almost like a religious conversion.' He tells Diana he is gay; she urges him to come out, and he does.

Diana likes to tell him that she, Barrymore and Paul Gascoigne are the three most famous people in Britain. Within a short time, she will be dead, and Barrymore and Gascoigne ruined.

One Friday, she appears distant. He asks her what is wrong. 'Oh, nothing,' she says. 'I've just been rushing around because I'm going off to Paris with Dodi … Do you want to meet next Wednesday?'

That Sunday morning, she dies in a car crash. He and Cheryl go together to her funeral, even though they have split up. Inside Westminster Abbey, Cheryl tells him to adjust his suit.

'Give it a break will you?' he snaps.

After the funeral, he moves away from Cheryl to go and chat to the crowd.

'It seemed the right thing to do,' he explains.

DIANA, PRINCESS OF WALES

LEARNS A LESSON FROM

PRINCESS GRACE

Goldsmiths' Hall, London EC2
March 3rd 1981

The engagement of HRH the Prince of Wales to Lady Diana Spencer was announced exactly a week ago. The future Princess's first public engagement is to be a musical recital at Goldsmiths' Hall in aid of the Royal Opera House.

The nineteen-year-old Diana is excited. She has chosen a black dress from the Emmanuels.* 'It was just a simple dress I had hanging in the show room,' recalls Elizabeth Emmanuel. 'It had actually been worn once by Liza Goddard. Lady Diana asked for something off the peg, which we didn't really do. She needed it quickly and there was no time to make a dress from scratch … We showed it to her, she tried it on and she looked sensational.'

'I thought it was OK because girls my age wore this dress,' is the way Diana remembers it. 'I hadn't appreciated that I was now seen as a royal lady, although I'd only got a ring on my finger as opposed to two rings. Black to me was the smartest colour you could possibly have at the age of nineteen. It was a real grown-up dress.' The dress is in stark contrast to the frumpy one she wore for her engagement photographs. One writer describes it as 'a black, very décolleté, strapless evening gown'; another, more excitable, calls it 'that nipple-busting, black taffeta eye-popper'.

Diana is due to attend the concert without her future husband by her side. She is nervous, but excited. Before she sets off, she appears at the door of his study. He looks at her, and drily comments that only people in mourning wear black. Diana tells him she has no other dress suitable for the occasion.

---

* In June 2010 the dress is bought at a London auction for £192,000 by a fashion museum in Chile.

This little spat knocks her confidence. Now she fears she will prove an embarrassment to the royal family.

When her car arrives at Goldsmiths' Hall, Diana steps out to a mass of flashing cameras. The same excitable writer describes it as 'the greatest moment of sexual theatre since Cinderella swapped her scuffed scullery clogs for Prince Charming's glass slippers'. Diana, already nervous, is taken aback. 'I was quite big-chested then and they all got frightfully excited.' Elizabeth Emmanuel is similarly surprised. 'We were overwhelmed by the impact it made when she stepped out of the limo, revealing all that cleavage. It knocked the Budget off the front page of every newspaper.' Even those without any great interest in current affairs take an interest in the dress. Leafing through *The Times* the next morning, the ancient society belle Lady Diana Cooper remarks to a friend, 'Wasn't that a dainty dish to set before a king?' An aide to Princess Grace of Monaco recalls, less jovially, 'Her breasts were on display and she was quite a wreck.'

As the evening progresses, Diana grows even more unsure of herself. 'It was an horrendous occasion. I didn't know whether to go out of the door first. I didn't know whether your handbag should be in your left hand or your right hand. I was terrified really – at the time everything was all over the place.'

A reception at Buckingham Palace follows. The fifty-two-year-old Princess Grace, the object of this sort of attention back in the 1950s, notices Diana's discomfort, and suggests they retire to the ladies' room for a little chat together. Diana tells Princess Grace that she is worried her dress is unbecoming. It is, she explains, two sizes too small. Her experience tonight has suddenly made her realise how unbearable it will be to have hundreds of people always looking at her. She sees stretching ahead of her a life without any form of privacy. She feels isolated, and fears for the future. What should she do? She bursts into tears.

Princess Grace puts her arms around her and pats her on the shoulder. She cups her cheeks in her hands and jokes, gently, 'Don't worry, dear. You'll see – it'll only get worse.'

The two women return to the throng, there to mingle and be assessed. 'I remember meeting Princess Grace and how wonderful and serene she was,' Diana later tells her confidant Andrew Morton. 'But there was troubled water under her, I saw that.'

Eighteen months later, Princess Grace is killed after her car fails to take a sharp corner on the serpentine D37 outside Monaco. Though the Prince of Wales sees no reason why Diana should attend the funeral, she is adamant that she should go. It will be the first time she has officially represented the royal family on her own.

By now, she has grown used to the hullabaloo surrounding her every appearance, and in some way appears to feed off it. For this occasion, she chooses to wear another black dress, far more demure, with a diamond-and-pearl heart necklace and a black straw boater.

On the way to the funeral, a number of things go wrong: the car breaks down, a lift gets stuck. But Diana remains poised and unflustered throughout. At the High Requiem Mass, she takes her place between Nancy Reagan and Madame Mitterrand. Other guests include many of the crowned heads of Europe, as well as Hollywood stars like Cary Grant, but for the worldwide TV audience of 100 million and the weeping crowd of onlookers outside the cathedral, Diana is the centre of attention. She doesn't put a foot wrong. 'My respect for her rose a hundredfold ... She was very hassled but behaved brilliantly,' says a fellow guest. At the reception afterwards, she speaks to Princess Caroline of Monaco about her mother. 'We were psychically connected,' she tells her.

At the end of a long, hot day, she flies back to Scotland. Exhausted and full of pent-up emotion, she bursts into tears. As they approach Aberdeen airport, she asks an aide, 'Will Charles be there to meet us?'

'We looked at her big eyes looking out of the aeroplane window in expectation,' the aide recalls. There is just one police car waiting.

'That means Charles isn't coming,' she concludes, and she is right.

PRINCESS GRACE

IS ALMOST PERSUADED BY

ALFRED HITCHCOCK

Grimaldi Palace, Monaco
Winter 1961

The last film Grace Kelly made with Alfred Hitchcock was *To Catch a Thief*, back in 1955. That December, Prince Rainier of Monaco proposed to her over a pudding of pears poached in wine. 'If you are to be at my side then you may need this,' he said, passing her a pictorial history of the Grimaldi family. Some say he lacks the romantic touch.

But Grace Kelly was not to be put off. In April 1956, the Oscar-winning Hollywood actress became the Princess of a country roughly the size of Hyde Park with a population of 38,000, roughly the same as Oswestry.* At the same time, she picked up so many titles – twice a Duchess, once a Viscountess, eight times a Countess, four times a Marchioness and nine times a Baroness – that she instantly became the most titled woman in the world.

But Monaco has its limitations. After five years there, Princess Grace is pining for her Hollywood days. Around the same time, Alfred Hitchcock convinces himself that his new movie, *Marnie*, is tailor-made for her.

He visits her at the Grimaldi Palace to discuss the matter. He has always got on well with Grace; some believe she represents his idea of the perfect woman. 'People have quite the wrong idea about Grace,' he once said. 'They think she is a cold fish. Remote, like Alcatraz. But she has sex appeal, believe me. It is ice that will burn your hands, and that is always surprising, and exciting too.' When working together, their relationship

---

* The wedding itself goes smoothly. Three miles of red carpet are laid throughout Monaco, and Aristotle Onassis hires a seaplane to drop thousands of red and white carnations over everyone. In return for documentary rights, MGM agree to pay for basic essentials such as the wedding dress, and on top of all this Rainier makes $450,000 from the sale of commemorative stamps. The only blot on the horizon is that Queen Elizabeth II sends a telegram refusing her invitation. 'The fact that we have never met is irrelevant,' harrumphs Rainier. 'This is still a slap in the face.'

was always chummy rather than romantic, and revolved around a shared sense of humour. Shooting *Dial M for Murder*, for instance, they had a running joke in which they would drop the first letter from the names of various stars: hence, Rank Sinatra, Lark Gable, Ickey Rooney and Reer Garson.

Is he in love with her? John Michael Hayes, the screenwriter of *Rear Window*, certainly thinks so. 'He would have used Grace in the next ten pictures he made. I would say that all the actresses he cast subsequently were attempts to retrieve the image and feeling that Hitch carried around so reverentially about Grace.'

Their lunch goes well. Hitchcock does not mention a script. 'I am too much of a gentleman to mention work to a Princess. That would be most uncouth. But I waited and finally she came to me.' Instead, he posts the new novel *Marnie*, by Winston Graham, to her agents in New York ('She always kept her agents, you know'), and they pass it on to her. She is instantly tempted, even though the book's subject-matter is hardly fit for a Princess, even of Monaco: it is the tale of a woman who has been left a frigid kleptomaniac by a childhood trauma involving the rape of her prostitute mother.

Prince Rainier considers the movies vulgar, and has good reason to distrust actors: William Holden, Ray Milland, Clark Gable, David Niven and Gary Cooper are just a few of Grace's many former lovers.* But he is moved by a letter from his mother-in-law, who says Grace hasn't been really happy since she stopped making films. Later that day, Rainier says to one of his aides, 'Well, she's doing a movie. God help us all, that's all I can say, when the news gets out. Run for cover, my boy, run for cover!'

A week later, Hitchcock is told by the Princess's agents that she will do it, though by now Prince Rainier has added the proviso that filming must take place during the family's customary holiday period, and should not interfere with Grace's official duties. An official announcement is made on March 18th 1962: 'Princess Grace has accepted an offer to appear during

---

* 'Grace had more lovers in a month than I did in a lifetime,' Zsa Zsa Gabor puts it modestly. Playing golf with David Niven, Prince Rainier asks him who, out of all her former lovers, was the best at fellatio. Without thinking, Niven replies 'Grace –' before quickly correcting himself, 'Gracie Fields.' But Noël Coward maintains that Niven did indeed mean Gracie Fields. 'It's absolutely true. It was a speciality of Rochdale girls,' he says. 'They called it the Gradely Gobble.'

her summer vacation in a motion picture for Mister Alfred Hitchcock, to be made in the United States … It is understood that Prince Rainier will most likely be present during part of the filmmaking depending on his schedule and that Princess Grace will return to Monaco with her family in November.'

A reporter from the *Daily Express* manages to waylay Hitchcock. He asks if there will be any love scenes. 'Passionate and most unusual love scenes, but I am afraid I cannot tell you anything beyond that. It's a state secret,' replies Hitchcock, injudiciously adding that the Princess's sex appeal is 'the finest in the world'.

Their Serene Highnesses have underestimated the priggishness of the Monegasques. They are in uproar, not least at the mention of sex. 'She would be slighting our country,' says one. They do not like the idea of their monarch kissing her leading man; little do they know that Hitchcock has plans for him to rape her as well. The Prince's mother is livid, and keeps hissing, '*C'est une américaine!*'

Grace is so upset by the reaction that she stops eating, and finds it hard to sleep. To butter up the people, the Palace issues a second statement, announcing that the $800,000 she will receive for the film will be donated to a charity for Monegasque children and athletes. But neither her subjects nor her mother-in-law are appeased.

Eventually, Grace gives an interview to a reporter from *Nice Matin* announcing her decision to abandon the film. 'I have been very influenced by the reaction which the announcement provoked in Monaco,' she says.

How upset is Hitchcock by her decision? He tells friends that when they had their lunch together in the Palace, he thought that a spark had gone out of her, and she seemed bored. Her new role as Princess has, he thinks, drained her of warmth.

A few months after her decision, in June 1962, Princess Grace writes to Hitchcock. 'It was heartbreaking for me to have to leave the picture,' she confesses. Hitchcock writes back: 'Yes, it was sad, wasn't it? … Without a doubt, I think you made not only the best decision, but the only decision to put the project aside at this time. After all, it was only a movie.'

ALFRED HITCHCOCK

WALKS OUT ON

RAYMOND CHANDLER

6005 Camino de la Costa, La Jolla, California
September 1950

Alfred Hitchcock sends Raymond Chandler *Strangers on a Train*, the new novel by Patricia Highsmith. Eight other writers have already turned it down, including Dashiell Hammett. 'None of them thought it was any good,' Hitchcock recalls. This is strange in itself, because it is a compelling story, the first in a series that is set to make Patricia Highsmith the world's finest suspense novelist.

Chandler says he finds it 'a silly enough story',* but grudgingly agrees to adapt it, partly for the money and 'partly because I thought I might like Hitchcock'. In early July, he signs a contract with Warner Brothers giving him $2,500 a week for five weeks' work. The contract contains a clause confirming that he need never leave home: he has always hated what he calls 'those god-awful jabber sessions' with executives. Like many novelists, Chandler is unhappy as a screenwriter. Hollywood feeds his paranoia and self-loathing. 'If my books had been any worse, I should not have been invited to Hollywood,' he maintains, 'and if they had been any better, I should not have come.'

Nevertheless, he has enjoyed a fair share of success (though, in his case, 'enjoy' is possibly too strong a word), and six years ago was nominated for an Oscar for *Double Indemnity*.

Alfred Hitchcock is easy with Chandler's contractual clause, and happy to be driven in his limousine to Chandler's house in La Jolla, generally accompanied by his executive producer, Barbara Keon.

At first, everything goes fine, and Chandler finds Hitchcock 'very considerate and polite'. But after a few of these meetings he starts to grow irritated

---

* 'Suspense as an absolute quality has never seemed to me very important,' he writes to Bernice Baumgarten while working on his screenplay. This might explain his lack of empathy with *Strangers on a Train*, both the book and the film.

by him. 'Every time you get set, he jabs you off balance by wanting to do a love scene on top of the Jefferson Memorial or something like that.'

Chandler's main gripe concerns Hitchcock's indifference to plausibility. He accuses him of being too ready 'to sacrifice dramatic logic (insofar as it exists) for the sake of a camera effect', preferring to work with a director 'who realizes that what is said and how it is said is more important than shooting it upside down through a glass of champagne'.

Oddly enough, plausibility has never played a particularly prominent part in Chandler's own work. Like Hitchcock's films, his novels exist on a level of heightened reality, akin to a dream or a poem. 'When in doubt have a man come through the door with a gun in his hand,' is his advice to aspirant crime writers.

He finds Hitchcock niggly and interfering. 'He is full of little suggestions and ideas, which have a cramping effect on a writer's initiative. You are in a position of a fighter who can't get set because he is continuously being kept off-balance by short jabs.'

In turn, Hitchcock finds Chandler increasingly touchy. 'We'd sit together and I would say, "Why not do it this way?" and he'd answer, "Well, if you can puzzle it out, what do you need me for?"'

Time is against them. Hitchcock wants to start filming before the autumn leaves begin to fall. It annoys Chandler that he did not mention this at their first meeting, when he insisted that there was 'no hurry at all'.

Hitchcock starts passing Chandler's completed pages to others for rewrites. Chandler hears about it, and sees red. 'What this adds up to is that I have no assurance, to put it rather bluntly, that anything much more is happening to me than that my brain is being picked for whatever may be in it, and that someone else or a couple of someone elses are at work behind the scenes, casting the stuff into a screenplay from the way he wants it,' he complains to his agent. He asks to change his salary to a lump sum, so that he can work at his own pace, and without interference. The studio refuses this request.

Hungover in the mornings, Chandler begins to resent Hitchcock's daily arrival. 'Look at that fat bastard trying to get out of his car!' he mutters to his secretary. She warns him he might be heard. 'What do I care?' he snaps.

On this particular morning in early September, Hitchcock arrives bang on time. Unknown to Chandler, he has decided that this meeting will be their last. As Hitchcock levers himself down into his usual chair, Chandler, already drunk, starts ranting. The film is inferior to the original book, he says, and why the hell doesn't Hitchcock just forget all his silly plot variations and daft camera tricks?

Hitchcock says nothing, even when Chandler falls silent. Realising that Hitchcock has sent Chandler to Coventry, Barbara Keon can't resist filling in the silences. This causes Chandler to resume his ranting, which in turn causes Hitchcock to stand up, walk out of the room, and exit through the front door without a backward glance. Keon hastily packs up her bits and pieces and chases after him.

The chauffeur opens the car door. Hitchcock lets Keon in first, then squeezes in beside her. As the car moves away, Chandler runs outside and screams abuse, employing his old phrase, 'Fat bastard!' and others too rude for repetition. 'It was personal, very personal,' recalls a friend of Keon.

As the car gathers speed, Hitchcock remains silent, staring out of the window with a poker face. He is clearly brooding. After a while, he just turns to Barbara Keon and mutters, 'He's through.'

Chandler and Hitchcock never speak again. Chandler can't understand why. 'Not even a telephone call,' he complains to a friend. 'Not one word of criticism or appreciation. Silence. Blank silence.'

But he carries on writing as though nothing has happened, mailing his completed script to the studio, special delivery, on September 26th. Hitchcock doesn't even bother to acknowledge its receipt. The next month, he hires a new writer, a young blonde. Hitchcock initiates their first script conference by holding his nose, picking up Chandler's script between his thumb and forefinger, and dropping it neatly into a wastepaper basket.*

---

* On December 6th 1950, Chandler writes a furious letter to Hitchcock after Warners have sent him a copy of the final script. 'In spite of your wide and generous disregard of my communications on the subject of the script of *Strangers on a Train* and your failure to make any comment on it,' he begins, 'and in spite of not having heard a word from you since I began the writing of the actual screenplay – for all of which I might say I bear no malice, since this sort of procedure seems to be part of the standard Hollywood depravity – in spite of this and in spite of this extremely cumbersome sentence, I feel that I should, just for the record, pass you a few comments on what is termed the final script … What I cannot understand is your permitting a script which after all had some life and vitality to be reduced to such a flabby mass of clichés, a group of faceless characters, and the kind of dialogue every screen writer is taught not to write …'

He never posts this letter.

RAYMOND CHANDLER

LOSES THE PLOT WITH

HOWARD HAWKS

Warner Brothers Studio, Burbank, Los Angeles
October 1944

Plotting has never come easy to Raymond Chandler. He sees it as his key flaw, and describes himself as 'a mystery writer with a touch of magic and a bad feeling about plots'. To a young novelist seeking advice, he writes, 'As to methods of plotting and plot outlines, I am afraid I cannot help you at all, since I have never plotted anything on paper. I do my plotting in my head as I go along, and usually I do it wrong and have to do it all over again.'

It worries him. 'I wish I had one of these facile plotting brains, like Erle Gardner or somebody,' he confesses to his publisher. 'I have good ideas for about four books, but the labor of shaping them into plots appals me … Most writers think up a plot with an intriguing situation and then proceed to fit characters into it. With me a plot, if you could call it that, is an organic thing. It grows and often it overgrows. I am continually finding myself with scenes that I won't discard and that don't want to fit in. So that my plot problem invariably ends up as a desperate attempt to justify a lot of material that, for me at least, has come alive and insists on staying alive. It's probably a silly way to write, but I seem to know no other way. The mere idea of being committed in advance to a certain pattern appals me.'

In his fifties, after years of struggle, his writing career has taken off. But success fails to make him any happier. A pessimist, he measures his income in tax returns: at the end of this financial year, he has to pay $50,000 in tax. He has just given up writing a screenplay of his own novel *The Lady in the Lake* because the process bored him stiff. He only feels creative when writing fresh material. 'For God's sake,' rants the producer, 'this is supposed to be an adaptation of something we bought from you. And you keep on writing different scenes!' In the end, Chandler insists that his name be removed from the credits. It will, he predicts, be 'probably the worst picture ever made'.

He is more optimistic, though, about the forthcoming production of his novel *The Big Sleep*, principally because he won't have to write the screenplay. He arrives at Warner Brothers in a cheery mood for a meeting with the director, Howard Hawks, the star, Humphrey Bogart, and the two screenwriters, a novice female crime writer called Leigh Brackett, and the great Southern novelist William Faulkner, many of whose own plots are every bit as hard to unravel as Chandler's, perhaps even more so.

The meeting goes well, as these preliminary meetings often do. Chandler admires both Hawks ('a very wise hombre') and Bogart ('the genuine article'), and tells Faulkner and Brackett that he likes their script, though he is less flattering about it in private ('"Twill do'). After this meeting, Hawks assures him that he shoots from the cuff, using the script merely as a starting point for his actors, and rewriting it himself as he goes along. What can possibly go wrong?

While they are filming, the plot, already dense, grows impenetrable. Faulkner's reliance on alcohol – after a night on the town with Hawks, he is spotted groping for cigarette stubs in a mint julep glass – makes his command of the plot shaky. This is possibly not helped by the unusual arrangement with his fellow screenwriter, whereby he is writing every other scene. Additionally, during filming, Lauren Bacall becomes so distressed by the brilliance of the unknown Martha Vickers, who plays her nymphomaniac sister, that to pacify her the studio cuts all but one of Vickers' scenes, leading to yet more gaps in the plotting.

The plot is further muddied by Hawks's impromptu revisions, which often involve going back to the original novel, and by the schmaltzy ending that a third screenwriter, brought in by the studio, has tacked on. Furthermore, the screenwriters have tried to anticipate the censors by editing out all allusions to homosexuality and pornography, thus obscuring the motives for blackmail and murder. Finally, the Hollywood Production Code will not allow a heroine to get away with being an accessory to murder, so that any killings originally ascribed to the nymphomaniac Carmen must now be placed at someone else's door. The plot, already scrambled, has by now gone completely haywire, involving no fewer than seven mysterious murders at the hands of an indeterminate number of assailants.

To sum up: the nymphomaniac Carmen did not, as Vivian supposed, kill Regan during a mental blackout; in fact he was killed by Eddie Mars, who believed him to be having an affair with Mars's wife; Lundgren killed Brody; Canino killed Jones; Marlowe killed Canino; and the chauffeur Owen Taylor killed the pornographer (or 'rare books dealer') Geiger.

But who killed the chauffeur Owen Taylor? He is lying dead in a limousine under ten feet of water at the end of the pier, but nobody – screenwriters, director, cast, crew – can work out why.*

Shooting grinds to a halt while everybody tries to puzzle it out. Hawks and Bogart get into an argument about it: Hawks is pretty sure Taylor was murdered, while Bogart assumes it is suicide. Eventually, Hawks decides to send a telegram to Raymond Chandler: he, of all people, must know.

Sitting at home, Chandler studies the telegram. He can't remember his novel well enough, so he goes back to it and rereads the crucial scenes. But by the end of the process he is none the wiser, so he sends back a telegram: 'I DONT KNOW.'

A few days later, Jack Warner, the parsimonious head of Warner Brothers, chances upon this telegram, and finds out that it cost the studio seventy cents. He immediately phones Howard Hawks. Was it really necessary, he asks, to spend money on a telegram about a silly little point like that?

---

* The final film includes this dialogue between Bogart and the gambler and blackmailer Brody:

Marlowe: Hmm, hmm. You know where that Packard is now? ... It's in the Sheriff's garage. It was fished out of twelve feet of water off Lido pier early this morning. There was a dead man in it. He'd been sapped. The car was pointed toward the end of the pier and the hand throttle pulled out.

Brody: Well, you can't pin that on me.

Marlowe: I could make an awful good try ... You see, the dead man was Owen Taylor, Sternwood's chauffeur. He went up to Geiger's place 'cause he was sweet on Carmen. He didn't like the kind of games Geiger was playing. He got himself in the back way with a jimmy and he had a gun. And the gun went off as guns will, and Geiger fell down dead. Owen ran away taking the film with him. You went after him and got it – how else would you get it?

Brody: All right, you're right. I heard the shots and saw him run down the back steps and into the Packard and away. I followed him. He turned west on Sunset and beyond Beverly he, uh, skidded off the road, and uh, came to a stop. So I came up and played copper. He had a gun, he was rattled, so I sapped him down. I figured the film might be worth something so I took it. That's the last I saw of him.

Marlowe: So you left an unconscious man in a car way out near Beverly someplace and you want me to believe that somebody conveniently came along, ran that car all the way down to the ocean, pushed it off the pier, and then came back and hid Geiger's body.

Brody: Well I didn't.

Marlowe: Somebody did.

HOWARD HAWKS

PLAYS GOLF WITH

HOWARD HUGHES

Lakeside Country Club, Burbank, California
July 1930

The Lakeside Country Club* is currently Hollywood's most fashionable golf course. Howard Hawks is about to tee off on a sunny afternoon in July when the golf pro comes running out.

'Howard Hughes is on the phone,' he says. 'He wants to play golf with you.'

Hawks is a fine golfer – he has a four handicap. This allows him to deal on equal terms with Hollywood executives who make other, less sporty, directors feel out of their depth. And, unlike most other directors, Hawks has even featured golf in his movies, capturing its contrary blend of commerce, exercise, competition and socialising. In *Bringing up Baby*, the lawyer Alexander Peabody hates talking business while playing golf, but in the middle of a game his golfing partner Dr Huxley tries to talk him into donating $1 million to his palaeontology museum. As Peabody prepares to play a shot, Huxley says, 'If you could use your influence with Mrs Random, that would be nice,' which enrages Mr Peabody. 'When I play golf, I only talk golf! And then only between shots!' he snaps.†

Howard Hawks himself stands by no such rules. He is happy to play golf and talk business at the same time. Small wonder, then, that the pro at the Lakeside Country Club is taken aback by the vehemence of Hawks's reply.

'Tell him I don't want to play golf with him!' he says.

The pro asks why.

'The son of a bitch is suing me, that's why!'§

---

* Now the Lakeside Golf Club.

† The golfing sequence in *Bringing up Baby* was shot at the Bel Air Country Club.

§ When W.C. Fields is invited to play at the Lakeside with someone he doesn't like, he replies, 'When I want to play with a prick, I'll play with my own.'

He isn't kidding. The two Howards are sworn enemies, currently locked in a vicious legal battle. Hughes is suing Hawks for plagiarism, claiming that Hawks lifted scenes from Hughes's air-battle film *Hell's Angels* and transplanted them into his own air-battle film, *The Dawn Patrol*. Hughes is also furious with Hawks for hiring the very same experts who have just finished working for him, and he is after retribution. In the view of Hal Wallis, Hughes 'raised competitiveness to the level of mania, trying to buy up all the World War I fighter planes that he didn't already own'.

A few weeks ago, Hughes turned up at Hawks's house and forbade him from filming a scene in which a fighter pilot is shot in the chest.

'Howard, I make pictures for a living and you make them for fun,' Hawks interrupted the twenty-five-year-old millionaire. 'I got a hangover. I'm not interested in talking about it.' In his subsequent legal deposition, Hawks pointed out that people shot in aeroplanes are almost invariably shot in the chest.

Hughes even persuaded one of his writers to bribe Hawks's secretary to leak a copy of the script; but the secretary passed the news on to Hawks, who had Hughes's writer arrested for theft. According to Hawks, 'Hughes called me up and said, "Hey, you've got my writer in jail." And I said, "That's where the so-and-so belongs." I said, "Why did you try to corrupt a perfectly nice girl by bribing her? If you wanted a script, I'd have given you one. Now, I don't give a damn about it."'

Hollywood feuds don't come much meaner: Hawks has been driven to issue a restraining order against Hughes. It seems unlikely that such a fierce dispute can be settled over a round of golf.

But golf plays an even more crucial role in the life of Howard Hughes, who is a five handicap. When he was a boy, his mother, a health-obsessive, encouraged him to play golf, as she believed golf courses to be free from infections. She worried about every aspect of her child's health: his feet, his teeth, his digestion, his bowels, the colour of his cheeks, his weight. She also worried about what she called his 'supersensitiveness'. Young Howard was extremely nervous, and unable to make friends with other children, perhaps because his mother was always worrying that they might pass an infection on to him.

When Hughes was sixteen, his mother died during minor surgery, leaving him with both lifelong hypochondria and a blind faith in the medicinal power of golf. Two years later, his father died from a heart attack, leaving Hughes heir to the larger part of his thriving tool company. Hughes immediately bought out his relatives, but was prevented from taking complete control of the company by a Texas state law which regards citizens as minors until they reach the age of twenty-one. It is possible for this law to be overruled by the courts, but only when the owner turns nineteen, so until that date Hughes conducted a clandestine campaign. At regular intervals he played golf with Judge Walter Monteith at the Houston Country Club. As they walked together around the course, he promised the judge that if the courts declared him an adult, he would enrol at Princeton University. On December 24th 1924, his nineteenth birthday, he filed his application. The result was a foregone conclusion: the judge declared him an adult, thus allowing him to take over the Hughes Tool Company. From that moment on, Howard Hughes never gave a second thought to enrolling at Princeton.

And so to this sunny July day. The pro goes back to the clubhouse, and returns two minutes later with Hughes's reply: he has agreed to drop his lawsuit, and is on his way.

A few minutes later, Hughes turns up, and the two enemies embark on their round. Golf works its peculiar magic. Across eighteen holes, they discover that they have a surprising amount in common. They are both tall and lanky, reserved and crafty. They enjoy breaking rules, and view themselves as Hollywood outsiders. They are also both great womanisers, though Hughes prefers the brassy type, and Hawks the more refined.*

By the time the round is over, their feud is at an end. Moreover, Howard Hawks has agreed to direct Howard Hughes's new film, *Scarface*, for $25,000.

Nobody knows what was said, but it might have helped that Hawks won their game of golf by seventy-one strokes to Hughes's seventy-two.

---

* When Katharine Hepburn is playing the tenth hole of the course in 1936, a two-seater plane lands in front of her. Out climbs Hughes, brandishing a bag of clubs and saying, 'Mind a third?' Their three-year affair begins later the same day.

HOWARD HUGHES

TALKS BRAS WITH

CUBBY BROCCOLI

7000 Romaine Street, Los Angeles
Spring 1940

In April 1983, Cubby Broccoli appears before a Supreme Court investigation into the affairs of the late Howard Hughes.

'Did you have occasion to meet Mr Hughes on a movie set?'

'Yes.'

'What was your first job?'

'My first job was to take a very lovely young lady on a train up to Flagstaff, Arizona.'

'Was that Jane Russell?'

'Yes.'

At this point, as Broccoli remembers it, 'there was a bit of a stir among the listeners which may have been envy'.

The son of a vegetable farmer,* Albert Romolo Broccoli took jobs in his cousin's Long Island Casket Company, as a salesman with the Paris Beauty Parlour Supply Company, and cleaning jewellery in Beverly Hills before joining Twentieth Century-Fox as a gofer.

In the spring of 1940, Howard Hawks takes him on as his assistant on the film *The Outlaw*, produced by his old rival Howard Hughes. The male leads have already been cast, but not the female. Hughes takes responsibility for casting. 'It was the general consensus at the time that Hughes was "a bosom man"', Broccoli recalls.

Hawks shows Broccoli a photograph of Ernestine Jane Geraldine Russell, who is at present employed as a receptionist to a chiropodist. She

---

* His grandfather Pasquale Broccoli arrives in New York from Calabria with only a packet of broccoli seeds. Other immigrants to America have tried planting broccoli, but with little success. But the Broccolis' broccoli – from the family de Cicco strain, which sells for $16 an ounce – proves triumphant. The family goes on to grow many other types of vegetable – spinach, carrots, radishes, cucumbers – but broccoli remains their pride and joy.

is tall and beautiful, with a thirty-eight-inch chest. Hawks asks Broccoli what he thinks of her. 'I think she's terrific,' he replies.

Hughes thinks the same, and hires Jane Russell at $50 a week. To Broccoli's delight, the night before she sets off on her long train journey to Flagstaff, Arizona, Hughes asks him to escort her.

'I'd appreciate it if you'd see to it that she gets everything she needs on the journey,' he adds.

'Sure, Howard.'

'Oh … and Cubby …'

'Yes?'

'Keep all the characters away from her.'

After two weeks' filming, Hughes declares himself dissatisfied with the early rushes: there are no clouds in the sky. He tells Hawks that he wants clouds, 'even if you have to wait for a little while'.

Hawks is impatient – he has a commitment to start directing his next film – and furious. 'You evidently don't like what I'm doing. Why don't you take over the picture?' he says, and walks out.

This rather suits Hughes, who has always been eager to take over the directing. But where Hawks was empathetic and instinctive, Hughes is distant and perfectionist. One scene alone requires 103 takes. The production, scheduled to last six to eight weeks, ends up taking nine months. Now promoted to Howard Hughes's assistant, Cubby Broccoli can't help noticing how much time the director takes studying Jane Russell's figure. 'His big preoccupation was how to get the maximum impact from Jane Russell's breasts.' It is almost as though he were treating them as stars in their own right. 'We're not getting enough production out of Jane's breasts!' Hughes barks at his cinematographer.

In one scene, Jane Russell is tied between two trees with leather thongs, and writhes around as though trying to escape. Hughes studies her through his viewfinder, and frowns. He summons Broccoli and complains that her brassière is giving her breasts an artificial look: as she twists about, its outline is clearly visible beneath her blouse. But Jane refuses to go bra-less; she is not that sort of girl.

Hughes won't let the matter go. 'This is really just a very simple engineering problem,' he tells Broccoli. He retires to his drawing board, suspending production while he redesigns Miss Russell's brassière.* 'What he was trying to do was to get a smooth look, a no-bra look,' remembers Russell. 'And as usual, Howard was right. He was way ahead of his time.'

Hughes comes up with a cantilevered underwired bra, with rods of curved structural steel connected to the shoulder straps and sewn into the brassière below each breast. It allows for virtually any amount of Jane Russell's generous bosom to be freely exposed; but when she tries it on, she finds it far too uncomfortable. 'I *never* wore his bra, and believe me, he could design planes, but a Mr Playtex he wasn't. Oh, I suppose given several years and a willing model he would have conquered the problem, but fortunately he had a picture to worry about.'

Russell hides her new bra behind her bed, puts her old one back on, covers the seams with Kleenex tissues, and pulls the straps over to the side. This crafty dodge worries her poor wardrobe mistress. 'What if we get fired?' she says.

'Nobody's going to tell,' replies Russell, putting her blouse back on.

Russell is tied back to the trees and given the signal to start struggling. Hughes spends a very long time looking through his viewfinder before saying, 'OK.' The shoot recommences, and Hughes is delighted with the result.

But the story does not end there. When the Hollywood censor sees the finished film, he is enraged. 'The girl's breasts, which are quite large and prominent, are shockingly uncovered,' he complains, recommending 108 separate cuts.

Hughes takes the matter to appeal. A master of publicity, he employs a Columbia University mathematician. With the aid of calipers, this expert goes along a line of blown-up photographs of leading actresses – Betty Grable, Rita Hayworth, Jean Harlow, Norma Shearer – measuring the average percentage of bust displayed, then comparing it with the percentage of Jane Russell's bust on view, eventually finding in favour of Jane Russell. The censorship board is won round, and agrees to just three cuts. Three years after the film started production, it is premiered in San Francisco, by which time Jane Russell is already one of the most famous

---

* He is meant to be designing a top-secret medium-range bomber capable of flying at 450 miles an hour for the US Air Force, but this has to take a back seat to Miss Russell's breasts.

actresses in America. 'The Picture That Couldn't be Stopped', reads one billboard, adding, 'Sex Has Not Been Rationed'. Other advertisements include a billboard asking, 'What are the Two Great Reasons for Russell's Success?' and a skywriting plane flying above Pasadena, leaving behind it the words 'THE OUTLAW', along with two giant circles, each with a dot in the centre.*

'It was all fun in those days,' reminisces Broccoli, half a century on.

---

* A later film Jane Russell makes with Howard Hughes, a 3D Technicolor musical called *The French Line*, is promoted with the slogans 'J.R. in 3-D. It'll knock BOTH your eyes out!' and 'Jane Russell in 3 Dimensions – and what dimensions!' The Archbishop of St Louis, where the film is premiered in 1953, issues a warning to his parishioners. 'Dearly beloved, since no Catholic can with a clear conscience attend such an immoral movie, we feel it our solemn duty to forbid our Catholic people under penalty of mortal sin to attend this presentation.' The Archbishop does not realise that this is exactly the reason Hughes chose to premiere the film in St Louis, with its 65 per cent Roman Catholic population.

CUBBY BROCCOLI

SHARES A BARBER WITH

GEORGE LAZENBY

Kurt's of Mayfair, London W1
November 1965

While Cubby Broccoli, now the producer of the James Bond films, is having his hair cut at Kurt's of Mayfair, he is struck by the occupant of the next chair, 'this handsome character with a strong jaw, great physique and a lot of self-assurance'. It crosses his mind that he might make a good Bond, but he imagines that anyone having his hair cut at such an expensive barber's must be a wealthy businessman. And anyway, the position is already filled.

In fact, the person in the next chair can't really afford to be there at all. He is a male model, born in Goulburn, Australia, the son of the greenkeeper at a bowls club. George Lazenby arrived in England last year and worked as a used-car salesman before drifting into modelling. He has had some success in his new career, modelling clothes and shampoo and fronting an advertising campaign for High Speed Gas. His most noticeable role is probably as the hero of the TV advertisement for Fry's chocolate, in which he strides across the screen like a gladiator, bearing a crate of chocolate on his shoulders.

Lazenby wants to launch himself as an actor, and entertains ambitions to be the next James Bond. To this end, he has been secretly plotting to bump into Broccoli. Having discovered that Broccoli has his hair cut regularly at Kurt's, he duly booked an appointment at the same time.

When Broccoli returns to his office, he instructs his secretary to call Kurt and find out the name of his suave customer. Broccoli jots down the name George Lazenby, thinking it might come in handy.

Three years later, Sean Connery decides to stop playing James Bond. The quest for a new Bond begins. Three hundred potential James Bonds are interviewed or screen-tested for the role, among them Jeremy Brett, James Brolin, Lord Lucan, Adam West (star of the television *Batman*) and

Peter Snow, later to become famous as the wielder of the election-night Swingometer.* Summoned to a meeting with Broccoli, Lazenby wears a Savile Row suit and a Rolex Submariner wristwatch. He is shameless. 'An actor would go into an audition for the role thinking of Connery, but I wasn't an actor. I was so arrogant, I had nothing to lose.'

Broccoli and his co-producer Harry Saltzman watch from their first-floor office as Lazenby crosses the road to their office. They are impressed by his self-assurance, and even more impressed when he darts past the receptionist and bolts upstairs, just like James Bond.

In his interview, he exudes a winning mix of defiance and indifference. When they offer him a screen test, he demands payment, and they agree to it. 'Everyone was impressed by Lazenby. The infallible litmus test was to parade him in front of the office secretaries. Their eyes lit up as he swung past their desks and through to our office. Six foot two inches tall – the same height as Connery – he was a 186-pounder who knew how to walk tall and put himself over,' says Broccoli.

Lazenby's cocky persona is not contrived. 'They tested three hundred actors on film and no one had what Connery had, that self-assurance with women, but I certainly did.† I'd been a model, had just hit London in the Swinging Sixties and was having a great time playing around with the girls there. I was always running around with a grin on my face.' His cockiness extends to fibbing: he tells the casting director he has already made movies in Russia, Germany and Hong Kong, though he has never acted before.

At the screen test, Broccoli asks him to perform a fight sequence with an assassin. In the heat of the moment, Lazenby punches the assassin – a professional wrestler – in the face, thus further impressing Broccoli with his manliness. The role is his.

Soon after the filming of *On Her Majesty's Secret Service* begins,§ Broccoli's admiration for Lazenby begins to wane. He dislikes the way he

---

* The unknown Timothy Dalton drops out of the running, believing himself, at twenty-one, too young for the part.

† To date, it is estimated that James Bond has killed more than 150 men and slept with forty-four women, three quarters of whom have tried to kill him.

§ In the original script, the switch from one James Bond to another is explained by Bond having undergone plastic surgery so as to disguise him from his enemies. In subsequent revisions, this explanation is dropped in favour of no explanation at all.

is already behaving like a superstar, demanding special treatment and quarrelling with chauffeurs. At one point, his co-star Telly Savalas takes him to one side and advises him to stop being so difficult. By the end, the director, Peter Hunt, will speak to him only through a middle man. As Broccoli watches him lord it over everybody, it occurs to him that Lazenby is sawing off the branch he is sitting on.

Nevertheless, he is judged to have acquitted himself reasonably well as James Bond, and they offer him $1 million to play the role again. Lazenby demands twice the amount. They turn him down, and he subsequently announces his retirement on *The Johnny Carson Show*. Both Carson and the audience burst into laughter, assuming he is joking. Watching on television, Broccoli and Saltzman are furious, believing it will cause damage at the box office. Lazenby further infuriates them by making no effort to look like Bond: he is dressed like a hippy, with long hair and a beard.

Years later, George Lazenby regrets his prima-donna behaviour. 'The trouble was I lived Bond out of the studios as well as in. I had to have a Rolls-Royce to go around in, and women just threw themselves at me if I stepped into a nightclub. I couldn't count the parade that passed through my bedroom. I became hot-headed, greedy and big-headed. I got on the bandwagon and said I must be who they say I am and demanded limousines and did the whole bit, which was obnoxious and arrogant and all the things you hate about those people. I got what I deserved and had a long slide down, which was much harder than going up.' He blames his decision to abandon Bond on his manager. 'Ronan advised me: "Bond is over, finished, anyway it's Sean Connery's gig and you cannot match that guy. We'll make other movies." I listened to him. I thought he knew what it was all about, but I was dumb. I missed out on everything.'*

---

* Lazenby's future work as an actor is sporadic. Over the years he has occasional roles on television, among them episodes of *Baywatch*, *Kung Fu* and *Hawaii Five-O*. In the 1990s, he appears in a number of the *Emmanuelle* movies.

GEORGE LAZENBY

NAMES NAMES TO

SIMON DEE

Studio 5B, London Weekend Television
February 8th 1970

The new James Bond, George Lazenby, is promoting *On Her Majesty's Secret Service*. He is booked to appear with his co-star, Diana Rigg, on the first half of *The Simon Dee Show*, before John Lennon and Yoko Ono come on for the second half. What can possibly go wrong?

Since he transferred from the BBC to LWT a month ago, Simon Dee has been feeling increasingly unwanted. 'I found myself not where I wanted to be, not on the television network I wanted, not on the day that I wanted, not with the guests that I wanted … and in a general state of mental decay.'

His BBC show, *Dee Time*, first broadcast in April 1967, made him one of the most famous men in Britain. Originally spotted when starring in an advertisement for Smith's Crisps, for three years he embodied the sixties dream, hosting his own chat show ('It's Siiiiiiimon Deeeee!'), dashing up and down the King's Road in an Aston Martin, hosting the Miss World competition, presenting an award to the Beatles and numbering Michael Caine ('Mike') and Roger Moore ('Rog') among his famous friends. Every Saturday evening, up to eighteen million viewers regularly tuned in to *Dee Time*.

But as his fame grew, so too did his sense of entitlement. He became more and more difficult with his colleagues, his bosses, his studio audiences. Before long, he insisted on choosing his guests, and threatened to walk out whenever he didn't get his way. When the time came to renew his contract, he strode into the office of the Head of BBC Light Entertainment and demanded more money. But Billy Cotton called his bluff, offering him 20 per cent less 'to test his loyalty'.

He failed the test, and left for London Weekend Television, but the audience for his new show – transmitted at 11 p.m. on Sunday nights

– rarely reaches a million. He is unhappy and increasingly paranoid. He has always been prone to constructing clandestine explanations for humdrum events, but his sense of a conspiracy is escalating. He complains that he has spotted men in black hunched behind hedgerows, taking photographs of him; he is also convinced his telephone is bugged. Some blame his paranoia on marijuana, but he argues that, on the contrary, it is marijuana that keeps him sane.

Dee greets his first guest in the green room. (Oddly enough, Dee too auditioned for James Bond; he tells friends he was rejected simply because he was too tall.) His first impression of Lazenby is that he looks nothing like he did as James Bond: he now sports a beard and long hair, and is dressed like a cowboy. But, ever the pro, Dee masks his surprise.

The interview begins very slowly. Lazenby is perhaps a little distant, but Dee sees no real cause for alarm. Then, out of nowhere, Lazenby dips into his pocket, pulls out a piece of paper, turns to the camera and shouts: 'I would like to draw everybody's attention to the fact that the following senators were involved in a plot to kill President Kennedy!'

He starts reciting a long list of names. Dee attempts to steer the interview onto another topic by bringing in Diana Rigg. 'That's very interesting, George. What does Diana make of all that then? Isn't she lovely!'

But Lazenby is furious at the interruption, and continues to read his list of murderous senators in a louder and louder voice. An enthusiast for conspiracies, Dee nevertheless realises that naming individual senators as conspirators in a presidential assassination is taking things too far. Across Lazenby's shoulder, he sees the studio floor manager making furious 'wind up' signals to him, but Lazenby proves unstoppable.

Dee attempts to distance himself from Lazenby's rants by saying, 'I really don't know anything about this subject, folks,' and finally says, 'Fascinating stuff, George. Thank you. And we'll be talking to two more fascinating people, John Lennon and Yoko Ono, in just two minutes!' This is the signal for an advertising break.

The show is recorded a few hours before transmission, so Dee imagines that any offending passages will be edited out. But for some reason they are not. On Monday morning, the newspapers are full of it.

Dee is summoned by Stella Richman, Managing Director of LWT. 'Who said you could talk about Kennedy?'

'I didn't talk about Kennedy. Lazenby did, and it happens to be his right as a guest to talk about anything he likes.'

Richman behaves, in Dee's opinion, 'like some demented puppet', accusing him of plotting the incident. 'If you ever mention Kennedy on air again I shall tear up your contract. Now leave!'

Dee is affronted. 'It really was an amazing moment. Here was this female terrier telling me that she had the right to tell me who I could or couldn't book on my show and what I was supposed to say to them! And if I disagreed with her then I was out of a job!'

The incident fuels Dee's already highly developed sense of conspiracy. Has he fallen into a carefully laid trap? Conspiracy piles upon conspiracy: he suspects Lazenby was put up to it by his old enemy Ronan O'Rahilly, who also talked Lazenby out of renewing his James Bond contract ('All that Bond stuff's on the wane, man. Look at *Easy Rider* and things, that's the way to go').

But Dee remains bullish. 'I don't give a damn. Last night, for this so-called disastrous programme, I had the highest viewing figures ever for a Sunday-night show. I'm supposed to feel ashamed of that? … So George made a fool of himself, not me. He died the death, baby, not me! It doesn't worry me, baby! I'm running my show, not anybody else.'

It is the beginning of the end for both host and guest. Soon afterwards, it is announced that this first series of *The Simon Dee Show* on LWT will also be the last.* Dee blames this on his opposition to Britain entering the EEC.

* A brand-new late-night chat show is hosted by a relative unknown, whose name is Michael Parkinson. Dee's slot on the BBC is given to the actor Derek Nimmo, in *If it's Saturday, it Must be Nimmo*. Among Nimmo's first guests is Basil Brush, a leading glove puppet.

SIMON DEE

TALKS OF HEAVEN AND HELL WITH

MICHAEL RAMSEY

Studio 5B, London Weekend Television
June 5th 1970

The meteoric career of Simon Dee, King of the Chat Show, is on the point of disintegration. Over the past few months he has rubbed everyone up the wrong way.* His paranoia has produced the enemies of which he had once only dreamed.

Tonight's show is to be his last. The only remaining topic for discussion is his severance pay. 'The company is in no mood to be generous with compensation,' reports the *Sunday Telegraph*.

Dee casts around for explanations of his downfall beyond his opposition to Britain's entry into the Common Market, and finds one in the looming presence of his rival chat-show host, David Frost: *Frost on Sunday* is broadcast in the prime evening slot of 7.25, whereas *The Simon Dee Show* goes out much later, and at no set time. Dee's guests are seldom advertised in advance, whereas Frost's always are. Moreover, Frost is given the heavyweight guests, while Dee has to make do with novelty acts: one of his recent shows featured Vincent Price poaching a haddock in a dishwasher.

Whenever Dee tries to make his show more interesting, he always seems to slip up. He detects David Frost's fingerprints on every banana

---

* One day, furious at not being allowed Matt Monro on his show, he decides to 'cause them a bit of bother by seeing how they manage to broadcast *The Simon Dee Show* without Simon Dee appearing on it'. He simply fails to show up. 'They phoned me every day if not every hour to try and find out when I might be back, but I answered – sounding perfectly fine, of course – that I was too ill to speak and needed to go back to bed. It was delicious!' He arrives at LWT at the last possible moment, just as his emergency replacement, Pete Murray, is preparing to go on. 'I came out and said, "Hello everyone, well, as long as you've got your health, what else matters, eh? And for those of you who tuned in tonight to see Pete Murray … sorry!" It got a big laugh from the studio audience and went on to be one of my best LWT shows.'

skin. 'I think he may have been rather worried that I might be better at it than he was. That he'd be beaten at his own game. Of course, he wasn't about to allow that.' Frost is a director of LWT, while Dee is the new boy, given his slot only after having fallen out with the BBC. When the two men pass each other in the corridor, no one ever sees them speak.

On screen, Dee remains as easy-going as ever, the epitome of Sixties Casual. But his end is nigh. Off screen he is more tense and difficult than ever. Only for his very last show is he permitted the sort of heavy-weight guest he claims always to have wanted: the Archbishop of Canterbury.

Dr Ramsey and Simon Dee sit opposite each other in leather armchairs, Ramsey in his purple cassock, Dee in his electric-blue suit with matching silk cravat. To the viewers, it looks like a clash between ancient and modern: the venerable Establishment figure, a devoted advocate of silence,* versus the slick and with-it young chat-show host.

And so, for the first few minutes of their conversation, it seems. Dee tries to get Ramsey onto the subject of sex, and succeeds. Ramsey says that he regrets 'the modern obsession, concentration and attention on nudity and sex. There's a kind of openness and frankness that is good and wholesome. But it's absolutely wrong and unnecessary to have this obsession.'

But when Dee decides to quiz him on other aspects of the permissive society, Ramsey shows himself more in tune with the times than Dee expected, and praises elements of the hippy culture. Dee questions him about 'the people who want peace, and because of their behaviour, and the fact that they don't fit into any particular slot, are rejected'. But Ramsey comes out in support of the counter-culture: 'The people are fed up with our civilisation, and the rot that's in it. They try to escape from it by going into another world.'

Dee affects surprise at these opinions, but Ramsey has, in fact, always been a liberal. Ten years ago, he defined the 'three outstanding moral

---

* 'He did not think that there was enough quiet in the world. To realise God you need silence. He loved spaces for silence, and places of silence. He encouraged the practice of retreats. He was an inspiring conductor of retreats. He thought of the religious communities as little havens of quiet scattered across society …'. From Owen Chadwick's memorial address.

issues' as the urgent need for disarmament, for radical changes in race relations, and for rich countries to help the poor. In the House of Lords, he has voted for liberalising the laws against homosexuality. He has called for military action against the Ian Smith regime in Rhodesia, and was a vociferous critic of General Pinochet in Chile. In 1967, when the proprietor of *Time* magazine made a jingoistic remark about the Vietnam war in his presence, Ramsey was outraged by his lack of compassion for suffering innocents, and showed him the door.*

Dee asks what he imagines to be a 'cheeky' question. 'A colleague of yours in the Anglican Church, another bishop, was recently quoted as saying that he imagined heaven to be the kind of place where Mozart is permanently being playing in the background by a kind of otherworldly orchestra and that delicious foie gras is permanently available on tap. Do you agree with him? Is that your vision of heaven too?'

Some of the team consider this a marvellously irreverent question. 'You should have seen the look on Ramsey's face!' says one. 'He just wasn't expecting to be asked that!'

In fact, Ramsey has a profound belief in heaven, enriched by his deep knowledge not only of Western Christianity – he was Regius Professor of Divinity at Cambridge – but also of the Eastern Orthodox Churches. If there is a look of astonishment on Ramsey's face, it is probably at the glibness of the question. 'He bubbled with ecstasy over the beatific vision. He had a real sense of joining with angels and archangels here and now in worship,' comments someone who hears him talk of heaven.

The Archbishop's definition of hell is simple. 'Hell,' he says, 'is stewing in one's own juice.' As it turns out, this is to be Dee's occupation for the next thirty-nine years.

A month after the show is broadcast, a courier from LWT arrives at Dee's Chelsea house with a briefcase containing £9,000, the remainder of

---

* At the end of the year, Ramsey flies to South Africa, where he preaches against apartheid. 'If we exclude a man because he is of another race or colour,' he asks, 'are we not excluding Christ himself?' He expresses these views even more vehemently in a frosty meeting with President Vorster. He is determined not to be photographed looking cheerful with the President, so before the meeting, 'I practised making one unpleasant face after another while shaving. I did it so I should get a sort of continuity of unpleasant faces.'

what he is owed. 'And that was it, more or less. I sort of died after that. It was the end of me.'*

Simon Dee is not seen on British television for another thirty-three years. In 2003, when Channel 4 offers him a one-off special, he suggests they invite some of his famous friends from the sixties. But they all refuse. 'Did you tell him that it was me, that it was my big comeback show?' he asks. The answer is yes. Dee says nothing, but looks disappointed.

Brewer's Dictionary of Rogues, Villains and Eccentrics defines 'Simon Dee Syndrome' as applying to 'someone who is remembered for having been forgotten'.

---

* For the next three decades, he attempts any number of comebacks, but they all end in tears. He walks out on the Radio 4 *Today* programme after just two broadcasts, from a Fairy Liquid commercial during lunchtime on day one, and from a Reading radio station on the very first morning, after refusing to interview Alvin Stardust. Over the years, he finds himself in court for, successively, shoplifting a potato peeler, non-payment of rates, smashing up a loo set in a shop, and assaulting a policeman outside Buckingham Palace after being told he cannot speak to the Queen. In 1974 he serves twenty-eight days in Pentonville Prison for non-payment of rates on his former Chelsea home.

'No bank will give me an account now,' he says to an interviewer in 2004. 'They say they don't know who Simon Dee is. I give them videos of Simon Dee on LWT and they absolutely say no, they can't accept that. I even faxed the chairman and told him what was going on, and he got in touch with the manager, and told him to keep throwing me out.' At the time of his death aged seventy-four in 2009, he is living in a one-bedroomed flat in Winchester with twenty-six scrapbooks stuffed with his newspaper cuttings, beginning in 1964 and ending in 1972.

MICHAEL RAMSEY

IS PUNISHED BY

GEOFFREY FISHER

The Headmaster's Study, Repton School, Derbyshire
May 1919

Michael Ramsey is unhappy at prep school. 'I never were more utterly miserable,' he writes to his mother in a letter home dated 'Tuesday Evening just after tea'. '… I cannot bear it any longer … I am just crying like anythinke. Come at once never mind anything else. I am utterly miserable.'

In 1918 he wins a scholarship to Repton, where, preferring books to sport, he is only a little more cheerful, and remains an outsider. His headmaster – distant, forceful, coolly efficient – is a young clergyman called Geoffrey Fisher. Ramsey nicknames him 'the little snipe'. In turn, Fisher marks Ramsey down as eccentric, bookish and scruffy; he notes with disapproval his habit of endlessly hitching up his trousers with his elbows.

As Ramsey grows older, he discovers a talent for debating, and develops an interest in politics. Like his parents, who voted Labour in the 1918 general election, he has a horror of jingoism and militarism; aged fifteen, he energetically opposes a debating motion to send British troops to fight Bolshevism in Russia. But he goes too far; when an assistant master speaks in support of the motion, Ramsey turns on him, and is excessively caustic, a punishable offence. There follows what Ramsey calls 'some unpleasantness': he is told to report to Geoffrey Fisher, who makes him learn and recite fifty lines of Greek from the play *Medea*.

He soon gets into further trouble for refusing to parade with the Officer Training Corps. He then enters into a battle of wills with Fisher – a battle which, perhaps surprisingly, he wins. Finding a loophole in the school rules, the pupil forces the headmaster to admit that military training cannot be regarded as compulsory, and, armed with a letter of support from his father, he is excused. When he leaves Repton at the end of 1922, his final report from Fisher is notably grudging in its praise: 'A boy with force of character who, in spite of certain uncouthnesses, has done good service on his own lines.'

Michael Ramsey goes into the Church, and swiftly gains promotion. The paths of the two men cross again when Fisher, now Bishop of Chester, agrees to take Ramsey on as his examining chaplain. For his part, Ramsey never quite manages to shake off his fear of his old headmaster. The two men are very different: Fisher, a leading Freemason, is brisk, efficient, bossy, conservative, a stickler for correct dress, and a keen advocate of gaiters at Matins; Ramsey is dreamy, liberal,* humorous, vague, scholarly, easily bored,† with a tendency to walk around with his shoelaces undone.

In 1945, Fisher is appointed Archbishop of Canterbury, succeeding another old Repton headmaster, William Temple. When the time comes for his own retirement, Fisher considers his former pupil entirely unsuited to succeed him, and advises the Prime Minister accordingly. 'Dr F is *violently*, even *brutally* opposed to Dr Ramsey,' notes Harold Macmillan in his diary.

Ramsey delights in telling friends the story. 'He said, "Oh, Prime Minister, I shall be retiring shortly, and I don't think the Archbishop of York, Dr Ramsey, would be entirely suitable as my successor." And Macmillan asked, "Why is that?" So Fisher said, "He was a boy under me at Repton, and I don't think he'd be very suitable." So Macmillan said, "Oh, Dr Ramsey *would* be suitable." And Fisher said, "Dr Coggan, the Bishop of Bradford, would be *very* suitable." So Macmillan said, "Well, Archbishop, you may have been Michael Ramsey's headmaster, but you're not mine, and I intend to appoint Dr Ramsey. Good afternoon."'§

---

* 'In 1975, a group of chaplains went to lunch,' recalls one of them, Father Stock, 'and afterwards I was sitting upstairs in the study and Michael began to talk about the Pope's attitude towards sex. "Masturbation, masturbation, so silly of the Pope to make such a fuss about masturbation. It's the sort of thing we all do, and we hope one day something more interesting will come along to take its place." Well, it was a warm day and the windows were wide open, and I thought, what on earth will people think if they hear all this!'

† The Bishop of Southwark, Mervyn Stockwood, remembers Ramsey at Church Assembly drawing up cricket teams composed of the greatest bores among his colleagues. For every five minutes they speak, they score a run. 'He's got a boundary today!' he exclaims whenever one of his bores exceeds himself.

§ In his diary, Macmillan also describes Fisher as 'a silly, weak, vain and muddle-headed man'. He complains of his meetings with Fisher, 'I try to talk to him about religion. But he seems quite uninterested and reverts all the time to politics.'

Michael Ramsey is duly installed as Archbishop of Canterbury. His relationship with the retired Fisher remains prickly. When Fisher accepts a peerage, Ramsey, a great one for nicknames, dubs him 'the Baron'. In turn, Fisher refuses to go quietly into retirement. He insists that he still be addressed as 'Your Grace', and from his new home in Trent, Dorset, floods Lambeth Palace with letters complaining about his successor's decisions.

'The Trent postmark always fills me with a feeling of doom,' Ramsey confides to friends, claiming that Fisher's letters always go straight into the wastepaper basket. A humorous man, he likes to picture Lady Fisher running down the street after her husband, trying to prevent him reaching the pillarbox. 'Yes, she tried to stop him. She used to run after him down the street, but all to no avail!'

When the new Archbishop of Canterbury returns one day from modelling for his waxwork at Madame Tussaud's, his staff find him extremely cheerful. 'They ran out of wax and had to melt down Geoffrey Fisher!' he exclaims jubilantly.

In 1974, when the time comes for his own retirement, Ramsey makes a witty speech at a dinner in his honour at New College. In it, he tells of a recent dream: he was in heaven, at a sherry party thrown for all the former Archbishops of Canterbury. One by one, they came up to talk to him. He met and embraced Anselm, the eleventh-century Archbishop, warming to him as a man who is 'primarily a don, who tried to say his prayers, and who cared nothing for the pomp and glory of his position. And just as Anselm and I seemed to be getting on so well together, who should come up to us but the Baron. "Now then, boys," said Fisher, "time to get back to work!"'

Yet his reveries about Fisher, though comical, operate as a form of defence, and spring from schoolboy fears. Secretaries at Lambeth Palace report that whenever one of Fisher's stern letters of admonishment arrives in his in-tray, Fisher goes into a tailspin of agony, and is unable to make any decisions for the rest of the day. Sometimes they try to hide the letters from him. Years later, when Robert Runcie is Archbishop of Canterbury, he is told by officials at Lambeth Palace that they finally hid an Epstein bust of Fisher 'because Michael trembled like a leaf every time he saw it'.

GEOFFREY FISHER

IS PHOTOGRAPHED BY

ROALD DAHL

Repton School, Derbyshire
Summer 1931

Geoffrey Fisher is in retirement in Dorset when he is contacted by one of his most illustrious old pupils from Repton, Roald Dahl. Less than a month ago, Dahl's seven-year-old daughter Olivia died suddenly of encephalitis; Dahl is distraught, and needs consoling.

Fisher invites Dahl down, and the two men talk. What passes between them? We have only Dahl's account to go by. Apparently, Fisher tells him that Olivia is in heaven. But for Dahl, this is not enough. He wants to know that her dog, Rowley, will join her there when he dies, but Fisher refuses to give him this assurance.

'His whole face closed up,' Dahl tells his other children, eight years later. 'I wanted to ask him how he could be so absolutely sure that other creatures did not get the same special treatment as us, but the look of disapproval that had settled around his mouth stopped me. I sat there wondering if this great and famous churchman really knew what he was talking about and whether he knew anything at all about God or heaven, and if he didn't, then who in the world did? And from that moment on, my darlings, I'm afraid I began to wonder whether there really was a God or not.'

But is Dahl's account to be trusted? The two men clearly part on amicable terms, as Dahl sends Fisher a copy of *Kiss Kiss*, his latest book of short stories, and encloses a photograph of Fisher beside a cricket pitch, looking towards the camera with an amused expression on his face. The photograph dates back over thirty years, to when Dahl snapped it as a schoolboy at Repton.

On the opening page of this copy of *Kiss Kiss*, he writes: 'The head-master was roaring with laughter. There was a "click" behind him. He looked round and saw the thin boy holding a camera in his hands. "Dahl," the headmaster said sternly, "if it is ribald you will suppress it!" Today, thirty-two years later, the boy is a little frightened that the headmaster will feel the same way about these stories. But he offers them, nevertheless, with gratitude and affection.'

The gratitude and affection are apparently still there when Dahl visits his old school in the 1970s to deliver a speech in which he praises Geoffrey Fisher, who has recently died, as a 'thoroughly good' man. This also accords with the view he took of him as a boy, in a letter home to his mother written at around the time he took his photograph. 'He's most frightfully nice but he's a religious fanatic. Far too religious for this place.'

These warm tributes, delivered in three different decades, are hard to square with what follows.

In 1984, now aged sixty-seven, Roald Dahl publishes *Boy*, an autobiography of his childhood. A chapter titled 'The Headmaster' begins: 'The Headmaster, while I was at Repton, struck me as being a rather shoddy bandy-legged little fellow with a big bald head and lots of energy but not much charm. Mind you, I never did know him well because in all those months and years I was at the school, I doubt whether he addressed more than six sentences to me altogether ...'

Dahl then tells how, after leaving Repton, this sadistic headmaster had 'bounced up the ladder ... to get the top job of them all, Archbishop of Canterbury! And not long after that it was he himself who had the task of crowning our present Queen in Westminster Abbey with half the world watching. Well, well, well! And this was the man who used to deliver the most vicious beatings to the boys under his care!'

Dahl goes on to describe a flogging Fisher meted out to Dahl's boyhood friend Michael. In Dahl's account, Fisher tells Michael to take down his trousers. 'The great man then gave him one terrific crack. After that, there was a pause. The cane was put down and the Headmaster began filling his pipe from a tin of tobacco. He also started to lecture the kneeling boy about sin and wrongdoing. Soon, the cane was picked up again and a second tremendous crack was administered upon the trembling buttocks. Then the pipe-filling business and the lecture went on for maybe another thirty seconds. Then came the third crack of the cane ... This slow and fearsome process went on until ten terrible strokes had been delivered, and all the time, over the pipe-lighting and the match-striking, the lecture on evil and wrongdoing and sinning and malpractice went on without a stop. It even went on as the strokes were being administered. At the end of it all, a basin, a sponge and a small clean towel were produced by the Headmaster, and the victim was told to wash away the blood before pulling up his trousers ... If someone had told me at the time that this flogging clergyman was one day to become the Archbishop of Canterbury, I would never have believed it ... If this person, I kept telling myself, was one of God's chosen salesmen on earth, then there must be something very wrong about the whole business.'

But Dahl is not telling the truth. Though Michael was beaten by a headmaster, it was by the next headmaster, a man called John Christie; Fisher had already left the school.

Why does Roald Dahl falsely identify Geoffrey Fisher as the cane-wielding, pipe-smoking, sanctimonious sadist? Is it, as some suggest, because accusing a former Archbishop of Canterbury of sadism is more newsworthy than accusing someone unknown? Or is it simply a case of mistaken identity? But if the latter is the case, and Dahl really believes Fisher guilty, why does he go to a man he believes to be a 'sanctimonious hypocrite' for spiritual guidance following the death of his little daughter? And why does he send him his book, with its loving inscription, and that photograph, taken all those years ago, of the man he described at the time as 'frightfully nice'?

ROALD DAHL

OFFERS WRITERLY TIPS TO

KINGSLEY AMIS

Iver Grove, Iver, Bucks
Summer 1972

Authors with money crave esteem. Authors with esteem crave money. Authors with neither crave both. Authors with both crave immortality. For these reasons, meetings between authors can be edgy.

Since the publication of *Lucky Jim* in 1954, Kingsley Amis has accrued sufficient money and esteem to arouse the envy of even his closest friends. Or *especially* his closest friends: 'It's not his *success* I mind so much as his immunity from worry and hard work, though I mind the success as well,' frets Philip Larkin to his girlfriend Monica Jones in 1955. '... He and Hilly struck me as a pair of DIRTY RICH CHILDREN – they have no worries, they REFUSE TO SUFFER ...'

In 1972, Amis is a guest at a summer party thrown by the wealthy, esteemed playwright Tom Stoppard at his beautiful Palladian villa. Within seconds, he is bristling with irritation. This is inevitable: he has long been both the victim and the laureate of irritation. Irritation is his muse. Before the party has got going, he has already been irritated by the monotony of his fellow guest Michael Caine, and by what he sees as the wrong-footing tactics of his host. Previously, Stoppard has always greeted him with a 'full Continental-style' embrace. Though Amis tends to dislike this 'when it comes from a man outside the family', he has tried to make allowances. 'Oh well, I had thought, the chap was a Czech, after all ... and obviously no queer, and it would be churlish to back off. So for the next couple of times, resigning myself, I had got off the embracing mark simultaneously with him. Then this time, or one like it, he stepped back from my outstretched arms with a muffled cry of shock or distaste.'

But a greater irritation is already approaching: hovering above Stoppard's seventeen acres is a helicopter, ready to deliver a late arrival. Amis's hackles really start to rise. 'I could not imagine why this form of transport had been thought necessary on a perfectly normal fine day, a Sunday as I remember, and nor was any explanation proffered.'

Out steps Roald Dahl, the most successful children's author in Britain, perhaps even in the world.

At some stage, 'not by my choice', Amis finds himself closeted with him. Dahl declares himself a great fan of Amis. 'What are you working on at the moment, Kingsley?' he asks. Amis starts to reply, but is interrupted by Dahl. 'That sounds marvellous,' he says, 'but do you expect to make a lot of money out of it however well you do it?'

'I don't know about a lot. Enough, I hope. The sort of money I usually make.'

'So you've no financial problems.'

'I wouldn't say that either, exactly, but I seem to be able to …'

Dahl shakes his head, and cuts Amis short once more. 'I hate to think of a chap of your distinction having to worry about money at your time of life. Tell me, how old are you now?'

Amis says that he is fifty.

'Yes. You might be able to write better, I mean even better, if you were financially secure.'

Amis, already bristling, attempts to turn the conversation around. 'Never mind, what have *you* got on the –'

Dahl is shaking his head. 'What you want to do is write a children's book. That's where the money is today, believe me.'

'I wouldn't know how to set about it.'

'Do you know what my advance was on my last one?' Dahl can't wait to tell Amis, who acknowledges that it certainly sounds like a large sum.

'I couldn't do it,' says Amis. 'I don't think I enjoyed children's books much when I was a child myself. I've got no feeling for that kind of thing.'

'Never mind,' replies Dahl. '*The little bastards'd swallow it.*'

Amis is the sole source for this conversation. He recalls it, nearly twenty years later, in his *Memoirs*, first published a year after Dahl's death in 1990. Has Dahl become the victim of the same sort of story-telling he once meted out to Geoffrey Fisher? 'Many times in these pages I have put in people's mouths approximations to what they said, what they might well have said, what they said at another time, and a few almost-outright inventions, but that last remark is verbatim,' declares Amis. He will never deviate from his insistence that 'Never mind, the little bastards'd swallow it' is an exact transcription of what Dahl said.*

In his account, Amis goes on to say that children are meant to be good at detecting insincerity, and would probably see through him. He may be boring Dahl a good deal, 'but that was perfectly all right with me'. At length, Dahl cuts in.

'Well, it's up to you. Either you will or you won't. Write a children's book, I mean. But if you do decide to have a crack, let me give you one word of warning. Unless you put everything you've got into it, unless you write it from the heart, the kids'll have no use for it. They'll see you're having them on. And just let me tell you from experience that there's nothing kids hate more than that. They won't give you a second chance either. You'll have had it for good as far as they're concerned. Just you bear that in mind as a word of friendly advice. Now, if you'll excuse me, I rather think I'll go in search of another drink.'

With what Amis describes as 'a stiff nod and an air of having asserted his integrity by rejecting some particularly outrageous and repulsive suggestion', Dahl walks away. Amis is left feeling he has been looking at a painting by Escher 'in which the eye is led up a flight of stairs only to find itself at the same level as it started at'.

That night, Amis watches the news on television, and notes it includes 'no report of a famous children's author being killed in a helicopter crash'.

---

* But it is easy to get these things wrong. Amis himself was once quoted in an interview with John Mortimer as admitting that he had 'hit his son with a hammer'; in fact, he had said that he had hit his *thumb* with a hammer. Likewise, his host, Tom Stoppard, was once quoted by Kenneth Tynan as saying, 'I am a human nothing'; Tynan went on to say that Stoppard's plays should be read as an attempt to come to terms with this bleak truth. Thirty years later, Stoppard writes a letter to the *Guardian* stating, with characteristic good humour, that what he in fact said was 'I am *assuming* nothing.'

Dahl's authorised biographer, Donald Sturrock, offers a paraphrase of the conversation and attempts a defence, arguing that 'many of Dahl's English literary contemporaries ... resented his skill at making money and disliked the pride he took in his own financial successes', adding that this 'frequently caused misunderstandings ... He knew that Amis, like most of the guests, did not respect children's writing as proper literature and this attitude made him vulnerable. Drunk and ill at ease, he probably felt that the only way to keep his head up was to talk money. The clash of attitudes was bitter and fundamental.' However, though he seems to go along with Amis's account, nowhere in his otherwise detailed rendition of their meeting does Sturrock either repeat or refute the words 'Never mind, the little bastards'd swallow it.'

KINGSLEY AMIS

IS DEPOSITED BY

ANTHONY ARMSTRONG-JONES

in Slough
November 1959

Queen magazine is planning to run a feature called 'Top Talkers', about the most brilliant conversationalists in the country. The top talkers all gather for lunch, together with a fashionable young photographer, Tony Armstrong-Jones, who has been hired to take the pictures. At one point, the editor of *Queen*, Mark Boxer, suggests it might be a nice idea to put a new photograph of Princess Margaret at the top of the feature, labelling it 'Top Inspirer'.

'I object strongly to that idea,' says Armstrong-Jones.

'So do I,' says the equally fashionable thirty-seven-year-old novelist Kingsley Amis.

'What don't you like about it, Tony?' asks Boxer.

'Well, I feel professionally that either I'm the photographer for the feature or I'm not, and it's a bit messy to have somebody else's work mixed up with mine.'

There the matter rests. No one thinks to ask Amis what his objections might be.

Some months later, Amis is hired by an advertising company to promote Long Life beer in a campaign which, in his own words, is intended to show 'a succession of supposed notables, including, I need hardly say, Humphrey Lyttelton, whose presence in such a series is apparently enforced by law, all swigging away at the relevant beer and crying up its merits'. The photographer, once again, is Anthony Armstrong-Jones.

The group of beer-swilling notables assembles for lunch one Friday in November. After cordial greetings, Amis says to Armstrong-Jones, 'I see that bloody colour-block of Princess Margaret got in after all, then.'

'Would you mind telling me why you were against the idea of its going in?' asks Armstrong-Jones.

'Well, just that the woman obviously has no mind at all – you remember that crap of hers about it not being any good our sending the products of our mind up into space while our souls remained stuck down below in the dives and the espresso bars – schoolgirl essay stuff. I just thought she didn't fit in very well with some of the people in the article in *Queen*. That's all.'

To which Armstrong-Jones replies crisply: 'I can assure you you're quite wrong. She is in fact an extremely intelligent and well-informed woman.'

'Oh, you know her, do you?'

'I have met her on several occasions.'

'Oh, I'm terribly sorry. I had no idea she was a great chum of yours. How tactless of me. I really didn't know.'

Amis seems to feel that he has settled their slight disagreement perfectly amicably. After lunch, the group reassembles in Armstrong-Jones's studio in Pimlico. The photographic session begins. Amis manages 'a number of sips and swallows of beer, pretended to have many more, looked at it, into, round, through glass after glass of it while Armstrong-Jones photographed'. After a while, Armstrong-Jones says, 'Don't go on drinking that filth. It's getting flat, too,' and asks his assistant to stir in some Eno's Liver Salts, to give it a frothy head.

As with most photographic sessions, this one lasts a good deal longer than planned. By the end, Amis has been joined by his wife, Hilly. Armstrong-Jones asks them what they are doing for the weekend. Amis says they are off to stay with his friend George Gale near Staines.

Armstrong-Jones declares that he is going to Bath, which is in the right direction, and insists on giving them a lift, if they wouldn't mind waiting for him to finish at the studio. Amis suggests he could take the southern road, and go via Staines – just a mile or two further on – and have a drink with the Gales before pressing on.

The finishing at the studio takes rather more time than Amis had imagined. Eventually, they pile into the car, and set off on the northern road via Slough, which is Armstrong-Jones's customary route. On the outskirts of Slough, he says he feels thirsty, and suggests they all pop into a pub. They stop and have a drink, and then, as Amis recalls, Armstrong-Jones 'said it had been fun and did the nearest thing possible to driving off leaving us standing on the pavement'.

The Amises are left to find a bus to Staines, wait for it, board it, and then be driven along a circuitous route before arriving at their destination nearly an hour and a half later than if they had set off by themselves.

A month or so passes. Amis is sitting in his study in Swansea when his guest, who has heard the story of their abandonment in Slough, tells him that it's just been announced that Princess Margaret is going to marry Tony Armstrong-Jones.

'Look, sonny,' says Amis, 'try and think of something a bit less obvious next time.' But it is true: the television coverage confirms it. Amis's friend George Gale later explains that 'It wasn't just a matter of him wanting a bit of company in the car and sod you. The devious bugger. What? I mean he was paying you back for insulting his girlfriend even though you didn't know she was his girlfriend. Pretty bloody impressive, you have to admit. He's upper-class, I keep telling you, which means he doesn't end up one down to the likes of fucking you.'

Amidst the chorus of jubilation greeting the news of the royal engagement, a single* sour note is sounded by Kingsley Amis, who suggests to an American friend that it is 'Such a symbol of the age we live in, when a royal princess, famed for her devotion to all that is most vapid and mindless in the world of entertainment, her habit of reminding people of her status whenever they venture to disagree with her in conversation, and her appalling taste in clothes, is united with a dog-faced tight-jeaned fotog of fruitarian tastes such as can be found in dozens in any pseudo-arty drinking cellar in fashionable-unfashionable London.' He adds that he is 'seriously considering forming a British Republican party to burn the happy couple in effigy on their wedding night. And why wasn't I sent an invitation? Eh?'

---

* Or not so single: when the Queen Mother telephones Cecil Beaton to tell him the news, he says, 'Oh, how wonderful, you must be thrilled ma'am, how simply marvellous, he's terribly clever and talented.' But when he puts down the phone, he turns to a house guest and exclaims, 'Silly girl! Not even a good photographer!'

LORD SNOWDON

IS MOTHERED BY

BARRY HUMPHRIES

Chez Moi, Addison Road, Holland Park, London W14
November 1966

Lord Snowdon is enjoying a quiet meal with friends at one of London's most chic restaurants when a man emerges from the gents', walks a few paces into the dining room, and drops his trousers.

The trouser-dropper in question is an up-and-coming Australian comedian called Barry Humphries, who is at present appearing in a weekly satire show on the BBC with Eleanor Bron, John Wells and the composer Stanley Myers.

One evening after work, Stanley Myers and his girlfriend and Barry Humphries and his wife go out to dinner together at Chez Moi, the swish new restaurant in Holland Park. Disconcerted that nothing vulgar has yet happened, Myers attempts to persuade Humphries to perform one of the practical jokes for which he is fast gaining a reputation.

Humphries is a long-time devotee of pranks, many of them elaborate. They emerge naturally from his Dada-ist period at Melbourne University, where his street work includes planting a roast chicken in a dustbin, coming along the next day dressed as a tramp, burrowing for the chicken in the bin, then pulling it out and guzzling it. This prank is later expanded and extended to aeroplanes: before boarding, Humphries fills a sick-bag with Russian salad, then pretends to be sick mid-flight and spoons the contents into his mouth.

He also used to enjoy planting an accomplice posing as a blind man on a Melbourne commuter train, bearing a white cane and with a leg in a plaster cast. The 'blind' man would then start reading a piano roll, as though it were braille. Stepping into the compartment bearing a foreign newspaper, Humphries would scream foreign gibberish at the man while destroying his piano roll and kicking at his plaster cast. 'Commuters were often transfixed in horror,' recalls Humphries. 'No one ever pursued me.

Mind you, I ran as fast as I could. People tried to comfort my blind friend. He would always say, "Forgive him." It was very funny to do and very hard not to laugh. It's a bit hard to say what effect the stunt was meant to have, since it was meant to amuse us, a kind of outrageous public act.'*

But it is the trouser trick that Stanley Myers particularly wants Humphries to perform on this particular evening in Chez Moi. It is, in Humphries' words, 'a simple, and perhaps juvenile, stunt which worked well only in a dignified or pretentious ambience. All that happened was that my pants fell down, apparently by accident, at a conspicuous moment. The "trick" was that I should exhibit a high degree of embarrassment.'

Humphries agrees to it. He retreats to the restaurant's loo in order to loosen his trousers in preparation for his grand entrance. Halfway back to the table, he times the release of the trousers to perfection: 'barely a diner in that crowded restaurant could have missed it'. With a tremendous show of shame 'and much bowing and shrugging', he returns to the table, where his friend Myers is convulsed with laughter.

But the joke doesn't afford much amusement to the other tables. Quite the opposite: the maître d' sidles over to Humphries. 'I am sorry, sir,' he says, 'but we must ask you please to leave the restaurant *immédiatement*. Lord Snowdon over zair is most offended by what just 'appen.'

Two waiters then lift Humphries bodily from his chair and carry him out of the restaurant with such speed that he has no time to catch even a sideways glimpse of Princess Margaret's horrified husband.

Out in the cold streets of Holland Park, he is obliged to loiter 'unwined and dined'. All he has to nibble on are a few sponge fingers, which he absent-mindedly placed in his pocket after an earlier lunch at Bertorelli's.

He tries to get back into the restaurant, but finds the door has been locked behind him. Through a chink in the curtains, he can see his wife and friends tucking into a delicious meal, 'relieved, no doubt, that I was out of the way'.

There and then, he plots his revenge. He walks to a telephone box on the corner of Addison Road and riffles through the directory for the phone number of Chez Moi. 'Ullo? Ullo?' says the maître d'.

---

* 'I was born with a priceless gift,' says Dame Edna Everage. 'The ability to laugh at the misfortunes of others.'

Humphries, an adept mimic, puts on the voice of an upper-class Englishwoman. 'This is the Countess of Rosse speaking. My son Lord Snowdon is dining in your restaurant. May I speak with him urgently?'

There is a long pause.

'Mother? How did you track me down here?'

'Tony, darling, there is a lovely and talented man in your restaurant tonight who has been far from well. His name is Barry Humphries and he has been accidentally locked out in the street. Please buy him and his party a large bottle of champagne and get the management to apologise.'

Throughout this monologue, Humphries hears Snowdon's voice going, 'What, Mother? Who is this? *Who is this speaking?*'

Humphries waits hopefully in the street, but to his disappointment, the doors of Chez Moi remain closed.

Ten years later, Barry Humphries is starring as Dame Edna Everage in his West End show, *Housewife, Superstar!*. The show is a triumphant success. *Vogue* magazine interviews Humphries, and arranges to send a photographer to the theatre.

Humphries arrives a little late. The photographer is already waiting by the stage door: it is Lord Snowdon. 'I'd like to take up most of your day on this job, if you can spare the time,' he says. 'Perhaps we could break somewhere for lunch?' Humphries suggests an Italian restaurant near the theatre.

'Oh no, thank you,' replies Snowdon. 'I want you to be *my* guest. There's an excellent French restaurant I know in Holland Park called Chez Moi. I wonder if you know it?'

'He gave me a broad Royal Doulton smile, and I think he might have even winked,' recalls Humphries. 'Otherwise, no subsequent reference was ever made to that evening, so long ago, when for two minutes I had been his mother.'

BARRY HUMPHRIES

TALKS ABORIGINAL TO

SALVADOR DALÍ

Gotham Book Mart, 41 West 47th Street, New York
November 1963

The twenty-nine-year-old Barry Humphries has spent the past year with his wife in New York, where the show in which he is appearing, *Oliver!*, is enjoying a successful run at the Imperial Theater on Broadway. He plays the relatively small role of the undertaker, though he is also understudying Fagin. They are living in a small apartment in Greenwich Village with no lift and no heating. Below it are Alex's Borscht Bowl and Ruth's Poodle Parlor. 'The mingled aromas of stewed beetroot and canine shampoo filtered up through our bare floorboards,' he recalls.

He loves New York. At the Village Vanguard, he sees Louis Armstrong and Sarah Vaughan; at Birdland, Count Basie. On Sunday nights he goes with Peter Cook, who is appearing in *Beyond the Fringe*, to watch the Supremes at the Apollo Theater in Harlem. In his favourite bar, the Ninth Circle, just a few doors away from his apartment, he chums up with a solitary drinker who always addresses him as 'the English poet'. Humphries takes him for a minor academic, as he has recently been seeking Humphries' advice on whether to accept an invitation to speak at Oxford University. After an all-night party in a furniture van, he at last catches the man's name: Jack Kerouac.

Early one afternoon, Humphries is standing on top of one of the ladders in the rare book room at the Gotham Book Mart when Salvador Dalí enters, ready for a signing session of his latest book. With him is his avaricious sixty-nine-year-old wife Gala, who is always on the lookout for young men; before long, her eyes stray up the ladder.

The Dalís are staying in their usual suite on the seventeenth floor of the St Regis Hotel on Fifth Avenue. Dalí likes to winter at the St Regis, where the staff are perfectly used to him walking his pet ocelot on a leash through the hall. It is said he once kept a bear in the hotel, but the bear was asked to leave after it surprised guests in the elevator and there were complaints. Dalí has been spotted taking live beetles to lunch with him in the hotel restaurant. He keeps them in a Perspex container and enjoys watching them climb up and down hills of sand. He says he finds them better lunch companions than humans.

While Dalí is in New York, he plans to attend the opening of his exhibition at the Knoedler Gallery of recent works, including the giant* *Galacidalacideoxyribononucleicacid*, which, he claims, is the longest one-word title in existence. The painting captures Gala looking out over a Spanish landscape, with the Prophet Isaiah behind her, and God the Father on a cloud presiding over the scene, with Christ and the Madonna just visible inside his head. It has already been bought by the New England Merchants Bank of Boston for $150,000. He is also promoting his new book, *The Diary of a Genius*, though he is said to be furious that, in the American edition, the appendix on farting has been suppressed. He blames it on the Protestants. A terrific farter himself, he points out that in Catholic countries you are allowed to fart to your heart's content.

Humphries is also a keen surrealist – his student works included *Pus in Boots*, consisting of two old shoes brimming with custard; a spoon containing the eye of a sheep, called *Eye and Spoon Race*; and a broken pram draped with raw meat, titled *Crèche Bang*† – so he shuttles down the ladder and 'somewhat obsequiously' introduces himself to the artist who has long been one of his idols.

The two men talk of Australia. Dalí tells Humphries of his great wish to visit the country and examine the cave paintings of the Aboriginals before breaking into what Humphries describes as 'a kind of gibberish, which was his fanciful version of Aboriginal speech'. The manager of the bookshop tries to butt in – he is anxious to start the signing session – but Gala Dalí has other plans. 'She began to stroke my none-too-lustrous hair and proposed that we all go back to the St Regis Hotel immediately so she could make certain tonsorial adjustments.'

---

* 305 x 345 cms.

† Others include *Her Majesty's Male*, a painting of Queen Elizabeth II with a 5 o'clock shadow, and *Cakescape*, a cake pressed between two panes of glass, looking a little like a Jackson Pollock.

Humphries is very excited by this unexpected encounter with the famous, 'yet not a little apprehensive', for Gala's reputation as a sexual predator precedes her. 'Only by having a constant succession of boys could she dispel her terror of growing old,' writes Dalí's biographer. 'And no sooner did she begin to tire of one than she used her astonishing sex appeal, her charm, her power and her money to acquire another.' Nevertheless, Humphries travels willingly with the Dalís to the St Regis Hotel. Throughout the entire journey, Dalí keeps up an unending stream of Aboriginal banter.

Gala shuts the door of the Dalís' suite behind them. She then produces a large pair of scissors, clasps the back of Humphries' head firmly in her left hand, and starts hacking away at his hair. 'Snip! Snip! The "glittering forfex" did its work, and a few stooks of mousy fibre fell into my lap. Dalí himself merely watched proceedings from an armchair, his head on one side and his hands resting on an elaborate walking stick.'

Humphries suspects that Gala is cutting his hair in this random fashion so as to keep up with, and perhaps outshine, her husband's descent into Aboriginal: by doing so, she hopes to establish her own credentials as an eccentric.*

Happily, he manages to wriggle out of her clutches without the loss of too much hair. Gala picks up a few of his shorn locks and inserts them into a copy of Dalí's autobiography, *The Secret Life of Salvador Dalí*. The Dalís then both inscribe it for him.

An hour or so goes by before Salvador and Gala descend into a furious and intimate argument, Salvador gesticulating wildly and screaming curses at Gala, and Gala returning the abuse in French.

'Feeling somewhat *de trop*', Barry Humphries slips away unnoticed, back to the real world.†

---

* 'Alas,' Humphries writes in one of his memoirs, 'rather like Yoko Ono, Senora Dalí lacked her husband's genius, and her surrealist postures were always rather humourless and uninspired.'

† He seems to have got off a good deal more lightly than the art critic Brian Sewell, who a few years later, whilst holidaying alone in Cadaqués, is invited back by Salvador Dalí, then taken to an olive grove, where he is required to lie naked in the foetal position and masturbate as Dalí takes photographs and fumbles in his own trousers. 'Sheepish and in silence', the two men then walk back to Gala, who is sitting in a giant eggshell in the garden.

SALVADOR DALÍ

SKETCHES

SIGMUND FREUD

39 Elsworthy Road, London NW3
July 19th 1938

The thirty-four-year-old painter Salvador Dalí has, over the years, made three attempts to meet Sigmund Freud, but each to no avail. Every time he calls at his house in Vienna, he is informed that Freud is out of town for reasons of health. He then walks around the city, eating chocolate tarts. 'In the evening, I held long and imaginary conversations with Freud; he came home with me once and stayed all night clinging to the curtains of my room in the Hotel Sacher.'

When *The Interpretation of Dreams* is first translated into Spanish in 1922, Dalí becomes a fanatical Freudian: 'It presented itself to me as one of the capital discoveries in my life, and I was seized with a real vice of self-interpretation, not only of my dreams but of everything that happened to me, however accidental it might seem at first glance.' From then on, his paintings become overtly and self-consciously Freudian, with intermingling sexual symbols set against strange dream landscapes.

In June 1938, Dalí is sitting in a restaurant in Paris, tucking into a dish of snails. By chance, he glances towards a fellow diner, and spots a photograph of Sigmund Freud on the cover of the newspaper in his hands: the world-renowned* founder of psychoanalysis has just arrived in the city, en route for London, after a last-minute flight from Nazi-occupied Vienna, where he has lived for seventy-nine years.

Dalí looks from the newspaper back to his plate of snails and utters a loud cry. 'I had just that instant discovered the morphological secret of Freud! Freud's cranium is a snail! His brain is in the form of a spiral – to be extracted with a needle!'

---

* Freud's recent eightieth birthday brought him greetings from, among others, Thomas Mann, H.G. Wells, Albert Schweitzer and Albert Einstein.

This improbable revelation causes Dalí to reinvigorate his campaign to meet his hero. Through the surrealist patron Edward James he contacts the author Stefan Zweig, who he knows to be both an admirer of his own work and a close friend of Freud. Zweig writes three letters to Freud on Dalí's behalf, suggesting that Dalí quickly draws a portrait of him. He explains that Dalí is 'the only painter of genius in our epoch', and that 'he is the most faithful and most grateful disciple of your ideas among the artists'.

In his third and final letter, written a day before their meeting, Zweig writes: 'For years it has been the desire of this real genius to meet you. He says that he owes to you more in his art than to anybody else … He is only here for two days from Paris (he is a Catalan) and he will not disturb our conversation … Salvador Dalí would have liked, of course, to show you his pictures in an exhibition. We know, however, that you only reluctantly go out, if ever, and therefore will bring his last, and, as it seems to me, his most beautiful picture to your home.'

The meeting takes place at Freud's first London home, near Primrose Hill, on July 19th. By chance, as Dalí approaches the house with Stefan Zweig and Edward James, he spots something extraordinarily significant, as he so often does: 'I saw a bicycle leaning against the wall, and on the saddle, attached by a string, was a red rubber hot-water bottle which looked full of water, and on the back of the hot-water bottle walked a snail!'

Sigmund Freud is eighty-two years old, and dying from the cancer of the jaw that has plagued him for the past sixteen years. He recently suffered an attack of deafness, so says very little to Dalí, who is at any rate unable to speak either German or English. But Dalí is unabashed by Freud's silence. 'We devoured each other with our eyes,' he says.

As agreed, Dalí shows Freud his recent painting *Metamorphosis of Narcissus*. It shows Narcissus naked in a barren landscape, staring at his own reflection in a pool, with, next to him, and echoing his contours, a stone hand holding an egg, from out of which a narcissus is hatching. There are various nude figures in the background, and a crab in the fore-ground. Freud studies it with his customary intensity. 'Until now,' he comments to Zweig the next day, 'I was inclined to regard the Surrealists – who seem to have adopted me as their patron saint – as 100 per cent fools (or let's rather say, as with alcohol, 95 per cent). This young Spaniard, with his ingenuous fanatical eyes, and his undoubtedly technically perfect mastership, has suggested to me a different estimate. In fact, it would be very interesting to explore analytically the growth of a picture like this …'

While Zweig and James talk to Freud, Dalí draws a portrait of his head in a sketch book, making it resemble at one and the same time both Freud and a snail. Worried that Freud might be shocked at how odd it makes him look, Zweig manages to prevent him from setting eyes on it.

Dalí is to recall his meeting with Freud as one of the most important experiences of his life. Whenever he can, he boasts that he forced the founder of psychoanalysis to reconsider his whole view of surrealism. In a letter to his fellow surrealist André Breton, he writes: 'He remarked (I showed him one of my pictures) that "in the paintings of the Old Masters one immediately tends to look for the unconscious, whereas when one looks at a Surrealist painting, one immediately has the urge to look for the conscious". Dalí adds that he thinks this proclamation is 'a death sentence on Surrealism as a doctrine, as a sect, as an "ism", while at the same time confirming the movement's validity as a "state of spirit".*

And what does Freud think of Salvador Dalí? As Dalí sketches the great psychoanalyst, his eyes blazing with excitement, Freud leans over to Edward James and whispers in German, 'That boy looks like a fanatic. Small wonder that they have civil war in Spain if they look like that.'†

---

* Ten years later, in an interview with Malcolm Muggeridge on the *Panorama* programme on BBC Television, Dalí appears to have moved on. 'All your wonderful jokes that we know about – taxi cabs with the rain inside and so on,' says Muggeridge, 'you're going to go on with those jokes?'

'Eh, thees correspond to le first period of my life,' replies Dalí. 'The moment of myself is very beeg interest in psychoanalysis, coming in London for meet le Doctor Freud. But now my only interest is about le treeee-mendous progress of nuclear recherches and nuclear physics.'

'And so really that represented a phase in your career, those jokes that we all know about, and now you move on, and all your life will be to the rhythm of atomic explosion?'

'Exactly, one new kind of, eh, atomic and nuclear mysticism.'

'Well, thank you very much, that's a fascinating phrase, nuclear mysticism.'

† Lucian Freud remembers his grandfather as someone who 'always seemed to be in a good mood. He had what many people who are *really* intelligent have, which is not being serious or solemn, as if they are so sure they know what they are talking about that they don't have the need to be earnest about it.'

SIGMUND FREUD

ANALYSES

GUSTAV MAHLER

Leiden, Holland
August 1910

Three times Gustav Mahler has made an appointment to see Sigmund Freud, and three times he has decided to cancel it. Freud makes it clear that if he cancels again, he will not be given another chance.

It is Mahler's wife, Alma, who is pushing him into a meeting. Their marriage, always wobbly, is in crisis. At fifty, Gustav is nearly twenty years older than Alma. When they were married eight years ago, few of their friends thought it would last. 'She is a celebrated beauty, used to a glamorous social life, while he is so unworldly and fond of being alone,' observed Mahler's friend, the conductor Bruno Walter.

Alma is gregarious and flirtatious,* Gustav withdrawn and ascetic. When they became engaged, Alma was interested in composing, but Gustav forbade her from pursuing it. 'You must give yourself *unconditionally*, shape your future life, in every detail, entirely in accordance with my needs … The role of composer falls to me – yours is that of loving companion.'

In July 1910, Gustav Mahler opens a letter wrongly addressed to himself.[†] It is in fact for Alma, from her young paramour Walter Gropius, saying he can't live without her, and urging her to leave her husband. Mahler confronts Alma, who shoves the blame back on him, telling him, 'I had longed for his love year after year and that he, in his fanatical concentration on his own life, had simply overlooked me.'

---

* She has relationships with, among others, Gustav Klimt, Max Burckhard, Alexander Zemlinsky and Oskar Kokoschka. She marries Gustav Mahler in 1902, Walter Gropius in 1915 and Franz Werfel in 1929.

[†] 'He was convinced at the time, and remained convinced for the rest of his life, that the architect had deliberately addressed the letter to him as his way of asking him for my hand in marriage,' wrote Alma much later.

Mahler promises to make amends; Alma agrees to stay. Having previously treated her with indifference, he develops a passionate jealousy of, in Alma's words, 'everything and everybody ... I often woke in the night and found him standing at my bedside in the darkness.' But she cannot shake off Gropius, and is again forced to choose. She decides to stay with Mahler, but only on condition that he seeks analysis.

Mahler has long been wary of psychoanalysis. Three years ago, when a friend mentioned Sigmund Freud's name, he snapped that psychoanalysis did not interest him, adding, 'Freud, he tries to cure or solve everything from *a certain aspect*.' The friend noted that 'apparently he was reluctant, in the presence of his wife, to use the appropriate word'.

Towards the end of August, Mahler finally keeps his appointment. Freud takes a break from his holiday on the coast to catch a tram to Leiden. They set off on a long walk through the town, talking for four hours.* To passers-by, they must look an odd couple: Freud is over six feet tall, and Mahler just five feet four inches; Mahler walks in a very unusual manner, with irregular strides interrupted by an odd little stamp.†

Having listened to Mahler's marital problems, Freud says the difference in the couple's ages, of which Mahler is so afraid, is precisely what attracts Alma to him. 'You loved your mother, and you look for her in every woman. She was careworn and ailing, and, unconsciously, you wish your wife to be the same,' he adds.

When Gustav reports these conclusions to Alma, she thinks Freud has hit the nail on the head: 'He was right in both cases. Gustav Mahler's mother was called Marie. His first impulse was to change my name to Marie in spite of the difficulty he had in pronouncing "r". And when he got to know me better he wanted my face to be more "stricken" – his very word. When he told my mother that it was a pity there had been so little sadness in my life, she replied, "Don't worry – that will come."' Alma also agrees with Freud's diagnosis of her father-fixation. 'I always looked for a

---

* Contemporary psychoanalysts seem to think that such a brief consultation cannot truly be classified as psychoanalysis. Yet it seems to have been in many ways more productive, and more constructive, than many courses of treatment that last a lifetime.

† At the Mahler wedding, his little niece Eleanor is caught mimicking Mahler's gait, and sent home in disgrace.

small, slight man, who had wisdom and spiritual superiority, since this was what I had known and loved in my father.'

Freud is likewise impressed by Gustav Mahler; he has never met anyone who grasped psychoanalysis so quickly.

'... Mahler suddenly said that now he understood why his music had always been prevented from achieving the highest rank through the noblest passages, those inspired by the most profound emotions, being spoilt by the intrusion of some commonplace melody. His father, apparently a brutal person, treated his wife very badly, and when Mahler was a young boy there was a specially painful scene between them. It became quite unbearable to the boy, who rushed away from the house. At that moment, however, a hurdy-gurdy in the street was grinding out the popular Viennese air "Ach, du lieber Augustin". In Mahler's opinion the conjunction of high tragedy and light amusement was from then on inextricably fixed in his mind, and the one mood inevitably brought the other with it.'*

Of course, this is what people admire in his music. It is what makes it innovative and modern. But it can be hard for artists to discriminate between their strengths and their weaknesses, as the two are so closely allied.

After they part, Gustav Mahler enters a state of elation. 'Feeling cheerful. Interesting discussion,' he wires Alma, and later, 'I am living everything as if new.' On the train back, he writes this verse about the meeting:

> Night shades were dispelled by one powerful word,
> The tireless throb of torment ended.
> At last united in one single chord
> My timid thoughts and my tempestuous feelings blended.

On his return, he looks again at Alma's compositions, and starts to sing them at the piano. 'What have I done? These songs are good. They're

---

* 'The use of the commonplace ... as a means of expression foreshadows the main trend in twentieth-century art,' writes Donald Mitchell in his essay 'Mahler and Freud' (1958). Freud himself is no judge of music: he is tone deaf.

excellent ... I shan't rest until you start working again. God, I was narrow-minded in those days.' Mahler dedicates his Eighth Symphony, which he unveiled on September 12th 1910, to her; he also has five of Alma's *lieder* published, with premieres in Vienna and New York.

Nine months later, on May 18th 1911, he dies of bacterial endocarditis.* Some months on, Freud suddenly realises he never sent an invoice for his consultation, so he writes one out, dating it 'Vienna, October 24 1911'. He attaches two stamps and sends it to Mahler's widow, Alma, 'for services rendered'.

---

* Alma lives for another fifty-three years.

GUSTAV MAHLER

REFUSES TO KNEEL BEFORE

AUGUSTE RODIN

Rue de l'Université, Paris
April 23rd 1909

A group of Mahler's admirers in Vienna has been persuaded by Alma Mahler's stepfather, the painter Carl Moll, to commission the great Auguste Rodin to sculpt the composer's head. At first, Rodin is indifferent. Only after being told that Mahler is a great composer, on the same level in music as he is in art, does Rodin agree to lower his regular price to 10,000 francs for a clay bust, with an additional charge for bronze casts.

Mahler is restless by nature, not the sort of man to agree to sit still for any length of time, so they appeal to his vanity, too, by telling him that the idea has come from Rodin himself, as Mahler's head interests him so much. Flattered, Mahler agrees.

He arrives in Paris from America. He is suffering from rheumatic heart disease, and has been unable to hike in the mountains, so can no longer 'wrest my ideas from Nature'. On April 22nd, their go-between Paul Clemenceau writes a letter to Rodin: 'If you are free to do so, please come tomorrow, Friday, at 12.30 to have lunch with us at the Café de Paris. Mahler will be there. We could arrange everything while dining. Remember that Mahler is convinced that it is your wish to do his bust, or he would have refused to pose.'

The lunch goes well. Though the two men barely exchange a word – Mahler speaks French only falteringly, and Rodin doesn't speak a word of German – Clemenceau is delighted by the way they get on. 'The first encounter between these two men of genius was extremely impressive. They didn't speak but only sized each other up, and yet they understood each other perfectly.'

Rodin gets down to work. Mahler has only a little time; he must leave for Vienna on May 1st. Each sitting lasts roughly an hour and a half. Rodin is a quick worker; he needs to be, because Mahler is such a fidget. In any game of musical statues, he would always be the first to lose. 'He couldn't keep still, even for a minute,' notes Alma.

Despite all this, sitter and sculptor strike up some sort of rapport. 'Rodin fell in love with his model; he was really unhappy when we had to leave Paris, for he wanted to work on the bust much longer,' observes Alma. 'His method was unlike that of any other sculptor I have had the opportunity of watching. He first made flat surfaces in the rough lump, and then added little pellets of clay which he rolled between his fingers while he talked. He worked by adding to the lump instead of subtracting from it. As soon as we left he smoothed it all down and next day added more. I scarcely ever saw him with a tool in his hand. He said Mahler's head was a mixture of Franklin's, Frederick the Great's and Mozart's.'

At each session, the Mahlers notice that one of the sculptor's mistresses is always lingering patiently in the next room while Rodin works away. 'Some girl or other with scarlet lips invariably spent long and unrewarded hours there, for he took very little notice of her and did not speak to her even during the rests. His fascination must have been powerful to induce these girls – and they were girls in what is called "society" – to put up with such treatment … Sometimes we were interrupted by a loud knocking on the door; it was *une amie* whom Rodin described as troublesome. She was obliged to wait for hours in the next room, and she kept on knocking, which made Rodin nervous and furious.'

Rodin works at a furious pace. 'He would step forward, then retreat, look at the figure in a mirror, mutter and utter unintelligible sounds, make changes and corrections,' writes Stefan Zweig, observing him at work.

Only once is there a clash between the two artists. It arises from a misunderstanding. Rodin needs to look at Mahler's head from above in order 'to gauge its volume and contour', so asks him 'perhaps rather brusquely' to get down on his knees. But Mahler is notoriously touchy, and misinterprets the instruction. Why should he abase himself? 'The musician thought it was to humiliate him that I asked him to kneel,' Rodin realises later.

Instead of kneeling as requested, Mahler flushes red with anger and storms out of the studio. As a conductor, he is more used to bossing than being bossed. What he says goes: he once declared that he would use only his eyes to conduct were he not so short-sighted. But, despite the language difficulties, the two men soon patch it up, and before Mahler sets off for Vienna, he has agreed to fit in some more sittings in October.

Rodin is thrilled by his own creation. 'There is a suggestion not only of Eastern origin, but of something even more remote, of a race now lost to us – the Egyptians in the days of Rameses,' he enthuses. He produces two busts of Mahler, one rougher and more expressionist, the other smoother and more naturalistic. On his fiftieth birthday, Mahler is presented with a book that has a photograph of his bust on its cover. Inside, there are tributes from his many admirers, including von Hofmannsthal and Zweig. Rodin himself writes the greeting, 'Au Grand Musicien G. Mahler'.

After Mahler's death, Rodin orders his assistant Aristide Roussaud to carve a marble version of the smoother bust. It can still be seen in the Musée Rodin. Bizarrely, it is labelled 'Mozart'. Alma Mahler ascribes this to a custodial error, but others point the finger at Rodin himself. Does he wish to somehow include Mahler's dying words, 'Mozart … Mozart!' in his portrait? Or, ever conscious of commerce, does he think that the public will be more likely to come and see a sculpture of the most popular of all composers rather than the moody, difficult, modern composer whom cynics have sometimes chosen to nickname Herr Malheur?

AUGUSTE RODIN

YEARNS FOR

ISADORA DUNCAN

Rue de la Gaîté, Paris
1900

Just recently, the twenty-three-year-old Isadora Duncan has grown aware that her body is 'something other than an instrument to express the sacred harmony of music'. Her bust, for a start, seems to be taking on a life of its own. 'My breasts which until then had been hardly perceptible began to swell softly and astonish me with charming and embarrassing sensations. My hips, which had been like a boy's, took on another undulation, and through my whole being I felt one great surging, longing, unmistakable urge, so that I could no longer sleep at night, but tossed and turned in feverish, painful unrest.'

So, having mesmerised London with her exuberant dancing, Isadora sets off for Paris with one aim in mind: to lose her virginity.

She proves as great a success in the French capital as she has already been in London. In her own eyes, she is 'a little, uneducated American girl ... who in some mysterious manner had found the key to the hearts and minds of the intellectual and artistic elite'. With Maurice Ravel playing the piano, she dances to the music of Chopin at Madame de Saint-Marceaux's Friday-night musical salons.

She is also taken up by an American lesbian in Paris, Winaretta Singer, heiress to the sewing-machine fortune. Winaretta's first marriage, to the Prince de Scey-Montbéliard, got off to an uncertain start after she speared him with an umbrella on their wedding night, threatening to kill him if he came any closer. (Her current marriage is to another Prince, Edmond de Polignac, who is also, conveniently, homosexual.) Princess Winaretta arranges a series of subscription concerts for Isadora, to which Parisian high society flocks, and from which everyone else is barred: asked at one of these events why she has not invited Coco Chanel, the Princess replies, 'I don't entertain tradespeople.' But Gabriel Fauré, Georges Clemenceau and Octave Mirabeau all come, as does the fifty-nine-year-old Auguste Rodin, who is immediately taken with Isadora Duncan, as she is with him. Others, more snobbish than Isadora, find Rodin humdrum socially. When Vita Sackville-West first met him, he struck her as 'a rather commonplace French bourgeois ... rather an unreal little fat man'. For her, it was only when Rodin began stroking his marble that this commonplace French bourgeois metamorphosed into a genius.

Rodin's attraction to Isadora is instant; he is desperate to sculpt her. He often gets carried away like this. 'Madame,' he cries while working on the bust of Mrs Mary Hunter, the ravishing sister of the composer Dame Ethel Smyth, 'your skin has the whiteness of turbot that one sees lying on the marble slabs of your amazing fishmongers! It looks as if it were bathed in milk! Ah, Madame!' And with this, he kisses Mary's hand, 'a little too greedily', according to her.

Isadora pursues the delighted Rodin to his studio in the rue de l'Université 'like Psyche seeking the God Pan in his grotto, only I was not asking the way to Eros, but to Apollo'. He is only too happy to show her around. 'Sometimes he murmured the names of his statues, but one felt that names meant little to him. He ran his hands over them and caressed them. I remember thinking that beneath his hands the marble seemed to flow like molten lead. Finally he took a small quantity of clay and pressed it between his palms. He breathed hard as he did so. The heat streamed from him like a radiant furnace. In a few moments he had formed a woman's breast that palpitated beneath his fingers.'

It does the trick. Isadora allows Rodin to take her outside. Hand in hand, the two of them glide to her studio in the rue de la Gaîté. Once there, she changes into her tunic and Rodin sits back while she dances an idyll of Theocritus:

> *Pan aimait la nymphe Echo*
> *Echo aimait Satyr.*

After dancing for a while, Isadora comes to a halt. She has developed various theories of dance that she is keen to share with Rodin, but she quickly discovers that a lesson in dance theory is very far from his thoughts. 'Soon I realised that he was not listening. He gazed at me with lowered lids, his eyes blazing, and then, with the same expression that he had before his works, he came toward me. He ran his hands over my neck, breast, stroked my arms and ran his hands over my hips, my bare legs and feet. He began to knead my whole body as if it were clay, while from him emanated heat that scorched and melted me. My whole desire was to yield to him my entire being and, indeed, I would have done so if it had not been that my upbringing caused me to become frightened, and I withdrew, threw my dress over my tunic, and sent him away bewildered.'

In later life, she comes to regret this sudden attack of the scruples, a seizure she ensures will never be repeated. 'What a pity! How often I have regretted this childish incomprehension which lost to me the divine chance of giving my virginity to the Great God Pan, the mighty Rodin. Surely Art and all Life would have been richer thereby!'

Despite missing his one and only chance (or perhaps as a result of it), for the rest of his life Rodin remains one of Isadora's most devoted admirers. A full fifteen years later, she is back on stage in Paris, and he is shouting fit to burst, his passion undimmed. As Isadora lies prone on the stage at the end of *Pathétique*, 'his arms went through the air like the wings of a windmill, and he seemed to shriek, although his voice was lost among the general shouting'.

Auguste Rodin never gets over her. 'Isadora Duncan is the greatest woman I have ever known!' he confides to a friend '... Sometimes I think she is the greatest woman the world has ever known. *Elle est suprème!*'

ISADORA DUNCAN

UPSTAGES

JEAN COCTEAU

Hôtel Welcome, Villefranche-sur-Mer
September 18th 1926

Now aged forty-nine, penniless and plump, Isadora Duncan has seen better days. 'I don't dance any more, I only move my weight around,' she says. The waspish New York wit Dorothy Parker nicknames her 'Duncan Disorderly'.

Isadora is living in a ramshackle studio at the far end of the promenade des Anglais in Nice. The block is surrounded by empty tin cans and discarded bicycles. Her front door is graffittoed with messages from friends and lovers. Next to its handle is a heart with 'Jean' written across it in Jean Cocteau's distinctive handwriting.

The studio is filled to bursting with clutter from her eventful life: Louis XV furniture from the Galeries Lafayette, dyed bulrushes in fake Sèvres vases, aspidistras in pots from Oriental bazaars. There is a rusting bathtub in her dressing room: in the old days, she is said to have bathed in champagne, but nowadays the tub is filled with yet more clutter. Her bed is swathed in ageing mosquito nets, the walls of her bedroom decorated with fading photographs of her many lovers. No one knows how many she has had, least of all Isadora. 'It became fashionable to boast of having had a week with Isadora,' reminisces Agnes de Mille. 'Whether true or false, the chance of contradiction was slight.'

Her love life is already the stuff of legend.* 'She was like a great flowing river through which the traffic of the world could pass,' says Edna St

---

* Once she gets going, she very much enjoys sex. 'I became a quivering mass of responsive senses in the hands of an expert voluptuary … Like a flock of wild goats cropping the herbage of the soft hillside, so his kisses grazed over my body, and like the earth itself I felt a thousand mouths devouring me,' she writes of her first liaison with Princess Winaretta's brother, Isaac Merritt Singer. She describes going to bed with the poet Mercedes de Acosta with similar gusto: '… A slender body, hands soft and white, for the service of my delight, two sprouting breasts round and sweet, invite my hungry mouth to eat, from whence two nipples firm and pink, persuade my thirsty soul to drink, and lower still a secret place where I'd fain hide my loving face …'

Vincent Millay, herself no slouch. There is a tall story that, ten years ago, Isadora begged George Bernard Shaw to have sex with her, saying that a baby with her body and his brains would be a world-beater. 'Yes,' Shaw is said to have replied, 'but suppose it had my body and your brains?'

She is a well-known sight in Villefranche, walking around the streets barefoot in a scarlet négligée, all topped off by hair of vivid magenta. She generally heads to the jetty, on the lookout for young men. Sometimes she attracts abuse from the less bohemian citizens of Villefranche. She imitates their tut-tuts: 'That Bolshevik! She's always carrying young men with her! She says he's her secretary! Have you heard of her last scandal! Such a vile woman!' Recently, when Isadora attended a dinner in Paris, a fellow guest, an American woman, turned to their host, Count Etienne de Beaumont, and exclaimed: 'My dear man, if I had known that you would have that red whore here, I would never have set foot in your home.' For a moment, Isadora looked taken aback, but then she turned to the butler, smiled, and said, 'Do you have something sweet in the house? I feel the need of it just now.'

On this particular day, a party is being thrown at the Hôtel Welcome to celebrate the seventeenth birthday of a painter called Sir Francis Rose. His mother, Lady Rose, has appointed Jean Cocteau master of ceremonies, and he has decided to make the most of it. Dressed in a beige suit lined with black satin, with his chair covered in red velvet, he has a bust of Dante on the table beside him.

The other guests are quite a mixed bag. The conventional Lady Rose has invited only English officers and their wives, but others have slipped through the net: a priest in purple socks with a vast Greek cross hanging around his neck, an author in a Spanish clerical hat, carrying a gramophone with a tortoise-shell trumpet, and the bulky Lady MacCarthy in a frilly green dress, giving her the appearance, according to Cocteau, of 'a cabbage reeling on tiny feet'. But some remain excluded: Lady Rose puts her foot down when an uninvited guest tries to bring his donkey in with him.

To the horror of Lady Rose, her son Francis,* crowned with roses, arrives at his own party arm-in-arm with Isadora Duncan, who is wearing

---

* It is Sir Francis Rose of whom Gertrude Stein is later to write 'A rose is a rose is a rose.'

a diaphanous Greek toga and is wreathed in flowers.* Cocteau describes her as 'very fat and slightly drunk', and 'enveloping the young man like a placenta'. The couple are accompanied by two gay young American men, who Isadora calls her 'pigeons'. Outside the hotel, fishermen are pressing their noses to the windows, ready to see what happens next.

A deathly silence turns the guests to statuary. Isadora laughs, and continues to drape herself over the birthday boy. 'She even dragged him into the window recess,' recalls Cocteau. 'It was then that Captain Williams, a friend of the family, played his part ... He strode across the dining room, approached the window, and shouted in a tremendous voice, "Old Lady, unhand that child!"' With that, the Captain hurls a large silver watch in her direction and brings down his cane on her head, blackening her eye and ripping her toga. Isadora falls to the floor.

But she has never been one to take things lying down. She has always been prone to rage, and her progress around the world has been marked by the splinters of hotel furniture. Sensing an eruption, one of her pigeons seeks to calm her down. Isadora picks up a lobster covered in mayonnaise and throws it at him.

Alas, she is a poor shot, and the lobster lands in the lap of Lady MacCarthy, showering her frilly green dress with mayonnaise. Lady MacCarthy is furious, and leaps from her chair, ready to launch herself at Isadora. At this point, Cocteau intervenes, restraining Lady MacCarthy from behind as her little fists pummel the air. A general affray ensues, with French and American sailors randomly taking sides. 'Mother remained indifferent and behaved as if nothing out of the ordinary was happening,' remarks Sir Francis several years later.

Eventually, peace returns to the Hôtel Welcome. The lobster is restored to the table, the mayonnaise renewed, and the guests all return to their seats, ready to tuck in. Only Captain Williams is missing. He is later

---

* Isadora prefers a bare minimum of clothes, if that. In Boston in 1922, she electrifies a room by lifting the folds of her scarlet tunic to reveal her naked body and crying, 'You don't know what beauty is! This – this is beauty!'

In Vienna, a distraught Princess Metternich asks why Isadora is dancing with so little on. 'I forgot to tell you how amiable our artiste is,' says her fellow dancer Loie Fuller. 'Her baggage has not yet arrived, but rather than disappoint us, she has agreed to appear in her practising costume.'

discovered spreadeagled on the balcony, covered in blood, a whisky bottle at his side.

JEAN COCTEAU

OVERWHELMS

CHARLIE CHAPLIN

The *Karoa*, South China Sea
February 1936

Jean Cocteau is riding high. Buoyed up by the success of his new film, *Le Sang d'un poète*, he plans to retrace the voyage of Phileas Fogg in *Around the World in Eighty Days*. Craftily, he has managed to persuade *Paris-Soir* to subsidise the trip; in return, he will send them a series of travel articles. Accompanied by his Moroccan boyfriend Marcel Khill, who he rechristens 'Passepartout', he travels from Rome to Brindisi to Athens to Cairo, from there to Aden and Bombay and Calcutta, and then on to Rangoon, Kuala Lumpur, Singapore and Hong Kong.

As he travels across the South China Sea from Singapore on an old Japanese freighter, the *Karoa*, Cocteau takes his usual peek at the passenger list. A fervent name-dropper, he is delighted to discover perhaps the most droppable name in the whole wide world: Charlie Chaplin, who is on a trip to the Orient with his wife, the actress Paulette Goddard, to celebrate the success of his own film, *Modern Times*.

Cocteau is cock-a-hoop. 'He amassed names chiefly to drop them,' writes his biographer, 'dropping them so familiarly, however, as to give the impression that there existed between him and various celebrities a kind of crazed empathy.' He loses no time in instructing his steward to take a note to Chaplin, inviting him to his cabin for an aperitif before dinner. At first, Chaplin does not know whether to reply, as he suspects a hoax. But having checked with the purser's office that Jean Cocteau is indeed aboard, he and Paulette Goddard pop their heads around the door of Cocteau's cabin at the suggested hour. Cocteau's own account of their encounter, which he shares with his readers in *Paris-Soir*, has a mystical, almost fairy-tale quality about it.

'Two poets follow the straight line of their destiny,' he marvels. 'Suddenly it comes to pass that these two lines transect and the meeting forms a cross or, if you prefer, a star … So many people planned that meeting and tried to be its organisers. Each time an obstacle arose, and chance – which has another name in the language of poets – throws us aboard an old Japanese freighter carrying merchandise on the China Sea between Hong Kong and Shanghai.'

He makes no mention of the nudge he has given destiny with his note to the steward.

'You cannot imagine the purity, the violence, the freshness of our extraordinary rendezvous, which we owed solely to our horoscopes,' he continues. 'I was touching the flesh and bone of a myth … As for Chaplin, he shook his white locks, removed his spectacles, put them on again, grasped me by the shoulder, burst out laughing, turned towards his companion, and said again and again, "Is it not marvellous? Is it not marvellous?"'

In Cocteau's account, the two men – both, aged forty-six – hit it off immediately. 'I don't speak English. Chaplin doesn't speak French. And we spoke without the slightest effort. What happened? What language was it? The language of life, more alive than any other, the language born from the desire to communicate at any cost, the language of mimes, of poets, of the heart.'

The two exchange all sorts of intimacies, according to Cocteau: Chaplin confesses to an inferiority complex, fills him in on all the details about his films and tells him about all his future projects. Their conversation goes on deep into the night. Over the next few weeks, so Cocteau says, they become inseparable. 'My meeting with Chaplin,' he assures his readers, 'remains the delightful miracle of this voyage.'

But Chaplin's version of the very same meeting is rather different, and, as far as one is able to judge, it has more of the ring of truth about it. According to him, 'the language of mimes, of poets, of the heart' in fact proved insufficient. All their communication took place through the faltering and haphazard translations of Marcel Khill: 'Meester Cocteau … he say … you are a poet … of ze sunshine … and he is a poet of ze … night.'

Chaplin agrees, however, that their initial meeting is a success, with the two men experiencing an immediate rapport, carrying on chatting into the early hours, and then agreeing to meet for lunch.

But they go too far, too soon. Upon waking, Chaplin feels he can't face any more of Cocteau at lunchtime, and sends him a note of apology. Over the next few days, Cocteau attempts to arrange another rendezvous, but each time they make an appointment, Chaplin contrives to miss it. From then on, he dines with Paulette, and Cocteau dines with Marcel. Before long, the two men have grown too embarrassed even to exchange glances. If one sees the other coming, he ducks into corridors and darts behind the nearest doors. Separately, the two of them grow familiar with parts of the ship they had never known existed.

'We had had more than a glut of each other,' Chaplin concludes in his autobiography. 'In the various stopping-off places we rarely saw each other, unless for a brief how-do-you-do or farewell. But when news broke that we were both sailing on the *President Coolidge* going back to the States, we became resigned, making no further attempts at enthusiasm.' Instead, Chaplin gets stuck into a new script; by the time the ship reaches California, he has written 10,000 words.

It is all a question of appetite. Cocteau's hunger for celebrities is insatiable, but Chaplin's is only fitful, and can fast turn to revulsion. On meeting Arnold Schoenberg or Albert Einstein or Thomas Mann, he feels an instant bond, but then retreats back into privacy. He has always possessed a remarkable ability to extract whatever he wants from a stranger in a very short time, but then feels replete. Strangers misinterpret this rapacity; what they take to be a firm bond invariably proves to be no more than a passing acquaintance: the prospect of a lifelong friendship suddenly reduced, as if by magic, to the memory of a chance encounter.

CHARLIE CHAPLIN

PLAYS STRAIGHT MAN TO

GROUCHO MARX

Beverly Hills Tennis Club, Los Angeles
July 14th 1937

Tennis has become the most fashionable sport in Hollywood: Clark Gable, Errol Flynn, Cary Grant, Spencer Tracy, Carole Lombard, David Niven, Norma Shearer and Katharine Hepburn all play. This prompts Fred Perry – the world no. 1 player for the past five years* – to turn professional and move to Los Angeles with his film-star wife Helen Vinson.

Perry buys the Beverly Hills Tennis Club with the American champion Ellsworth Vines. To mark its opening, the two of them play in one of the very first pro-celebrity tournaments: Perry partners Charlie Chaplin and Vines partners Groucho Marx.

Charlie Chaplin (b.1889) is just a year older than Groucho Marx (b.1890), but the gap seems infinitely wider: the two men are separated by sound. Chaplin is the king of silent comedy, Marx the king of the fast-talking wise-crack. Chaplin spends a lot of time fretting that he belongs to the past; at lunch before the game, he shares these fears with his opponent.

'Charlie turned around to me and said, "Gee, I envy you,"' recalls Groucho, a quarter of a century on, 'and I said, "You envy me? Why?" He said, "I wish I could talk on the screen the way you do." I found this such an ironical statement. Here was the greatest comedian that there's ever been, there's never been anyone like him, and he's sitting there envying me because I can talk.'

It is not hard to detect an undertow of triumph beneath this outward show of sympathy. Groucho has always been a very competitive man, and Chaplin is known as the world champion in their shared field of comedy. But by the time Groucho looks back on this conversation, silent comedy has come to seem as out-of-date and quaint as the penny-farthing.

---

* And is still, in 2011, the last Englishman to have won Wimbledon.

The two vexed comedians compare notes. 'There we were, two neurotics sitting, and talking, completely terrified about life and their careers. You would think that by this time Chaplin would be more or less convinced that he had a remarkable talent. But no! He was just as frightened as he had been when he first came to me and asked my advice.'

That first meeting took place sixteen years ago, when the Marx Brothers were travelling from Minneapolis to Edmonton. With three hours to kill between trains in Winnipeg, Groucho walked up the main street to the Empress Theatre, where Chaplin happened to be playing. He heard great gusts of laughter coming from inside. 'I've never heard an audience laugh so forcefully in my life.' He went backstage, introduced himself to Chaplin and invited him to come and see the Marx Brothers perform.

Chaplin accepted. As a prank, he chose to sit in the front row, reading a newspaper all the way through the show. The Marx Brothers said nothing about it at the time, but when Chaplin invited them to see his show, they switched places in their box with four Orthodox rabbis, all extravagantly bearded. Assuming that the rabbis were the Marx Brothers in disguise, Chaplin picked on them, whereupon all four rabbis stormed out in protest.

When their paths crossed again in Salt Lake City, the Marx Brothers persuaded Chaplin to visit a brothel with them, but he proved too sheepish to take an active role, preferring to chat to the madam and play with her dog. Afterwards, he told the brothers that he had just refused an offer of $500 a week from Hollywood. 'No comedian is worth five hundred a week,' he explained. 'If I sign up with them and don't make good, they'll fire me.'

They didn't run into Charlie Chaplin again for another five years, by which time he had become a major Hollywood star, well known for his many lovers, some of them very young. When the brothers came to dinner at his mansion, uniformed butlers stood behind each of their chairs.

For the rest of their lives, Groucho Marx and Charlie Chaplin maintain an edgy relationship, their admiration tempered by competitiveness.* Like Chaplin, Groucho is forever looking over his shoulder for fear of being overtaken. When *Monkey Business* and *City Lights* come out at the

---

* Groucho dies on August 19th 1977, Chaplin four months later, on Christmas Day 1977.

same time, he notes ruefully that while *City Lights* is acclaimed an instant classic, *Monkey Business* is seen as 'the usual Marx Madhouse ...'

On this summer's day in 1937, it is as though the edgy competition between the two most famous comedians in the world has been formalised. Chaplin Chaplin prides himself on his tennis: as well as being a member of the Beverly Hills Club, he has his own court at his home, where he throws tennis parties for fellow stars like Greta Garbo and Clark Gable. When newsreel photographers turn up, he always plays that little bit harder. Groucho is much less proficient with a racket. Unable to compete in tennis, and incapable of being seen in public without playing his buffoonish on-screen character, he decides to compete for laughs. He turns up with a huge suitcase and a dozen tennis rackets, curls up in a sleeping bag, then brandishes a ping-pong bat.

Chaplin and Perry win the first game with ease, and the second game too. At this point, Groucho tells the crowd that he is going to have a lunch break ('Vines can do all my playing for me!'). He dips into his suitcase and produces a tablecloth and a range of sandwiches, which he proceeds to spread on the ground. 'Will you join me for a spot of tea?' he shouts to Chaplin, playing to the crowd.

Charlie Chaplin feigns laughter, but is quietly seething: he wants to get on with the match. 'I didn't come here to be your straight man,' he hisses into Groucho's ear.

Groucho omits this comment from his memoirs. In newsreel footage, Chaplin can be seen smiling at Groucho's shenanigans, but this is only for the cameras. Years later, he has still not forgiven Groucho for casting himself in the role of funny guy. After all, given the choice, who wants to play stooge?

GROUCHO MARX

WANTS TO BE TAKEN SERIOUSLY BY

T.S. ELIOT

3 Kensington Court Gardens, London W8
June 1964

Early in 1961, T.S. Eliot and his young wife are disembarking from a glass-bottomed boat in Jamaica when, much to their delight, they spot Groucho Marx and his wife preparing to embark.

Prompted by this coincidence, Eliot sends a letter to Groucho a few weeks later. In it, he says how much he admires him and asks for a signed photograph.

Groucho is pleasantly surprised; like many comedians, he is an intellectual *manqué*. Accordingly, he posts Eliot a studio portrait of himself looking serious, without his cigar and his comedy moustache. Eliot thanks him, promises him that it 'will soon appear in its frame on my wall with other famous friends such as W.B. Yeats and Paul Valéry', and sends a photograph of himself.

'I had no idea you were so handsome,' replies Groucho. 'Why you haven't been offered the lead in some sexy movies I can only attribute to the stupidity of the casting directors.'

The pair embark on a correspondence based on mutual admiration. In a letter written in February 1963, Eliot mentions that Groucho's portrait is now framed on his office mantelpiece, 'but I have to point you out to my visitors as nobody recognises you without the cigar and rolling eyes. I shall try to provide a cigar worthy of you.'

To clear up the problem, Groucho sends Eliot another photograph, this one of himself in full comic attire. Eliot now has two photographs. 'I like them both very much and I cannot make up my mind which one to take home and which one to put on my office wall. The new one would impress visitors more, especially those I want to impress, as it is unmistakably Groucho. The only solution may be to carry them both with me every day.'

Their correspondence rumbles on, with its slightly effortful jocularity, but the two men are prevented by illness from meeting. First Eliot is in hospital, then Groucho. In June, 1963, Groucho writes to say that 'by next May or thereabouts, I hope to be well enough to eat that free meal you've been promising me for the past two years'. But his letter includes a small note of hurt: he mentions that, in a tribute to T.S. Eliot by Stephen Spender in the *New York Times Book Review*, there is a long list of the many portraits on the wall of his study, but 'one name was conspicuous by its absence'.

Eliot writes a somewhat defensive letter in response. 'I think that Stephen Spender was only attempting to enumerate oil and water colour pictures and no photographs – I trust so,' he says. He is looking forward to their meeting in the spring. 'If you do not turn up I am afraid that all of the people to whom I have boasted of knowing you (and of being on first name terms at that) will take me for a four flusher.'

Recently, he adds, he and his wife went to *The Marx Brothers Go West*, which they had never seen before. 'It was certainly worth it,' he adds.

Groucho finally arrives in London in June 1964, to host a TV panel show called *The Celebrity Game*.* Dinner is duly arranged. Eliot writes to confirm that he has ordered a taxi to take Groucho and his wife from the Savoy, where they are staying, to the Eliots' flat in Kensington Court Gardens. 'The picture of you in the newspapers saying that, amongst other reasons, you have come to London to see me has greatly enhanced my credit in the neighbourhood, and particularly with the greengrocer across the street. Obviously I am now someone of importance.'

Groucho revises hard before the dinner with the man he refers to as 'my celebrated pen pal'. He reads *Murder in the Cathedral* twice, *The Waste Land* three times, and 'just in case of a conversational bottleneck' he also brushes up on *King Lear*.

Over cocktails before dinner, there is a momentary lull of the kind that is, recalls Groucho, 'more or less inevitable when strangers meet for the first time'. To fill the gap, Groucho tosses in a quotation from *The Waste Land*. 'That, I thought, will show him I've read a thing or two besides my press notices from Vaudeville.'

---

* The panellists are Kingsley Amis, Brian Epstein, Susan Hampshire and Groucho's third wife, Eden Hartford. The pilot goes badly, and the show is never aired.

Eliot smiles faintly, 'as though to say he was thoroughly familiar with his poems and didn't need me to recite them'. So Groucho tactfully steers the conversation onto *King Lear*. 'I said the king was an incredibly foolish old man, which God knows he *was*; and that if he'd been *my* father I would have run away from home at the age of eight – instead of waiting until I was ten.'

But this conversational ploy also fails to catch fire: Eliot clearly wants to talk about comedy, not literature. 'He seemed more interested in discussing *Animal Crackers* and *A Night at the Opera*. He quoted a joke – one of mine – that I had long since forgotten. Now it was my turn to smile faintly. I said I was not going to let anyone – not even the British poet from St Louis – spoil my Literary Evening.'

So Groucho doggedly continues with his condemnation of King Lear. He refers to the disowning of Cordelia as 'the height of idiocy'. The Eliots listen politely. Mrs Eliot defends Shakespeare, and Mrs Marx takes her side. But Eliot remains determined to switch the subject back to comedy. 'He asked if I remembered the courtroom scene in *Duck Soup*. Fortunately, I'd forgotten every word. It was obviously the end of the Literary Evening, but very pleasant none the less.'*

In a letter to his brother Gummo describing the evening, Groucho says that Eliot and he have three things in common: an affection for good cigars, a love of cats, and a weakness for puns. The Marxes

---

* Twenty-five years later, I am present at a similar meeting, between Anthony Burgess and Benny Hill.

Watching old Benny Hill shows in Monaco (long after they had fallen out of fashion in Britain), Anthony Burgess has become an unabashed admirer of the comedian. Reviewing a new biography of Hill, *Saucy Boy*, in the *Guardian* in 1990, he declares him 'one of the great artists of our age'.

The two men meet for the first time shortly after the review appears. I am lucky enough to be present at this bizarre but historic encounter. Both of them prove to be remarkably as they are on television. Hill arrives first, as perky as can be, apparently over the moon at having been driven by a female taxi-driver ('Oooh, I said, you can take me ANYWHERE, my love!'). Burgess – histrionic, loquacious, with deep voice and furrowed brow, putting the emphasis on unexpected words – behaves just like a slightly hammy actor playing the part of Anthony Burgess.

The two of them are full of praise for each other, but never quite find common ground. All in all, the encounter follows a similar pattern to T.S. Eliot's meeting with Groucho Marx: the author wanting to show off his knowledge of comedians, the comedian wanting to show off his knowledge of authors. By the end of the dinner it seems to me unlikely they will ever meet again, and as far as I know, they never do.

But then, neither man has long to live. Hill dies in 1992; Burgess in 1993.

leave reasonably early, as 'we both felt he wasn't up to a long evening of conversation – especially mine'. The poet, adds the comedian, is 'a dear man and a charming host'.

T.S. ELIOT

PROVOKES GIGGLES FROM

QUEEN ELIZABETH
THE QUEEN MOTHER

Aeolian Hall, 135–137 New Bond Street, London W1
April 14th 1943

T.S. Eliot has agreed to take part in a grand wartime poetry reading at the Aeolian Hall, 'to keep the arts alive'. Organised by Osbert Sitwell, it is in aid of Lady Crewe's French in Britain Fund. Early on, Sitwell has persuaded Queen Elizabeth to be patron; he has been keeping her abreast of developments for some weeks. Her Majesty has even promised to bring the two little Princesses along with her.

A formidable line-up of poets has been assembled, among them C. Day Lewis, Louis MacNeice, Vita Sackville-West, Walter de la Mare, John Masefield and Osbert's sister Edith, who has helped to organise the event. The Sitwells have jointly directed rehearsals, timing the poets with a stop-watch so as to be sure they do not go on too long. Edith invites her fellow poet Dorothy Wellesley to join in, for two reasons: a) she is a woman and b) she is sure not to outshine Edith. But Edith almost immediately regrets asking her, as Wellesley starts 'being beyond any words tiresome ... Practically every day I get letters worrying me about something. She sends me all the tripe she writes.' Why on earth, she wonders, did W.B. Yeats include her in his last anthology of poetry? 'The old man's mind must have been going for him to think her any good at all as a poet.'

On the big night, the hall fills up. Queen Elizabeth and her daughters, Elizabeth and Margaret, both wearing mittens, are each presented with a programme by the celebrity programme-seller, the comic actress Beatrice Lillie, before being escorted to the front row. The recital kicks off with John Masefield, the Poet Laureate, paying tribute to Laurence Binyon, who died in March. Queen Elizabeth and her daughters look duly grave. From then on, the poets take to the stage in strict alphabetical order:

Edmund Blunden, Gordon Bottomley, Hilda Doolittle. Each of them stands behind a Victorian lectern, picked up by Sitwell in the Caledonian market, so large that only the heads of the very tallest poets can be spotted above it.

E is for Eliot. At five feet eleven inches, he is clearly visible. He has chosen to read the final section, 'London Bridge is Falling Down', from *The Waste Land*:

> *I sat upon the shore*
> *Fishing, with the arid plain behind me*
> *Shall I at least set my lands in order?*

Queen Elizabeth is certainly no highbrow – decades later, the socialite Nicky Haslam recalls the choreographer Frederick Ashton doing 'a brilliant imitation' of her 'having to sit through a Wagner opera and wanting to go to the lav' – but she has always tried to maintain a healthy interest in literature.* Nevertheless, she and her daughters find it hard to keep straight faces through Mr Eliot's more outlandish efforts:

> *London Bridge is falling down falling down falling down*
> *Poi s'ascose nel foco che gli affina*
> *Quando fiam ceu chelidon – O swallow swallow*
> *Le Prince d'Aquitaine à la tour abolie*

---

* The British royal family traditionally views writers and artists as more to be endured than enjoyed. Queen Elizabeth's father-in-law, King George V, perhaps the most philistine of all monarchs, once came across a painting by Cézanne at an art exhibition. 'Come over here, May,' he said, summoning his wife, 'here's something that will make you laugh.'

His son, King George VI, commissions John Piper, well known for his brooding, stormy pictures, to paint a series of Windsor Castle. The artist duly delivers the paintings, but hears nothing. Some time later, he is presented to the King at a garden party. 'Ah yes ... Piper,' says the King. 'Pity you had such awful weather.'

Royal encounters with writers and poets rarely go smoothly, and often end in conversational cul-de-sacs. When Robert Graves goes to the Palace to receive the Queen's Medal for Poetry, he says to the Queen, 'You realise, ma'am, that you and I are descended from the prophet Mohammed.' 'Oh, really?' says the Queen. 'Yes.' 'How interesting.' 'I think that you should mention it in your Christmas message, because a lot of your subjects are Mohammedans.'

Almost half a century on, Queen Elizabeth – now the Queen Mother – sits next to the novelist A.N. Wilson at a private dinner.* They have been talking about literature. Wilson has asked her what she reads for pleasure. 'I am very fond of detective stories. I like P.D. James, but it takes me about two months to finish one of her books. I really prefer Dorothy L. Sayers. Oh, and Barbara Pym I love.'†

The Queen Mother asks Wilson if he can get his daughters to read. 'Difficult to stop them, ma'am,' he replies.

'I remember dear Osbert – did you know him?' says the Queen Mother. 'Alas not.'

'I thought the girls ... you see, they were marooned in Windsor Castle for most of the war, and I was not sure that they were having a very good education, and kind Sachie and Osbert said they would arrange a poetry evening for us. Such an embarrassment. Osbert was wonderful, as you would expect, and Edith, of course, but then we had this rather lugubrious man in a suit, and he read a poem ... I think it was called *The Desert*. And first the girls got the giggles, and then I did, and then even the King.'

'*The Desert*, ma'am?' asks Wilson. 'Are you sure it wasn't called *The Waste Land*?'

'That's it. I'm afraid we all giggled. Such a gloomy man, looked as though he worked in a bank, and we didn't understand a word.'

'I believe he DID once work in a bank, ma'am.'

Following T.S. Eliot's reading, Walter de la Mare takes to the stage, but is too small to reach the lectern. W.J. Turner is next up, but his reading greatly exceeds his allotted six minutes, and he is heckled by some of his fellow poets. Then comes the interval; the Queen mixes informally with

---

* Wilson comes in for heavy and immediate criticism for betraying the confidences of the dinner table. His host, Lord Wyatt of Weeford, complains that it is 'a shabby trick' and that Wilson 'is boastfully shameless in being a scoundrel ... his underhand behaviour does not square with the Christian ethics he professes. Nor with those of a gentleman, which I had naïvely thought him to be.' Nicholas Soames MP condemns it as 'an intolerable betrayal ... For Mr Wilson to have broken every convention of civilised society in this regard is bad enough. Worse, it shows an appalling want of chivalry.'

Before his death, Wyatt arranges for the posthumous publication of his diaries, which, co-incidentally, contain detailed reports of many private conversations with the Queen Mother.

† By chance, she welcomes the novelist Kazuo Ishiguro to Balmoral during his gap year in 1973, but only as a beater.

all the poets in an ante room. But outside in the hall, an unfortunate incident is taking place.

Dorothy Wellesley, never easy, has had too much to drink, and is creating a disturbance. Earlier, she informed Osbert Sitwell that she was too drunk to read, but she has now changed her mind, and is determined to perform an impromptu recital. The ever-game Beatrice Lillie has put down her programmes and is struggling to enfold her in a jujitsu grip. Stephen Spender leaps to the aid of Lillie, and tries to pin down the errant poetess. Harold Nicolson steps forward to help; Wellesley promptly whacks him with her stick, mistaking him for Osbert Sitwell. At last the critic Raymond Mortimer lures her outside onto Bond Street, where, according to Edith Sitwell, she sits down on the kerb, bangs her stick on the pavement and uses 'frightful language about a) the Queen and b) me'.

The whole evening provides a conversational ice-breaker for the royal family in the coming months. They have always delighted in extracting merriment from things that go awry. Soon afterwards, when Rex Whistler comes to stay at Sandringham, Queen Elizabeth talks about 'that fantastic *poetry-reading orgy*' and simply cannot stop laughing.

QUEEN ELIZABETH
THE QUEEN MOTHER

TALKS KITCHENS WITH

THE DUCHESS OF WINDSOR

Windsor Castle
June 5th 1972

They have met perhaps half a dozen times in the past thirty-five years, and have never got on. Some suspect the awkwardness between them has festered into something closer to hatred.

The little Princesses' governess Marion Crawford is at Royal Lodge in April 1936 when the new King and his American lady friend Mrs Simpson drop in for a visit. She finds Mrs Simpson bossy and tactless: 'I remember she drew him [the King] to the window and suggested how certain trees might be moved, and a part of a hill taken away to improve the view.' This goes down badly with the then Duke and Duchess of York, as the Duke has had a hand in the garden's design. 'The atmosphere was not a comfortable one,' concludes Miss Crawford.*

Later that year, when the Yorks go to dinner at Balmoral, Mrs Simpson extends her hand, but Elizabeth brushes past her, announcing brusquely,

---

* Opinion among staff remains divided. 'She is quiet and easy to please,' an unnamed female employee of Raymond's hairdressing salon is quoted as saying in 1949. But in 2002, a former Buckingham Palace footman, Guy Hunting, recalls the dislike for the Duchess of Windsor felt by the Duke's former valet, Walter Fry. 'It was not the fact that she was foreign or divorced or untitled that rankled, it was simply that she did not seem to know how they [the servants] should be treated. The worst example of this was her behaviour at table. At lunch or dinner most people react immediately when they are aware that someone is standing beside them holding a dish of meat or vegetables. The well-mannered turn slightly, without breaking off conversation, and help themselves to whatever is offered. Wallis Simpson's habit was to ignore poor bent (no pun intended) footmen for as long as possible. When Walter realised that this was a game she enjoyed playing at every opportunity, he decided that she must be taught a lesson. During dinner one evening he waited patiently beside her to see if she was up to her usual tricks. When she failed, yet again, to acknowledge the presence of the large dish of roast pheasant that was getting heavier and heavier, he moved it sightly to the left until it brushed gently against the bare flesh of her upper arm. The heat of the silver generated an immediate response, and a withering glance from the lady from Baltimore. After that little incident she played by the rules, and Walter was a hero.'

'I came to dine with the King.' The dinner is sticky, with the Yorks the first to leave.

Over the next few decades, relations between the pair go from bad to worse. In 1938, when the Duke and Duchess of Windsor, as they now are, plan a tour of America, King George VI is determined that they should not be allowed to stay at the British Embassy, and the new Queen is even more adamant. 'When the men spoke in terms of indignation, she spoke in terms of acute pain and distress, and deeply felt ... All her feelings were lacerated by what she and the King were being made to go through,' the British Ambassador recalls. Their proposed tour never takes place.

A year later, the Duke of Windsor is not invited to the dedication of the tomb of his late father, though he himself paid for half of it. When he reads of the ceremony in the newspapers, with no acknowledgement of his own half-share in the costs, his fury boils over. 'I greatly regret that it should have taken so sacred an occasion to disclose so much that is unpleasant, and to destroy the last vestige of feeling I had left for you all as a family,' he writes to his mother.

And so the feud bubbles on: later that year, the Windsors visit England, but they are not invited to the Palace. 'I had taken the precaution to send her a message before they came, saying that I was sorry I could not receive her,' says Queen Elizabeth. 'I thought it more honest to make things quite clear. So she kept away, & nobody saw her. What a curse black sheep are to a family!' In 1940, she attempts to block the Duke of Windsor's appointment as Governor of the Bahamas, arguing that the Duchess 'is looked upon as the lowest of the low'.*

The two women do not meet again for a quarter of a century. Absence makes neither heart grow fonder. The Duchess tends to call Elizabeth 'the fat Scotch cook', 'the dumpy Duchess' or just plain 'cookie'. James Pope-Hennessy notes her 'facial contortion, reserved for speaking of the Queen Mother, which is very unpleasant to behold, and seemed to *me* akin to frenzy'. The Queen Mother is more tight-lipped in her dislike, but no less

---

* Less chummily, the Duke of Windsor describes his mother and his sister-in-law as 'ice-veined bitches'.

passionate. If ever the forbidden topic comes up, she refers to the Duchess of Windsor only as 'that woman'.*

They meet, briefly, at the dedication of a memorial plaque to Queen Mary in June 1967. At first, the Queen Mother refuses to attend if the Duchess of Windsor is to be present, but she relents. The Duchess fails to curtsey to her; the two women shake hands but do not exchange kisses. 'How nice to see you,' says the Queen Mother, moving smartly on. After the ceremony the Queen Mother says, 'I do hope we meet again.' 'When?' asks the Duchess, but no reply is forthcoming.

Five years on, in 1972, the Duke of Windsor dies of throat cancer. Throughout his final illness, the Queen Mother fails to make contact, but when the Duchess arrives at Heathrow Airport for the funeral, she is greeted by Lord Mountbatten, who delivers the message, 'Your sister-in-law will receive you with open arms. She is deeply sorry for you in your present grief and remembers what it was like when her own husband died.' According to Mountbatten, this 'comforted her a lot'.

After the funeral, there is a reception at Windsor Castle. 'It's so difficult, because she hardly knows anyone,' says Queen Elizabeth II as everyone shuffles in.

Before lunch, the two old enemies, both in their seventies, sit side by side on a sofa. The Duchess is showing signs of losing her mind. Princess Margaret eavesdrops on their conversation.

'Do you have an upstairs or a downstairs kitchen?' the Duchess asks the Queen Mother. The Queen Mother is nonplussed: Princess Margaret thinks she might be unsure as to her kitchen's exact location. But the Duchess tactfully fills the gap in conversation by replying to her own question. 'We tried both,' she says, 'and I prefer the upstairs as there is so much less moving about. Naturally it depends upon how many guests you are entertaining.'

At lunch, the Duchess sits between Prince Philip and Lord Mountbatten. 'Well, what are your plans?' asks Prince Philip. 'You going back to America, then?' The Duchess feels like saying, 'Why should I?' Instead she says, 'I

---

* Like a pantomime character, the Duchess of Windsor continues to arouse fierce reactions, both for and against. Nicky Haslam writes in 2009, 'On the day the Duchess died, I was dining with David Westmorland, Master of the Horse to the Queen, and his wife, Jane. The dinner was for Princess Margaret. I summoned up the courage to ask her what she felt about the Duchess. The Princess replied simply: "It wasn't her we hated, it was him."'

won't be coming back to England if that's what you're afraid of, except to visit the grave.' She is determined that the royal family should not see her grieve, and amused by the gusto with which they all tuck into their puddings.

When lunch is over, the two women again sit side by side. After a few drinks, the Queen Mother is more talkative, and expresses her sympathies. The Duchess pauses awhile, and seems to be searching for a suitable topic. At last, she finds one.

'Do you have an upstairs or a downstairs kitchen?' she asks.

THE DUCHESS OF WINDSOR

TAKES TEA WITH

ADOLF HITLER

Berchtesgaden, the Bavarian Alps
October 22nd 1937

'The two people who have caused me most trouble in my life,' recalls the Queen Mother in her old age, 'are Wallis Simpson and Hitler.'

Her two principal troublemakers meet just the once. Adolf Hitler feels the Duke and Duchess of Windsor have been ill-treated by the British, and invites them to Germany. 'The real reason for the destruction of the Duke of Windsor was, I am sure, his speech at the old veterans' rally in Berlin, at which he declared that it would be the task of his life to effect a reconciliation between Britain and Germany,' the Führer explains to dinner guests; '… the subsequent treatment of the Duke of Windsor was an evil omen; to topple over so fine a pillar of strength was both foolish and wicked.'

Together, the Windsors accept Herr Hitler's invitation. 'His Royal Highness wanted to see honour and glory paid to the woman he adored,' explains his equerry, Sir Dudley Forwood, years later.

The Windsors' train pulls into Berlin's Friedrichstrasse station on the morning of October 11th. No effort has been spared to make them feel at home. The station is decorated with strings of Union Jacks neatly alternating with swastikas. As the Duke and Duchess alight, a band strikes up a hearty rendition of 'God Save the King', and the crowd cheers 'Heil Edward!' and 'Hoch Windsors!'

Dr Robert Ley, the leader of the National Labour Front, presents the Duchess with a box of chocolates, complete with a card saying 'KÖNIGLICHE HOHEIT', or 'Royal Highness'.* A few minutes later, the

---

* The Windsors' circle always style her 'Your Royal Highness', even though it is not, strictly speaking, correct. Early on, this causes a dilemma for those torn between loyalty to the past and present Kings. When speaking to the Duchess, should they address her as Your Royal Highness or not? The high-society diarist Harold Nicolson records the anxiety of those staying as guests with W. Somerset Maugham at the Villa Mauresque in the South of France in August 1938 as

Third Secretary from the British Embassy hands the Duke a letter explaining that the Ambassador has been called away unexpectedly, and the Embassy is taking no official notice of their visit. The Windsors interpret this, quite accurately, as a slight. 'Both the Duke and Duchess were very, very hurt,' notes Sir Dudley.

They leave the station in a black Mercedes, with four SS officers hanging on the running boards. A specially invited crowd welcomes them to the Kaiserhof Hotel with a merry song specially composed by the Propaganda Ministry, under the aegis of Dr Goebbels. The next few days are spent in a whirl of guided tours. The Duchess is taken around a Nazi Welfare Society workhouse, where she watches women sewing clothes for the poor; the Duke is guest of honour at a concert given by the Berlin Labour Front Orchestra, ending with lusty renditions of 'Deutschland Über Alles', 'The Horst Wessel Song' and 'God Save the King'. Nazi newsreel cameras catch the Duke raising his arm in the Nazi salute. He will execute the same salute several times before he leaves. 'Nothing more than good manners,' explains Sir Dudley.

Their first evening is spent at a party at Dr Ley's country estate. Guests include the SS leader Heinrich Himmler, Hitler's deputy Rudolf Hess and his wife Ilse, and Josef and Magda Goebbels, whom the Duchess describes as 'the prettiest woman I saw in Germany'. Ilse Hess remembers the Duchess as 'a lovely, charming, warm and clever woman with a heart of gold'.

The sightseeing continues: here a visit to the training school of the Death's Head Division of the elite squad of the SS, there a trip to Goering's country estate, where they admire the lavish model railway he has assembled in his barn. The Duchess is impressed by 'the deftness with which the Field Marshal directed the trains up and down the tracks, opening and closing switches, blowing whistles, and averting collisions'. In turn, Emmy Goering is impressed by the Duchess. 'I could not help thinking that this

---

they prepare to greet the Windsors: 'We stood sheepishly in the drawing room. In they came ... Cocktails were brought and we stood around the fireplace. There was a pause. "I am sorry we were a little late," said the Duke, "but Her Royal Highness couldn't drag herself away." He had said it. The three words fell into the circle like three stones into a pool. Her (gasp) Royal (shudder) Highness (and not one eye dared to meet the other) ...'

woman would certainly have cut a good figure on the throne of England.'*

On October 22nd the Duke and Duchess are welcomed by the Führer himself. Herr Hitler's private train whisks them to Berchtesgaden; from there, they are driven in an open-topped Mercedes up the mountain at Obersalzberg to Hitler's Berghof.

As they admire the view over the Bavarian Alps from the large drawing room, an aide appears and whisks the Duke off to meet the Führer. The Duchess feels peeved at being left out. She has to make do with Rudolf Hess, who vainly attempts to break the ice with small-talk about music. After an hour or more, Hitler and the Duke return, and they all have tea in front of the fire.†

'I could not take my eyes off Hitler ... at close quarters he gave one the feeling of great inner force,' the Duchess remembers, thirty years on. 'His hands were long and slim, a musician's hands,§ and his eyes were truly

---

* The Duchess's looks struck several of those who met her as peculiar. 'This is one of the very oddest women I have ever seen,' observes her mother-in-law's biographer, James Pope-Hennessy, after going to stay with the Duke and Duchess in 1958. '... She is, to look at, a phenomenon. She is flat and angular, and could have been designed for a medieval playing-card. The shoulders are small and high; the head very, very large, almost monumental ... Her jawbone is alarming, and from the back you can plainly see it jutting beyond the neck on each side.' Nicholas Haslam recalls meeting her in a restaurant in New York in the early 1960s: 'Across the restaurant – cheek-kissing, air-kissing, winking, waving – comes this minute figure, the flat cubist head made higher and wider by black bouffant hair parted centrally from the brow to the black grosgrain bow at the nape, dressed in an impossibly wide-weave pink angora tweed Chanel suit, concertinaed white gloves, black crocodile bag and shoes ... "Oh, the Beatles. Don't you just love 'em? 'I give her all my love, that's all I do-oo,'" she sings. "Adore 'em. Do you know them? Oh, you are lucky."'

Margaret, Duchess of Argyll remembers meeting the then Mrs Ernest Simpson at a luncheon party in the mid-1930s: 'She was not outstanding in any way, not well dressed. Her hair was parted down the middle, arranged in "earphones", and her voice was harsh. My impression was of quite a plain woman with a noticeably square jaw, and not particularly amusing. But she was a pleasant person, and we were to remain friends.'

† Deborah Mitford, later the Duchess of Devonshire, also takes tea with Hitler in 1937. He is a friend of her sister Unity. 'He isn't very like his photos, not nearly so hard looking,' she writes in her diary. On a visit to his bathroom, she notices that he has 'some brushes there, with "AH" on them'. Through her sister Diana Mosley, the Duchess also encounters the Duchess of Windsor: 'I could not like her, she seemed so brittle, her face bony, angular and painted, her body so dangerously thin she might snap in half.'

§ In his memoirs, Sir Alec Douglas-Home confesses to a different impression of the Führer: 'I noticed that his arms swung low, almost to his knees. It gave him a curiously animal appearance.'

extraordinary – intense, unblinking, magnetic, burning with the same peculiar fire I had earlier seen in the eyes of Kemal Ataturk. Once or twice I felt those eyes turned in my direction. But when I tried to meet their gaze, the lids dropped, and I found myself confronted by a mask. I decided that Hitler did not care for women.'

At one point, though, he does make a memorable remark. The Duchess has just complimented him on the splendid architecture she has seen over the past ten days. 'Our buildings will make more magnificent ruins than the Greeks,' he replies, eerily.

On their way back to Munich, the Duchess waits until they are alone before asking her husband whether he had an interesting talk with Hitler. 'Yes, very,' he answers, riffling through the pages of a magazine. 'Now darling, you know my rule about politics. I'd certainly never allow myself to get into a political discussion with him!'

'You were with him one hour. What did you talk about?'

'He did most of the talking.'

'Well, what did he talk about?'

'Oh, the usual stuff. What he's trying to do for Germany and to combat Bolshevism.'

'What did he say about Bolshevism?'

'He's against it.'

For his part, Adolf Hitler comes away with a high opinion of the Duchess of Windsor. 'She would have made a good Queen,' he remarks later that day of their fleeting one on one.

AUTHOR'S NOTE

My work as a humorist relies on distortion. However, I have tried to keep this book on the straight and narrow: everything in it is documented. When accounts of the same meeting differ, as they almost always do, I have sided with the most likely.

To lend order to a book that revolves around chance, I have described each of the 101 meetings in exactly 1001 words, which makes *One on One* 101,101 words long. The acknowledgements, prefacing quotes, author's blurb, book's blurb and list of my other books each consist of 101 words, as does this note.

C. B.

ACKNOWLEDGEMENTS

Special thanks to Robert Lacey for his patience and expertise and to Gervase Poulden for his help with digging up information on, among others, James Dean, Gorky, Tchaikovsky and Frank Lloyd Wright. Thanks also to my agent Caroline Dawnay and to Olivia Hunt, Nicholas Pearson, Johnny and Mary James, Robin and Liz Summers, Francis Wheen, Susie Dowdall, Hugh Browton, Susanna Gross, Clare Gittins, Terence Blacker, Matthew Sturgis, Andrew Barrow, Anna Herve, Ian Irvine, Rebecca McEwan, Jonathan and Kalyani Katz, Hugo Vickers, the late Hugh Massingberd, and to everyone who remembered, however hazily, once reading something about someone meeting someone else.

BIBLIOGRAPHY

1) Adolf Hitler + John Scott-Ellis 1931
Obituary of Baron Howard de Walden, *Guardian* July 1999
Obituary of Baron Howard de Walden, *Independent* July 1999
Earls Have Peacocks: The Memoirs of Howard de Walden (Haggerston Press 1992)
The Rise and Fall of the Third Reich by William L. Shirer (Simon and Schuster 1959)
Hitler: A Study in Tyranny by Alan Bullock (Odhams 1952)
Wait for Me!: Memoirs of the Youngest Mitford Sister by Deborah Devonshire (John Murray 2010)

2) John Scott-Ellis + Rudyard Kipling 1923
Rudyard Kipling by Andrew Lycett (Weidenfeld and Nicolson 1999)
A Mingled Measure: Diaries 1953–1972 by James Lees-Milne (John Murray 1994)
Earls Have Peacocks: The Memoirs of Lord Howard de Walden (Haggerston Press 1992)

3) Rudyard Kipling + Mark Twain 1889
The Penguin Book of Interviews edited by Christopher Silvester (Viking 1993)
Rudyard Kipling by Andrew Lycett (Weidenfeld and Nicolson 1999)
The Faber Book of Writers on Writers edited by Sean French (Faber and Faber 1999)
Mark Twain: A Life by Ron Powers (Scribners 2005)

4) Mark Twain + Helen Keller 1909
Helen Keller: A Life by Dorothy Herrmann (University of Chicago Press 1998)
Midstream: My Later Life by Helen Keller (Doubleday 1929)
The Story of My Life by Helen Keller (Hodder and Stoughton 1903)
Mark Twain: A Life by Ron Powers (Scribners 2005)
YouTube: Helen Keller & Anne Sullivan (1930 newsreel footage)

5) Helen Keller + Martha Graham 1952

Merce Cunningham: The Modernizing of Modern Dance by Roger Copeland
 (Routledge 2004)

Blood Memory by Martha Graham (Macmillan 1992)

Helen Keller: A Life by Dorothy Herrmann (University of Chicago Press 1998)

6) Martha Graham + Madonna 1978

Blood Memory by Martha Graham (Macmillan 1992)

New York Times

New York Post

Madonna: An Intimate Biography by J. Randy Taraborrelli (Sidgwick and Jackson
 2001)

Martha Graham: A Dancer's Life by Russell Freedman (Clarion 1998)

'Madonna Makes Dance!' article by Madonna, *Harper's Bazaar* May 1994

7) Madonna + Michael Jackson 1991

Madonna: An Intimate Biography by J. Randy Taraborrelli (Sidgwick and Jackson
 2001)

Madonna: Blonde Ambition by Mark Bego (Harmony Books 1992)

Michael Jackson: The Magic and the Madness by J. Randy Taraborrelli (Sidgwick
 and Jackson 2003)

8) Michael Jackson + Nancy Reagan 1984

Michael Jackson: The Magic and the Madness by J. Randy Taraborrelli (Sidgwick
 and Jackson 2003)

The Reagan Diaries edited by Douglas Brinkley (HarperCollins 2007)

The Ronald Reagan Presidential Library

New York Times

New York Daily News

9) Nancy Reagan + Andy Warhol 1981

Independent

Andy Warhol: His Controversial Life, Art and Colourful Times by Tony Scherman
 and David Dalton (JR Books 2010)

The Andy Warhol Diaries edited by Pat Hackett (Warner Books 1989)

America's Queen: The Life of Jacqueline Kennedy Onassis by Sarah Bradford
 (Viking 2000)

Daily Telegraph August 21st 2009

Ronnie and Nancy: Their Path to the White House 1911–1980 by Bob Colacello
 (Warner Books 2004)

The Andy Warhol Diaries edited by Pat Hackett (Warner Books 1989)
My Turn: The Memoirs of Nancy Reagan by Nancy Reagan with William Novak
  (Weidenfeld and Nicolson 1989)

10) Andy Warhol + Jackie Kennedy 1978
The Andy Warhol Diaries edited by Pat Hackett (Warner Books 1989)
America's Queen: The Life of Jacqueline Kennedy Onassis by Sarah Bradford
  (Viking 2000)

11) Jackie Kennedy + Queen Elizabeth II 1961
The Mitfords: Letters Between Six Sisters edited by Charlotte Mosley (Fourth Estate
  2007)
America's Queen: The Life of Jacqueline Kennedy Onassis by Sarah Bradford
  (Viking 2000)
Palimpsest: A Memoir by Gore Vidal (André Deutsch 1995)
In Tearing Haste: Letters Between Deborah Devonshire and Patrick Leigh Fermor
  edited by Charlotte Mosley (John Murray 2008)

12) Queen Elizabeth II + The Duke of Windsor 1972
Royal: Her Majesty Queen Elizabeth II by Robert Lacey (Little, Brown 2002)
The Duchess of Windsor: The Uncommon Life of Wallis Simpson by Greg King
  (Aurum 1999)
The Prince of Wales: A Biography by Jonathan Dimbleby (Warner Books 1994)
The People's King: The True Story of the Abdication by Susan Williams (Allen Lane
  2003)
Redeeming Features: A Memoir by Nicholas Haslam (Jonathan Cape 2009)
Behind Closed Doors: The Tragic, Untold Story of the Duchess of Windsor by Hugo
  Vickers (Hutchinson 2011)

13) The Duke of Windsor + Elizabeth Taylor 1968
Rich: The Life of Richard Burton by Melvyn Bragg (Hodder and Stoughton 1988)
Elizabeth: The Life of Elizabeth Taylor by Alexander Walker (Grove Press 2001)
Furious Love by Sam Kashner and Nancy Schoenberger (JR Books 2010)
Palimpsest: A Memoir by Gore Vidal (André Deutsch 1995)
The Unexpurgated Beaton introduced by Hugo Vickers (Weidenfeld and Nicolson
  2002)

14) Elizabeth Taylor + James Dean 1955
Elizabeth: The Life of Elizabeth Taylor by Alexander Walker (Grove Press 2001)
James Dean: A Biography by John Howlett (Plexus 2005)

Liz: An Intimate Biography of Elizabeth Taylor by C. David Heymann (Citadel 1995)

James Dean: Little Boy Lost by Joe Hyams and Jay Hyams (Arrow 1994)

James Dean: The Mutant King by David Dalton (Plexus 1989)

A Passion for Life: The Biography of Elizabeth Taylor by Donald Spoto
(HarperCollins 1995)

Kevin Sessums, The Daily Beast March 23rd 2011

15) James Dean + Alec Guinness 1955

Alec Guinness: The Authorised Biography by Piers Paul Read (Simon and Schuster
2003)

The Parkinson Show October 10th 1977

Blessings in Disguise by Alec Guinness (Hamish Hamilton 1985)

deathofjamesdean.com

16) Alec Guinness + Evelyn Waugh 1955

Alec Guinness: The Authorised Biography by Piers Paul Read (Simon and Schuster
2003)

The Diaries of Evelyn Waugh edited by Michael Davie (Weidenfeld and Nicolson
1976)

The Letters of Evelyn Waugh edited by Mark Amory (Weidenfeld and Nicolson
1980)

Blessings in Disguise by Alec Guinness (Hamish Hamilton 1985)

Edith Sitwell: A Unicorn Among Lions by Victoria Glendinning (Weidenfeld and
Nicolson 1981)

17) Evelyn Waugh + Igor Stravinsky 1949

Stravinsky: The Second Exile – France and America 1934–1971 by Stephen Walsh
(Jonathan Cape 2006)

Tom Driberg in the *Observer* magazine May 20th 1973

*I Once Met … Chance Encounters with the Famous and Infamous from the Pages of
the Oldie* (Oldie Publications 2008)

Memories and Glimpses by A.L. Rowse (Methuen 1986)

Dialogues by Igor Stravinsky and Robert Craft (University of California Press
1982)

'The Only Member of his Club' by Penelope Fitzgerald, *New York Times*
September 13th 1992

'Yours affec: Evelyn', essay by Ann Fleming in *Evelyn Waugh and his World* edited
by David Pryce-Jones (Weidenfeld and Nicolson 1973)

Evelyn Waugh: Portrait of a Country Neighbour by Frances Donaldson
(Weidenfeld and Nicolson 1967)

18) Igor Stravinsky + Walt Disney 1939

New York Times January 14th 1990

City of Nets: A Portrait of Hollywood in the 1940s by Otto Friedrich (Headline 1987)

Walt Disney: The Biography by Neal Gabler (Aurum 2006)

Stravinsky in Pictures and Documents by Vera Stravinsky and Robert Craft (Hutchinson 1979)

Stravinsky: The Second Exile – France and America 1934–1971 by Stephen Walsh (Jonathan Cape 2006)

19) Walt Disney + P.L. Travers 1964

Mary Poppins, She Wrote: The Life of P.L. Travers by Valerie Lawson (Aurum 1999)

Walt Disney: The Biography by Neal Gabler (Aurum 2006)

20) P.L. Travers + George Ivanovich Gurdjieff 1949

Mary Poppins, She Wrote: The Life of P.L. Travers by Valerie Lawson (Aurum 1999)

Gurdjieff: The Anatomy of a Myth by James Moore (Element Books 1991)

Feet of Clay: A Study of Gurus by Anthony Storr (HarperCollins 1997)

21) George Ivanovich Gurdjieff + Frank Lloyd Wright 1934

Frank Lloyd Wright: A Biography by Meryle Secrest (Chatto and Windus 1992)

Gurdjieff: The Anatomy of a Myth by James Moore (Element Books 1991)

Many Masks: A Life of Frank Lloyd Wright by Brendan Gill (Heinemann 1988)

'Gurdjieff at Taliesin' by Frank Lloyd Wright, article in the *Capitol Times*, Madison, Wisconsin, August 26th 1934

22) Frank Lloyd Wright + Marilyn Monroe 1957

'Frank Lloyd Wright: Architecture Design Style' by Robert Green, *Wall Street Journal* April 19th 2007

Timebends by Arthur Miller (Methuen 1988)

The Genius and the Goddess by Jeffrey Meyers (Hutchinson 2009)

Many Masks: A Life of Frank Lloyd Wright by Brendan Gill (Heinemann 1988)

23) Marilyn Monroe + Nikita Khrushchev 1959

K Blows Top by Peter Carlson (Public Affairs Books 2010)

Timebends by Arthur Miller (Methuen 1988)

The Genius and the Goddess by Jeffrey Meyers (Hutchinson 2009)

Monroe Confidential by Lena Pepitone and William Stadiem (Pocket Books 1980)

Spectator July 3rd 2010

24) Nikita Khrushchev + George Brown 1956

Khrushchev: A Political Life by William Thomson (St Martin's Press 1995)

Khrushchev: The Man and his Era by William Taubman (W.W. Norton 2003)

Tired and Emotional: The Life of Lord George Brown by Peter Paterson (Chatto and Windus 1993)

In My Way by George Brown (Victor Gollancz 1971)

The Diaries and Letters of Harold Nicolson, Volume III: The Later Years, 1945–1962 edited by Nigel Nicolson (Atheneum 1968)

The Labour Government, 1964–70: A Personal Record by Harold Wilson (Weidenfeld and Nicolson 1971)

The Macmillan Diaries, Volume II edited by Peter Catterall (Macmillan 2011)

25) George Brown + Eli Wallach 1963

Tired and Emotional: The Life of Lord George Brown by Peter Paterson (Chatto and Windus 1993)

The Diaries of a Cabinet Minister by Richard Crossman (Hamish Hamilton 1978)

1963: Five Hundred Days by John Lawton (Hodder and Stoughton 1992)

In My Way by George Brown (Victor Gollancz 1971)

26) Eli Wallach + Frank Sinatra 1974

The Good, the Bad and Me: In My Anecdotage by Eli Wallach (Harcourt 2005)

'The Godfather Wars' by Mark Seal, *Vanity Fair* March 2009

Sinatra: The Life by Anthony Summers and Robbyn Swan (Doubleday 2005)

His Way: The Unauthorized Biography of Frank Sinatra by Kitty Kelley (Bantam Press 1986)

Eli Wallach in conversation with Niall Macpherson, National Film Theatre, October 10th 2007 (BFI archive)

Letter from Victor Gold, *Vanity Fair* May 2009

27) Frank Sinatra + Dominick Dunne 1966

Dominick Dunne: After the Party (documentary DVD)

New York Daily News

Sinatra: The Life by Anthony Summers and Robbyn Swan (Doubleday 2005)

Jim Morrison: Life, Death, Legend by Stephen Davis (Gotham 2004)

28) Dominick Dunne + Phil Spector 2007

Various articles by Dominick Dunne, *Vanity Fair*

Tearing Down the Wall of Sound: The Rise and Fall of Phil Spector by Mick Brown (Bloomsbury 2007)

29) Phil Spector + Leonard Cohen 1977

Tearing Down the Wall of Sound: The Rise and Fall of Phil Spector by Mick Brown (Bloomsbury 2007)

Awopbopaloobop Alopbamboom by Nik Cohn (Paladin 1970)

BBC News website

Guardian

30) Leonard Cohen + Janis Joplin 1967

Various Positions: A Life of Leonard Cohen by Ira B. Nadel (Bloomsbury 1996)

Leonard Cohen by Stephen Scobie (Douglas and MacIntyre 1978)

At the Chelsea by Florence Turner (Hamish Hamilton 1986)

Love, Janis by Laura Joplin (Villard 1992)

Scars of Sweet Paradise: The Life and Times of Janis Joplin by Alice Echols (Virago 1999)

Going Down with Janis by Peggy Caserta (Dell 1974)

Leonardcohenfiles.com

Songwriters on Songwriting by Paul Zollo (Da Capo Press 1997)

31) Janis Joplin + Patti Smith 1970

Just Kids by Patti Smith (Bloomsbury 2010)

At the Chelsea by Florence Turner (Hamish Hamilton 1986)

Interview with Patti Smith by Jeffrey Brown, PBS *Newshour* December 2010

32) Patti Smith + Allen Ginsberg 1969

Ginsberg: A Biography by Barry Miles (Viking 1989)

Just Kids by Patti Smith (Bloomsbury 2010)

Obituary of Allen Ginsberg by James Campbell, *Independent* April 7th 1997

Obituary of Allen Ginsberg, *Daily Telegraph* April 7th 1997

33) Allen Ginsberg + Francis Bacon 1957

Profile of Francis Bacon, BBC *Arena* 1986

'Bacon Agonistes' by John Richardson, *New York Review of Books* December 17th 2009

Francis Bacon: Anatomy of an Enigma by Michael Peppiatt (Weidenfeld and Nicolson 1998)

The Gilded Gutter Life of Francis Bacon by Daniel Farson (Century 1993)

Ginsberg: A Biography by Barry Miles (Viking 1989)

Literary Outlaw: The Life and Times of William Burroughs by Ted Morgan (Bodley Head 1991)

The Penguin Book of the Beats edited by Ann Charters (Penguin 1992)

34) Francis Bacon + Princess Margaret 1977
The Rise and Fall of the House of Windsor by A.N. Wilson (Sinclair-Stevenson 1993)
The Gilded Gutter Life of Francis Bacon by Daniel Farson (Century 1993)
Princess Margaret: A Life Unravelled by Tim Heald (Weidenfeld and Nicolson 2007)
Princess Margaret: A Life of Contrasts by Christopher Warwick (André Deutsch 2000)
Adventures of a Gentleman's Gentleman by Guy Hunting (John Blake 2002)
Man with a Blue Scarf: On Sitting for a Portrait by Lucian Freud by Martin Gayford (Thames and Hudson 2010)
'Francis Bacon 1909–1992' by Caroline Blackwood, *New York Review of Books* September 24th 1992

35) Princess Margaret + Kenneth Tynan 1968
The Life of Kenneth Tynan by Kathleen Tynan (Phoenix 1988)
Princess Margaret: A Life Unravelled by Tim Heald (Weidenfeld and Nicolson 2007)
Palimpsest: A Memoir by Gore Vidal (André Deutsch 1995)
The Diaries of Kenneth Tynan edited by John Lahr (Bloomsbury 2001)
The Sixties: Diaries, Volume II, 1960–1969 by Christopher Isherwood edited and introduced by Katherine Bucknell (Chatto and Windus 2010)

36) Kenneth Tynan + Truman Capote 1970
The Life of Kenneth Tynan by Kathleen Tynan (Phoenix 1988)
Capote: A Biography by Gerald Clarke (Hamish Hamilton 1988)
The Diaries of Kenneth Tynan edited by John Lahr (Bloomsbury 2001)
Truman Capote by George Plimpton (Picador 1998)
Shadow Box by George Plimpton (Simon and Schuster 1989)

37) Truman Capote + Peggy Lee 1979
Capote: A Biography by Gerald Clarke (Hamish Hamilton 1988)
Truman Capote by George Plimpton (Picador 1998)
Fever: The Life and Music of Miss Peggy Lee by Peter Richmond (Henry Holt 2006)
The Paris Review Interviews, Volume I (Canongate 2007)

38) Peggy Lee + Richard Nixon 1970
'Peggy Lee's Back on Top – Is that All There is?' by Judy Klemesrud, *New York Times* April 26th 1970
'Dead Silence on Human Rights' by Hugh Sidey, *Life* magazine March 26th 1970
Fever: The Life and Music of Miss Peggy Lee by Peter Richmond (Henry Holt 2006)

The Reagan Diaries edited by Douglas Brinkley (HarperCollins 2007)
Tammy Wynette: Tragic Country Queen by Jimmy McDonough (Simon and
   Schuster 2010)

39) Richard Nixon + Elvis Presley 1970

Elvis by Bobbie Ann Mason (Weidenfeld and Nicolson 2003)
Careless Love: The Unmaking of Elvis Presley by Peter Guralnick (Little, Brown
   1999)
The Day Elvis Met Nixon by Egil 'Bud' Krogh (Pejama Press 1994)
Groucho by Stefan Kanfer (Allen Lane 2000)
Getting High: The History of LSD, History Channel documentary, interview with
   Grace Slick

40) Elvis Presley + Paul McCartney 1965

Elvis by Bobbie Ann Mason (Weidenfeld and Nicolson 2003)
John Lennon: The Life by Philip Norman (HarperCollins 2008)
Careless Love: The Unmaking of Elvis Presley by Peter Guralnick (Little, Brown
   1999)
Can't Buy Me Love: The Beatles, Britain and America by Jonathan Gould (Portrait
   Books 2007)
The Love You Make: An Insider's Story of the Beatles by Peter Brown and Steven
   Gaines (Macmillan 1983)
The Beatles: A Day in the Life compiled by Tom Schultheiss (Omnibus 1980)
The Beatles Anthology, DVD

41) Paul McCartney + Noël Coward 1965

The Faber Book of Pop edited by Hanif Kureishi and Jon Savage (Faber and Faber
   1995)
The Orton Diaries edited by John Lahr (Methuen 1986)
The Letters of Noël Coward edited by Barry Day (Methuen 2007)
The Noël Coward Diaries edited by Graham Payn and Sheridan Morley (Da Capo
   Press 2000)
Noël Coward by Philip Hoare (Chatto and Windus 1995)
Paul McCartney: Many Years from Now (Secker and Warburg 1997)
John Lennon: The Life by Philip Norman (HarperCollins 2008)
The Beatles: A Day in the Life compiled by Tom Schultheiss (Omnibus 1980)

42) Noël Coward + Prince Felix Youssoupoff 1946

The Noël Coward Diaries edited by Graham Payn and Sheridan Morley (Da Capo
   Press 2000)

The Life of Noël Coward by Cole Lesley (Jonathan Cape 1976)

The Murder of Rasputin by Greg King (Century 1996)

The Duff Cooper Diaries edited and introduced by John Julius Norwich
(Weidenfeld and Nicolson 2005)

43) Prince Felix Youssoupoff + Grigori Rasputin 1916

The Murder of Rasputin by Greg King (Century 1996)

The Life and Times of Grigorii Rasputin by Alex de Jonge (Collins 1992)

Rasputin: His Malignant Influence and his Assassination by Prince Youssoupoff
(Jonathan Cape 1927)

Lost Splendour by Felix Youssoupoff (Jonathan Cape 1953)

Rasputin: The Man Behind the Myth by Maria Rasputin and Patte Barham
(Prentice Hall 1977)

44) Grigori Rasputin + Tsar Nicholas II 1915

A Lifelong Passion: Nicholas and Alexandra, Their Own Story by Andrei Mylunas
and Sergei Mironenko (Weidenfeld and Nicolson 1996)

The Life and Times of Grigorii Rasputin by Alex de Jonge (Collins 1982)

Nicholas II: The Last of the Tsars by Marc Ferro (Viking 1991)

The Man Who Killed Rasputin by Greg King (Century 1996)

45) Tsar Nicholas II + Harry Houdini 1903

Handcuff Secrets by Harry Houdini (George Routledge and Sons 1909)

Nicholas and Alexandra by Robert K. Massie (Victor Gollancz 1968)

The Secret Life of Houdini: The Making of America's First Superhero by William
Kalush and Larry Sloman (Atria Books 2006)

The Orson Welles Sketchbook, BBC TV December 2009

46) Harry Houdini + Theodore Roosevelt 1914

Presidential Anecdotes by Paul F. Boller, Jr (Oxford University Press 1981)

Obituary of Houdini, *New York Times* November 1st 1926

Clips from a Life by Denis Norden (Fourth Estate 2008)

47) Theodore Roosevelt + H.G. Wells 1906

The Time Traveller: The Life of H.G. Wells by Norman and Jeanne Mackenzie
(Weidenfeld and Nicolson 1973)

An Experiment in Autobiography, Volume II by H.G. Wells (Victor Gollancz
1934)

The Invisible Man: The Life and Liberties of H.G. Wells by Michael Coren
(Bloomsbury 1993)

Theodore Rex by Edmund Morris (HarperCollins 2002)
The Future in America: A Search After Realities by H.G. Wells (Chapman and Hall 1906)

48) H.G. Wells + Josef Stalin 1934
Stalin: The Court of the Red Tsar by Simon Sebag Montefiore (Weidenfeld and Nicolson 2003)
The Penguin Book of Interviews edited by Christopher Silvester (Viking 1993)
An Experiment in Autobiography, Volume II by H.G.Wells (Victor Gollancz 1934)
Comrades by Robert Service (Macmillan 2007)
The Invisible Man: The Life and Liberties of H.G. Wells by Michael Coren (Bloomsbury 1993)
The Time Traveller: The Life of H.G. Wells by Norman and Jeanne Mackenzie (Weidenfeld and Nicolson 1973)

49) Josef Stalin + Maxim Gorky 1936
Comrades by Robert Service (Macmillan 2007)
Stalin: The Court of the Red Tsar by Simon Sebag Montefiore (Weidenfeld and Nicolson 2003)
Gorky by Henri Troyat (Allison and Busby 1991)

50) Maxim Gorky + Leo Tolstoy 1900
Maxim Gorky: Selected Letters selected, translated and edited by Andrew Barratt and Barry P. Scherr (Clarendon Press 1997)
Literary Portraits by M. Gorky translated by Ivy Litvinov (Foreign Languages Publishing House 1900)
Gorky by Henri Troyat (Allison and Busby 1991)
Gorky's Tolstoy and Other Reminiscences translated, edited and introduced by Donald Fanger (Yale University Press 2008)

51) Leo Tolstoy + Pyotr Il'ich Tchaikovsky 1876
www.tchaikovsky-research net
Tolstoy by A.N.Wilson (Hamish Hamilton 1988)
Tolstoy by Henri Troyat (W.H. Allen 1968)
Tchaikovsky by Herbert Weinstock (Da Capo Press 1981)
The Life and Letters of Peter Ilich Tchaikovsky by Modeste Tchaikovsky (University Press of the Pacific 2004)
Diaries of Tchaikovsky edited by Wladimir Lakond (W.W. Norton 1945)
Tchaikovsky: A Biography by Alan Kendall (Bodley Head 1988)

52) Pyotr Il'ich Tchaikovsky + Sergei Rachmaninoff 1888
Sergei Rachmaninoff: A Lifetime in Music by Sergei Bertensson and Jay Leyda
(George Allen and Unwin 1965)
www.tchaikovsky-research.net

53) Sergei Rachmaninoff + Harpo Marx 1931
Sergei Rachmaninoff: A Lifetime in Music by Sergei Bertensson and Jay Leyda
(George Allen and Unwin 1965)
Harpo Speaks! by Harpo Marx with Rowland Barber (Geis Associates 1961)
The Real Nick and Norah by David L. Goodrich (2001

54) Harpo Marx + George Bernard Shaw 1928
Harpo Speaks! by Harpo Marx with Rowland Barber (Geis Associates 1961)
The Secret Lives of Somerset Maugham by Selina Hastings (John Murray 2009)

55) George Bernard Shaw + Bertrand Russell 1895
City of Cities: The Birth of Modern London by Stephen Inwood (Macmillan 2005)
A Bernard Shaw Chronology by Anthony Matthews Gibbs (Palgrave Macmillan
2001)
Back to Methuselah by George Bernard Shaw (Constable 1921)
Bernard Shaw by Michael Holroyd (Chatto and Windus 1997)
Portraits from Memory by Bertrand Russell (George Allen and Unwin 1958)
The Spirit of Solitude by Ray Monk (Jonathan Cape 1996)
Analysis of the Mind by Bertrand Russell (1921)
An Outline of Philosophy by Bertrand Russell (1927)
On Education by Bertrand Russell (1926)

56) Bertrand Russell + Sarah Miles 1964
Serves me Right by Sarah Miles (Macmillan 1994)
Bertrand Russell: The Ghost of Madness by Ray Monk (Jonathan Cape 2000)
Face to Face, BBC TV box set

57) Sarah Miles + Terence Stamp 1961
Serves me Right by Sarah Miles (Macmillan 1994)
Double Feature by Terence Stamp (Bloomsbury 1989)
Olivier by Terry Coleman (Bloomsbury 2005)

58) Terence Stamp + Edward Heath 1968
Edward Heath: The Authorised Biography by Philip Ziegler (Harper Press 2010)
Edward Heath: A Biography by John Campbell (Jonathan Cape 1993)

John Fowles: The Journals, Volume II edited by Charles Drazin (Jonathan Cape 2006)

Survey of London, Volumes 31 and 32: St James Westminster Part 2, general editor F.H.W. Sheppard (Survey of London 1963)

'Piccadilly Piccalilli' by Nicholas Hill, *Tatler* May 1982

The Bachelor of the Albany by Marmion Savage (Harper and Brothers 1848)

'Profile of Albany' by Hywel Williams, *New Statesman* December 1998

The Times February 2nd 2001

White Heat: A History of Britain in the Swinging Sixties by Dominic Sandbrook (Little, Brown 2006)

59) Edward Heath + Walter Sickert 1934

Edward Heath: A Biography by John Campbell (Jonathan Cape 1993)

Edward Heath: The Authorised Biography by Philip Ziegler (Harper Press 2010)

The Tories: Conservatives and the Nation State 1922–1997 by Alan Clark (Weidenfeld and Nicolson 1998)

Music: A Joy for Life by Edward Heath (Sidgwick and Jackson 1976)

Walter Sickert: A Life by Matthew Sturgis (HarperCollins 2005)

Cold Cream by Ferdinand Mount (Bloomsbury 2008)

Diaries 1942–1943: Ancestral Voices by James Lees-Milne (Chatto and Windus 1975)

Listening for a Midnight Tram: Memoirs by John Junor (Chapmans 1990)

The Strange Death of Tory England by Geoffrey Wheatcroft (Allen Lane 2005)

The Kenneth Williams Diaries edited by Russell Davies (HarperCollins 1993)

A World of my Own: A Dream Diary by Graham Greene (Reinhardt Books 1994)

Article by Andrew Graham-Dixon, *Independent* November 24th 1992

60) Walter Sickert + Winston Churchill 1927

Clementine Churchill: The Biography of a Marriage by Mary Soames (Houghton Mifflin 1979)

Winston and Clementine: The Personal Letters of the Churchills by Mary Soames (Doubleday 1998)

Walter Sickert: A Life by Matthew Sturgis (HarperCollins 2005)

Sir Winston Churchill: His Life and his Paintings by David Coombs and Minnie S. Churchill (Running Press 2004)

In Search of Churchill by Martin Gilbert (HarperCollins 1994)

61) Winston Churchill + Laurence Olivier 1951

Olivier by Terry Coleman (Bloomsbury 2005)

Laurence Olivier by Donald Spoto (HarperCollins 1991)

Confessions of an Actor by Laurence Olivier (Weidenfeld and Nicolson 1982)

62) Laurence Olivier + J.D. Salinger 1951

J.D. Salinger: A Life Raised High by Kenneth Slawenski (Pomona Books 2010)
In Search of J.D. Salinger: A Biography by Ian Hamilton (Random House 1988)
Dream Catcher: A Memoir by Margaret A. Salinger (Washington Square Press 2000)
The Catcher in the Rye by J.D. Salinger (Little, Brown 1952)
Olivier by Terry Coleman (Bloomsbury 2005)
The Times February 13th 2010
Westport Patch March 20th 2010
Guardian January 27th 2011

63) J.D. Salinger + Ernest Hemingway 1944

'Liberating France Hemingway's Way' by Michael Taylor, *San Francisco Chronicle* August 2004
'When Papa Met Salinger' by Bradley R. McDuffie, *Edmonton Journal* July 2010
In Search of J.D. Salinger: A Biography by Ian Hamilton (Random House 1988)
Dream Catcher: A Memoir by Margaret A. Salinger (Washington Square Press 2000)
J.D. Salinger: A Life Raised High by Kenneth Slawenski (Pomona Books 2010)
The True Gen: An Intimate Portrait of Hemingway – by Those Who Knew Him by Denis Brian (Grove Press 1988)
Ernest Hemingway: A Life Story by Carlos Baker (Charles Scribner's Sons 1969)
Interview with Lillian Ross, *Observer* December 12th 2010

64) Ernest Hemingway + Ford Madox Ford 1924

A Moveable Feast by Ernest Hemingway (Jonathan Cape 1964)
Ford Madox Ford by Alan Judd (HarperCollins 1990)
Hemingway by Frank Lynn (Simon and Schuster 1987)
Hemingway: The Paris Years by Michael Reynolds (Blackwell 1989)
Hemingway: A Life without Consequences by James R. Mellow (Hodder and Stoughton 1993)

65) Ford Madox Ford + Oscar Wilde 1899

Memories and Impressions: A Study in Atmospheres by Ford Madox Ford (Harper and Brothers 1911)
Return to Yesterday by Ford Madox Ford (Victor Gollancz 1931)
Oscar Wilde by Richard Ellmann (Hamish Hamilton 1987)
The Complete Letters of Oscar Wilde edited by Merlin Holland and Rupert Hart-Davis (Fourth Estate 2000)
An Innkeeper's Diary by John Fothergill with an introduction by Craig Brown (Folio Society 2000)

66) Oscar Wilde + Marcel Proust 1891
Oscar Wilde by Richard Ellmann (Hamish Hamilton 1987)
The Complete Letters of Oscar Wilde edited by Merlin Holland and Rupert Hart-Davis (Fourth Estate 2000)
Marcel Proust by William C. Carter (Yale University Press 2000)
Marcel Proust: A Biography by George D. Painter (Chatto and Windus 1989)
Marcel Proust: Selected Letters, Volume IV edited by Philip Kolb (HarperCollins 2000)

67) Marcel Proust + James Joyce 1922
A Night at the Majestic by Richard Davenport-Hines (Faber and Faber 2006)
James Joyce by Richard Ellmann (Oxford University Press 1959)
Written Lives by Javier Marias (Canongate 2006)

68) James Joyce + Harold Nicolson 1931
Harold Nicolson: Diaries and Letters 1930–39 edited by Nigel Nicolson (Atheneum 1966)
Harold Nicolson: A Biography by James Lees-Milne (Chatto and Windus 1980)
James Joyce by Richard Ellmann (Oxford University Press 1959)

69) Harold Nicolson + Cecil Beaton 1967
Beaton in the Sixties: More Unexpurgated Diaries by Cecil Beaton, edited by Hugo Vickers (Weidenfeld and Nicolson 2003)
Cecil Beaton by Hugo Vickers (Weidenfeld and Nicolson 1985)
Harold Nicolson: A Biography by James Lees-Milne (Chatto and Windus 1980)

70) Cecil Beaton + Mick Jagger 1967
Beaton in the Sixties: More Unexpurgated Diaries by Cecil Beaton, edited by Hugo Vickers (Weidenfeld and Nicolson 2003)
Cecil Beaton by Hugo Vickers (Weidenfeld and Nicolson 1985)
Life by Keith Richards (Weidenfeld and Nicolson 2010)
The Stones by Philip Norman (Elm Tree Books 1984)

71) Mick Jagger + Tom Driberg 1967
Tom Driberg: His Life and Indiscretions by Francis Wheen (Chatto and Windus 1990)
Mick and Keith by Chris Salewicz (Orion 2002)
Faithfull by Marianne Faithfull with David Dalton (Michael Joseph 1994)
The Stones by Philip Norman (Elm Tree Books 1984)

72) Tom Driberg + Christopher Hitchens 1976

'Reader, He Married Her' by Christopher Hitchens, *London Review of Books* May 10th 1990

Hitch-22: A Memoir by Christopher Hitchens (Atlantic 2010)

Tom Driberg: His Life and Indiscretions by Francis Wheen (Chatto and Windus 1990)

Memoirs by Kingsley Amis (Hutchinson 1991)

Messengers of Day by Anthony Powell (Heinemann 1978)

73) Christopher Hitchens + George Galloway 2005

Gorgeous George: The Life and Adventures of George Galloway by David Morley (Politico's 2007)

Hitch-22: A Memoir by Christopher Hitchens (Atlantic 2010)

YouTube: George Galloway debates Christopher Hitchens at Baruch University, New York

Independent September 16th 2005

Guardian September 16th 2005

Guardian May 18th 2005

Weekly Standard May 24th 2005

The Times September 15th 2005

Christopher Hitchens in *Slate* magazine September 13th 2005

74) George Galloway + Michael Barrymore 2006

Guardian January 13th 2006

The Times January 24th 2006

BBC News website

Awight Now by Michael Barrymore (Simon and Schuster 2007)

Barrymore: A Man Possessed by Phil Taylor and Paul Nicholas (Metro Publishing 2002)

75) Michael Barrymore + Diana, Princess of Wales 1996

Awight Now by Michael Barrymore (Simon and Schuster 2007)

Barrymore: A Man Possessed by Phil Taylor and Paul Nicholas (Metro Publishing 2002)

Interview with Michael Barrymore, *Observer* December 29th 2002

Interview with Cheryl Barrymore, *Daily Mail* July 31st 1999

Diana by Sarah Bradford (Viking 2006)

76) Diana, Princess of Wales + Princess Grace 1981

Interview with David and Elizabeth Emmanuel, *Sunday Mirror* August 16th 1998

Diana: Story of a Princess by Tim Clayton and Phil Craig (Hodder and Stoughton 2001)

The Diana Chronicles by Tina Brown (Century 2007)

Once Upon a Time: The Story of Princess Grace, Prince Rainier and their Family by J. Randy Taraborrelli (Sidgwick and Jackson 2003)

Diana by Sarah Bradford (Viking 2006)

Diana: Her True Story – in Her Own Words by Andrew Morton (Michael O'Mara 1992)

77) Princess Grace + Alfred Hitchcock 1961

Hitchcock and the Making of Marnie by Tony Lee Moral (Manchester University Press 2002)

Grace: The Secret Lives of a Princess by James Spada (Sidgwick and Jackson 1987)

Once Upon a Time: The Story of Princess Grace, Prince Rainier and their Family by J. Randy Taraborrelli (Sidgwick and Jackson 2003)

Ned Sherrin's Theatrical Anecdotes (Virgin 1991)

Alfred Hitchcock: A Life in Darkness and Light by Patrick McGilligan (Wiley 2003)

78) Alfred Hitchcock + Raymond Chandler 1950

The Life of Raymond Chandler by Frank MacShane (Hamish Hamilton 1986)

Selected Letters of Raymond Chandler edited by Frank MacShane (Jonathan Cape 1981)

Alfred Hitchcock: A Life in Darkness and Light by Patrick McGilligan (Wiley 2003)

The Raymond Chandler Papers edited by Tom Hiney and Frank MacShane (Hamish Hamilton 2000)

The Oxford Book of American Literary Anecdotes edited by Donald Hall (Oxford University Press 1981)

The Oxford Book of Literary Quotations edited by Peter Kemp (Oxford University Press 1997)

79) Raymond Chandler + Howard Hawks 1944

The Life of Raymond Chandler by Frank MacShane (Hamish Hamilton 1976)

Selected Letters of Raymond Chandler edited by Frank MacShane (Jonathan Cape 1981)

Howard Hawks: The Grey Fox of Hollywood by Todd McCarthy (Grove Press 1997)

The Thirsty Muse: Alcohol and the American Writer by Tom Dardis (Abacus 1989)

80) Howard Hawks + Howard Hughes 1930

Howard Hawks: The Grey Fox of Hollywood by Todd McCarthy (Grove Press 1997)

Howard Hughes: His Life and Madness by Donald L. Barlett and James B. Steele (André Deutsch 1979)

Howard Hughes by Peter Harry Brown and Pat H. Broeske (Little, Brown 1996)

81) Howard Hughes + Cubby Broccoli 1940

When the Snow Melts: The Autobiography of Cubby Broccoli (Boxtree 1998)

Howard Hughes by Peter Harry Brown and Pat H. Broeske (Little, Brown 1996)

Citizen Hughes by Michael Drosnin (Hutchinson 1985)

Howard Hughes by John Keats (Random House 1966)

Howard Hughes: His Life and Madness by Donald L. Barlett and James B. Steele (André Deutsch 1979)

An Autobiography by Jane Russell (Sidgwick and Jackson 1986)

82) Cubby Broccoli + George Lazenby 1965

When the Snow Melts: The Autobiography of Cubby Broccoli (Boxtree 1998)

Interview with George Lazenby on *Entertainment Tonight* September 1992

83) George Lazenby + Simon Dee 1970

Whatever Happened to Simon Dee? by Richard Wiseman (Aurum 2006)

Obituary of Simon Dee, *The Times* January 2nd 2004

Obituary of Simon Dee, *Independent* January 2nd 2004

Brewer's Dictionary of Rogues, Villains and Eccentrics by William Donaldson (Cassell 2002)

84) Simon Dee + Michael Ramsey 1970

Michael Ramsey: A Portrait by Michael De-la-Noy (HarperCollins 1990)

Michael Ramsey: A Life by Owen Chadwick (Oxford University Press 1990)

Whatever Happened to Simon Dee? by Richard Wiseman (Aurum 2006)

Daily Sketch June 5th 1970

Brewer's Dictionary of Rogues, Villains and Eccentrics by William Donaldson (Cassell 2002)

85) Michael Ramsey + Geoffrey Fisher 1919

Michael Ramsey: A Portrait by Michael De-la-Noy (HarperCollins 1990)

Michael Ramsey: A Life by Owen Chadwick (Oxford University Press 1990)

Robert Runcie: The Reluctant Archbishop by Humphrey Carpenter (Hodder and Stoughton 1996)

The Macmillan Diaries: The Cabinet Years 1950–1957 edited by Peter Catterall (Macmillan 2003)
Macmillan 1957–1986 by Alistair Horne (Macmillan 1989)

86) Geoffrey Fisher + Roald Dahl 1931
Storyteller: The Life of Roald Dahl by Donald Sturrock (Harper Press 2010)
Boy by Roald Dahl (Jonathan Cape 1984)
Archbishop Fisher: His Life and Times by Edward Carpenter (Canterbury Press 1991)

87) Roald Dahl + Kingsley Amis 1972
Memoirs by Kingsley Amis (Hutchinson 1991)
Storyteller: The Life of Roald Dahl by Donald Sturrock (Harper Press 2010)
Letters to Monica by Philip Larkin, edited by Anthony Thwaite (Faber and Faber 2010)
The New Oxford Book of Literary Anecdotes edited by John Gross (Oxford University Press 2009)

88) Kingsley Amis + Anthony Armstrong-Jones 1959
Memoirs by Kingsley Amis (Hutchinson 1991)
Snowdon: The Biography by Anne de Courcy (Weidenfeld and Nicolson 2008)
Princess Margaret: A Life Unravelled by Tim Heald (Weidenfeld and Nicolson 2007)

89) Lord Snowdon + Barry Humphries 1966
More Please: An Autobiography by Barry Humphries (Viking 1992)
My Life as Me: A Memoir by Barry Humphries (Michael Joseph 2002)
Snake Charmers in Texas: Essays 1980–87 by Clive James (Jonathan Cape 1988)
Dame Edna Everage and the Rise of Western Civilisation by John Lahr (Flamingo 1992)

90) Barry Humphries + Salvador Dalí 1963
More Please: An Autobiography by Barry Humphries (Viking 1992)
My Life as Me: A Memoir by Barry Humphries (Michael Joseph 2002)
The Shameful Life of Salvador Dalí by Ian Gibson (Faber and Faber 1997)
Diary of a Genius by Salvador Dalí (Doubleday 1965)
New York Times
Dirty Dalí: A Private View by Brian Sewell, screened by Channel 4 June 1997

91) Salvador Dalí + Sigmund Freud 1938

The Death of Sigmund Freud by Mark Edmundson (Bloomsbury 2007)

The Shameful Life of Salvador Dalí by Ian Gibson (Faber and Faber 1997)

The Secret Life of Salvador Dalí by Salvador Dalí (Dial Press 1942)

Panorama, BBC 1955

Man with a Blue Scarf: On Sitting for a Portrait by Lucian Freud by Martin
    Gayford (Thames and Hudson 2010)

92) Sigmund Freud + Gustav Mahler 1910

Gustav Mahler: Memories and Letters by Alma Mahler (second edition, John
    Murray 1968)

Mahler by Michael Kennedy (J.M. Dent 1974)

Mahler by Kurt Blaukopf (Allen Lane 1973)

Why Mahler? How One Man and his Symphonies Changed the World by Norman
    Lebrecht (Faber and Faber 2010)

The Life and Work of Sigmund Freud by Ernest Jones (Basic Books 1953–57)

93) Gustav Mahler + Auguste Rodin 1909

The World of Yesterday by Stefan Zweig (Cassell 1953)

The Penguin Book of Art Writing edited by Martin Gayford and Karen Wright
    (Viking 1998)

Rodin by Frederick V. Grunfeld (Hutchinson 1988)

Gustav Mahler: Memories and Letters by Alma Mahler (John Murray 1946)

94) Auguste Rodin + Isadora Duncan 1900

The Penguin Book of Art Writing edited by Martin Gayford and Karen Wright
    (Viking 1998)

My Life by Isadora Duncan (Victor Gollancz 1968)

Isadora: The Sensational Life of Isadora Duncan by Peter Kurth (Little, Brown
    2001)

Portraits of a Lifetime by J.E. Blanche (1937), quoted in *The Faber Book of Art
    Anecdotes* edited by Edward Lucie-Smith (Faber and Faber 1992)

A Book of Secrets by Michael Holroyd (Chatto and Windus 2010)

95) Isadora Duncan + Jean Cocteau 1926

Loving Garbo by Hugo Vickers (Jonathan Cape 1994)

An Impersonation of Angels: A Biography of Jean Cocteau by Frederick Brown
    (Longmans 1969)

Isadora: The Sensational Life of Isadora Duncan by Peter Kurth (Little, Brown
    2001)

96) Jean Cocteau + Charlie Chaplin 1936

An Impersonation of Angels: A Biography of Jean Cocteau by Frederick Brown
(Longmans 1969)

Professional Secrets: An Autobiography of Jean Cocteau (Farrar, Straus and Giroux
1972)

Chaplin: His Life and Art by David Robinson (Penguin 2001)

My Autobiography by Charles Chaplin (Bodley Head 1964)

97) Charlie Chaplin + Groucho Marx 1937

Manitoba History No. 16 Autumn 1988

Monkey Business: The Lives and Legends of the Marx Brothers by Simon Louvish
(Faber and Faber 1999)

Groucho: The Life and Times of Julius Henry Marx by Stefan Kanfer (Allen Lane
2000)

98) Groucho Marx + T.S. Eliot 1964

The Groucho Letters: Letters from and to Groucho Marx (Michael Joseph 1967)

99) T.S. Eliot + The Queen Mother 1943

Queen Elizabeth the Queen Mother: The Official Biography by William Shawcross
(Macmillan 2009)

Elizabeth the Queen Mother by Hugo Vickers (Hutchinson 2005)

The Diaries and Letters of Harold Nicolson, Volume II: The War Years, 1939–45
edited by Nigel Nicolson (Collins 1967)

The Journals of Woodrow Wyatt, Volume II edited by Sarah Curtis (Macmillan
1999)

The Book of Royal Lists by Craig Brown and Lesley Cunliffe (Routledge and Kegan
Paul 1982)

The Spectator Annual edited by Fiona Glass (HarperCollins 1991)

Edith Sitwell: A Unicorn Among Lions by Victoria Glendinning (Weidenfeld and
Nicolson 1981)

100) The Queen Mother + The Duchess of Windsor 1972

Elizabeth the Queen Mother by Hugo Vickers (Hutchinson 2005)

Behind Closed Doors: The Tragic, Untold Story of the Duchess of Windsor by Hugo
Vickers (Hutchinson 2011)

Queen Elizabeth the Queen Mother: The Official Biography by William Shawcross
(Macmillan 2009)

Point to Point Navigation: A Memoir 1964 to 2006 by Gore Vidal (Little, Brown
2006)

The Duchess of Windsor: The Uncommon Life of Wallis Simpson by Greg King (Aurum 1999)

Redeeming Features: A Memoir by Nicholas Haslam (Jonathan Cape 2009)

Adventures of a Gentleman's Gentleman by Guy Hunting (John Blake 2002)

101) The Duchess of Windsor + Adolf Hitler 1937

The Heart has its Reasons by the Duchess of Windsor (Tandem 1969)

The Duchess of Windsor by Michael Bloch (Weidenfeld and Nicolson 1996)

The Duchess of Windsor: The Uncommon Life of Wallis Simpson by Greg King (Aurum 1999)

A Lonely Business: A Self-Portrait of James Pope-Hennessy edited by Peter Quennell (Weidenfeld and Nicolson 1981)

The Book of Royal Lists by Craig Brown and Lesley Cunliffe (Routledge and Kegan Paul 1982)

Hitler's Table Talk 1941–44 edited by Hugh Trevor-Roper (Oxford University Press 1988)

Harold Nicolson: Diaries and Letters 1930–39 edited by Nigel Nicolson (Atheneum 1966)

The Rise and Fall of the House of Windsor by A.N. Wilson (Sinclair-Stevenson 1993)

Behind Closed Doors: The Tragic, Untold Story of the Duchess of Windsor by Hugo Vickers (Hutchinson 2011)

Redeeming Features by Nicholas Haslam (Jonathan Cape 2009)

Forget Not by Margaret, Duchess of Argyll (W.H. Allen 1977)

Wait for Me!: Memoirs of the Youngest Mitford Sister by Deborah Devonshire (John Murray 2010)

The Way the Wind Blows by Sir Alec Douglas-Home (Collins 1976)

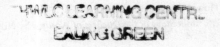